Red Friends

Red Friends

Internationalists in China's
Struggle for Liberation

John Sexton

VERSO

London • New York

First published by Verso 2023
© John Sexton 2023
All rights reserved

1 3 5 7 9 10 8 6 4 2

Verso
UK: 6 Meard Street, London W1F 0EG
US: 20 Jay Street, Suite 1010, Brooklyn, NY 11201
versobooks.com

Verso is the imprint of New Left Books

ISBN-13: 978-1-78873-566-7
ISBN-13: 978-1-78873-568-1 (UK EBK)
ISBN-13: 978-1-78873-569-8 (US EBK)

British Library Cataloguing in Publication Data
A catalogue record for this book is available from the British Library

Library of Congress Cataloging-in-Publication Data
A catalog record for this book is available from the Library of Congress

Typeset in Minion by Hewer Text UK Ltd, Edinburgh
Printed and bound by CPI Group (UK) Ltd, Croydon, CR0 4YY

For Yang Li

Contents

Acknowledgements

I would like to especially thank Greg Benton, who had the idea for the book. Other scholars I am indebted to include Tom Grunfeld, Frederick Litten, Shen Zhihua, Ye Lishu, Yu. V. Chudodeyev, Larry Hannant, Roderick and Sharon Stewart, June Teufel Dreyer, and Robbie Barnett. I owe special thanks to Isabel Crook and her sons, Carl, Michael, and Paul, who were extraordinarily generous with their time and spoke openly and frankly about their family's fascinating past. Fred Engst gave me invaluable information about his parents, Joan Hinton and Erwin 'Sid' Engst, as well as about his own experience of growing up during the Cultural Revolution. Jane Su helped me understand the daily lives of foreign residents who were outside the 'foreign experts' system. Colin MacKerras provided insights into the situation of foreigners in China during the 1960s, based on his experience as a volunteer teacher. Jenny Clegg told me fascinating details about her father, Arthur Clegg, who did so much to organise solidarity with China during the War of Resistance against Japan. Neil Redfern helped me with biographical details of British Communists who were drawn into the Cultural Revolution. Gregor Kneussel helped with German-language sources and provided valuable nuggets on Otto Braun, Agnes Smedley, and others. Alexander Pantsov was of enormous help in navigating the Russian archives and answered some crucial questions. Pang Li provided equally important assistance by tracking down Chinese texts. David Ferguson shared his experiences as a modern foreign expert in Beijing.

I must also thank my wife, Yang Li, for her patience as well as her assistance, especially when my Chinese failed me. It is unfortunately just too late to thank Sid Rittenberg for his generous help, as he has recently gone to meet Marx, but I would like to mention him here. I hope his shade thinks I have been fair to him.

26 February 2021

Preface

In the century of its existence, the Chinese Communist Party (CCP) has grown from a group whose supporters could be counted, generously, in dozens, to an organisation with not far off one hundred million members.[1] No ordinary political party, it is in effect the ruling apparatus of the People's Republic of China, a state in which the few other parties permitted to exist do so on its sufferance. Among the Communist Party's tens of millions of members, finding any who adhere to its founding ideals is difficult. Many party members join for career reasons, for, while it is possible for non-members to hold middling positions in government and elsewhere, party membership smooths the path to advancement. It is commonplace, and considered normal, for owners and top managers of private companies to be party members, and even to serve as secretaries of the party branches that are now compulsory in most firms.

Since its foundation, not only the membership but also the declared aims and ideals of the party have changed beyond recognition. While the patriotic aim of national salvation was among the motives of its founders, they looked abroad for inspiration and imported ideas of democracy, liberalism, feminism, anarchism, socialism, and the application of scientific methods to solve social problems. One of the mainsprings of the New Culture and May Fourth movements that gave birth

1   The CCP is the second-largest party in the world. The honour of first place goes to India's Bharatiya Janata Party.

to the party was the desire to cast off the suffocating patriarchal ideology of official Confucianism. A simple demand that young people, above all young women, be allowed to marry the person of their choice motivated many recruits.

In today's party, nationalism has eclipsed other concerns. The task the Communist Party has set itself is the Great Revival of the Chinese People. The socialism it espouses is one 'with Chinese characteristics'. Traditional culture has been rehabilitated. While it was once compulsory to denounce Confucianism as a reactionary hangover, for the past several years the Chinese government has been invoking the name of the great sage to build its soft power around the world. At home, a seemingly harmless cosplay fad, the Han Clothing Movement, has attracted unpleasant right-wing ideologues.

Recently 'socialism with Chinese characteristics' has acquired the qualifier 'for a new era'. It is not hard to discern that the new era is one in which China has risen to parity with the other great powers, and the United States in particular. China, according to most forecasts, will soon surpass the United States to become the world's largest economy. It therefore demands a 'new type of great power relations' that reflects and respects this pre-eminence.

The Chinese Communist Party has changed profoundly since its early years. When it was founded, the party was internationalist in outlook, seeing itself as part of a world movement for the propagation of proletarian revolution – so much so that its leaders were reluctant to embrace the anti-imperialist alliance with the nationalist Kuomintang (KMT) urged on them by Communist International advisors. Party leaders also recognised the rights of China's national minorities, to the extent of being prepared to relinquish territory.[2]

Today, questioning the sacred unity of the territory of the People's Republic has become almost the most grievous offence of which one can be accused. Even oblique hints that all is not harmonious among the country's fifty-six officially recognised ethnic groups can lead to arrest and imprisonment.[3] It was not always thus. The following extract is from Article 14 of the constitution of the Chinese Soviet Republic that was

---

2   The PRC eventually adopted the Soviet nationalities policy but omitted the right to secede – the mechanism by which the USSR was dissolved in 1991.

3   The most sensitive areas are Taiwan, Tibet, Xinjiang, and Inner Mongolia.

formed in 1931 in Jiangxi Province, and whose chairman was Mao
Zedong.

> The Soviet government of China recognises the right of self-determi-
> nation of the national minorities in China, their right to complete
> separation from China, and to the formation of an independent state
> for each national minority. All Mongolians, Tibetans, Miao, Yao,
> Koreans, and others living on the territory of China shall enjoy the
> full right to self-determination, i.e. they may either join the Union of
> Chinese Soviets or secede from it and form their own state as they
> may prefer.

This was boilerplate Comintern policy, derived from the constitution
of the Soviet Union and ultimately from Vladimir Lenin's writings on
the self-determination of nations. It was unthinkable that the Chinese
Communist Party, in its early years, would differ from orthodoxy on
such a fundamental issue. As late as 1936, in an interview with the journalist Edgar Snow, Mao let it be known that he was prepared to let
Taiwan go its own way once it had thrown off the yoke of Japanese
imperialism.[4]

The intellectuals who made up the initial core of the new party were
attracted by the internationalism and generosity of Soviet Russia in its
relations with China. The Soviet stance not only contrasted with that of
tsarist Russia which had flagrantly encroached on Chinese territory, but
also with that of China's supposed allies at Versailles who, despite China's
participation on their side in the war, awarded a chunk of Chinese territory to Japan. The award led to Chinese disillusionment with the United
States, and President ▬▬▬▬▬▬ in particular, whose apparent
commitment to the principle of self-determination was shown to be
hollow by his approval of the settlement.

The Soviet stance was expressed in the 1919 Karakhan Manifesto,
which renounced all territory and privileges ceded by China to tsarist
Russia. To be sure, before too long, realpolitik, not for the last time,
trumped idealism in Soviet policy. Faced with a military threat from
Japan, the Soviets later equivocated on the return to China of the strategic China Eastern Railway which, straddling Manchuria, connected two

4   Interviews with Mao, July–September 1936. Available at marxists.org.

parts of Soviet territory. But Vladimir Vilensky's pamphlet *China and Soviet Russia*, included as an appendix, contains the original text of the manifesto that offered to return the railway unconditionally.

This book is not about those who were inspired by Chinese Communism and especially by the ideas of Mao Zedong to make revolution elsewhere. Julia Lovell's recent scholarly book *Maoism* is a survey of them. It is about foreigners on the left who offered support to China's revolutionaries and to the Chinese people in their resistance to foreign invaders. It is not a comprehensive account. In general, I have tried to shed light on comparatively lesser-known persons and episodes. One is Vladimir Vilensky, mentioned above. Others include George Hardy, an old-style itinerant labour activist and one-time leader of the Industrial Workers of the World, whose battle for the emancipation of the working class 'on five continents', included risking his life in the Wuhan and Shanghai underground. Verda Majo, a Japanese Esperantist, broadcast impassioned pleas to her own country's soldiers to desert. Exiled writers Kaji Wataru and Ikeda Yuki organised Japanese prisoners of war into detachments of the Chinese army. Nosaka Sanzo, based in Yan'an, organised many more Japanese prisoners than Kaji and Ikeda. Two thousand Soviet pilots who fought for Nationalist China against Japan during the first phase of the War of Resistance have received comparatively little attention in English-language accounts. Others include a British hereditary peer who helped build the Red Army's radio network and an American nuclear scientist who spent most of her life in China designing agricultural machinery.

Until 1927, the influence of the Comintern on the Chinese Communist Party was overwhelming. Its policies, if not exactly imposed by decree, carried the day after heavy persuasion and despite the misgivings of the Chinese leadership. The first generation of agents, – Voitinsky, Sneevliet, Borodin, Blyukher, and others – were largely transmitters of decisions taken in Moscow. But, in this role, they had a profound effect on Chinese history. Their successors in the underground – George Hardy, Arthur Ewert, Manfred Stern, and so on – exercised considerable influence on the much-reduced Chinese party. But some in the CCP had already learned the lesson that Moscow's advice could lead to disaster. By the late 1930s, the leadership could hardly be unaware that Joseph Stalin favoured the Soviet relationship with the KMT government over that with the CCP. A slow estrangement between the CCP and Moscow began. Foreign advisors began to be used as scapegoats when things went wrong – most notably in the case of Otto Braun discussed later in this book.

After the foundation of the People's Republic, foreign experts and advisors would never again be allowed a decisive voice in Chinese affairs. During the 1950s, Soviet economic advisors were welcomed and treated with great respect, but their role was technical, not political. Other foreign experts were mainly restricted to translating and editing work. During the Cultural Revolution, some foreign Communists thought they were taking part, in some cases even a leading part, in a renewed upsurge of the world revolution, but they were soon removed from the stage – often to a prison cell. After being released, most remained loyal to China and Mao. With some exceptions, they remained staunch Stalinists, somewhat ironically since Stalin had liquidated almost the entire first generation of agents who had actually made a difference to Chinese history.

For those unfamiliar with CCP history, here is a very brief, incomplete summary. The CCP was formed in 1921 by Chen Duxiu and Li Dazhao following a Soviet mission led by a young print worker called Grigory Voitinsky. Following a 1923 agreement between Soviet diplomat Adolph Joffe and the KMT leader Sun Yat-sen, the CCP formed an alliance, known as the First United Front, with the KMT, that lasted from 1924 until 1927. Beginning in 1925, anti-imperialist uprisings, mainly directed against the British, developed into a mass movement of workers and peasants for their own social demands. The CCP grew rapidly and threatened to eclipse its KMT partner, an outcome not planned or foreseen by the Comintern. In April 1927, Chiang Kai-shek, the KMT leader after Sun's death, turned his forces, which had been financed, armed, and trained by the Soviet Union, against his erstwhile allies. From then until 1937, the CCP existed underground in some cities, mainly in Shanghai, and in a few isolated strongholds in the countryside. In 1934, facing defeat by Chiang's forces, the party abandoned its bases in southeast China and set off on the Long March which took it to northwest China. In 1937, following a revolt by sections of his army and facing a full-scale Japanese invasion, Chiang Kai-shek agreed to a Second United Front with the CCP. Although the Soviet Union gave massive military aid to Chiang Kai-shek, the Second United Front had fallen apart in all but name by 1941. After Japan's defeat, Chiang restarted the civil war against the CCP, but political corruption of his regime and demoralisation in the army, which was vastly superior on paper, led to his defeat and the proclamation of the People's Republic of China in 1949.

Under Mao Zedong's leadership, the party carried out a series of campaigns, notably the Anti-Rightist Campaign, the Great Leap Forward, and the Cultural Revolution, that are now largely seen as disastrous. In 1979, Deng Xiaoping began a process of Reform and Opening Up that successive leaders have more or less continued. The crushing of student-led protests in June 1989 brought an end to hopes of democratisation while economic reforms continued to push the country in the direction of capitalism. In 2012, the accession of Xi Jinping to the leadership marked an apparent return to one-man rule. Xi has emphasised ideological conformity at home and asserted China's growing clout on the world stage.

It would be easy to dismiss some of the people portrayed in this book as irredeemable Stalinists. Two examples who have indeed been written off in this way are George Hardy and Arthur Clegg. This is an oversimplification. Hardy belonged to a pre–World War I generation of leftist internationalists who rallied to the Russian Revolution, Clegg to a later generation drawn in by the conjuncture of the Great Depression and the rise of fascism. The Comintern's struggle against the fascists (although inconsistent and inept) and the decisive role of the Red Army in defeating Hitler hardened their commitment. For many in both generations, loyalty to the Soviet Union became an article of faith that no evidence could undermine. (When forced to choose, many transferred that loyalty to the PRC.) Just as the Wars of Religion and the Spanish Inquisition do not invalidate the good works done by Catholics in the service of their faith, Stalin's crimes do not cancel out the trade union and other campaigning work of Hardy, Clegg, and indeed the millions of loyal adherents of the Communist movement.

Understanding and nuance do not imply exoneration. As far as I am aware, neither Clegg nor Hardy condemned, or even took into serious consideration, the fact that among Stalin's hundreds of thousands of victims, were many Soviet and other foreign revolutionaries who served in China in the 1920s. They never referred to his cynical murder of air force general Pavel Rychagov, hero of the Spanish Civil War and China's

War of Resistance against Japan.[5] It is possible they did not know, but just as likely that they chose to look the other way. However, their guilt should not be exaggerated. Cognitive dissonance is not unique to old Communists. Liberals and centrists, to say nothing of those who celebrate past empires, also have selective memories.

---

5   They were also happy to let the CCP's first leader, Chen Duxiu, carry the can for Stalin's misdirection that propelled the mediocrity Chiang Kai-shek to power. Without Soviet arms and advisors, Chiang would have remained, at best, a minor provincial warlord.

1

Agents and Diplomats

In 1912, after China's imperial court was overthrown, Lenin, enthused by the fall of an autocracy even older than the tsarist regime, extravagantly praised Sun Yat-sen, the provisional president of the newborn Chinese republic, as a 'revolutionary democrat, endowed with the nobility and heroism of a class ~~that is rising, not declining~~'. The Xinhai Revolution[1] had proved that '~~in Asia, there is still~~ a bourgeoisie ~~capable of championing sincere, militant, consistent democracy~~, a worthy comrade of France's great men of the Enlightenment and the great leaders of the close of the eighteenth century'.[2]

Lenin's paean to Sun reflected his internationalism and, contrary to later myth, his early hopes for revolution in China and the colonial world. However, he was overly optimistic. Unlike the Romanovs in 1905, the Qing dynasty perished, but China's bourgeois-democratic revolution, such as it was, was aborted. Sun had prestige but no army and, in a matter of weeks, handed the presidency to a general of the old regime, Yuan Shikai. Although Yuan had defeated the rebels in bloody fighting, he changed sides when he saw that the Qing dynasty was politically doomed.[3] After Sun realised, too late, that Yuan planned a personal

---

1   Xinhai is a traditional date form denoting the year 1911.
2   Vladimir Lenin, 'Democracy and Narodism in China', *Collected Works*, Vol. 18, Moscow: Progress Publishers, 1975, 165.
3   Around 200,000 people were killed in the revolution.

dictatorship, he attempted a revolt but was defeated and fled to Japan. In 1915, Yuan declared himself emperor of a new dynasty, but he had over-played his hand, and a military revolt forced him to back down. When he died soon afterwards – of despair, natural causes, or poisoning – the country fragmented into warlord fiefdoms.[4]

After the defeat of the revolution, China's reformist intellectuals – among them Hu Shi, Lu Xun, Li Dazhao, and Mao Zedong – coalesced around the magazine *New Youth*. Its editor was the iconoclastic Chen Duxiu. Like Sun Yat-sen, Chen had spent time in exile in Japan, but he refused to join Sun's Tongmenghui, the forerunner of the Kuomintang (KMT), because he was repelled by Sun's atavistic attachment to secret society ideas and practices.[5] Chen was a thoroughgoing moderniser who believed that only 'Mr Science and Mr Democracy' could save China. *New Youth* became the house journal of the New Culture Movement that repudiated Confucianism and celebrated new, imported ideas of liberalism, anarchism, socialism, and feminism. They even challenged the legitimacy of the classical form of the Chinese language espoused by officialdom. Believing the archaic official usage fettered thought, they wrote in the vernacular and advocated radical language reform.[6]

The First World War, above all the Versailles Treaty that ended it, revived China's revolutionary movement. In August 1914, days after declaring war on Germany, the British Empire asked its ally, Japan, to attack German interests in East Asia. Eyeing Germany's thriving Chinese colony, the port of Qingdao, Japan readily agreed.[7] The British imperial-ists, with territorial ambitions of their own, accepted that Japan should be rewarded with Qingdao and contributed three warships and 1,500 troops to the invasion force. Thousands of miles from home and

---

4   There are several theories about Yuan Shikai's death, the most accepted being that he died of the kidney disease uremia.

5   Sun was attached to atavistic ideas of expelling the 'alien' Manchu Qing dynasty and restoring the 'native' Ming dynasty. He also demanded that Tongmenghui members swear an oath of personal loyalty to him.

6   Some wanted to replace Chinese characters with an alphabet; the most radical wanted to abandon the Chinese language altogether in favour of Esperanto or English. One aphorism, often attributed to Lu Xun, was *hanzi bu mie, zhongguo bi wang* – 'Characters must go, or China is lost'.

7   Germany seized a Chinese naval base in Qingdao in 1897 and by 1914 had built a modern city.

hopelessly outnumbered, the Germans held out for two and a half months but were ultimately forced to surrender. London celebrated this act of international piracy, fought on Chinese soil without permission and morally equivalent to Germany's original land grab, as 'the greatest prize' of the war so far.[8] The British lost a dozen troops. The Japanese lost a few hundred, most of them when their British-built cruiser *Takachiho* was sunk. It was the only serious fighting Japan did in the war.[9]

By comparison with the slaughter in Europe, the battle of Qingdao was little more than a skirmish, but it changed Chinese history.[10] China, weak and divided, was pressured by the allies to join the war effort. More than 200,000 Chinese served on the Russian front and 135,000 on the Western front in labour battalions. In 1917, the Beijing government finally declared war on Germany.[11] By the end of the war, the Chinese felt they had done enough to earn fair treatment, but at the Paris Peace Conference, the victorious powers awarded Qingdao and its Shandong hinterland to Japan. The decision caused uproar in China. Believing the government had signed the peace treaty, Beijing students trashed ministers' houses; strikes and boycotts spread throughout the country. The May Fourth Movement, as it became known, radicalised a whole generation. Its leader – commander in chief, in Mao Zedong's words – was Chen Duxiu. Before May Fourth, Chen believed a new generation of intellectuals would accomplish social reform. Henceforth he looked to the masses to carry out a social revolution.

Within weeks of May Fourth, the Soviet deputy foreign minister, Lev Karakhan, announced Russia's unilateral renunciation of all privileges and concessions previously ceded by China to the tsarist regime.[12] With

---

8   Foreign secretary Lord Grey wrote that Japan would be given Chinese territory in return for helping defeat Germany, just as Britain 'would naturally get compensation in [other] parts of the world.' See Jonathan Fenby, *The Siege of Tsingtao*, Melbourne: Penguin, 2015.

9   Japanese troops also helped Britain suppress the 1915 Singapore mutiny by Indian troops.

10   The battle is, however, commemorated on British war memorials.

11   Of the Chinese in Russia, around 40,000 later joined the Red Army. See Gregor Benton, *Chinese Migrants and Internationalism: Forgotten Histories, 1917–1945*, London: Routledge, 2011, 20–9; and Mark O'Neill, *From the Tsar's Railway to the Red Army*, Melbourne: Penguin, 2014.

12   See Appendix A: *China and Soviet Russia* for the full text of the Karakhan Manifesto.

Soviet Russia still fighting the civil war, the Karakhan Manifesto had no practical effect, but, as a propaganda coup, it had a significant impact on Chinese public opinion. Woodrow Wilson had impressed the world with his declarations in favour of self-determination. However, his heavily hedged Fourteen Points had not stopped him accepting the handover of Shandong, the birthplace of Confucius, to Japan. Wilson had even blocked a racial-equality clause the Japanese wanted to include in the Versailles Treaty. Some Chinese intellectuals who had formerly admired the United States and democracy began to pay attention to Soviet Russia and communism.[13]

Although signed by Karakhan, the manifesto was drafted by Vladimir Vilensky, a leader of the Bolshevik Party's Far Eastern Bureau.[14] Vilensky, known by his pseudonym Sibiriakov (the Siberian),[15] was a textbook professional revolutionary. Born in Tomsk in 1888, he grew up in extreme poverty, became a foundry worker, and took part in the 1905 Revolution. In 1908, he was sentenced to four years hard labour, then exiled to Yakutsk after completing his prison term. Freed by the 1917 Revolution, he fought throughout the civil war in Siberia and founded the Red Army's first military academy. In 1919 he wrote a radical pamphlet, *China and Soviet Russia*, that included the Karakhan Manifesto as an appendix. The Soviets sent him to negotiate with the Chinese, hoping that the manifesto's generous terms would persuade China to establish diplomatic relations. He met with Chinese officials in Irkutsk and Vladivostok, but the talks failed, mainly because the other big powers, determined to avoid a precedent that might compromise their own historic privileges, pressured the Chinese to rebuff the Soviet initiative.

In early 1920, Vilensky sent Grigory Voitinsky to investigate the situation in China and contact sympathetic intellectuals. Voitinsky's mission exceeded expectations. Indeed, probably no foreigner played a bigger role in helping to establish the Chinese Communist Party (CCP). Voitinsky, a typesetter who had spent a decade in the United States, was

---

13   The Soviets later backtracked over the question of control of the strategic China Eastern Railway.

14   Leong Sow-Theng. *Sino-Soviet Relations: The first phase, 1917–1920*, Canberra: Australian National University, 1971, 4.

15   Tony Saich, 'The Chinese Communist Party during the Era of the Comintern (1919–1943)', Amsterdam: International Institute of Social History, n.d., 9.

only twenty-seven years old when he arrived in Beijing. He spoke no Chinese, but his fluent English served as a lingua franca. He had returned to Russia after the October Revolution and, like Vilensky, fought in the civil war in Siberia. He was captured and jailed by the Japanese on Sakhalin Island but organised a prisoner revolt and escaped. As his civil war record suggests, he was courageous and resourceful. A colleague described him as fearless and 'a first-class conspirator and an exemplary underground worker, the man who filled all the requirements of the revolutionary movement in China at that stage'.[16] Voitinsky was also tactful, modest, and thoughtful – qualities that endeared him to China's radical intellectuals who, although they rejected conservative ideas, ~~valued old-fashioned politeness.~~ valued conservative politeness/

Voitinsky assembled a small team that included his wife, M. F. Kuznetsova, an interpreter called Yang Mingzhai, twenty-four-year-old I. K. Mamaev, and Mamaev's wife, M. Sakh'ianova, who was an ethnic Buryat.[17] Through an émigré Russian professor, they met Li Dazhao. Li gave them a letter of introduction to Chen Duxiu, who had relocated to the International Settlement in Shanghai after serving a jail sentence for his part in the May Fourth Movement. Chen, in turn, introduced Voitinsky to Sun Yat-sen, who told Voitinsky he was keen to pursue an alliance with the Soviets.[18] Sun's fellow KMT leader, Liao Zhongkai, was so taken with the idea that he began studying Russian.

In the light of Voitinsky's progress, in July 1920, Vilensky called a meeting in Beijing that decided to widen the scope of the mission to include the establishment of a Chinese Communist Party.[19] Chen Duxiu supported the project and relaunched *New Youth* as a publication of the Communist International. Within a few months, the fledgling party had recruited about sixty members. In Shanghai, Voitinsky set up a Sino Russian News Agency and a language school where Kuznetsova taught Russian to the recruits to prepare them for cadre training in Moscow.

16   Marc Kasanin (Kazanin), *China in the Twenties*, Moscow: Nauka Publishing House, 1973, 224.

17   Steve Smith, *A Road Is Made: Communism in Shanghai, 1920–1927*, Honolulu: University of Hawaii Press, 2000, 12.

18   Alexander Pantsov, *The Bolsheviks and the Chinese Revolution 1919–1927*, Honolulu: University of Hawaii Press, 2000, 45.

19   Saich, 'Chinese Communist Party', 9.

Sun Yat-sen now headed a southern government based in Canton that he planned to use as a springboard for a northern expedition to unify China. In January 1921, Vilensky visited Canton for discussions with Sun and his sometime ally, the 'anarchist general' Chen Jiongming, who was governor of Guangdong Province.[20] The following August, in an article for Russian broadsheet *Izvestia*, Vilensky called for a Congress of the Peoples of the Far East. Soviet Russia, along with defeated Germany, had been pointedly excluded from the Washington Naval Conference called by President Warren Harding.[21] Moscow hoped to attract China to a rival intergovernmental conference, but the Beijing government declined to take part. The congress nevertheless went ahead in January 1922 as a conference of revolutionary parties, rebadged as the Congress of the Toilers of the Far East.

The Congress was a follow-up to the second congress of the Comintern where Lenin presented his famous Theses on National and Colonial Questions, calling on Communists to fight alongside anti-imperialist movements. Many delegates to the Second Congress were sceptical of such alliances, seeing their 'own' bourgeois nationalists as rivals rather than potential allies. Their spokesperson was the Indian revolutionary M. N. Roy who, paradoxically, was a recent convert from pure nationalism.[22] Roy had been a militant nationalist since his schooldays. During the First World War, he had tried to run guns to India using German money. When the plan fell through, he fled to San Francisco, at the time a haven for Indian nationalists. After the United States joined the war in 1917, he took refuge in Mexico, where he was recruited by the Latvian Comintern agent Mikhail Borodin and set up a Mexican Communist Party. The party was so small that it was derided by an opponent as 'six members and a calico cat', but it was Roy's ticket into the Comintern congress.[23] Lenin received Roy's challenge respectfully, debated him on

---

20 At this time, Chen Jiongming was generally regarded as more left wing and closer to the Communists than Sun Yat-sen. The two men had very different strategies for reforming China. Sun Yat-sen planned a Northern Expedition to unify the country by force. Chen Jiongming proposed a federal solution that Sun feared would leave power in the hands of the warlords.

21 President Harding called the Washington Conference (November 1921 – February 1922) to curb a naval arms race among the great powers and to demonstrate the growing authority of the United States following World War I.

22 Manabendra Nath Roy. His real name was Narendra Nath Bhattacharya.

23 Carleton Beals, *Glass Houses*, Philadelphia: J. B. Lippincott Company, 1938, 30.

the floor of the congress, and appointed a commission to amend his theses to include some of Roy's points; the commission secretary was the Dutch Communist Henk Sneevliet. The actions of these three – Roy, Borodin, and Sneevliet – helped determine the outcome of China's twentieth-century political conflicts.

Sneevliet arrived in China in time to attend the Chinese Communist Party's founding congress held in Shanghai in July 1921. While Voitinsky had laid the groundwork for the formation of the party, and Chen Duxiu was elected party secretary, neither attended the congress; the latter had been invited by Chen Jiongming to be education director of Canton, and Voitinsky had gone to Russia. Thus, in place of Voitinsky, Sneevliet represented the Comintern at the congress. The Dutchman was the most influential foreign revolutionary in the early years of the CCP and, argu-ably, played a pivotal role in Chinese history. He devised, proposed, and enforced the 'bloc within' tactic under which CCP members joined the KMT and submerged their own party's identity in an attempt to capture the host party from within. The 'bloc within', combined with the Soviet policy of building up the KMT armed forces, led to the disastrous defeat of 1927, the decimation of the CCP in the cities, and its retreat to the countryside.

Sneevliet held a week-long meeting with Sun Yat-sen in Guilin, at which they discussed the common ground between Soviet socialism and Sun's Three Principles of the People. Sun agreed to send a delegate to the Congress of the Toilers of the Far East.[24] In turn, Sneevliet went on to Canton, where, fortuitously, he arrived during a seamen's strike and was impressed by the links between organised labour and the KMT. Based on these favourable signs, he decided that the tiny CCP should downgrade its independent activity and work within the KMT.[25]

The CCP leaders resisted Sneevliet's proposal to submerge their new party in the KMT. They regarded the KMT as a clique of opportunists,

---

24   Dov Bing, 'Sneevliet and the Early Years of the CCP', *The China Quarterly*, No. 48 (1971), 677–97, 681. Sun's representative at the Congress of the Toilers of the Far East, Zhang Qiubai, met Lenin in the Kremlin but caused a stir in the congress by claiming that the KMT was a Communist Party in all but name and that, consequently, China had no need for another one. Zhang was a slightly clownish figure who was ridiculed by the other Chinese delegates. With hindsight, however, they should have heeded his warning that the KMT would not tolerate another party on its patch.

25   Ibid., 683.

putschists, and warlords loosely linked to Sun Yat-sen by personal ties rather than principles. But Sneevliet would not take no for an answer. Despite his limited experience of China, he insisted they follow his line. Sneevliet, physically imposing and domineering, could scarcely have been less like the even-tempered Voitinsky. According to Zhang Guotao, one of the CCP's early leaders, he behaved like a Prussian officer about to challenge his opponent to a duel.[26] He did not hesitate to overrule Chen Duxiu, one of China's leading intellectuals and a veteran of three revolutions.[27] However, the party leaders did not yield.

Sneevliet believed that the tiny Chinese Communist Party would not be able to grow on its own by accretion. It had been created too early – 'fabricated' by the Russians. Determined to have his way, he went back to Russia and returned to China in the summer of 1922, armed with a Comintern order signed by Voitinsky requiring the CCP Central Committee to immediately relocate from Shanghai to Canton and 'do all its work in close contact with Comr. Phillipp', that is to say, Sneevliet. With the authority and the funds of the Comintern behind Sneevliet, the CCP leaders had no choice but to comply.

To understand why Sneevliet was fixated on his 'bloc within' tactic, we need to look into his background. Sneevliet has been judged severely for his imposition of a failed line on the CCP. But whatever else can be said about him, he was a revolutionary and an internationalist. He was a senior trade union official with a comfortable career ahead of him, but he gave it up on a point of principle, emigrating to the Dutch Indies to oppose the colonial regime. He had been chairman of the Dutch railway workers' union and a prominent figure in the Social Democratic Workers Party (SDAP). He was one of the first and youngest socialists to be elected to municipal office. Nevertheless, in 1912 he resigned from both the union and the party in protest at their betrayal of the great international seamen's strike of 1911. Influenced by the leftist poet Henriette van der Schalk, shortly before leaving for the Indies, he joined the Marxist Social-Democratic Party, which later became the Dutch Communist Party.

---

26 Zhang Guotao, *The Rise of the Chinese Communist Party*, Lawrence: University Press of Kansas, 1971, 137–9.

27 The Xinhai Revolution of 1911–12, the 'second revolution' of 1913, and May Fourth, 1919.

Sneevliet settled in Semarang, capital of Central Java – an industrial city and the centre of radicalism in the Netherlands' vast Indonesian colony. With almost religious zeal, he set about building the Indies Social Democratic Association (ISDV). At first, it was a discussion group of expatriates. But Sneevliet, still only thirty years old, was not interested in creating a talking shop. Determined to mobilise the indigenous population against colonialism, he persuaded the local railway union to recruit local, unskilled workers. To turn the ISDV into a revolutionary movement committed to ending Dutch rule, he began to look for local allies.

After some false starts, he turned his attention to a large but amorphous nationalist movement, Sarekat Islam (Islamic Union), that had attracted several hundred thousand members under the slogan 'Our Homeland, Our Religion, Our Nation'. Sneevliet sent young activists from the railway union to join Sarekat Islam and win its members to socialism. Economic disruption caused by the war helped his cause: the price of rice rose sharply, and Sarekat Islam activists began describing capitalism as sinful, while becoming increasingly receptive to the arguments of the ISDV. Sneevliet's 'bloc within' Sarekat Islam was a success. Within a few years, Sneevliet's young protégé, a railway worker called Semaun, emerged as leader of the breakaway Red Sarekat Islam, taking with him a large chunk of the membership that became the core of the Indonesian Communist Party – which was, for some time, the largest in East Asia.

After the February Revolution in Russia, Sneevliet wrote a radical article titled 'Zegepraal' (Triumph) that celebrated the overthrow of the tsar and predicted that the colonial regime in the Indies would soon go the same way. He was arrested for sedition, but, at his trial, gave a nine-hour speech denouncing colonialism and was acquitted.[28] Alarmed by his growing influence, the colonial authorities deported him in 1918. The following year, when he represented the Indonesian party at the second congress of the Comintern, his reputation preceded him. Lev Trotsky himself translated as he addressed a large crowd outside the Winter Palace during the opening ceremonies. As such, he was already a celebrated activist when the Comintern sent him to China eighteen months later. Although he clashed with the Chinese Communists, his

28 Ruth McVey, *The Rise of Indonesian Communism*, Jakarta: Equinox, 2006, 26.

differences with them were tactical, rather than matters of principle. It was understandable that he would see China through the prism of his Indies experience and seek to repeat it. What is less easy to explain, however, is how he conflated the militaristic KMT with the loosely organised Sarekat Islam.

Voitinsky's and Sneevliet's wooing of Sun Yat-sen culminated in the 1923 Sun-Joffe agreement.[29] In January that year, Adolph Joffe, as 'special envoy plenipotentiary of the Soviet Union', signed a joint manifesto with Sun, by which the Soviet Union agreed to help Sun achieve 'national unification and . . . full national independence', and acknowledged that under the present conditions, it was 'not possible to carry out either Communism or even the Soviet system in China'. The manifesto reaffirmed Karakhan's earlier commitment to renounce all privileges granted 'under duress' by the Chinese to tsarist Russia[30] and agreed a form of words on Mongolia that satisfied both sides.[31]

When Sun signed the agreement, he was in a weak position, following his ouster from Canton in a June 1922 coup led by Chen Jiongming. The Soviets gave two million Mexican dollars to Sun as a down payment on the vastly greater sums they would deliver over the next few years – money which enabled Sun to retake Canton from Chen Jiongming. By the end of 1923, Soviet financial and military aid was flowing into Canton along with military and political advisors.[32] The Sun-Joffe

---

29   Adolph Joffe, a close friend and political ally of Trotsky, was one of the Soviet Union's most experienced diplomats. A leading Soviet delegate at Brest-Litovsk, he also negotiated the treaty of Rapallo with Germany. He supported closer ties with China to the extent that he saw Soviet backing for Mongolian independence as 'a new edition of the tsarist policy'. He doubted it was 'worthwhile, for the sake of two million Mongols who do not have any role to play in the world, to damage our entire policy and relationship with four hundred million Chinese'. Liu Xiaoyuan, *Reins of Liberation: An Entangled History of Mongolian Independence, Chinese Territoriality, and Great Power Hegemony, 1911–1950*, Washington, DC: Woodrow Wilson Center Press, 2006, 60.

30   The strategically important China Eastern Railway was a sticking point. It crossed Chinese territory but was part of the Trans-Siberian and linked two parts of Russian territory. The Soviets backtracked on handing full control of the line to China, although they had explicitly offered it in the first version of Karakhan Manifesto, as published in Vilensky's pamphlet *China and Soviet Russia*. See Appendix A.

31   The full text of the Sun-Joffe Manifesto can be found in Conrad Brandt, Benjamin I. Schwartz, and John King Fairbank, *A Documentary History of Chinese Communism*, Cambridge, MA: Harvard University Press, 1952, 71–2.

32   By mid-1924 two dozen military advisors had arrived and by 1926 there were nearly sixty. See C. Martin Wilbur and Julie Lien-ying How, *Missionaries of Revolution:*

agreement was, on the face of it, very favourable to Sun. He received substantial aid and recognition of his status as a government leader. The aid would allow him, for the first time, to create a substantial military force of his own and free him from dependence on unreliable warlord allies. He had also extracted an acknowledgement that China had formal (albeit unenforceable) jurisdiction over Mongolia. But the key concession was the political agreement that China was not ready for Communism, or even the formation of soviets as instruments of struggle. Sneevliet's tactic of forming a 'bloc within' the KMT to build a revolutionary party had been transformed into an alliance between a state and a quasi-state and, in the process, the independence of the CCP had effectively been bartered away.[33]

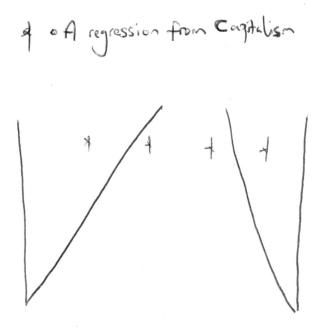

Soviet Advisers and Nationalist China, 1920–1927, Cambridge, MA: Harvard University Press, 1989, 7.

33   Vilensky also held talks with Wu Peifu, one of Sun Yat-sen's arch-rivals and later the main target of Chiang Kai-shek's Northern Expedition. The CCP initially viewed Wu favourably, but he was dropped after, in February 1923, he massacred railway workers who had called a strike on a railway under his control. See Leong, *Sino-Soviet Relations*, 222–4.

2

Advisors and Soldiers

Mikhail Borodin was chosen to head the Soviet mission in Canton. On 31 July 1923, the Soviet Politburo approved a proposal to send him to China as political advisor to Sun Yat-sen. Borodin's terms of reference, set out by Stalin, are of particular interest:

> ~~Instruct Comrade Borodin that in his work with Sun Yat-sen~~ he should be guided by the interests of the Chinese national liberation movement and should under no circumstances ~~be~~ ~~carried~~ away into schemes to implant communism in China.[1]

Borodin would be the Soviet point man in Canton, but he was to report to Moscow's plenipotentiary in Beijing, Lev Karakhan, who was dispatched, at the same time, to negotiate the reopening of diplomatic relations with the Beijing government.[2] Karakhan had recommended Borodin for the Canton post, and the two men ~~set off for China~~ ~~together~~.[3]

---

1   Russian State Archive of Socio-political History (RGASPI), 17.3.369.6, author's translation.

2   That is to say, the government Sun Yat-sen hoped to replace. Such duplicity was and remains commonplace in international relations.

3   There is no indication of opposition to Stalin's proposal. The other full members of the Politburo were Lenin (who was already incapacitated), Zinoviev, Kamenev, Rykov, Tomsky, and Trotsky. Apart from Lenin, they were all later killed by Stalin. (Tomsky shot

Karakhan's 1919 manifesto smoothed his path in Beijing. It helped
that he was handsome, charming, and eloquent. Especially popular
among students and intellectuals, he spent much of his time making
speeches and giving public lectures in universities. By May 1924, he had
persuaded Beijing to recognise the Soviet Union and was appointed
ambassador. Amusingly, since the other diplomats in Beijing were mere
ministers in charge of legations, Ambassador Karakhan outranked
them, and these sworn enemies of Communism were obliged to defer to
him on formal occasions.[4]

During Karakhan's tenure, the Beijing embassy buzzed with activity.
Soviet advisors were constantly passing through in transit to and from
Canton. Comintern agents and Soviet spies used it as their base.[5] The
CCP and local workers' committees met on the premises; the embassy
opened its doors as a cultural centre. Discussion groups on all sorts of
issues were open to the public. The embassy staff even put together a
jazz band featuring a Hawaiian guitar – an instrument that was all the
rage at the time. The star of the cultural scene was the constructivist
writer Sergei Tretyakov, who spent a year in China lecturing on Russian
life and literature. His embassy colleagues later recalled how he brought
social events to life with his effervescent wit. His play, *Roar China*, about
foreign gunboats bullying Chinese shipping on the Yangzi River, was
later performed on Broadway, and Bertolt Brecht regarded him as his
mentor.

While Borodin's early period in Canton was a success, Sun Yat-sen's
position was still precarious. The self-styled generalissimo
commanded almost no troops of his own and relied on the loyalty of
fickle warlords. His most dangerous rival, Chen Jiongming, now
supported by the British, was attempting a comeback.[6] Sun was ready
to flee, but Borodin and Liao Zhongkai persuaded him to fight.

---

himself before he could be arrested on charges of 'terrorism.') There were also four
candidate members, two of whom, Bukharin and Rudzutaks, were shot. Kalinin died of
cancer in 1946. Of the eleven full candidate members, only Molotov outlived Stalin.

4   Karakhan's diplomatic mission was not the first sent by the Soviets. The Far
Eastern Republic, a short-lived Siberian state spawned by the civil war, had earlier sent
a mission to Beijing. See Appendix B.

5   The embassy was considered relatively secure at this time, but in 1927 it was
sacked by warlord troops.

6   English language newspapers in China referred to Chen Jiongming as the leader
of the White Kuomintang.

Borodin mobilised a volunteer force of 500 Socialist Youth, forcing Chen Jiongming to back down. Sun, suitably impressed, expressed his gratitude, calling Borodin his Lafayette.[7] Drawing on the momentum created by the victory, Borodin pushed through a reorganisation of the KMT along Soviet lines. The party held its first-ever congress in January 1924, adopting a programme drafted by Borodin. Liao Zhongkai persuaded the delegates to allow CCP members to join. In May, the Whampoa Military School was established to train an officer corps for a new model army.

Chiang Kai-shek, recently returned from the Soviet Union an apparently committed revolutionary, was appointed head of the military school. Its chief advisor was General Vasily Blyukher, a hero of the Russian Civil War. Blyukher directed a series of victories that consolidated Sun's hold on Canton and extended it throughout Guangdong Province. In October 1924, the Whampoa cadets crushed the reactionary Canton Merchant Corps. Then, in the months that followed, two Eastern Expeditions finished off Chen Jiongming's army and forced him to flee to Hong Kong. In June 1925, Blyukher led a lightning campaign against the Yunnan and Guangxi warlords – former allies who had turned against Sun. Buoyed by these successes, the KMT renamed its armed forces the National Revolutionary Army (NRA) and announced the formation of a national government.

The imperialists were, naturally, horrified. A headline in the *North China Herald*, a mouthpiece of British interests in China, screamed 'Comrade Borodin Now Dictator in Canton', quoting an anonymous, possibly fictitious Chinese general pleading for foreign troops to occupy the city.[8] According to another article, Borodin had exerted a 'malign influence' on Sun Yat-sen that led him down 'the path of terrorism and extortion, until in the end, by dint of hard working on the waning mind of the leader, Borodin became Dr Sun's *alter ego*'. [9] The *Daily Mail*, for its part, denounced Borodin as a 'Lettish Jew' out to 'destroy the British Empire'.[10]

---

7   In response to a hostile journalist who asked if he knew Borodin's real, Jewish, surname.

8   *North China Herald*, 5 September 1925.

9   *North China Herald*, 3 October 1925.

10   Percival Phillips, *Daily Mail* article reprinted in the *North China Herald*, 23 January 1926.

Radicalised
Juventil

Among ~~~~~~~~~~~~~, Borodin inspired devotion that approached worship. The American journalist Vincent Sheean described him as 'the directing genius of the mass movement', a man with 'the natural dignity of a lion or a panther' who deserved 'the name of greatness'.[11] According to the military advisor Alexander Cherepanov, Borodin had extraordinary analytical powers that allowed him to discern patterns of cause and effect where others saw only 'a stormy train of events'. Rayna Prohme, the American editor of the KMT newspaper the *People's Tribune*, said Borodin was 'the biggest man in China today . . . a social force . . . He has the power of throwing on his search light and making things stand out in bold relief, so the irrelevant disappears'.[12] Her colleague Milly Bennett was simply smitten; Borodin was 'big, handsome . . . calm . . . benign . . . melodramatic, witty . . . a man to capture the imagination and the heart as well'.[13] It amounted to a minor personality cult. André Malraux portrayed him as a shadowy hero in his 1928 novel of the Chinese revolution, *Les conquérants*. Echoing Malraux, Borodin's American biographer Bruce Jacobs described him as 'the Bolshevik conqueror of half of China'.[14]

However, in 1927, Borodin was forced to flee ignominiously across the Gobi Desert in a makeshift motorcade. Meanwhile, the revolutionary movement was being wiped out by KMT generals. It was not only Chiang Kai-shek. One of the most enthusiastic participants in the slaughter was General Tang Shengzhi, on whose army Borodin had until recently relied.[15] On any interpretation, Borodin's mission in China ended in disaster.

The United Opposition led by Trotsky, Lev Kamenev, and Grigory Zinoviev had, correctly if belatedly,[16] warned of the dangers of hitching the fortunes of the CCP to the KMT. They had no time for Borodin.

---

11   Vincent Sheean, *Personal History*, London: Hamilton, 1969 [1935], 203, 226.

12   Baruch Hirson, Arthur Knodel, and Gregor Benton, *Reporting the Chinese Revolution: The Letters of Rayna Prohme*, London: Pluto Press, 2007, 72–3.

13   Milly Bennett and Tom Grunfeld, *On Her Own: Journalistic Adventures from San Francisco to the Chinese Revolution, 1917–1927*, London: Routledge, 2015, 221–2.

14   Dan Jacobs, *Borodin: Stalin's Man in China*, Cambridge MA: Harvard University Press, 1981, 1.

15   Hirson et al., *Reporting the Chinese Revolution*, 80.

16   See Alexander Pantsov and Gregor Benton, 'Did Trotsky Oppose Entering the Guomindang from the First?', *Republican China*, Vol. 19, No. 2 (1994), 52–66.

Trotsky was particularly scathing, dismissing Borodin as a bad actor posturing on the world stage:

> Here is the political biography of Borodin: in 1903, at the age of 19, he emigrated to America; in 1918, he returned to Moscow . . . Having quit Russia *before* the first revolution and having returned *after* the third, Borodin appeared as the consummate representative of that state and Party bureaucracy which recognized the revolution only after its victory . . . People of this type assimilate without difficulty the gestures and intonations of 'professional revolutionists'.[17]

Borodin's real name was Mikhail Gruzenberg. He was born in 1884 into a poor Jewish family in Vitebsk. His mother tongue was Yiddish, but he was schooled in Russian and mastered German and Latvian after moving to Riga where he worked as a logger and boatman. He joined the Bund as a teenager, but abandoned it for the Russian Social Democratic Labour Party (RSDLP) after a couple of years.[18] In 1903, he backed Lenin in his dispute with the Mensheviks. The same year, he left Russia, not for the United States (as Trotsky said), but for Switzerland to work for Lenin. When the 1905 Revolution broke out, he returned to Riga and represented the city's small Bolshevik contingent on the city's joint revolutionary council.[19] He had some standing in the Bolshevik faction. He sat on the praesidium at the 1905 Tammerfors conference and was a delegate to the Stockholm Congress of the RSDLP in April 1906. After the defeat of the revolution, he moved to St Petersburg but was arrested and deported, ultimately settling in Chicago.

Trotsky's assessment of Borodin was wrong in detail, but it is true that in the United States, Borodin temporarily abandoned politics. He married a fellow Latvian called Fanny Orluk. They had two sons, to whom they gave typically American names – Fred and Norman. Borodin quickly mastered English and, after a period teaching fellow immigrants at Jane Addams's Hull House, he became a successful educational entrepreneur, owner of the Berg Progressive Preparatory School. But, like

---

17   Les Evans and Russell Block, eds., *Leon Trotsky on China*, New York: Pathfinder Press, 2018, 641–2.

18   i.e., the Jewish Labour Bund.

19   Constitutional Democrats.

many former revolutionaries, he was re-energised by the February Revolution. As secretary of an émigré organisation called Friends of Russian Democracy, he hovered between the various factions, trying to reconcile supporters of the Provisional Government with supporters of the Petrograd Soviet.[20] However, after the October Revolution, he threw in his lot with the Bolsheviks again, and in 1918 he sailed for Russia.

Borodin's facility with languages made him an ideal candidate for clandestine courier work. Therefore, he was sent to the United States, Germany, Switzerland, the Netherlands, Mexico, Spain, and Britain, often carrying large sums of money.[21] One notable mission was to Mexico, where, in addition to recruiting M. N. Roy, he held talks with President Venustiano Carranza on establishing diplomatic relations with Soviet Russia.[22] His last mission before being sent to China was to Britain, where he helped lay the basis for the Minority Movement. But Special Branch detectives swooped on him as he was about to address a meeting in Glasgow. He was jailed for six months, then deported.[23]

Vasily Blyukher was a worker from a peasant background. While still in his teens, he was jailed for leading a strike in a steel factory. Drafted into the army at the start of World War I, he won the Cross of St George

20   According to some fellow militants, Borodin had become hostile to Lenin. On 9 June 1927, the *Springfield Leader and Press* claimed that in 1917, he was not a Communist but a supporter of Kerensky.

21   Because of the blockade on the early Soviet state, funds were smuggled by couriers. Borodin was embarrassed when jewellery he was carrying to the United States to finance Comintern work went missing. He had entrusted it to a sympathiser – an Austrian army officer – to avoid a customs inspection, but the officer disappeared. There are various versions of how the situation was resolved (one involving Éamon de Valera), but Borodin was exonerated.

22   Carranza expressed sympathy but declined to recognise the Soviets, saying he feared, probably correctly, that it would provoke an invasion from the north. The United States had been carrying on a low-intensity war on Mexico since 1910. In 1916, General Pershing led 10,000 troops in a year-long unsuccessful campaign to capture Pancho Villa.

23   More than twenty detectives swooped on the meeting. For a fuller account of Borodin's British mission, see Jacobs, *Borodin*, 101–7. Interestingly, while in London, Borodin warned James Connolly's son Roddy Connolly that it would be suicidal for the IRA to launch a civil war against the Free State. 'What the hell do they want a Republic for?' Borodin asked him. Borodin's advice may have reflected a softening of Soviet policy towards Britain following the 1921 Anglo-Soviet Trade Treaty that Lord Curzon hoped would result in 'a cessation of Bolshevik hostility in parts of the world important to us.' See Jérôme aan de Wiel, 'Ireland and the Bolshevik Revolution', *History Ireland*, Vol. 25, No. 6 (2017), 38–42.

– a medal only granted for 'undaunted courage'. Wounded and subsequently invalided out, he joined the Bolshevik Party soon afterwards. After enlisting in the Red Guards, he served on the Military Revolutionary Committee in Samara. During the civil war, he commanded a partisan army and turned out to be a natural military genius, earning the first-ever award of the Order of the Red Banner.[24] In 1921, when only thirty years old, he was appointed commander of the armed forces of the Far Eastern Republic. According to an aide, he 'personified the romance of the revolution . . . all the men were in love with him, they called him an eagle'.[25]

In China as in Russia, Blyukher did not shy away from the front line. Indeed, he regularly joined reconnaissance missions over enemy territory in ramshackle aircraft nicknamed 'flying coffins'. His Chinese pseudonym, Galen, became a byword for courage and expertise. An advisor sent from Beijing to investigate the situation in Canton reported that 'Galen has acquired for himself an incredibly high prestige. The Chinese had absolute confidence in Com. Galen, so that his every statement pertaining to military operations was considered to be a law'.[26]

Blyukher, like Borodin, became a public face of the Soviet mission in Canton, often speaking at mass rallies.[27] Although he was popular with the rank and file, there was another side to Blyukher. A stickler for protocol, he was high handed with colleagues. When Marc Kazanin was assigned to Blyukher's staff, he was shocked to learn he was expected to stand up when the general entered the room. The military advisor Vladimir Akimov recounted how horse-riding with Blyukher was torture since he would lag behind and check his officers were maintaining the correct posture. Blyukher also liked to play the gallant officer, once terrifying his lover's landlady by visiting with an armed escort.[28] More seriously, he irritated Borodin, his nominal superior, by turning

24   Blyukher's first Red Banner was awarded when, commanding a partisan army, he broke an encirclement in forty days of fighting and linked up with the Red Army. See Vera Vishnyakova-Akimova, *Two Years in Revolutionary China*, Cambridge, MA: Harvard University Press, 1971, 223.

25   M. I. Kazanin, *Zapiski sekretaria missii: Stranichka istorii pervykh let sovetskoĭ diplomatii* [*Notes of a mission secretary: Pages from the history of the first years of Soviet diplomacy*], Moscow: Izd-vo vostochnoĭ lit-ry, 1962, 26–7.

26   Wilbur and How, *Missionaries of Revolution*, 524–5.

27   Vishnyakova-Akimova, *Two Years in Revolutionary China*, 223.

28   Ibid., 281–2.

up to meetings in an ostentatious uniform with Mauser-toting guards on the running boards of his car. Relations between the two became so bad that Blyukher took an extended break in Russia, pleading illness. The dispute seems to have been purely about status; as a military man, Blyukher tried to keep out of 'politics'.

Borodin's early successes and his good relationship with Sun Yat-sen seemed to have cemented the Soviet-KMT alliance, but events soon turned against him. According to Sneevliet, three 'super-warlords' dominated Chinese politics: Sun Yat-sen; Wu Peifu, who was favoured by the United States and Britain; and the Manchurian strongman Zhang Zuolin. In late 1924, Wu Peifu and Zhang Zuolin went to war for control of the Beijing government. The Comintern regarded Zhang Zuolin as an illiterate bandit in the pay of Japan,[29] but, despite Borodin's pleas, Sun Yat-sen sided with Zhang and assembled an army to march north.[30] In the event, Sun's forces were not needed; the outcome was decided when the so-called 'Christian general' Feng Yuxiang, hitherto loyal to Wu Peifu, defected and seized Beijing. One result of the war was that the Soviets gained another unreliable ally. After discussions with Karakhan, Feng Yuxiang renamed his forces the Guominjun (Nationalist Army), and the Soviets began sending him supplies and advisors.

Sun went north for reunification talks with the new Beijing government, accompanied by Borodin. But shortly after arriving in Beijing, Sun Yat-sen fell ill with liver cancer and died on 12 March 1925. His death removed a cornerstone of the Soviet-KMT alliance. In the succession battle around his deathbed, Borodin was little more than a spectator to the battle over his legacy between Sun's in-laws, the powerful Song family; his son from a previous marriage, Sun Fo; Chiang Kai-shek; and others. But it was events that began in Shanghai two and a half months later that would strain the alliance to breaking point. On 30 May, British police gunned down a group of anti-imperialist demonstrators in Shanghai. Amid nationwide outrage, the conflict escalated rapidly. On 23 June, British and French troops fired on marchers in Canton from the Shamian Island concession, killing fifty and wounding hundreds. A quarter of a million workers in Hong Kong walked out, leaving the colony a ghost town. A hundred thousand strikers relocated to Canton,

---

29   See John Sexton, *Alliance of Adversaries*, Chicago: Haymarket, 2019, 75–6, 276.
30   Wilbur and How, *Missionaries of Revolution*, 119.

where armed pickets enforced a boycott of Hong Kong shipping. The strike committee became an alternative government with courts, jails, newspapers, schools and even a small navy of half a dozen gunboats.[31] The great Hong Kong–Canton Strike lasted for nearly a year and a half. Within a few months, the combined membership of the Chinese Communist Party and its Youth Corps grew from three thousand to twenty thousand, and the old Bolshevik Borodin found himself in the middle of a revolutionary situation.

Borodin's brief was to help the KMT carry out the national revolution and steer clear of proletarian revolution. But mass mobilisation on this scale threatened the script written in Moscow. From the KMT's point of view, stipends paid to strikers diverted money from the army and threatened to bankrupt the government. Even supposed leftists in the KMT leadership like Eugene Chen and Wang Jingwei regarded the eruption of the masses as an inconvenience to be calmed as soon as possible. Before long, Borodin joined Wang Jingwei in an effort to negotiate an end to the strike.[32] It was, on the face of it, a paradoxical development. If ever there was a mass anti-imperialist movement in China, it was the Hong Kong–Canton strike. But here was a Bolshevik trying to call it off.

Despite Borodin's efforts to cool the mass movement, right-wingers quickly lost patience. At the height of the crisis, Borodin's strongest supporter in the KMT, Liao Zhongkai, was assassinated. The KMT rightist Hu Hanmin was suspected, and Chiang Kai-shek, still apparently a revolutionary, arrested him.[33] Although Hu was cleared, he was packed off to Moscow to remove him from the political scene. Whether by luck or design, Chiang had eliminated a rival, and the list of candidates likely to succeed Sun had been whittled down to two – Wang Jingwei and Chiang Kai-shek.

On 20 March 1926, Chiang Kai-shek launched an anti-communist coup in Canton, arrested CCP members, put the Soviet advisors under house arrest, and disarmed the workers' militia. When Chiang struck, Borodin was away in Beijing, where he had given a characteristically fluent and impressive progress report to a Soviet commission of enquiry

---

31   Jacobs, *Borodin*, 182.

32   Jacobs claimed that Borodin regarded the strikers as riffraff, although he provided no source, and it seems unlikely. Ibid., 182.

33   Chiang at this time still projected a radical image. He was known to be impulsive: during the Shamian crisis, he had threatened to declare war on the British Empire.

chaired by Andrei Bubnov.[34] Bubnov had since travelled south and was among those detained in Canton. Wang Jingwei, who was nominally in charge of the army, protested that Chiang had deployed troops without authorisation. However, at an emergency meeting of the KMT Executive, Chiang prevailed and Wang Jingwei was 'invited' to take a vacation in Europe. With his last rival gone, Chiang now controlled the Canton government, the party, and the army. But, without Soviet military aid, the long-planned Northern Expedition to unify China had no hope of success. Therefore, having achieved his objectives, he apologised profusely and tried to explain away the crisis as a misunderstanding,[35] claiming his action had been provoked by an unauthorised manoeuvre of the warship *Zhongshan*, whose commander, Li Zhilong, was a CCP member. To demonstrate goodwill, he arrested the right-wing police chief, Wu Tiecheng, and sacked a few other rightists. It was enough for the Soviets. Bubnov negotiated an abject settlement, as part of which he agreed to hand over a complete list of CCP members in the KMT, government and military.

When Borodin returned to Canton, he not only endorsed the agreement but also claimed, absurdly, that it had 'dealt a sharper blow to the rightists than the Communists'.[36] Borodin's more than reasonable attitude was appreciated in an unlikely quarter – the *North China Herald*, where the anti-communist George Sokolsky wrote, 'From all persons, that I have been able to gather, from Chinese and foreigners in Canton, both Mr. and Mrs. Borodin were conserving forces in Canton, whose advice was always against excess.'[37] Elsewhere, the paper celebrated 'Chiang Kai-shek's Determined Campaign against Bolshevists' and crowed that 'strike pickets [are] to be curbed'.[38]

Chiang Kai-shek had every reason to feel pleased with the result of his pronunciamiento. He had clipped the wings of the Communists and eliminated his last rival for the leadership of the KMT – and he had

---

34 According to a British intelligence report, the commission was tasked with finding out why so much money had been spent in China for so little gain. See UK National Archives, KV-2-3037. PF589/SAV1 Mikhail Borodin.

35 According to an account by Eugene Chen's daughter-in-law, it was Chen, together with the antique dealer and KMT rightist Zhang Jiangjiang, who persuaded Chiang Kai-shek not to burn his bridges with Moscow.

36 Pantsov, *Bolsheviks*, 93.

37 George Sokolsky, *North China Herald*, 24 April 1926.

38 *North China Herald*, 29 May 1926.

done so without losing the all-important support of the Soviet Union. But the Soviet response to the March coup was, on the face of it, inexplicable. Chiang Kai-shek had shown his hand. The leaders in Moscow could scarcely have been given a clearer signal that they should reassess their strategy. Chiang was, in Marxist terms, a textbook Bonapartist. Indeed, it was a standing joke among the advisors that he saw himself as Napoleon.[39] A report on the March coup by the military advisor General V. A. Stepanov suggested as much but reached exactly the wrong conclusion:

> He is definitely not an ordinary militarist but a militarist with revolutionary interests . . . I have personally heard him speak of the achievements of Washington, Napoleon, and Lenin . . . He is filled with revolutionary ideas . . . trivial details of his behavior are but signs of his weakness for self-aggrandizement and self-glorification. They may be overlooked.[40]

The weak Soviet response allowed 20 March 1926 to became a dress rehearsal for 12 April 1927, when Chiang turned on the Shanghai workers and initiated a massacre of leftists, workers, and peasants throughout China.

Why did the Soviets continue to support Chiang Kai-shek after his démarche against them? One possibility is simple inertia. After all, so much money and effort had been thrown into the Canton mission that it had acquired a momentum of its own. But the Bubnov commission had been sent to China precisely to investigate why so much had been spent for such meagre results. And, if British intelligence files can be considered reliable evidence, Borodin had recently been instructed to warn Chiang Kai-shek that if he continued to cause trouble, he would be relieved of his command.[41] If the Soviet leadership suspected Chiang before the March coup, it was all the more culpable for continuing to support him afterwards. Another explanation is that China had become a factor in the Kremlin power struggle between Stalin and the United Opposition led by Trotsky, Kamenev, and Zinoviev. Following the coup,

---

39   Vishnyakova-Akimova, *Two Years in Revolutionary China*, 166.
40   Wilbur and How, *Missionaries of Revolution*, 705–15.
41   UK National Archives, KV-2-3037. PF589/SAV1 Mikhail Borodin.

Trotsky, for the first time, called for the CCP to withdraw from the KMT.[42] However, precisely because their authority was contested, Stalin and Nikolai Bukharin doubled down on their line that the coalition with the KMT must be preserved. The Soviet debate over China was couched in terms of grand theories: permanent revolution, the democratic dictatorship of the proletariat and the peasantry, the characterisation (by the Stalinists) of the KMT as a 'bloc of four classes', and so on. But common sense dictates that continuing to arm an 'ally' who has unmasked himself as an opponent is political stupidity.

Following Chiang Kai-shek's launch of the Northern Expedition on 9 July 1926, the NRA took Changsha within a month and Wuhan by the end of the year. In turn, the KMT government relocated from Canton to Wuhan. The campaign succeeded because it was planned and led by Blyukher and because the NRA was regularly resupplied by six Soviet ships running a shuttle service.[43] As such, Jacobs' overblown description of Borodin as the Bolshevik conqueror of half of China could more realistically be applied to Blyukher. Indeed, Chiang Kai-shek, a Bonaparte without Napoleon's military talent, rarely took a tactical decision without consulting him.[44]

However, Chiang kept a firm grip on political decisions. He was determined not to be controlled by the Wuhan government; therefore, instead of continuing north, bypassing the armies of Sun Chuanfang, commander of the so-called League of Five Provinces,[45] as Blyukher planned, he insisted on striking east to take Nanchang, capital of Jiangxi Province. In so doing, he aimed to establish an independent power base, far from Wuhan with its radical workers' movement and the Left KMT government. It nearly ended disastrously for him when Sun Chuanfang counterattacked, recaptured Nanchang, and massacred hundreds of students and other suspected leftists.[46] Chiang fell to pieces, threatened

42   Pantsov, *Bolsheviks*, 92.

43   Wilbur and How, *Missionaries*, 314.

44   Vishnyakova-Akimova, *Two Years in Revolutionary China*, 212, 223. Borodin left Blyukher in charge of Canton when he went to Beijing with Sun Yat-sen. When Borodin returned, a turf war broke out and Blyukher returned to Russia. One of Chiang's demands after his March 1926 coup was that Blyukher be sent back to China. He returned to Canton in May 1926.

45   The eastern provinces of Zhejiang, Anhui, Jiangsu, Jiangxi, and Fujian.

46   In 1935, Sun Chuanfang was assassinated by Shi Jianqiao, the daughter of one of his victims. The KMT government pardoned her.

to shoot himself, and begged Blyukher to take over. Blyukher subsequently directed a second, successful assault. Once the city was secured, Chiang recovered his composure and claimed credit for the victory.[47]

In Red Wuhan, workers joined trade unions and struck for higher pay and shorter hours. In the surrounding countryside, peasants demanded land reform. A huge crowd occupied the British concession area – which the British never regained. Borodin seemed to be at the height of his powers.[48] Although Wuhan had the appearance of a city where a revolution had already taken place, the economy suffered as business owners decamped down the Yangzi. Most ominously, the KMT generals, overwhelmingly from the propertied classes, were turning against the revolution[49] – a problem that became more acute as the NRA absorbed surrendering warlord troops and their officers.

Meanwhile, Blyukher had accompanied Chiang Kai-shek almost as far as Shanghai. As the NRA prepared to take the city, the CCP attempted to seize control of its Chinese quarter in a series of uprisings, and Blyukher asked Chiang to speed up the advance to assist the Communists. When he refused, Blyukher resigned as Chiang's advisor, despite the latter's tearful pleas.[50] But even without his indispensable aide, by now nothing could prevent Chiang Kai-shek from taking Shanghai. He did so after a final, successful uprising, led by Zhou Enlai, Chen Duxiu and Voitinsky, drove out Sun Chuanfang's troops and allowed the NRA to advance into the city unopposed. But soon afterwards, as is well known, on 12 April 1927, Chiang, in league with criminal gangs, turned his guns on the workers' movement and massacred thousands. Once again, the disarray of the CCP and the Comintern in the face of the slaughter is hard to explain. They had received hard intelligence of the impending coup from a dissident general, Xue Yue, who offered to pre-empt it by arresting Chiang but was rebuffed.[51] In February, Voitinsky had warned

---

47 Vishnyakova-Akimova, *Two Years in Revolutionary China*, 251–2.

48 According to the Chen family, Borodin, a 'man of a thousand faces', was indecisive throughout the confrontation with the British. See Chen Yuan-tsung, *Return to the Middle Kingdom*, New York: Union Square Press, 2008, 209.

49 Of fifty-six generals, fifty-one were large landowners. Ibid., 244.

50 Vishnyakova-Akimova, *Two Years in Revolutionary China*, 280.

51 Harold Isaacs, *The Tragedy of the Chinese Revolution*, Chicago: Haymarket Books, 2009 [1938], 146. Xue Yue had several subsequent clashes with Chiang Kai-shek but remained within the KMT fold and ended his days in Taiwan aged one hundred and one.

the Kremlin of Chiang's plans.[52] But, eight days before the coup, Stalin and Bukharin hailed the KMT as a 'cross between party and soviets' and a 'revolutionary parliament'.[53]

More capital blunders followed. It should have been clear by now that Chiang Kai-shek had become the most dangerous enemy of the revolution, but the Wuhan government, with Borodin's approval, sent its best troops north to fight Wu Peifu and Zhang Zuolin, leaving the city virtually defenceless. At the battle of Zhumadian, the Wuhan army won a significant victory that was raucously celebrated by 30,000 workers in Wuhan. The aged Tom Mann, visiting China on behalf of the Comintern, delighted the crowd by galloping across the stage to ridicule the retreating enemy. However, the victory was won at a huge cost. Wuhan lost 14,000 men – a fifth of its troops. Hardest hit was the elite Fourth Corps, the so-called Ironsides, where CCP-supporting officers and men were concentrated.[54]

While Borodin was constrained by Comintern policy, he was also indecisive in a crisis. When the reactionary general Xu Kexiang captured Changsha with a few hundred troops, prompt action could have recovered the city, but Borodin dithered. He ordered a counterattack by peasant militias, then changed his mind, but too late to inform all the insurgents. The half-cocked revolt was thus easily suppressed.[55] He then led a delegation to appease Xu but turned back en route, retreating to Wuhan. At this point, he seems to have suffered a mental breakdown. Milly Bennett found 'the big man . . . shrunken in his clothing', rambling incoherently.[56] After his mind cleared a little, he compared the Russian and Chinese revolutions: 'Our revolution was big, big, but nothing compared to this. We work blindly, we lift the curtain and are frightened by the immensity of the scene. This revolution will kill many a Borodin.'[57]

---

52   Pantsov, *Bolsheviks*, 240.

53   Zinoviev, *Theses on the Chinese Revolution*, presented to the Politburo, 15 April 1927.

54   Vishnyakova-Akimova, *Two Years in Revolutionary China*, 321; Isaacs, *Tragedy of the Chinese Revolution*, 229. Fourth Corps officers carried out the Nanchang Uprising on 1 August 1927, now celebrated as the founding of the People's Liberation Army. Ironically, their commander, Zhang Fakui crushed the uprising.

55   Vishnyakova-Akimova, *Two Years in Revolutionary China*, 319.

56   Chen, *Return to the Middle Kingdom*, 2008, 247; Bennett and Grunfeld, *On Her Own*, 242.

57   Bennett and Grunfeld, *On Her Own*, 243.

If Borodin had suffered a nervous breakdown, it would perhaps have been understandable. His wife had been captured in February and handed over to Zhang Zuolin, who intended to execute her after a show trial in Beijing. In the event, she was released when a judge, probably bribed by the Comintern, acquitted her, then promptly fled the country in fear of his life. Soviet agents smuggled her to Vladivostok.

Short of arming the workers and peasants – an option ruled out so long as he was obliged to preserve the alliance with the KMT – Borodin's last remaining hope was Feng Yuxiang and the Guominjun. In June, Wang Jingwei, who had returned from his Paris exile in April, led a delegation from Wuhan to meet Feng in Zhengzhou.[58] But Feng, who had previously shown himself to be a turncoat, did so again.[59] Throwing in his lot with Chiang Kai-shek, he gave the delegation an ultimatum: break with the Communists and expel Borodin, or he would march on Wuhan.

In Moscow, Stalin, realising the old strategy was on the point of collapse, ordered a swing to the left and sent M. N. Roy, a radical by instinct, to Wuhan to implement the new line. But, far from improving the parlous situation, Roy made matters worse.[60] After a secret meeting of the Executive Committee of the Communist International, Stalin sent a message to Roy and Borodin ordering them to arm the CCP, raise a 50,000-strong army and set up a revolutionary tribunal to try disloyal NRA officers. The Soviet advisors and the CCP leadership were dumbfounded by this 'fairy tale from overseas'. No one in Wuhan believed it could be implemented. In all likelihood, neither did Stalin, for whom it was an alibi to be produced as necessary in his battle against the Opposition. But Roy, who knew little about China and adhered to the Kremlin line, had faith in the leaders of the Left KMT. He therefore showed the message to Wang Jingwei, Eugene Chen, and Madame Sun, hoping to reassure them that they still had Soviet support. Far from being reassured, they were horrified and terrified. To calm the storm,

---

58 Wang had travelled via Moscow, where he received a 'handsome welcome'. Wilbur and How, *Missionaries of Revolution*, 402.

59 Feng had betrayed Wu Peifu by carrying out a coup in Beijing on 23 October 1924.

60 See John P. Haithcox, 'The Roy-Lenin Debate on Colonial Policy: A New Interpretation', *Journal of Asian Studies*, No. 23 (1963), 93–101.

Borodin asked Moscow to recall Roy.[61] But it seems the incident convinced Wang Jingwei that it was time to break with the Communists.[62]

Across China, a chain reaction of counter-revolution was taking place. In Beijing, Zhang Zuolin stormed the Soviet embassy and lynched Li Dazhao and nineteen others. In Canton, the former capital of the revolution, General Li Jishen, unleashed his troops against the Left. Thousands of workers were rounded up and paraded through the streets. The Whampoa academy was closed, and hundreds of cadets were confined on prison ships. Amid the mayhem, Solomon Lozovsky, general secretary of the Red International of Labour Unions, arrived to take part in a pan-Pacific trade union conference. He hurriedly left for Wuhan where, following the new Moscow line at the rescheduled conference, he gave a rousing speech calling for social revolution.[63] Milly Bennett, accustomed to Borodin's careful cultivation of the KMT leadership, ridiculed him as a 'cartoon Bolshevik' and described him, rather fatuously, as a 'mouthpiece for the mechanistic world revolutionary theory of Leon Trotsky'.[64]

Red Wuhan took one last surreal gasp of the revolutionary wind. On 20 June, hundreds of delegates assembled for the Fourth All-China Congress of Trade Unions. The Congress, decked with red flags, lasted ten days and called for a punitive expedition to destroy the counter-revolutionary Chiang Kai-shek. Then, in one of the 'most egregious errors of that period', on Borodin's orders, the workers' militia voluntarily disarmed itself 'in plain view of the delegates' so that it could be more easily absorbed as worker and peasant detachments into the forces of Zhang Fakui – a supposed Wuhan loyalist. Immediately afterwards, troops occupied Wuhan's trade union offices.[65]

---

61   Jacobs, *Borodin*, 269–71; Samaren Roy, *M. N. Roy: A Political Biography*, New Delhi: Orient Longman, 1997, 76–8.

62   To be sure, Wang Jingwei had other reasons; he had opposed sending the Ironsides north – a decision he said left Wuhan 'a sitting duck.' With no reliable troops to defend the city, he may have felt a rapprochement with Chiang Kai-shek was his only viable option left. See Bennett and Grunfeld, *On Her Own,* 202.

63   Vishnyakova-Akimova, *Two Years in Revolutionary China*, 258–9, 317.

64   Bennett and Grunfeld, *On Her Own*, 255. Lozovsky was, in fact, a particularly slavish supporter of Stalin, which did not, however, save his life. Furthermore, if any theory was mechanistic, it was the Stalin-backed 'stages theory.'

65   Vishnyakova-Akimova, *Two Years in Revolutionary China*, 324; Jacobs, *Borodin*, 282–3. Zhang Fakui, commander of the Fourth Corps Ironsides, later sided with Chiang and crushed the Nanchang uprising and the Canton Commune.

The Soviet advisors in Wuhan were now in mortal danger. Soon after, Blyukher was poisoned. While he recovered, one of his aides died.[66] In mid-July, Borodin fled to a nearby resort with Song Qingling, Rayna Prohme, and others, as General He Jian's troops shot up his headquarters in Wuhan. The situation was, of course, much worse for the rank-and-file Chinese revolutionaries:

> The central leadership, evidently no longer able to control the situation, simply left comrades to their own devices . . . Since there was no longer any revolution in which to participate many of them were forced to beg for their living on the streets and await arrest and execution.[67]

On 15 July, Wang Jingwei called a KMT Central Executive Committee meeting to formally break the alliance with the Communists and expel Borodin. Only Eugene Chen and Liao Zhongkai's widow dissented.[68] Twelve days later, Wang and his officials bade Borodin a hypocritical farewell at the railway station. It had been decided that Borodin should travel overland to Russia, since Chiang Kai-shek's hatred made the river passage via Shanghai too dangerous. On the way, Borodin and his companions made a risky stop at Zhengzhou, Feng Yuxiang's stronghold. Meanwhile, Stalin tried to retrieve the situation by ordering an uprising. The futile and hastily conceived seizure of Nanchang lasted only a day, provoking Wang Jingwei to ask Feng Yuxiang to arrest Borodin. Feng, however, keeping his options open and no doubt hoping for a resumption of Soviet aid, allowed him to continue unhindered.

The trip through northern China in cars and trucks was long and difficult. Among Borodin's thirty-strong party were Eugene Chen's two sons, Jack and Percy, and the prolific American journalist Anna Louise Strong, who, after arriving in Wuhan as the revolution crumbled, had badgered Borodin to take her with him so she could write his biography. Borodin was understandably depressed, but, freed of his responsibilities, he spoke openly and frankly to Strong. The KMT,

---

66   Vishnyakova-Akimova, *Two Years in Revolutionary China*, 325.

67   Wang Fanxi, *Memoirs of a Chinese revolutionary*, New York: Columbia University Press, 1991, 37, 42.

68   Song Qingling was not a member of the CEC.

he said, was 'a toilet, which, however often you flush it, still stinks'. As for the 'Left' Wuhan government, it was 'a rabbit before an anaconda, trembling, knowing it is going to be devoured'.[69] When Borodin arrived in Ulan Bator, the Mongolians, not quite knowing what to do with him, gave him a hero's welcome. After these last days in the limelight, he flew on to Russia, and an uncertain fate, in a tiny plane with Jack Chen.

Blyukher was one of the last Soviet advisors to leave China. Chiang Kai-shek, who had developed an odd (and unreciprocated) affection for him, insisted on bidding him farewell in Shanghai. Unknown to Chiang, Blyukher had helped plan the 1 August Nanchang Uprising.[70] When they met, Chiang, a man who was admittedly not noted for empathy, wondered why Blyukher looked depressed. Bizarrely, he later described the meeting 'as one of the most moving partings of my life'.[71]

Borodin was not the out-and-out imposter caricatured by Trotsky. Rather, he was an old Bolshevik who shared the strengths but also the weaknesses of that type, including a tendency to think schematically and faithfully adhere to the party line, even when it flew in the face of common sense. He implemented Stalin's policy, not his own, but he carried it out faithfully. He also, no doubt for reasons of self-preservation, went along with the cynical attempt to pin the blame on Chen Duxiu and the CCP. For these, he is culpable. More charitably, he was a man of some abilities who was over-promoted and out of his depth.

Sneevliet can be forgiven for seeing China through the prism of his Indies experience. Indeed, it was not wrong to advise the CCP to look for political allies. As he explained to a student conference in 1920, his aim in the Dutch Indies had been to turn Sarekat Islam 'into a communist organisation, an organisation that will be a member of the Third International'.[72] But the KMT was a militaristic clique, not a mass party.

---

69   Anna Louise Strong, *China's Millions*, New York: Coward-McCann, 1928, 38–9.

70   As he bid farewell to Chiang, he was requesting an arms shipment of 15,000 rifles, 10 million rounds, and thirty machine guns to be sent to Communist forces retreating from Nanchang.

71   Wilbur and How, *Missionaries of Revolution*, 423.

72   Quoted in Dov Bing, 'Lenin and Sneevliet: The Origins of the Theory of Colonial Revolution in the Dutch East Indies', *New Zealand Journal of Asian Studies*, Vol. 11, No. 1 (2009), 153–77, 159.

Unlike Sarekat Islam, it did not even have a reservoir of potential recruits. Its mass membership was instead created from scratch by the CCP. As the CCP member Zheng Chaolin put it: 'It was the experience, funds and firepower of the Soviet proletariat that fashioned a new political party, modelled on the organisation of the Russian Bolsheviks, under the old and vacant sign-board of the Kuomintang.'[73]

The CCP leaders understood the KMT far better than Sneevliet; thus, his refusal to accept their advice and criticism was unforgivable. Perhaps he had become accustomed to obedience from his young Indonesian supporters, including the aforementioned Semaun, who addressed him as 'my guru'. Whatever his qualities as a revolutionary and an internationalist, Sneevliet's arrogance helped steer the CCP into a blind alley. The Soviets ended up supporting Sun Yat-sen's militarist project to unify China by force and in doing so created an army that destroyed their own party.

Karakhan was skilful, personable, and astute but toed the party line and lacked political judgment. In 1925, he offered military aid and advisors to the serial turncoat Feng Yuxiang. But it was Feng's defection to Chiang Kai-shek that delivered the final blow to Red Wuhan.

Like most military advisors, Blyukher kept out of politics. But, to his credit, he was wary of Chiang Kai-shek and had suggested it might be necessary to clip his wings by removing troops from under his command. And he quit his post as advisor – albeit belatedly – before Chiang's Shanghai coup.

Voitinsky was more sceptical of the KMT than Borodin and keener on preserving the independence of the CCP. At one point, he reported to Stalin that Borodin was in danger of liquidating the party. He helped organise the Hong Kong strike and the Shanghai uprisings, acquiring the reputation of something of a wild man among the KMT lefts like Eugene Chen. Nevertheless, he remained a leadership loyalist, representing the 'left wing' of official policy. He introduced the standard anti-Trotskyist motion at a CCP congress and never joined the opposition.

Roy liked to think of himself as a man of action, but all his actions failed – from his gun-running in World War I , a rather adventurist

---

73   Zheng Chaolin and Gregor Benton, *An Oppositionist for Life: Memoirs of the Chinese Revolutionary Zheng Chaolin*, Atlantic Highlands, NJ: Humanities Press, 1997, 72.

1920 scheme, endorsed by Lenin and Trotsky, to invade British India
from Afghanistan, to his blunder in China. Indeed, he arrived in China
knowing virtually nothing of the country and the situation but convinced
he knew all the answers. And while his bit part did not change anything
fundamentally, it provided Stalin with another convenient scapegoat.
Afterwards, he remained convinced he had been right all along.

3
Journalists

The American journalist Rayna Prohme, editor of the Wuhan government's official newspaper, the *Hankow People's Tribune*, was the brightest star in Mikhail Borodin's circle of admirers. In addition to working on the *Tribune*, she acted as Borodin's unofficial press secretary. Reporters seeking an interview with the great man therefore had to negotiate with Rayna, his indispensable assistant and gatekeeper. She had daily meetings with 'Bee', as she called him, and developed a profound admiration for him. Among less scrupulous journalists, their close association became food for gossip, of all-night drinking parties, even an affair. She laughed the rumours off, but told a friend 'the high advisor, Borodin . . . has impressed me more than any person I have met in a long time . . . Bill thinks I am utterly dominated by him. I imagine I am.'[1] Bill was Rayna's husband, chief editor of the KMT news agency.

Both Rayna and Bill Prohme were workaholics. From 1925 to 1927, they worked tirelessly and at the expense of their health to tell the story of the Chinese Revolution. When they met, both were radicals but lacked well-defined political affiliations. Rayna was studying economics at Berkeley, and Bill was working as a journalist in San Francisco. They became close, although both were already married. It is not clear whether they had begun an affair when Rayna, seeking adventure, left for China

---

1   Baruch Hirson, Arthur Knodel, and Gregor Benton, *Reporting the Chinese Revolution: The Letters of Rayna Prohme*, London: Pluto Press, 2007, 72.

in 1923, intending to stay five years. But her departure precipitated a health crisis for Bill, who suffered from tuberculosis. Rayna returned from China as soon as she heard Bill's condition had worsened. After she nursed him back to health, they returned to China together. Soon after they arrived in Beijing, Eugene Chen hired Bill to run his recently established KMT News Agency, and before long, both Bill and Rayna were working together on Chen's *Peking People's Tribune*.[2]

Soon after the Prohmes arrived in China, the political situation in Beijing soured. The supposedly enlightened Feng Yuxiang had seized control of the capital in alliance with the KMT, but his other ally was the reactionary Manchurian strongman Zhang Zuolin. In August 1925, Eugene Chen was arrested and brutalised by Zhang's troops. He wound up the Beijing office, and Rayna and Bill left for Canton, where Bill continued running the KMT News Agency and Rayna worked on the official government newspaper, the *Canton Gazette*.

Rayna came from a wealthy family. Her father was vice-president of the Chicago Board of Trade, and she had a gilded childhood and adolescence. From an early age, she gathered a circle of admirers attracted by her intense and engaging personality, which was matched by her bright red hair. A friend described it as 'a flaming aureole, with sun and brightness in it. Her eyes were large, reddish brown and warm, with interest and laughter in them.'[3] Rayna married her high school sweetheart, Samson 'Raph' Raphaelson, later famous for writing the Broadway play *The Jazz Singer*, which was adapted as the world's first talking picture. They were introduced to radical politics by the fashionable Greenwich Village set around Max Eastman's monthly *The Masses*. When Rayna moved to Berkeley, she became part of another leftish circle around the anthropologist Alfred Kroeber, famous for his study of Ishi, the last member of the Yahi indigenous people.[4] Raph followed Rayna to California. Their marriage did not last long, but, after an amicable divorce, they remained lifelong friends.

In China, Rayna and Bill drove themselves to the brink of exhaustion. But, whereas Rayna was spontaneous, bordering on chaotic in her style of work, Bill was dour and almost Prussian in his insistence on order

2   Eugene Chen, foreign minister of the southern government, set up the agency in 1925 with finance provided by the banker Farstan Song, an associate of Feng Yuxiang.

3   Hirson et al., *Reporting the Chinese Revolution*, 19.

4   Ishi's biography, *Ishi in Two Worlds*, Berkeley: University of California Press, 1961, was written by Alfred Kroeber's wife, Theodora.

and routine. The press pack, cynical and dismissive of the revolution, knew Rayna was as 'red as they come', but they were charmed by her. By contrast, they regarded Bill as humourless, vehement, and dogmatic. Despite their contrasting personalities, they were a devoted couple, as testified by Rayna's endearing letters to Bill.

Milly Bennett, Rayna's colleague on the People's Tribune, was a close but critical friend. She was less committed to the cause than Rayna and allowed a note of resentment to creep into her description of Rayna, who 'got a daily pep talk from Bee. I did not. This was the difference between being a fascinating dame with bright red hair and an unfascinating dame without red hair'.[5]

In 1927, the celebrity journalist Vincent 'Jimmy' Sheean blundered into the Prohmes' marriage. Sheean had made his reputation as a reporter by clandestinely entering the short-lived Republic of the Rif to interview its leader, Abd el-Krim el-Khattabi.[6] Subsequently, the North American Newspaper Alliance sent him to report on the Chinese Revolution and, after a brief stays in Shanghai and Nanjing, he sailed upriver to see Red Wuhan for himself. When he met Rayna to ask for an interview with Borodin, he immediately fell in love with her. He was enchanted by her 'red-gold hair', her 'frivolous turned-up nose', and her laugh, which he described as 'the gayest, most unselfconscious sound in the world. You might have thought that it did not come from a person at all, but from some impulse of gaiety in the air'.[7]

Sheean began turning up at the People's Tribune office every day to see Rayna. If he missed a day, he felt uneasy and bereft. Milly Bennett, recognising that he was writing sympathetic stories about the revolution, tolerated him. But Rayna called him a spoiled child and told him to 'sober up and get out of town'. She instructed Bennett to tell Sheean she was out of the office when he called, but he would simply hang around until Rayna showed her face. Although Rayna tolerated him as a sometimes-amusing pest, it is clear from her letters that there was never an affair.

---

5   Milly Bennett and Tom Grunfeld, *On Her Own: Journalistic Adventures from San Francisco to the Chinese Revolution, 1917–1927*, London: Routledge, 2015, 247.

6   Abd el-Krim el-Khattabi was a Berber guerrilla leader who fought against Spanish colonialists and held out for five years (1921–26) before being defeated by a joint Spanish and French force that used chemical weapons.

7   Vincent Sheean, *Personal History*, London: Hamilton, 1969 [1935], 214.

Besotted and obsessed, Sheean dismissed Rayna's husband as 'an emotional Red' whose 'violent revolutionary enthusiasm' masked an inability to argue logically. The two men could scarcely have been more different. While Bill was workmanlike, committed, and dependable, Sheean was, by his own admission, an irritating young man. He was tall, handsome, wore ostentatious white silk suits, smoked Egyptian cigarettes, drank expensive Scotch whisky, and affected the air of a lethargic dilettante for whom success came without exertion. He was a prolific name-dropper who claimed to be friends with Ernest Hemingway, Dorothy Parker, Louise Bryant, Gertrude Stein, and other celebrities. He played up his status as a foreign correspondent and, indeed, helped define the role; Alfred Hitchcock's eponymous 1940 film was based on Sheean's best-selling autobiography, written precociously when he was just thirty-four. The irony is that although he was celebrated as a journalist, Sheean was careless with facts. Having had ten years to check, he wrote that Sun Yat-sen died in 1924, not 1925. He recalled Chiang Kai-shek as a young man of thirty from a poor background in Guangdong Province who, despite having no education, had risen through the ranks from private to general. None of that was true. Chiang was forty when Sheean interviewed him. Born into a well-off merchant family in Zhejiang Province, he had trained as an officer at the Baoding Military Academy. Sheean claimed that Eugene Chen was mixed race. He was not, although his children were. In fact, the mixed-race rumour was invented by Eugene Chen's political enemies.[8] It should be said, also, that Sheean's assessment of Borodin was superficial and impressionistic – based on Borodin's personal mannerisms and turns of phrase.

When Borodin fled China, Rayna expected to be invited to travel with him. Instead, he ordered her to accompany Song Qingling and Eugene Chen back to Russia via Shanghai. Though Song Qingling affected a friendly and informal manner in private, she was a grand personage in a position to make demands. In order to rebut rumours that she was having an affair with Eugene Chen, she needed a chaperone, as any suggestion of impropriety would undermine her standing as the official widow of Sun Yat-sen. She was an important political asset who appeared to justify the Left KMT and later the CCP claim to an unbroken line to 'the father of modern China'. In Shanghai, her party,

---

8   Ibid.,193, 197, 207.

including Chen's daughters, were allowed to board a Soviet steamer for Vladivostok. Chiang Kai-shek was not secure enough to risk a move against Madame Sun. Bill was planning to go with them but, at the last minute, Eugene Chen high-handedly told him to stay in Shanghai to do unspecified liaison work. It is possible Chen feared that, with Bill aboard, their party would look like two couples instead of a man, a woman, and a chaperone. In any case, it was an unfortunate decision. Bill would never see Rayna again.

In Moscow, Madame Sun and Eugene Chen were welcomed as heroes. They were given suites in the luxurious Metropole Hotel, feted as celebrities, taken to ballets and operas, and invited to lavish parties hosted by Bukharin and other senior leaders. Somewhat surreally, two of Eugene Chen's children, Jack and Silan, won a Charleston competition. But things soon turned sour for Rayna. Despite the initial warm reception given to the Chinese, behind the scenes, Moscow had written off the Chinese Revolution. Stalin's attention was focused on finishing off the Opposition and preparing a grand celebration of the tenth anniversary of the October Revolution. Rayna's salary, which had been paid by the Comintern, was abruptly cut off, as was Bill's. She had hoped she could find Bill a job with the Soviet news agency TASS in Moscow, but that was now impossible. He decided to move from Shanghai to Manila to find work.

Sheean, lovesick, arrived in Moscow in mid-September, just as Rayna's situation took another turn for the worse. She had been living with Eugene Chen and Song Qingling in the Sugar Palace, an old bourgeois mansion, but relations in the household had become strained. Her chaperoning duties completed, Rayna had served her purpose and was an encumbrance. Song and Chen set off for a holiday in a southern resort, leaving Rayna, who had no winter clothes, to freeze in Moscow. Before leaving, they made it clear to Rayna that she was no longer welcome – possibly because, as one of Chen's daughters later maintained, the rumours of an affair were true. Rayna was forced to find a place to live with what little money she had, in a city with an endemic housing crisis. Nevertheless, she wrote to Bill, she was glad to leave, as she 'was never accepted there as a legitimate member of the group from China, but as a sort of super-menial, something that the cat dragged in'.[9] Sheean helped

9   Letter from Rayna Prohme to Bill Prohme, 25 September 1927; Hirson et al., *Reporting the Chinese Revolution*, 114.

Rayna find a room with the wife of a Russian diplomat based in Beijing
and left for London soon afterwards. In letters to Bill, Rayna acknowledged that this was 'one good thing' Sheean had done, but complained
that, despite knowing her desperate situation, he had borrowed money
from her:

> It is cold here already and I shiver. The devil of it is that I foolishly
> trusted Sheean, who arrived here without a lot of money. I let him
> take some and he was to pay it back by buying me some warm things
> in Berlin or London. And, of course, he will. But I hadn't figured that
> it would be cold so soon. Also Jimmie is a selfish beast.[10]

Rayna found living with the diplomat's wife intolerable. She moved
several times but never found comfortable accommodation. Worse, she
was by now seriously ill – suffering from headaches, feelings of confusion, and blackouts. She still held out hope that 'the chief', Borodin,
would come up with some new project for her and Bill, but Borodin had
been ordered to keep his distance from 'the Chinese' and was in no position to help.

Sheean returned to Moscow in November, during the celebrations for
the tenth anniversary of the revolution. The atmosphere was tense.
Trotsky was nowhere to be seen, having been expelled from the party.
Sheean and Rayna had to pass through cordons of soldiers to get to Red
Square, where they saw Stalin saluting the anniversary parades. They
heard rumours that a group of Chinese students had been arrested after
unfurling a banner that read 'Long Live Trotsky' and that Trotsky's close
friend Adolph Joffe, who had signed the fateful agreement with Sun
Yat-sen, had committed suicide. But, despite the warning signs that the
revolution was degenerating, Rayna had decided to enrol at the
Comintern's Lenin Institute for training in clandestine work. Sheean
was horrified and several times kept her up till the early hours trying to
dissuade her, despite her increasingly severe headaches.

Having failed to seduce Rayna or dissuade her from enrolling at the
Lenin School, Sheean decided to leave Moscow. He asked Rayna to put
on her most beautiful gold qipao and join him for one last 'bourgeois'

---

10   Letter from Rayna Prohme to Bill Prohme; Hirson et al., *Reporting the Chinese
Revolution*, 129.

meal at the Grand Hotel, although earlier that day she had fainted in a friend's apartment. Rayna then dragged Sheean to a ceremony where the aged Klara Zetkin was to receive the Order of the Red Banner in recognition of her lifetime of struggle. Rayna was moved to tears, but Sheean was busy ridiculing the tubby figure of Béla Kun, standing next to Zetkin on the platform. Rayna flared up at him. 'Oh, damn you,' she said. 'Can't you feel it at all?'

The next day, Rayna collapsed. After Sheean fetched a doctor from the German embassy, she briefly recovered, and Borodin and others came to visit her. However, she soon relapsed and died on 21 November 1927. The autopsy was inconclusive, but it's possible Rayna had suffered a series of strokes brought on by overwork and stress.[11] Having abandoned her in life, the Comintern gave her a state funeral. As the procession marched through snow-covered Moscow in silence, Madame Sun, perhaps contrite about the way she had treated her friend, refused to ride in the limousine provided for her despite the cold. Sheean walked beside her, seeing visions of Rayna through the falling snow. Though Borodin did not attend, he visited Sheean that evening to explain that on principle, he never went to funerals. He was moved by Rayna's death but could only manage a few banal remarks, including his favourite phrase about taking the long view. The next day, Sheean left for Berlin.

When Bill Prohme arrived in Moscow, nearly a month after Rayna's funeral, he was unable to find out exactly what had happened to her. Thereafter, his tuberculosis prevented him from getting regular work, and he spent time in a Swiss sanatorium before eventually moving to Hawaii. When Sheean revealed the intensity of his feelings for Rayna in his 1935 autobiography *Personal History*, Bill was enraged and told Sheean so in a series of letters. Although, in the book, Sheean hypocritically claimed to have come to value Bill as a friend, a vindictive and self-pitying letter to one of Rayna's friends tells an entirely different story:

> He is not a particularly intelligent man, and I know *all* about his relationship with Rayna ... and I know that he knew and understood nothing of her last phase. Yet a violent, angry, vituperative, childish letter from this rather stupid man, who is very ill and obviously not

11   Bennett and Grunfeld, *On Her Own*, 312.

quite himself, has the power to paralyze me for good chunks of time . . . If he were well I could make short work of him; but he is ill, and I have to take everything he says and turn the other cheek.[12]

Bill Prohme killed himself on the anniversary of Rayna's death, in the year Sheean's book came out. Both he and Rayna, loyal foot soldiers of the revolution, were ill used by its 'great leaders', scarcely any of whom, ironically, showed any aptitude for the roles they claimed for themselves. The Prohmes were particularly badly let down by Eugene Chen who, when they left Beijing for Canton in 1925, had thanked them profusely and promised them that 'the KMT never forgets'. At the time, they had no idea they would ever have to call in Chen's promise, joking about his theatrical farewell. By contrast with the Prohmes, Sheean, who used Rayna's story to decorate his autobiography, his reputation made by the Hitchcock semi-biopic, became a role model for future generations of journalists.

---

12   Letter from Vincent 'Jimmy' Sheean to Helen Freeland, 24 September 1935; Hirson et al., *Reporting the Chinese Revolution*, 155.

4

A Knight of Labour in Shanghai

After the 1927 defeat, the remnants of the CCP-controlled armed forces retreated to remote mountain areas where they set up bases, most notably in Jiangxi Province. In the cities, the party and the trade unions were reduced to a clandestine existence. Many foreigners worked alongside their Chinese comrades in the underground, mainly in Shanghai, where the foreign concession areas provided some limited space for organisation. Among them was the itinerant British Communist George Hardy.

In August 1927, the Red International of Labour Unions (RILU)[1] sent Hardy to Wuhan to take charge of the Pan-Pacific Trade Union Secretariat (PPTUS), which had been established there in May. Hardy's partner, Patricia 'Paddy' Ayriss, who had previously worked at the headquarters of the Communist Party of Great Britain (CPGB) on King Street, went with him.[2] By the time they arrived, the revolution had already collapsed. Borodin and most of the Soviet advisors had left or were on their way out of China, and Wuhan had made its peace with Chiang Kai-shek. Leftists across the country were being killed with impunity by Chiang and his allies. The 1 August armed

---

1   Often referred to as the Profintern, its Russian abbreviation. See Glossary.

2   Paddy Ayriss's real name was Jessie Emma Garman. She was working at the CPGB headquarters on King Street when she and Hardy began an affair. Hardy's first wife, Edith, threatened to go to the newspapers, so in order to avoid a scandal, the party sent Hardy and Ayriss to Moscow. Ayriss worked for the Soviet embassy in London from 1937 to 1941.

uprising in Nanchang failed after a few days, and the troops who had taken part were being hunted down by their former commander Zhang Fakui. The official Moscow line, however, remained that the revolution had merely suffered a setback and a renewed upsurge was imminent.

By the time Hardy and Ayriss arrived in Wuhan in late September, it was clear that continuing the work of the secretariat in Wuhan, even on a clandestine basis, would be next to impossible. The old staff left after as soon as they arrived. For safety, Hardy and Ayriss took lodgings in the former British Concession, now a jointly administered 'Special Area'. Arrests, beatings, and executions of radicals and ordinary workers were commonplace, although there was still sporadic resistance. After six female students were executed, a crowd seized the Kuomintang officials responsible and killed them on the spot. Despite the precarious situation, Hardy and Ayriss managed to produce five editions of the secretariat's journal *Pan-Pacific Worker*. Because the post office refused to handle them, they had to smuggle them out of Wuhan.

The bloody suppression of the Canton Commune ended all possibility of work in Wuhan. Stalin, hoping to confound the Opposition with good news, paying little attention to conditions on the ground in China, ordered the Canton uprising to coincide with the fifteenth congress of the Soviet Communist Party. Two agents he had recently sent to China, Vissarion Lominadze and Heinz Neumann, organised the action.[3] Around 6,000 insurgents were killed, including the leader of the uprising, Zhang Tailei. At the time, Hardy defended the uprising – a position he later repudiated: 'This was a serious error on my part . . . With the betrayal of the national revolution so complete, Canton surrounded by

---

3 Neumann joined the KPD in 1920. He was one of the party's leading theoreticians, editor-in-chief of the *Rote Fahne*, and was elected to the Reichstag. He initially supported the ultra-left line that the SPD and Nazis were equally dangerous but changed his mind in 1932 and fell out of favour in the party. In 1935 he was deported from Switzerland to the Soviet Union, where Stalin had him shot in 1937. Lominadze was a former first secretary of the Georgian Communist Party. Having long been a loyal Stalinist, he joined the Trotskyist opposition in 1932 and shot himself in 1935 when he was about to be arrested. Regarding the Canton uprising, Victor Serge went so far as to suggest that Stalin knew in advance that it was doomed, but Trotsky believed that the leadership, however deluded, was hoping for success. See Susan Weissman, *Victor Serge: The Course Is Set on Hope*, London: Verso, 2013, 104–5.

Chinese and imperialist armed forces, it was a leftist action facing inevitable defeat.'[4]

Hardy and Ayriss left for Shanghai, where they would spend the next three years (apart from a short break from September to October 1928, when Hardy was sent to Britain on a Comintern assignment). Of necessity, their work was strictly underground; the authorities in the International Settlement regularly handed suspected radicals over to the KMT to be imprisoned or executed, and any Chinese known to be associated with a foreign agent of the Comintern or RILU would be immediately arrested. Agents, therefore, had a limited shelf life. Fearing his presence was endangering his Chinese comrades, Hardy reluctantly decided to leave.

Hardy was one of the Comintern's most experienced activists. While not literally a member of the Knights of Labor – that pioneering American workers' organisation had virtually disappeared in the 1890s – he was a knight errant of the early labour movement in the mould of Tom Mann or James Larkin. Before he joined the Communist Party, Hardy had been a roving labour activist for a decade and a half. He had protested against racist atrocities in the Belgian Congo, been jailed for anti-war activities in the United States, and, for a brief period, been general secretary of the Industrial Workers of the World (IWW).

Hardy was born in Yorkshire in 1884, his father an illiterate but radical farmworker, his mother a Baptist who read the newspaper to her husband. He left school at twelve – top of his class but barely literate, as he put it. After brief stints as a farmworker and a plater's mate in a shipyard, he sought escape from a drudgery by joining the Hussars. A skilled horseman and crack shot, he could not stand the discipline and quit after punching a sergeant. Soon afterwards, he emigrated to Canada. Along with fifty other young 'assisted' emigrants, the restless and rebellious twenty-two-year-old marched to the railway station accompanied by a brass band. According to the local paper, they were off to 'consolidate the unity of the Dominions on which the sun never sets.'[5]

After arriving in Canada penniless, he took a succession of jobs around Toronto as a farm worker, on the railways, and in a tractor factory. In all of them, he clashed with management and quit or was

4   George Hardy, *Those Stormy Years*, London: Lawrence & Wishart, 1956, 201.
5   Ibid., 19.

fired. In his next job, he joined the International Brotherhood of Teamsters but was reported as an 'agitator' by a fellow worker and fired. Blacklisted, recently married, his wife pregnant, Hardy moved to British Columbia, where a Swedish lumberjack who was a member of the IWW introduced him to Marxism. After reading *Value, Price, and Profit* and then graduating to *Capital*, he joined the Socialist Party of Canada, organised a branch of the Teamsters union, and led a successful strike. After a second strike failed, noting that the Socialist Party had disdained to involve itself in this purely economic struggle and the Teamsters union had offered no help, he cut his ties with both and joined the IWW, taking his Teamsters branch with him.

For the next decade, Hardy travelled the world as an activist with the syndicalist IWW. Arriving in Australia in 1912, he was unimpressed by the world's first workers' government, which had been formed by the Australian Labor Party in 1910. The Labor leaders, he observed, were 'masters of double talk' who hamstrung trade unions with complicated arbitration procedures.[6] When he returned to Canada, by now a well-known agitator, he was initially refused entry.

During the Vancouver miners' strike for union recognition that lasted from September 1912 until the summer of 1914, Hardy led the trades council and the Miners Liberation League. When the employers brought in scabs and the government sent heavily armed troops to arrest hundreds of strikers, he denounced the British Columbia premier, Richard McBride, to his face and accused the attorney general, William Bowser, of murder. Shortly before the start of World War I, the strike ended in defeat as many leftists succumbed to patriotic fever. Hardy, however, stood firm and joined the internationalists organised around the Chicago anti-war paper *International Socialist Review*. The war would nevertheless bring personal tragedy when his two brothers, ignoring his pleas, joined up and were subsequently killed.

Back in Yorkshire during the war, Hardy worked on the Hull docks and campaigned against conscription. Horrified by stories of atrocities in the Belgian Congo related, approvingly, by a Belgian seafarer, he decided to see for himself and signed on a ship bound for Boma, the capital of the colony. He found an armed camp, where 'sentries . . . with fixed bayonets' stood guard as African dockers were beaten mercilessly

---

6   Ibid., 45.

for trivial offences – or simply on a whim. Writing in 1956, during the Mau Mau uprising, Hardy compared British atrocities in Kenya to the Belgian practice of castrating Congolese, related in E. D. Morel's *Red Rubber*. Thanks to recent court cases, we now know that during the uprising the British also used castration as a weapon of terror.[7]

Hardy signed on a cargo ship back to Boston in 1916 and was elected general secretary of IWW-affiliated Marine Workers Industrial Union on the Great Lakes. During a strike on Lake Superior, the employers hired gunmen to attack workers. Hardy resisted calls to arm strike pickets, but, after the United States entered the war, Woodrow Wilson launched a full-scale assault on the labour movement, targeting its internationalist wing in particular. Emboldened employers attacked strikers across the country with impunity. In August, IWW activist Frank Little was lynched in Butte, Montana, by detectives working for the Anaconda Copper Company.

Hardy called for a conference of miners, seamen, and steelworkers to put a stop to the 'bloody slaughterhouse in Europe',[8] but he was arrested in a general sweep of IWW members carried out by the FBI and locked up in Cook County Jail. When Hardy and the fifty-odd other Wobblies in the jail heard about the October Revolution, they kept their spirits up by singing, 'All hail to the Bolsheviki / We will fight for our class and be free.'

Hardy was put on trial with one hundred other members of the IWW, including its leader Big Bill Haywood. Because guilty verdicts were predetermined in the four-month trial, the defendants used it as a propaganda platform. Haywood was sentenced to twenty years.[9] Hardy got a year and a day, and on his release, Haywood told him to go to Britain to organise a solidarity campaign. His arrival was announced by George Lansbury in the *Daily Herald*. On the return journey, Hardy signed on as a stoker on a White Star boat in Liverpool and sneaked into the United States by sliding down a baggage chute.

After the Bolshevik success in Russia, syndicalists in the IWW, Hardy among them, began to rethink their opposition to 'politics' and the need

---

7 See, for example, 'Kenya's Mau Mau Uprising: Victims Tell Their Stories', *BBC News*, 6 June 2013, bbc.co.uk.

8 Hardy, *Those Stormy Years*, 73.

9 Haywood was released pending an appeal. In 1921, he skipped bail and fled to Soviet Russia, where he died in 1928.

for a revolutionary party. With all the former IWW leaders in jail or in exile, Hardy was elected general secretary at the May 1920 general convention. Later that year, while representing the IWW at a conference in Berlin, he was invited to Moscow to meet Lenin. He had to travel clandestinely and first took a ship to Estonia, where he disembarked disguised as a returning Russian prisoner of war. According to his account of his meeting with Lenin, he persuaded the Soviet leader to accept the programmatic compromises – for example avoiding calls for insurrection – necessary to launch a legal party in the United States.[10] Whatever his tactical hesitations, once back in America, Hardy tried to persuade the IWW to affiliate to the Red International of Labour Unions (RILU), but the tension between the syndicalists and Communist sympathisers in the IWW was building towards a split. In 1922, Hardy was expelled from the IWW, joined the Communist Party, and began working full time for the RILU.

Once he changed his allegiance, Hardy never wavered in his loyalty to the Communist movement. He resumed his travelling activism, now on behalf of the RILU. Back in Britain, he was one of the key leaders of the National Minority Movement, heading its transport workers' section. Sent to China to take charge of the PPTUS, Hardy's main task was to assist Chinese trade unionists in the All-China Federation of Trade Unions, now reduced to a clandestine existence. Low wages and dreadful working conditions meant that strikes were frequent, though intense repression meant that political meetings had to be organised with elaborate security. In these circumstances, it is not clear how much Hardy was able to accomplish. According to his own assessment, one of his greatest successes was a 1929 May Day rally of four hundred workers held in a guild-hall in the International Settlement. It was, he said, 'the biggest single feat of illegal organisation in these years'. Workers were instructed to arrive at different times in small groups of three or four. There was a tense moment when a policeman wandered into the hall to ask what was going on; he was 'arrested' and released after the meeting dispersed. But, a fortnight later, near the same spot, police fired on a workers' demonstration, killing one of the marchers, and a press photographer covering the event was lynched by White Russians.

---

10   Hardy claims in his memoir that he disagreed with Lenin.

In 1929, Hardy organised a second Pan-Pacific Conference. The secretariat had hoped to hold the conference in Australia despite possible difficulties with its whites-only immigration laws. However, Prime Minister Stanley Bruce banned the conference, and the venue was changed to Vladivostok. Because travel there was equally difficult for some delegates, Hardy chaired a parallel conference held clandestinely in Shanghai. It seems the secretariat had the greatest success in the relatively liberal environment of the Philippines, which was then a colony of the United States. On May Day 1930, PPTUS affiliate the Congreso Obrero de Filipinas (COF) was able to organise a demonstration of 50,000 workers in Manila.

Whatever their accomplishments, Hardy and Ayriss were risking their lives, as was illustrated by the case of two of their contemporaries in the Shanghai underground, a couple who became known to the world as the Noulens. Arrested in a joint operation by the Shanghai Municipal Police and the French Concession Police, they were handed over to the KMT authorities amid a lurid press campaign accusing them of planning to 'bolshevise' China. Despite a worldwide campaign to free them organised by Willi Münzenberg's League against Imperialism, supported by leftist celebrities like Henri Barbusse, Maxim Gorki, and Klara Zetkin, as well as Albert Einstein and other left-leaning liberals,[11] 'Hilaire Noulens' was sentenced to death and his wife to life imprisonment. However, the death sentence was commuted to a life sentence, thanks to a general amnesty proclaimed when the Japanese attacked Shanghai in January–March 1932. The Japanese saved the couple once again in 1937 when the jails were opened after the invasion. Song Qingling arranged passage for them to the Soviet Union.[12] Had Hardy – who left China a year before the Noulens were arrested – been put on trial in a Chinese court with no amnesties in force, he may well have been executed.

---

11   Einstein's association with the campaign and, more generally, with the League against Imperialism, of which he was honorary president, led to an FBI investigation and his exclusion from the Manhattan Project to build the atom bomb.

12   It seems that they were reluctant to go – understandably, as Stalin's purges were in full swing. The Noulens were suspected by some – including Freda Utley, Song Qingling, and Agnes Smedley – of supporting the Opposition. In the event, they were not arrested. After the collapse of the Soviet Union, the Noulens' real identities were revealed by their son as Yakov Rudnik and Tatyana Moiseenko, both Soviet citizens. See Freda Utley, *Last Chance in China*, Indianapolis: Bobbs-Merrill, 1947, 25–6; and Frederick Litten, 'The Noulens Affair', *China Quarterly*, No. 138 (1994): 492–512, 498.

Hardy's time in China coincided with a left turn by the Comintern under the slogan of the Third Period, and the pre-eminence of the leftist Li Lisan in the CCP. Li was one of the main advocates of the failed Nanchang Uprising and continued to follow a putschist line. In 1930, he led a rerun of the Nanchang failure in Hunan Province. Communist troops took the provincial capital, Changsha, on 25 July, but by 6 August the city was back in government hands. The CCP also followed a leftist line in trade union work, organising small 'red' unions at the expense of work in the KMT's legal 'yellow' unions. Hardy, who had vast experience as a trade unionist, complained to Moscow that 'the Party as a whole has not even fully grasped the full significance of trade union work'. He seems to have argued for a more pragmatic approach, supporting 'red' unions where appropriate but also advocating work inside the 'yellow' unions. At the tenth plenum of the Executive Committee of the Comintern (ECCI), despite its own leftist line, Osip Piatnitsky criticised the CCP's extreme sectarianism:[13]

> [Why] do the Chinese comrades still waver on the question as to whether to work or not to work in the Kuomintang unions? What is the result? The Red unions are small outfits and the Kuomintang unions are mass organisations.

At some point, the ECCI and the RILU seem to have lost patience with the CCP leadership and decided Hardy could be put to better use elsewhere.[14] But the CCP leaders, who valued Hardy's work despite their policy differences, resisted the reassignment, saying that he was one of the few foreign agents who understood conditions in China.[15] When Hardy was eventually redeployed in late 1930, it was to Hamburg, to work for a classic 'red' union – the short-lived International of Seamen and Harbour Workers.

---

13   Piatnitsky was head of the Comintern's International Liaison Department (OMS). A Bolshevik since 1903 who was jailed several times by the tsarist regime, he was executed in October 1938 for denouncing Stalin's purges.

14   David McKnight, *Espionage and the Roots of the Cold War*, London: Routledge, 2014, 110–12.

15   Ibid., 109. Although more flexible than the CCP, Hardy generally followed the Stalinist line. In a 1927 *Pan-Pacific Worker* article, he denounced the International Federation of Trade Unions as an 'appendage of imperialism,' and the relatively left-wing International Transport Workers' Federation as 'social-fascist.'

In 1937, after Japan launched its full-scale invasion of China, Hardy was appointed trade union organiser for the London-based China Campaign Committee (CCC). It was a difficult time for him. Shortly after taking the job, he learned that his son had been killed while fighting for the International Brigade in Spain.[16] Hardy called on dockers and seamen to boycott Japanese ships, but, apart from some isolated instances of largely spontaneous strikes in 1937 and 1938, he had little success in promoting industrial action. Right-wing trade union leaders like Walter Citrine and Ernest Bevin clamped down hard on anything that smacked of a political strike, and workers were wary of risking their jobs for a faraway cause, however worthy.[17] For these reasons, Hardy's successes were limited to propaganda and education. He travelled continuously, speaking to trade union branches and trades councils, dozens of which passed resolutions condemning Japan. In the spirit of the Popular Front, he organised a speaking tour for Zhu Xuefan, the Chinese government's delegate to the International Labour Organisation, who was a member of both the KMT and the Green Gang. However, the announcement of the Molotov–Ribbentrop Pact in August 1939 caused an abrupt change of line by the CPGB and threw the CCC into crisis. Middle-class supporters withdrew funding, and Hardy lost his job as Trade Union Organiser.[18] Characteristically, he fought against accusations that the Communists had betrayed China by pointing out, correctly, that the Soviet Union was the only country sending military aid to Chiang Kai-shek.

In 1951, Hardy visited China as part of a labour movement delegation. The last chapter of his autobiography is a rapturous description of the New China, cleansed of child labourers, rickshaw pullers, and arrogant imperialists. It was, of course, a stage-managed tour. The only beggars he saw were a couple who, it was explained to him, were too old to change their ways. He was taken to model farms and factories. He saw 'workers standing at their machines . . . with no fear on their faces' and heard stories of landlord oppression in the now 'peaceful and poetic scene of the Chinese countryside'. He saw a march of students in

16 Arthur Clegg, *Aid China 1937–1949: A Memoir of a Forgotten Campaign*, Beijing: New World Press, 1997, 60.

17 Tom Buchanan, *East Wind: China and the British Left, 1925–1976*, Oxford: Oxford University Press, 2012, 71–2.

18 Clegg, *Aid China*, 143.

Shanghai near the place where, in 1929, the worker and photographer were killed. He compared the new cooperatives to Robert Owen's utopian socialist experiments. Speaking to meetings in Shanghai and Beijing, he warned his audience to be vigilant against agents of 'the Chiang gangsters sheltering in their last hideout under the protection of the American fleet'. One of the delegation's hosts was Zhu Xuefan who had completed a remarkable political evolution, and survived a KMT assassination attempt in 1946, to become minister for post and telegraphs in the People's Republic of China.[19] Liu Shaoqi, who remembered Hardy from his years in the underground, paid him this tribute: 'Comrade Hardy, too, came to us in 1927, and helped very much. He lived secretly . . . if he had been caught, they would have murdered him. Now he comes to China under different conditions.'[20]

A partly humorous account of the 1951 delegation describes Hardy dismissively as a 'seasoned Stalinist'.[21] It is, of course, undeniable that he was a Stalinist: his autobiography contains several allusions to 'Trotskyite' treachery and spies, and in a 1937 report to the ECCI from South Africa, he warned against underestimating the danger from Trotskyists who were organising around the Vanguard bookshop in Johannesburg.[22] It was the Soviet dictator's toady-in-chief Dmitri Manuilsky who persuaded him to write a memoir of his life in the movement 'on five continents'.[23] But to label Hardy a Stalinist tout court would be a serious oversimplification.

Hardy's lifetime of labour activism began long before the Russian Revolution. He was an instinctive rebel, opinionated, forceful, and argumentative – a Bolshevik to whom the epithet 'bolshy' was entirely applicable. A man who claimed to have argued with Lenin was unlikely to show much respect for the leadership of the CPGB. He despised Willie Gallagher, with whom he clashed repeatedly, and had little time for the party leader Harry Pollitt. Although he remained a member, he regarded

---

19   Ibid., 177.

20   Hardy, *Those Stormy Years*, 255.

21   Patrick Wright, *Passport to Peking: A Very British Mission to Mao's China*, Oxford: Oxford University Press, 2010, 82.

22   Russian State Archive of Socio-political History (RGASPI), 495.20.662.87.

23   Stalin joked to Dimitrov that Manuilsky was particularly slavish because he had once been a Trotskyist. Dimitrov et.al., *The Diary of Georgi Dimitrov 1933-1949*, New Haven: Yale University Press, 2018, 104.

the British party as parochial, even chauvinist. Hardy was the kind of hardliner for whom 'Stalinism' stood for a refusal to compromise and having no truck with reformism or watering down the party programme. It meant internationalism, in the sense of unequivocal and practical support for anti-colonial struggles even, and indeed especially, if it meant opposing your own country. It also required you to believe all sorts of nonsense, such as that the entire leadership of the October Revolution had turned out to be counter-revolutionaries, along with those who fought against Franco in Spain and alongside the CCP during the revolution of 1925–27. But how and why Hardy remained loyal despite Stalin's dictatorship, even throughout the Great Purges, is a question that can be asked of an entire generation of revolutionaries.[24] Hardy remained politically active until his death in 1966. He spent his final years in Sussex, where the CPGB branches were notoriously hard line, campaigning for pensioners' rights.

---

24   Che Guevara, for example.

5

Neither Patriot nor Traitor

On 6 May 1950, the American journalist and author Agnes Smedley died in Oxford, following an operation to remove a stomach ulcer. Six months earlier, she had fled from the United States to escape a vociferous campaign instigated by Major General Charles Willoughby, the ultra-reactionary head of US military intelligence in East Asia, to have her indicted as a Soviet spy. Smedley was one of several journalists, academics, and State Department employees being pursued by MacArthur's 'pet fascist' Willoughby and others for having 'lost China'.[1] She stayed for several months in the London flat of Hilda Selwyn-Clarke, a Fabian socialist she had met in Hong Kong. Selwyn-Clarke had worked with Song Qingling's China Defence League in the colony before being interned by the Japanese. Although ill, Smedley was in a characteristically argumentative mood, railing to her politically moderate host against the 'authoritarian' Soviets, the 'fascist' Americans, and Britain's determination to hold on to Hong Kong. By mid-April, she had outstayed her welcome and moved to Oxford to stay with another friend. Soon afterwards, her health worsened, and she was admitted to hospital. The US government had placed restrictions on her passport that meant a hoped-for return to China was impossible, but, in one of her final letters she requested that, should she fail to recover, her ashes should be sent to

---

1   Andrew Gordon, *A Modern History of Japan*, Oxford: Oxford University Press, 2003, 239.

Zhu De, commander-in-chief of the People's Liberation Army, to be buried in China. The following year, a group of supporters took them to Beijing, where they were interred in the Babaoshan Revolutionary Cemetery. Her gravestone carries an inscription, in Zhu De's calligraphy, praising his biographer as an American revolutionary and friend of China.[2]

For two decades, Smedley was more or less forgotten. However, when the left revived in the 1970s, young activists began mining the history of the movement for role models. Smedley, an authentically working-class socialist and feminist, was an obvious candidate. In 1973, her autobiographical novel *Daughter of Earth* was republished by the Feminist Press. Three years later, the same publisher brought out a selection of her writings, *Portraits of Chinese Women in Revolution*, with an introduction by Janice and Steve MacKinnon. The MacKinnons produced a full-length biography that appeared in 1988. In China, a Smedley-Strong-Snow Society, no doubt intended to contribute to the warming relations with the United States, was established in 1983. Before leaving the United States, Smedley, helped by the high-powered lawyer O. John Rogge and a campaign mounted by sympathisers, had extracted an apology from the War Department for having fingered her as a Communist agent. The MacKinnon biography stuck to Smedley's account that, although a Communist sympathiser, she had never been a member of any Communist Party and had never worked for Soviet intelligence or the Communist International. When the Soviet archives were opened, however, they revealed that Smedley had indeed worked for the Comintern. In 2005, another biographer, Ruth Price, drew the less-than-startling conclusion that the author of *China's Red Army Marches* and a biography of Zhu De, who had lived in the Soviet Union and been a lover of the Soviet master spy Richard Sorge, was a Communist. But Price, a former press secretary to Democratic congresswoman Bella Abzug, went further. Smedley had not only worked for the Comintern but also for the Soviet military's Main Intelligence Directorate

---

2   Smedley's unfinished biography of Zhu De, *The Great Road*, was published in 1956. The chairman of the House Un-American Activities Committee, Congressman Harold Himmel Velde, claimed that Communists murdered Smedley to prevent her testifying before the committee. Janice MacKinnon and Stephen MacKinnon, *Agnes Smedley: The Life and Times of an American Radical*, Berkeley: University of California Press, 1988, 347.

(GRU), often referred to as the Fourth Department of the Red Army. She backdated Smedley's treachery to before the existence of the Comintern when, during the First World War, as a supporter of Indian nationalists who accepted German aid, she was 'on our wartime enemy's payroll'. When Smedley was arrested, this 'master of deception' fooled liberals and progressives that she was a victim of 'wartime hysteria'.[3] Her right-wing accusers, according to Price, 'did not know the half of her involvement'.[4]

Smedley arrived in China in 1928 with a decade-and-a-half career as a revolutionary internationalist behind her. Brought up in a poor family, as a child she witnessed the Colorado Labor Wars of 1903–4 and sympathised with striking miners, most of whom were Mexicans or first-generation European immigrants. While studying in Arizona in 1912, she was introduced to left-wing ideas by Thorberg Brundin and her brother Ernest, children of Swedish immigrants and members of the Socialist Party. Smedley followed the Brundins to California where, a few months later, she married Ernest. She was an unconventional twenty-year-old who carried a gun and a knife and, having discovered she was one-eighth Cherokee, insisted on being called Ayahoo. In California, she encountered radical Indian nationalists of Har Dayal's Ghadar Party, mainly poor Sikh immigrants from the Punjab, and became passionately committed to the Indian cause.[5]

At the end of 1916, Smedley's marriage collapsed, and she was fired from her teaching job when her Socialist Party membership card was discovered. She moved to Greenwich Village and joined Margaret Sanger's birth control movement. While working as secretary to Lajpat Rai, a Congress Party member, she maintained links with the radical

---

3 According to Price, she initially set out to clear Smedley's name. See Ruth Price 'Agnes Smedley: On Proving What Her Worst Enemies Had Claimed (Much to My Regret)', *History News Network*, April 2005, historynewsnetwork.org.

4 Ruth Price, *The Lives of Agnes Smedley*, Oxford: Oxford University Press, 2005, 8.

5 Har Dayal was a free-thinker who, as well as seeking to expel the British, was an advocate of women's rights, a student of Marx and Bakunin, and a member of the IWW. Dayal was from a well-to-do Hindu family and had studied at Oxford. He fled to Berlin after being arrested in 1914. According to a 1929 FBI report cited by Price, Smedley met him before he left and by August 1914 was an active worker for the Ghadr Party. Dayal died in Philadelphia in 1939 at the age of fifty-four. Some supporters suspected he was poisoned.

Ghadarists, including M. N. Roy and his wife, Evelyn Trent.[6] In 1917, Roy and Trent fled to Mexico to evade Woodrow Wilson's Red Scare, but Smedley was arrested the following year and spent several months on remand before being released on bail. In 1920, with indictments against her still pending and without a passport, she signed on to a Polish freighter as a stewardess, subsequently jumping ship in Danzig (Gdansk).[7] Virendranath 'Chatto' Chattopadhyaya, leader of the Indian nationalists in Berlin, used his government connections to have her brought to the capital, after which Chatto and Smedley became lovers and were unofficially married.[8] Their relationship, although difficult and marked by spells apart, would last until shortly before she left for China.

In 1921, Smedley had her first encounter with the Soviets when she and Chatto attended a conference of Indian nationalists in Moscow. It was not a happy experience. Soviet Russia was exhausted by civil war and famine; the Bolsheviks had just crushed the Kronstadt uprising and introduced the New Economic Policy. Smedley wrote in upbeat style for Max Eastman's *Liberator* magazine that 'Moscow is the center of the class-conscious world. From the four winds of the earth the revolutionaries are gathering.'[9] However, she was privately dismayed by what she found, writing to her close friend Florence Lennon, 'The prisons are jammed with anarchists and syndicalists who fought in the revolution ... Any Communist who excuses such things is a scoundrel and a blaggard ... everybody is under surveillance. You never feel safe.'[10] She befriended Emma Goldman, by then world famous for her writings and activism, who was also disillusioned with the revolution after Kronstadt and was living in difficult circumstances with her lover Alexander Berkman. Goldman was taken by the younger woman, who shared her anarcho-syndicalist views.

If Smedley found a friend in Goldman, in Moscow she demonstrated her lifelong knack for making enemies. The Indian revolutionaries were

6   Rai, known as the 'lion of Punjab', died in 1928 from injuries inflicted by a British policeman during a demonstration. Congress supported the British in World War I, while Ghadar planned uprisings with German aid.

7   MacKinnon and MacKinnon, *Agnes Smedley*, 68.

8   Unofficially, because Chatto was already married to an Irish woman who had become a nun and refused to divorce him.

9   Agnes Smedley, The Parliament of Man, *Liberator*, October 1921, 13.

10   Letter from Agnes Smedley to Florence Lennon, quoted in MacKinnon and MacKinnon, *Agnes Smedley*, 74.

split between followers of Roy and Chatto. Roy, in the minority, advocated a socialist programme to appeal to the poor, while Chatto emphasised national liberation. The two men were competing for the patronage of the Comintern, but it was an unequal struggle. Lenin had been impressed by Roy at the second Comintern congress and invited him to the Kremlin for a one-to-one meeting. Chatto and two others from his group were eventually invited to meet the Soviet leader but left 'disappointed and even angry'. Smedley desperately wanted to be part of the delegation to meet Lenin, but only Chatto supported her.[11] Thereafter, she bore a grudge against Roy that he found inexplicable. In her *Liberator* article, Smedley also denounced the British Communists – who, following Lenin's lead, backed Roy – as 'colonialists' who would only cooperate with 'simon-pure Communists', and wanted to 'manage' the Indian Revolution.[12]

Other attacks were simply personal and gratuitous. The famous trade union activist Ella Reeve Bloor was in Moscow with her lover, Earl Browder,

> a young, dainty man . . . who wore baby-blue silk Russian smocks . . . and long black silk ribbons . . . and with his baby white skin . . . posed in Moscow as the delegate from the Kansas miners . . . I was so disgusted . . . I hate female men above all. And then to have them say they represent miners when I know they haven't been within a thousand miles of a mine.[13]

The problem for Smedley was that, in 1934, Browder became general secretary of the Communist Party USA. His later moves against her suggest he was aware of, and had not forgotten, her withering assessment of him.

Smedley never lost her talent for offending people. *Daughter of Earth* was published in 1929 to glowing reviews. It was a passport into literary circles, making her a minor celebrity. Mike Gold, the CPUSA's artistic commissar, was especially enthusiastic, praising it as that holy grail:

11 M. N. Roy, *M. N. Roy's Memoirs*, Bombay and New York: Allied Publishers, 1964, 482.

12 Smedley, The Parliament of Man, 14.

13 Letter from Agnes Smedley to Florence Lennon, 23 October 1921, quoted in 'Earl Browder', Spartacus Educational website, spartacus-educational.com.

genuine proletarian literature.[14] Gold was finishing his semi-fictional autobiography *Jews without Money*. When it came out, however, Smedley did not return the compliment but called it 'strained and artificial'.[15] She wrote to Langston Hughes to tell him his novel *Not without Laughter* was individualistic.[16] She dismissed Ernest Hemingway as a braggart. She even criticised Lu Xun for 'vacillating'.[17] Indeed, she could not care less whose toes she trod on.

But her words sometimes had consequences, as the following episode illustrates. Gold had a brother called Max Granich.[18] In 1934, Browder sent Granich and his wife Grace to Shanghai to help Smedley publish an anti-imperialist journal in the concession areas. It turned out, however, that the Graniches saw themselves as editors and Smedley as their assistant. While Smedley took this as an unendurable slight, Song Qingling backed the Graniches, and since Song sat at the centre of the Comintern's web in Shanghai, Smedley had to concede. But she did so with bad grace, falling out with Song (or Madame Sun, as she called her) in the process, and they were never reconciled. It was a split that had been a long time coming, as the MacKinnon biography confirms: 'Sun was genteel, emotionally restrained, and taciturn, whereas Smedley was coarse, tempestuous, and outspoken'. The break would soon lead to Smedley's excommunication from the Comintern.[19]

Smedley wrote *Daughter of Earth* partly as therapy. Her relationship with Chatto was as troubled as her marriage to Ernest. Although he genuinely loved Smedley, Chatto was simultaneously controlling and dependent. 'He can't endure *anything* which doesn't come from himself. He crushes me,' she wrote. He was even jealous of her previous lovers, although she gave him plenty of reasons to be jealous of present ones. During one of their temporary separations, she had an affair with one of his young acolytes. Smedley suffered from chronic anxiety about sex that she attributed to her puritanical upbringing when she had seen

---

14 'Semi-proletarian' might be a better description. Although Smedley's family was poor, her father was a failed entrepreneur as well as a worker. He was variously a travelling salesman, mine operator, haulage contractor, and a deputy sheriff, in which role he may have clashed with striking miners.

15 Price, *The Lives of Agnes Smedley*, 191.

16 Ibid., 211.

17 Ibid., 195.

18 Gold's real name was Itzok Granich.

19 MacKinnon and MacKinnon, *Agnes Smedley*, 167–9.

working-class women worn down by endless childbearing. She had been attracted to Ernest but was terrified of pregnancy and had two abortions before leaving him when it became clear he wanted children. In 1923, after begging money from Margaret Sanger, she began seeing a psychoanalyst.[20] The sessions, she told Florence, made her reflect on 'my contempt for women as a sex and at the same time my bitter feminism. Likewise my lifelong man-ishness.'[21] In 1925, on a trip to Denmark, she met the novelist Karin Michaelis, who encouraged her to write her life story. As well as helping her to work through her psychological problems, Smedley hoped the book would make her rich. Unfortunately, while praised by critics, it was not a bestseller. Her money problems remained chronic, and she continued to depend on handouts from well-off friends.

Quite apart from their personal conflicts, Chatto and Smedley's lives in Berlin were precarious. The Weimar government no longer welcomed them, and they were forced into a semi-underground existence. Political violence was rising, all parties maintained militias, and Smedley took to carrying a gun. She wrote despairingly to Florence that she could see no difference between monarchists drilling in Bavaria and Communists drilling elsewhere. They were both 'men preparing to murder their own kind for the sake of an idea [and] not their own idea either'.[22] Once again Smedley's remarks implied a more critical attitude to the Communist movement than she is usually credited with.[23] Indeed, in the mid-1920s, Smedley and Chatto were still attracted to anarchism and attended meetings with Goldman and others. However, things changed with the formation of the League against Imperialism in 1927. Chatto was invited to be its Secretary. He accepted and joined the German Communist Party (KPD). Smedley began attending classes on Marxist economics but, critical of the Communists' backwardness on feminism and sexual freedom, she wrote to Florence that she would

20 Ibid., 98.
21 Ibid., 91–4. The psychoanalyst, Elizabeth Naef, was an orthodox Freudian who, in the fashion of the time, suggested Smedley had penis envy.
22 Ibid., 84.
23 For those who believe Smedley was a supreme deceiver who fooled everyone, even her closest friends, everything she wrote is suspect. But that is an unfalsifiable article of faith.

never join the party.[24] Her relationship with Chatto was finally ending, and she decided to leave Germany, planning to go first to China and then India. On the way, she passed through Moscow, where she met Song Qingling.

Was Smedley an agent? The short answer is yes. It is surprising that anyone would feel it necessary to deny the obvious – that the author of *China's Red Army Marches*, who in her last letter swore loyalty to the Chinese Revolution and cursed the American government, was not only a Communist but also had organisational links to the movement. However, the traditional position of the American left was that those accused by McCarthyites were framed. They were innocent, not in the sense that they should not have had to hide their Communist affiliations, but in the sense that they were not Communists. Smedley's denials and her lawsuit against the US Army were intended to save herself from financial ruin and imprisonment. For reasons of self-preservation, outright denial remained a sensible policy for the left for several decades. But the MacKinnons' biography was published nearly forty years after her death, when the need for clandestinity was long past.

The MacKinnons also downplayed the significance of her love affair with Richard Sorge by diminishing the latter's significance as an operative. They dismissed the idea that he warned the Russians about Operation Barbarossa as 'absurd, since Sorge was arrested in 1941', and complained about the emergence of a 'Sorge industry'.[25] But Sorge was not arrested until October 1941, and we can read his warnings in published extracts from the GRU archive. On 1 June 1941, for example, Sorge reported to the Soviet general staff that Berlin had informed his principal source, the ambassador in Tokyo, Eugen Ott, that Germany would attack the Soviet Union in the second half of June, and that Ott was 95 per cent certain that war was imminent.[26]

Having admitted that Smedley was an agent – the Comintern archive records unequivocally that, in 1934, she was sent on an assignment

---

24   Ibid., 121.

25   Ibid., 326, 366.

26   Report from agent Ramsay in Tokyo to the head of intelligence of the General Staff of the Red Army, 1 June 1941. Quoted in Gavrilov, *Dokumenty Razvedupravleniya Krasnoi Armii. Janvar' 1939-Iyun' 1941 g.* / (Seriya 'Rossiya. XX vek. Dokumenty') [*Documents of the Intelligence Directorate of the Red Army, January 1939 – June 1941*] (Russia 20th Century Documents), 2008, 657–8, available at docs.historyrussia.org/ru.

(*komandirovka*) to China to publish an anti-imperialist newspaper – two questions remain. What agencies did she serve, and when?

Price maintains that she was an agent of both the Comintern and the GRU, and that her career as an agent began in 1928 when she was sent to China by the International Liaison Department (OMS)[27] of the Comintern. The evidence offered is the 1951 testimony of an FBI informant, the Hungarian Communist Laszlo Dobos, better known by his pseudonym Louis Gibarti. Gibarti was a close comrade of Willi Münzenberg, who quit the Communist movement in protest at Münzenberg's expulsion. He told the FBI that in the late 1920s, Smedley was in 'very high standing' with Alexander Abramov-Mirov, head of the OMS.[28] Evidence from defectors cannot be discounted, but they often give interrogators the answers they are looking for, and Gibarti's recollection of twenty-year-old events was perhaps imperfect.[29] Either way, it seems he was mistaken. If Smedley was sent to China by the OMS in 1928, there should be a record in the Comintern files. But a March 1930 letter to the ECCI from Ignace Rylsky, who had recently returned from China complaining about poor communication between Shanghai and Moscow mentions, as an example, an unanswered query about the bona fides of a 'Miss Smedley', *Frankfurter Zeitung* correspondent in Shanghai, who had helped pass messages and claimed to represent the League against Imperialism. If Smedley was an OMS agent, Rylsky should have known since, before being sent to China in 1929, he was Abramov-Mirov's deputy.[30]

In other evidence, Price says Smedley was 'up to her ears' in preparations for the founding conference of the League against Imperialism, but the reference given – to Smedley's *Battle Hymn of China* – merely notes the founding of the League, and that Chatto was involved.[31] Smedley did not even attend the conference. Many other non-Communists did, however, including Nehru and George Lansbury, who was

27   Otdel Mezhdunarodnoy Svyazi.

28   Price, *The Lives of Agnes Smedley*, 7.

29   Gibarti was a busy man. Between 1921 and 1927, he travelled to ten countries on Comintern business.

30   For Rylsky's reference to Smedley, see M. L. Titarenko et.al., eds., VKP(b), *Komintern i Kitai: Dokumenty* [The CPSU, the Comintern, and China: Documents], 5 Vols., Moscow: ROSSPEN, 1994–2007, Vol. 3, 827. Both Rylsky and Abramov-Mirov were later shot as 'Trotskyists.' See docs.historyrussia.org/ru.

31   Price, *The Lives of Agnes Smedley*, 153.

elected its first president. Albert Einstein sent greetings and was elected
honorary president. It is surely obvious that none of them, although as
'up to their ears' as Smedley, were Comintern agents. If we accept that
Smedley helped organise the conference, it would at best show she was
a sympathiser, as was already evident.

Price suggests that Smedley accepted the Comintern assignment 'to
give her life [a] deeper meaning'.[32] But she had other reasons for going
to China. An American friend, David Friday, subsidised her trip on the
understanding she would establish a birth control clinic there. There
were also journalistic opportunities. The *Frankfurter Zeitung* creden-
tialled her as a reporter in China, and she also wrote for the *Nation* and
the *New Republic*. One might reasonably ask why she did not go straight
to India, the country with which she had been so long associated; but
had she done so, she would probably have been immediately arrested by
the British. She was an absentee defendant in the three-year Meerut
conspiracy trial that lasted from 1929 until 1933. Smedley herself implies
that a clean break from Chatto was her main reason for leaving Berlin
and that she did, indeed, intend to eventually go to India:

> In an effort to free myself from him [Chatto] totally, I had spent a
> number of months of 1927 in Denmark and Czechoslovakia, where I
> wrote my first book. *Daughter of Earth*. This book was a desperate
> attempt to reorient my life. I returned to Berlin in 1928 to teach at the
> university, but as soon as vacation time came I left for France, where I
> completed plans to go first to China and then to India.[33]

The evidence of Smedley's work as an agent is far from clear cut.
There are several more mentions of her in the Comintern archive. On 15
November 1932, in connection with a plan to hold an international anti-
war conference in Shanghai, an ECCI directive listed among those who
would need to be involved 'representatives of anti-war committees of
the major countries and foreign journalists in China (Smedley and
others)'. [34] The conference was banned by both foreign and Chinese
authorities in Shanghai, but, in October 1933, seventy of the planned

32   Ibid., 161.
33   Agnes Smedley, *Battle Hymn of China*, London: Gollancz, 1944, 23.
34   RGASPI 495.4.221.5–6, 8–9.

300 delegates, including Baron Marley, the Labour Party's chief whip in the House of Lords, managed to assemble at a secret location.[35]

Earlier, in May 1932, Sorge wrote to his old Comintern boss, Piatnitsky, complaining that Comintern work was diverting his group from its proper tasks. It seems Sorge had to step in to fill gaps left by the arrest of the Noulens, but he told Piatnitsky, 'Your apparatus is improving again and . . . the time has come for your people to take over this work.' He asks to be relieved of 'this overload . . . We are poor little technicians. We are not qualified to act as political controllers . . . and I am already compromised enough.'[36] He expresses surprise that Piatnitsky has not taken up his suggestion that Smedley should be given responsibility for 'international newspaper work' rather than the inexperienced operatives the Comintern had been sending out. Smedley, he says, could do three times as much and would cost three times less. Finally, he demands that Smedley be paid for work she did for *Moscow News* and other literary work, as she is flat broke.[37]

Then, in mid-May 1933, Arthur Ewert wrote to Piatnitsky, asking him to talk to Smedley about her future work in China: 'Up to now, both we and our neighbours have been using her. It would be advisable to change the situation. The best thing would be to give her long-term literary assignments that would enable her to stay in China and be of use in general work as before.' ('Our neighbours' refers to Sorge and the GRU.) Ewert also asked Piatnitsky to arrange for Smedley to take a vacation in the Caucasus so she could complete work on a book about China; Smedley left for Moscow almost immediately. Sorge had already left Shanghai in January for Berlin (via Moscow) to create a pro-Nazi cover story, as GRU head Berzin wanted him to set up an espionage operation in Tokyo. Sorge and Smedley would never meet again.

Smedley was, in fact, working on two books: *China's Red Army Marches*, a novelistic account of the Jiangxi Soviet, and a selection of

---

35   'Anti-war Conference Blocked, Not Wanted in China', *Advocate*, 4 October 1933, available at trove.nla.gov.au.

36   RGASPI 495.19.573.13.

37   Titarenko, *The CPSU, the Comintern, and China*, Vol. 4, 153–5. It is possible that 'international newspaper work' is a euphemism. But he is writing to Piatnitsky – a Comintern official. Even the date of Sorge's recruitment to the GRU is not entirely certain. The leader of the Red Orchestra, Leopold Trepper, said it was 1933, not 1929. If that is correct, it rules out the possibility that Smedley worked for the GRU, even unknowingly. See Leopold Trepper, *The Great Game*, London: Sphere Books, 1979, 73.

essays entitled *Chinese Destinies*. After the Communist press refused to publish the latter on grounds it was considered too hostile to Chiang Kai-shek, Vanguard Press, an independent left-wing publisher, brought it out. But on 3 April 1934, the Political Commission of the Political Secretariat of the ECCI resolved to send Smedley back to China to publish a replacement for *China Forum*, following the break with its Trotskyist editor Harold Isaacs.[38] This is definite proof that Smedley worked for the Comintern. But the sequence of messages suggests that, in the period 1932–34, the Comintern moved to regularise what had been, until then, informal work on its behalf by Smedley; it thus undermines the theory that she was sent to China by the OMS in 1928.

Price contends that Smedley worked not only for the Comintern but also for the GRU, and that she did so consciously and with full knowledge of which agency she was working for. She quotes a December 1941 police interrogation during which Sorge says he 'made her [Smedley] a member of the Comintern headquarters staff', which meshes with his 1932 letter to Piatnitsky. The MacKinnons also record this, but they dismiss it because of its source.[39] Nowhere, however, did Sorge say he recruited her to the GRU. The closest he came was – again under interrogation – when he said that Smedley's work with him was done 'with her full understanding'. Price suggests that this means that, unlike the other members of Sorge's ring, Smedley knew that her activities went beyond the boundaries of Comintern work. There is no particular reason to think so, however. Branco Vukelić and Miyagi Yotoku, who died in Japanese prisons, and even Ozaki Hotsumi, who was hanged along with Sorge in 1944, believed throughout that they had been working for the Comintern.[40] Sorge was perfectly capable of fooling people, especially, one suspects, someone as besotted with him as Smedley was.[41] Ewert's choice of words – we have been 'using' her – would seem to back this up. What is more, Sorge, as we saw above, really was working for the Comintern – albeit unwillingly.

38   RGASPI 495.184.283.37,39. Quoted in Titarenko, *CPSU*, 585–6.

39   MacKinnon and MacKinnon, *Agnes Smedley*, 147–8.

40   Robert Whymant, *Stalin's Spy: Richard Sorge and the Tokyo Espionage Ring*, London: I. B. Taurus, 2013, 65.

41   She wrote to Florence that she was in 'a big, broad, all-sided friendship and comradeship' with the 'he-man' Sorge, and that she felt married to him, although she feared it would not last. MacKinnon and MacKinnon, *Agnes Smedley*, 147.

Sorge joined the GRU on the understanding that it was a professional spy organisation and that his work should be entirely unconnected to that of local Communist parties and the Comintern. But, immediately after arriving in Shanghai, he broke his own rule by contacting Smedley, a well-known correspondent for Germany's most respected newspaper and a known Communist sympathiser who was being watched by every agency in the city. He did not make contact discreetly but began an affair with Smedley, roaring around Shanghai with her on the back of his motorbike – often while drunk. As we saw from his message to Piatnitsky, he felt burdened and distracted by Comintern work. Just how heavily involved he was is illustrated in an extraordinary report by an agent called Lesse who describes how, in November 1931, Song Qingling, after visiting the Noulens in prison in Nanjing, went to see her brother-in-law Chiang Kai-shek to plead for their release. Chiang not only refused but ordered Deng Yanda, a dissident military officer and leader of the so-called Third Party, to be shot the same day. Outraged, Song Qingling met with Sorge and asked him to organise one hundred armed Communists to spring the Noulens from jail.[42] It seems that this somewhat hare-brained scheme was not attempted.

All the foreign leftists in Shanghai knew each other through the overlapping circles of Lu Xun and Song Qingling, the Zeitgeist bookshop run by Irene Weidemeyer, or the bars they frequented. Smedley was at the heart of the network. If, by a small chance, people did not know each other, she would introduce them. She launched the League of Left-Wing Writers with Lu Xun. She was friends with Hu Shi and had an affair with the romantic poet Xu Zhimo. She was a great recruiter for the cause – Rewi Alley and George Hatem were among those she won over. Loud and full of herself, she passed herself off as *the* Comintern representative and let it be known she was a personal friend of Piatnitsky. As such, her frenetic networking and name dropping made her a security risk.

A visiting CPUSA member, Rudy Baker,[43] who met Smedley several times, complained of Arthur Ewert's heavy drinking and 'frivolous' attitude to security. N. N. Herbert, sent to sort out the aftermath of the

---

42   Report of K. Lesse to the OMS on his work in China, Moscow, 14 January 1932, RGASPI 495.19.118. 9–24. Quoted in Titarenko, *CPSU*, 112.

43   Rudy Baker was born Rudolph Blum in Croatia. He was a CPUSA member and the party's link with the ECCI. See F. I. Firsov, Harvey Klehr, and John Earl Haynes, *Secret Cables of the Comintern, 1933–1943*, New Haven: Yale University Press, 2014, 34.

Noulens affair, reported that Smedley and even Song Qingling were frequent guests at drunken parties at Ewert's home – where Ewert kept vital secret documents. 'How can one combat this?', Herbert wrote in despair. Smedley's plan for launching the Comintern's replacement for *China Forum* was discovered when 'thirty or forty' CCP members were rounded up. On 5 May 1935, the ECCI, noting that Smedley, contrary to instructions, was openly mixing with underground foreigners, risking their security and that of the Chinese comrades, resolved to suspend Smedley's work and immediately recall her from China.[44]

Though Smedley's indiscipline would seem to rule her out for espionage work, Price suggests, without providing any evidence, that it was a deliberate pose to put people off the scent that she was a spy.[45] However, the material in the Comintern archives demonstrates that Smedley's carelessness and indiscipline were only too real. As Song Qingling reported later: 'She had the best of intentions, but her methods were detrimental to our interests.'[46] In the many biographies of Sorge, Smedley is often portrayed as a key member of his spy ring because she introduced him to Ozaki Hotsumi – his closest and most valuable confederate in Japan. But Ozaki was not some anonymous foreign office official; he was a well-known left-wing journalist who frequented the Zeitgeist bookshop and was translating *Daughters of Earth*. Some accounts say Smedley also introduced Sorge to Ruth Werner, real name Ursula Kuczynski, later famous as 'Red Sonja', Klaus Fuchs's handler. But other versions have it that Werner, who was already a KPD member, visited Sorge in hospital after he crashed his motorbike.[47] Either way, Werner, younger than Smedley, soon replaced her as Sorge's pillion passenger and lover. After all, making a few introductions does not amount to building a network. In any case, one thing must be stressed: Smedley was never an agent in the same sense as were the Red Army colonels Sorge and Kuczynski.

Wisely, Smedley did not return to the Soviet Union, where she would likely have been liquidated along with her ex-husband Chatto and

44   Piatnitsky, Dimitrov, Kuusinen, Wang Ming, and others made the decision. See minutes No. 450 (B) of a meeting of the Political Commission of the ECCI Political Secretariat, Moscow, 5 May 1935, RGASPI. 495.4.348. 3, 6.

45   Price, *The Lives of Agnes Smedley*, 162.

46   Letter from Song Qingling to Wang Ming, 26 January 1937, RGASPI. 495.74.281.34–35. Quoted in Titarenko, *CPSU*, 1092–4.

47   See, for example, Whymant, *Stalin's Spy*, 37.

countless others. But the Comintern was unhappy with her work. The definitive break came at the turn of 1936–37 in Xi'an, where, for a time, she found herself the only foreign correspondent in the city when Chiang Kai-shek was taken hostage by his warlord underlings Zhang Xueliang and Yang Hucheng. They had been dragging their feet in the campaign against the Red Army, and Chiang had arrived to lay down the law. When the rebels made their move, Smedley was staying in the same guesthouse as Chiang's staff officers, and Yang's troops roughed her up and stole her money.[48] During the Xi'an Incident, which electrified the world, Smedley's journalistic instincts took over. She was in her element. With the help of a CCP contact, she set up a radio transmitter and began broadcasting a blow-by-blow account of the crisis.

The broadcasts revived her notoriety in the United States, where respectable journalists painted her as a 'Red Peril' and a potential 'White Empress over yellow-skinned millions'.[49] But Smedley's words also enraged the Comintern. Whereas Mao's instinct was to put Chiang on trial, Stalin's goal was to sign a treaty with Nationalist China to counter Japan. Smedley, contrary to policy, not only excoriated Chiang but also revealed top-secret details of the agreement that freed him. This time, the clamour within the Comintern to cut links with Smedley was overwhelming. On 23 January 1937, Song Qingling wrote to Wang Ming, after her brother T. V. Soong told her that Chiang Kai-shek was incandescent about the breach of confidence and was threatening to renege on his commitments. Song repeated Smedley's perennial faults – keeping unwise company, profligate spending, compromising safe houses, and so on. She assured Wang Ming that she had 'passed on your instruction to isolate her and I cannot understand why our comrades gave her a job in Xi'an'.[50] Wang Ming wired the CCP Central Committee from Moscow to accuse Smedley of divulging secrets to 'British circles'.[51] The CPUSA, for its part, denounced her in the *Daily Worker*, while the ECCI hinted she might be a Trotskyist: 'Serious attention must be paid to the intrigues of the Trotskyist servants of the Japanese invaders whose provocations in Xian and throughout China are aimed at undermining the

---

48 They also killed her friend, a German dentist and CCP sympathiser called Herbert Wunsch.

49 MacKinnon and MacKinnon, *Agnes Smedley*, 177.

50 RGASPI 495.74.281.34–35, reproduced in Titarenko, *CPSU*, 1092–4.

51 RGASPI 495.74.281.31.

anti-Japanese united front. We find Agnes Smedley's activities quite suspicious.'[52]

Nevertheless, in Xi'an, Smedley carried on as usual. She was delighted to be reunited with her friend, the left-wing writer Ding Ling, who had been presumed dead after being kidnapped by KMT agents. She followed Ding Ling to the CCP's new base in Yan'an where, in interviews with her idol Zhu De, she gathered material for her posthumously published biography. She was initially repelled by Mao – one of the feminine men she disliked – and she noted that while Zhu was loved, Mao was respected.[53] Although she felt she had found her spiritual home in the Communist capital, it was not long before, true to her turbulent nature, like the Monkey King, she 'caused havoc in heaven'. An influx of young female students from KMT areas had already unsettled the wives of the leaders, and when Smedley started organising dance evenings, their suspicions grew. Even though ten people had been recently arrested for forming a Free Love Club,[54] Smedley was unconcerned. She teased the men, telling them to liberate themselves from their 'feudal-minded' wives. It was only a matter of time before puritan Yan'an blew a fuse.

The denouement came when Mao began visiting Smedley's cave to flirt with her neighbour, a beautiful actress called Lily Wu. Mao's wife, He Zizhen, dragged him out of Lily Wu's cave and began beating him up outside Smedley's entrance. She then attacked Lily Wu, and finally Smedley, calling her an imperialist. Characteristically, Smedley floored her with a single punch. To resolve the scandal, Mao banished He Zizhen to Russia. Ding Ling and Lily Wu were sent to join a travelling propaganda team. Perhaps hoping to ride out the crisis, Smedley applied to join the CCP but was rejected.[55] She soon became more unpredictable than usual, falling off her horse after challenging other riders to a race. Carried out of Yan'an on a stretcher bound for Xi'an, her relationship with the Communist movement ended in farce.

Still, she had not yet given up. In Xi'an, with the United Front now official, she was given a war reporter pass and travelled to Shanxi hoping to rejoin the Eighth Route Army. Zhu De met her but refused to let her

---

52   Telegram to the CC of the CCP, 19 January 1937, RGASPI 495. 74. 281, 17–18.
53   Agnes Smedley, *The Great Road*, New York: Monthly Review Press, 1972, 121.
54   Smedley, *Battle Hymn of China*, 119.
55   This was the only time she applied to join a Communist party.

go to the front, sending her to instead to besieged Hankou. She made a typically dramatic appeal: 'Hankow means spiritual death for me . . . cities are swamps – cesspools . . . your army is pure of soul . . . and of purpose. These have been the only happy days of my whole life.' [56] However, Zhu was unmoved, and she left on 4 January 1938.

In Hankou, Smedley, true to form, took an instant dislike to Norman Bethune when he arrived in China. When W. H. Auden and Christopher Isherwood first met her, they found her 'grim and sour', but later, buoyed by Gollancz's decision to publish *China Fights Back*, she became 'cheerful and triumphant'.[57] She remained persona non grata with the Comintern, however. *China Fights Back* was proscribed for downplaying the United Front and, as a result, sold badly. She continued reporting on the war and, ignoring Comintern hostility, spent a year with the New Fourth Army along the Yangzi River. Not one to rely on bar-room gossip for stories, Smedley walked for days to track down the army's Storm Guerrillas, with whom she lived for weeks – experiences recounted in the book *Battle Hymn of China*.[58]

Meanwhile, in paranoid Moscow, the GPU agent Mordvinov lamented that the 'lessons' of the Moscow trials had not been learned. He suggested that both Smedley and Edgar Snow were Trotskyists whose 'exaggerated' accounts of Red Army exploits constituted a 'provocation'.[59] In the context of the Soviet Union at the time, this amounted to a death threat.

In September 1940, Smedley, helped by Hilda Selwyn-Clarke and the Red Cross, crossed into Hong Kong. Selwyn-Clarke was working with Song Qingling's China Defence League, but Smedley would have nothing to do with either Song or the League. She happily met with both the other Song sisters, however. She quarrelled with the Red Cross which had sponsored her entry and would have to facilitate her return to the mainland. Dejected and angry, she suffered a heart attack. For weeks, first Hilda and then Bishop Hall looked after her in their homes. Eventually, Evans Carlson, who had met her in Yan'an, lent her

---

56   Agnes Smedley, *China Fights Back*, London: Gollancz, 1938, 269.

57   Price, *The Lives of Agnes Smedley*, 326.

58   Gregor Benton, *New Fourth Army: Communist Resistance along the Yangtze and the Huai, 1938–1941*, Richmond: Curzon Press, 1999, 20.

59   Memorandum from G. I. Mordvinov to Georgi Dimitrov, 19 August 1939, RGASPI 495.74.295.7–40.

money to buy a ticket to America. Rewi Alley saw her off on 6 May 1941.

In America, she depended on her former husband, Ernest, and his new wife for food and lodging. But she was disgusted by the shallowness of suburban life and alienated friends and relatives by trying to recruit them to the cause – although what cause was unclear. She denounced the Stalin-Hitler Pact and the CPUSA. The only Communists she could stomach were the Chinese. As usual, she was penniless, getting by on loans and some paid lectures. She began work on *Battle Hymn of China* and, despite quarrels with publishers, Hollywood showed interest in it.

Price's harshest judgment on Smedley was her support for 'our enemies' in World War I. But, arguably, Smedley's stand with the Indian nationalists against Woodrow Wilson's segregationist government was her finest hour. She refused to break with the radical Ghadarists who, with German aid, planned an uprising in the Punjab in 1915.[60] Among those she collaborated with were Taraknath Das and Salindranath Ghose. After the October Revolution, the Indian revolutionaries saw the Bolsheviks as an alternative to the Germans, and Ghose and Das wrote to Trotsky to ask for help. Smedley subsequently worked with Ghose to create a new Indian National Party with the aim of setting up a government in exile.[61] In March 1918, she was arrested, charged under the new Espionage Act, and remanded in Manhattan's notorious Tombs jail. Smedley's bail was set at 10,000 dollars, which supporters had raised by the summer.[62] However, she was jailed again in October, and only released a few weeks after the Armistice was signed.

Undeterred, she founded Friends of Freedom for India to campaign against the persecution of nationalists in the United States. This took great courage, but, for Price, it was all too terrible to contemplate. In her eyes, Smedley was guilty as hell – as, presumably, were Roger Casement and the leaders of the Easter Rising – for the Indians, as far as Smedley was concerned, were only doing what the Irish did; indeed, the Punjab uprising, although nipped in the bud, preceded the Easter Rising. Given the choice of participating in a senseless slaughter in Europe or striking

---

60   The uprising was thwarted after British agents uncovered the plan, but a revolt in Singapore was brutally crushed with the help of Japanese troops.

61   MacKinnon and MacKinnon, *Agnes Smedley*, 41.

62   Equivalent to approximately 200,000 2023 dollars.

a blow for freedom, 'extremists' in India and Ireland chose the latter. The uprisings failed, but the Home Rule strategy of the 'moderate' national-ists was not cost free. A million Indians, urged on by Congress, went to war for the British Empire, and seventy-five thousand were killed. Thousands of Irishmen were killed at Suvla Bay and Sudelbar before Connolly and Pearce led the 1916 Easter Rising.

As noted earlier, Price indicts Smedley for hoodwinking naive liber-als such as Margaret Sanger and Roger Baldwin into campaigning for her release. But Sanger and Baldwin were scarcely naive; in fact, they were the sort of people from whom most modern members of the Democratic Party would run a mile. Sanger had worked with the IWW to organise the 1912 Lawrence textile workers' strike and the 1913 Paterson silk workers' strike. She wrote for the Socialist Party's newspa-per *The Call* and had supported Eugene Debs's 1912 presidential run.[63] Baldwin, another 'liberal', whose National Civil Liberties Bureau partly paid Smedley's legal expenses, was a member of the IWW, refused to register for the draft in World War I, and was jailed for a year in 1918. He was also a founding director of Vanguard Press which, in 1928, published his *Liberty under the Soviets*, a rather rose-tinted account of the Soviet Union in which he wrote, revealingly,

> While I found myself agreeing with the majority – an unusual state of mind for me – on the issue of the Trotskyist Opposition, my sympa-thies were all with the suppressed Trotsky minority, and my hopes in enough Party democracy to keep it in the Party as a critical force.[64]

One of the most sensational claims in Price's biography is that Smedley was raped by M. N. Roy. The basis for the claim is a passage in *Daughter of Earth* that describes a traumatic assault by an Indian nation-alist on the Smedley character Marie Roberts, after which she attempts suicide. Roberts's attacker in the book is called Juan Diaz and described as a light-skinned, half-Portuguese Christian who went on to betray the cause to the British. It is not clear why Price identifies Diaz as represent-ing Roy, since, as a glance at any photo reveals, he was rather dark skinned. Furthermore, he was neither half Portuguese, nor a Christian,

63   Adam J. Sacks. 'The Socialist Pioneers of Birth Control', *Jacobin*, August 2019.
64   R. N. Baldwin, *Liberty under the Soviets*, New York: Vanguard Press, 1928, 270.

but a Hindu Brahmin from Bengal, and he never betrayed the cause. Presumably anticipating this objection, Price adds that the Diaz character is a composite of Roy and another nationalist called Herambalal Gupta. Gupta was no more Portuguese or Christian than Roy, but he did eventually defect to the British.

The evidence Price cites for identifying Roy as the attacker is a 1988 letter from Samaren Roy, an Indian historian who wrote three books about his namesake. Although Price gives no details, she intimates that Samaren Roy told her that Roy was attracted to Smedley. This on its own goes nowhere near establishing the case. More damningly, however, Samaren Roy's biography of M. N. Roy, published in 1997, a full eight years before Price's book appeared, explicitly identifies Roy not with the Juan Diaz character, but with a completely different character in *Daughter of Earth* – Viren – whose portrayal in the novel fits much better with what we know of Roy.[65] Like the real Roy, Viren is tall, handsome, proud, arrogant, and argumentative. Furthermore, in the novel, Viren, along with Amand, who represents Smedley's husband Chatto, vehemently denounces Juan Diaz. If, as Samaren Roy maintains and indeed seems likely, Smedley intended Viren to represent Roy, Price's case is undermined. Since Samaren Roy's undisclosed correspondence was Price's principal evidence, her accusation would seem to be not just unproven, but unfounded.

The MacKinnons say the perpetrator was Gupta. They offer as evidence the fact that, like the fictional Diaz, Gupta turned traitor. He was in the United States at the time the incident took place (Roy was in Mexico). They also note that Gupta used the pseudonym Juan Lopez. This is more convincing than anything Price offers. But, as Alan Wald points out, their case is also far from conclusive. Wald also makes the rather obvious point that one should be cautious about drawing factual conclusions from what is, after all, a fictionalised autobiography.[66]

Smedley has been described as a Stalin worshipper.[67] But, once again, the evidence is unclear. She was, for a period, good friends with the

---

65   Samaren Roy, *M. N. Roy: A Political Biography*, New Delhi: Orient Longman, 1997, 17. Samaren Roy died in 2007.

66   Alan Wald, 'Inconvenient Truths: The Communist Conundrum in Life and Art', *American Literary History*, Vol. 21, No. 2 (2009), 368–403, 372–4.

67   See, for example, Alexander Pantsov with Steven Levine, *Mao: The Real Story*, New York: Simon & Schuster, 2013, 306.

Trotskyists Harold Isaacs and Frank Glass. In 1931, she was close enough to them to ask them to stay in her flat as bodyguards when she felt threatened by KMT and imperialist agents. When she proposed Isaacs as editor of *China Forum*, she could hardly have been unaware of his views. Glass at the time, although openly Trotskyist, worked for the Russian TASS news agency. But everything changed in 1933 when Hitler came to power, aided by the Comintern's sectarian Third Period policy. Trotsky abandoned his previous strategy of working as a faction to reform the official Communist parties from within. Declaring the KPD politically bankrupt, he called for a new party to be built in Germany and moved in the direction that would lead to the formation of a new International. In May 1934, Isaacs publicly broke with the CCP. When Smedley came back from her trip to the Soviet Union, she was fanatically anti-Trotskyist and began describing Trotskyists as Japanese agents.[68] Glass reacted furiously:

Then came Agnes Smedley, the sob-sister of the Chinese revolution, with her *China's Red Army Marches*. This lady, who in recent years has developed into a vicious vilifier of the Fourth Internationalists (the time of her development along this line coincided with a visit to Moscow, where she lived happily for about a year as a pensioner of the State Publishing House), gathered all the material for her book in her foreign-style apartment in Shanghai during the course of conversations with a functionary of the Communist party . . . Neatly inserted into it, of course, were the usual slanderous diatribes against the Trotskyists, whom, in accordance with what her informant told her and without any effort to check, she labelled as spies and *provocateurs*.[69]

Smedley, for her part, sided with the official Comintern, reproduced its standard attacks on the Trotskyists, and added venom of her own.

---

68   Just how fanatical is illustrated by the fact that, passing through New York on her return to China, she ended her long friendship with Florence Lennon because she had a Trotskyist boyfriend. MacKinnon and MacKinnon, *Agnes Smedley*, 160–1.

69   Frank Glass (Li Fu-jen), 'A Liberal in China', *New International*, Vol. 4, No. 3 (March 1938), 89–90, available at marxists.org. While correct about her anti-Trotskyism, Glass's charge that Smedley got her material secondhand from the comfort of her apartment was a cheap shot and quite unfair. *China's Red Army Marches* was published in 1934, by New York-based Vanguard Press.

She was undoubtedly motivated in part by personal spite – against Isaacs in particular. In 1935, she wrote to Edgar Snow,

> Yes, Isaacs is an Isaacs-ist . . . the Japanese secret anti-Communist service are glad to announce among themselves that they are now working with the Trotskyists through spies who pretend to be Trotskyists. They are – really, and the Trotskyist gang here hate me so much that they have told everything they know about me to them . . . Every Communist fears them more than active KMT spies.[70]

Smedley's accusations, which were entirely false and reprehensible,[71] might well have led to the deaths of her former friends. On the other hand, her books contain precious little praise of Stalin. The Soviet dictator is mentioned only a handful of times and in neutral terms. In Xi'an, as we saw, Smedley openly defied the official Soviet line of collaboration with Chiang Kai-shek, and later, in 1948, she backed Tito in his dispute with Stalin.

How are we to assess Smedley? The evidence presented here from the Soviet archives of her fraught relationship with the Comintern should dispel wild flights of fancy, such as the contention, in an episode of PBS's NOVA TV series, that she was one of the most prolific spies of the twentieth century.[72] At best, such claims are journalistic hyperbole.[73] At worst, they are attempts to conflate activism and rebellion with espionage – which was, and remains, the aim of the Espionage Act under which she was charged in 1918. Smedley was undoubtedly a flawed character, impulsive, and often downright reckless. Her political views were instinctive rather than thought through. Although a Communist, she dismissed Marxist theory: 'Who cares if I read all that trash? I know

---

70   Letter from Agnes Smedley to Edgar Snow, quoted in Price, *The Lives of Agnes Smedley*, 261.

71   Snow also included in his books the ritual denunciations of the Trotskyists required by the Comintern, but confined himself to criticising their mistakes and stopped short of calling them spies.

72   See 'Agnes Smedley', Secrets, Lies, and Atomic Spies, NOVA Online, pbs.org.

73   There are many biographies of Sorge. Whymant, on page 36 of *Stalin's Spy*, literally puts words in Sorge's mouth: 'Can you [Smedley] introduce to me a Japanese to help improve my knowledge of Japan's policy towards China?' Whymant, by his own admission, invented this dialogue. It is difficult to understand why.

who the enemy is, and that's enough.'[74] Her upbringing left her psychologically scarred, and her friendships and sexual relationships were difficult. She argued vehemently and pointlessly with benefactors and excommunicated long-term friends whose views offended her. Though she was capable of great kindness, she sometimes expressed it in grand gestures intended to shame her companions as much as aid the beneficiary.[75] A feminist pioneer, she nevertheless espoused views that would be regarded as homophobic and, frankly, sexist today. Her writing was propagandistic and exaggerated to the extent that it was not only her Western editors who asked her to turn down the dial; indeed, the Comintern chose the more credible Snow over her as its propaganda vehicle.

Interestingly, both the MacKinnon and Price biographies frame Smedley's story in the context of American patriotism. For the MacKinnons she was an *American* radical, which is to say a patriot. For Price, she was a great deceiver who led a double life as a calculating agent of a foreign power. Neither of these pictures does her justice. For all her many faults, Smedley was a courageous and unwavering internationalist who would have rejected the label of patriot as readily as that of traitor. We might leave the last word to Leopold Trepper, who would surely have seen her as one of 'the thousands of communists who regarded themselves not as spies but as fighters in the vanguard of world revolution . . . civilians who were devoting themselves to a cause just as they might have done in a labor union'.[76]

---

74   Price, *The Lives of Agnes Smedley*, 186.
75   For example, making her intellectual friends swap places with their rickshaw pullers.
76   Trepper, *The Great Game*, 70–1.

6

Germans

In official Chinese accounts, the German Communist Otto Braun, known in China by his pseudonym Li De, is depicted as the foreign advisor whose military blunders led to the loss of the Communist Party's stronghold in Jiangxi Province in 1934. According to this narrative, when Braun arrived in Ruijin, capital of the Chinese Soviet Republic in late 1933, he was given command of the Red Army by his sponsor, the youthful general secretary of the party, Bo Gu (Qin Bangxian) – one of the so-called twenty-eight Bolsheviks of Moscow, returnees opposed to Mao Zedong. Chiang Kai-shek had recently begun the fifth in a series of 'encirclement campaigns' to suppress the southern Soviets. Braun, who had little practical military experience, relied on abstract textbook strategies that favoured 'positional warfare'. In turn, his missteps led to serious defeats and eventually the loss of the entire base area.

As a result of these blunders, in October 1934, Braun was forced to order the retreat that became the Long March. What is more, his complacent and passive leadership during the first months of the retreat led to chaos and massive losses that continued until he was ousted, along with Bo Gu, by Mao Zedong at the Zunyi Conference in January 1935. Nearly ninety years later, this remains the line officially endorsed by the CCP:

Braun did not speak a word of Chinese, nor did he possess any background information about China. Instead of carefully analyzing the

real situation on the ground, he simply applied military academy
doctrines. The results of his foolish command were disastrous: heavy
casualties and a substantial part of Communist territory lost . . .

The Zunyi Meeting, free from Comintern intervention, is regarded
as a critical turning point in CPC history. It was the first time the CPC
made an independent strategic decision about the direction of the
Chinese revolution. Braun was dismissed from military command
and the first CPC leadership with Mao at the core began to take
shape.[1]

Braun was overbearing and dismissive of objections to his strategy.
Poring over maps in his study, he behaved like a 'foreign imperial envoy'
and refused to listen to advice from field officers. His position was unas-
sailable since he was 'the emperor's father' – the power behind the throne
– the emperor being the inexperienced Bo Gu, who was just twenty-
seven years old and accepted Comintern advice as if it was holy writ.[2]

It is not just government websites; scholarly works also endorse the
same verdict. For instance, one historian of the period contends,

Because the Provisional CC comprised young students who had
returned from the Soviet Union, it did not trust Mao Zedong, or the
other founders of the base area and it gave command authority to the
young German who only understood military dogma. As a result, the
Red Army could no longer rely on flexible and mobile tactics or on its
ability to rapidly move back and forth, including fighting behind the
enemy lines.[3]

As if incompetence and arrogance were not enough, Braun lived a life
of luxury while his Chinese comrades endured Spartan conditions

---

1   State Council Information Office, English-language website, china.org.cn.
2   The CCP narrative was widely accepted outside China. See for example, the
Encyclopaedia Britannica entry on the Long March, which states that the Red Army
fought off the first four encirclement campaigns 'using guerrilla warfare [tactics]
developed by Mao.' In the fifth campaign, Mao having been sidelined, the leadership
reverted to conventional 'positional warfare tactics' against the superior KMT forces and
as a result were forced to abandon the Soviet. See 'Long March', *Encyclopaedia Britannica*,
britannica.com.
3   Shen Zhihua, *A Short History of Sino-Soviet Relations, 1917–1991*, Singapore:
Palgrave Macmillan, Springer Nature Singapore, 2020, 51–2.

without complaining. He was given special quarters – a house of his own set in fields – and supplied with all sorts of luxuries.[4]

Despite the harsh living conditions in Ruijin with the Red regime beleaguered . . . the CPC central committee spared no effort to look after Braun. He was provided with secretaries, interpreters, body-guards, an exclusive doctor and chefs. Coffee and cigars which he loved were obtained for him from big cities like Shanghai and Guangzhou.[5]

Scandalously, Braun also violated the puritan code of the revolution-ary base by making advances to women comrades, not even bothering to check if they were married. On one occasion, wearing a flashy uniform, he leapt from his horse like a gallant cavalry officer and began paying compliments, in German, to a young woman. Not speaking a word of German, the woman nevertheless understood Braun's inten-tions. Just then, her husband who happened to speak German arrived on the scene, rebuked Braun, and led his wife away. Or so the story goes, as related in the memoirs of General Chen Shiju, who surmised that, absurd as such behaviour was in revolutionary China, it was probably considered acceptable in Germany.[6]

That then is the charge sheet. Let us examine the accused. Otto Braun was born near Munich in 1900. His mother, who was widowed when he was a child, sent him to a Catholic orphanage. He was drafted into the army in 1918, too late to see action in World War I. According to a curriculum vitae he wrote in 1969, the army dismissed him in December 1918 for 'unreliability', perhaps because he had joined the Communist youth organisation, the Free Socialist Youth. In April 1919, he joined the KPD, taking up arms in support of the short-lived Bavarian Soviet Republic. He was arrested but released soon afterwards and moved to Berlin where, in 1921, he became a full-time worker for the KPD. He joined the party's paramilitary organisation and at the time of the disastrous March Action of 1921,

---

4   Whether the house was a luxury or not is a matter of perspective; Braun called it an 'isolated farmhouse'. See Otto Braun, *A Comintern Agent in China*, London: C. Hurst, 1982, 31.

5   State Council Information Office, English-language website, china.org.cn.

6   State Council Information Office, Chinese-language website, china.com.cn.

he is said to have been the head of its intelligence branch in Central Germany.[7]

Not long afterwards, Braun made headlines. In July 1921, disguised as a policeman, together with several comrades he called at the home of an émigré Russian, a certain Colonel Freyburg, who was an associate of the notorious Siberian Cossack warlord, Grigory Semyonov.[8] The fake police searched Freyburg's flat, confiscated his extensive files, and passed them to Soviet intelligence. However, they were arrested soon afterwards, after Braun carelessly left an incriminating briefcase in a taxi. Their trial became a cause célèbre for the left. Conservatives who initially denounced the defendants as Communist agents were wrong footed when Braun astutely claimed to be a right-wing activist. He was granted bail and immediately went into hiding.

In 1926, Braun was rearrested and held on remand in Berlin's Moabit prison for a year and a half until he hit the headlines again. On Wednesday, 11 April 1928, his twenty-year-old fiancée, Olga Benário, sprang him from jail in an audacious coup. Benario had been in a relationship with Braun since she was sixteen. Braun, eight years her senior, had left his wife for her. In turn, she had left her middle-class Jewish family to be with him and had visited him regularly in Moabit. This time, she brought him a bunch of primroses and an orange, possibly as a pre-arranged signal. The visit was supervised by a judge, accompanied by two warders. Braun was eating the orange when seven men armed with pistols and clubs burst into the judge's office, overpowered the guards, held a gun to the judge's head and calmly strolled out of the prison with the couple, discarding their weapons on the way.[9]

---

7 The KPD military wing, called the Red Front from 1924, was one of many paramilitary groups in Weimar Germany. Right-wing militias included the various groups of demobilised soldiers known as the Freikorps, the Steel Helmet League of the German National People's Party, and the Nazi Party's SA. On the left, in addition to the Red Front, the Social Democrats had the Black, Red, and Gold Reichsbanner militia that evolved into the Iron Front.

8 At the time, Semyonov was still fighting against the Soviets. He fled Russia in September 1921 and tried to settle in the United States but was denounced as a mass murderer by the former head of the United States intervention force in Russia, General William S. Graves. He was captured by Soviet forces in Manchuria in 1945 and hanged.

9 The 2004 Brazilian feature film *Olga* depicts Benário pulling a gun in a packed courtroom.

The jailbreak made newspapers around the world. The story had two irresistible angles: it was an act of great daring carried out by a young woman for love. Furthermore, her lover was a dangerous Communist with whom she had consorted despite coming from a respectable family. Several newspapers reported that the couple had gone through 'a Communist wedding ceremony', and that Benário had planned the operation.[10] The couple won public sympathy, especially when it turned out that the guns used in the escape were not loaded. Despite a five-million-mark price on their heads, Braun and Benário were able to evade the police until July when they left, by separate routes, for the Soviet Union.

In Moscow, Benário and Braun enrolled in the International Lenin School to train as professional Comintern cadres. Braun later continued his studies at the Frunze Military Academy and joined the Moscow Proletarian Rifle Division of the Red Army. He probably joined the GRU – Soviet Military Intelligence – at the same time. Olga Benário studied military science at the Zhukovsky Air Force Academy where, it is said, she trained as a pilot and a paratrooper.

They were now agents in the service of world revolution and the Soviet Union, liable to be assigned to any location at a moment's notice. Perhaps their feelings for each other faded, or they suppressed them for the cause. By choice or on orders, they separated in 1931 when Olga was sent on missions to France and Britain. In 1934, she was ordered to accompany the Brazilian leftist leader Luís Carlos Prestes, an army officer turned guerrilla leader, to Rio de Janeiro as his bodyguard. En route, the two fell in love and married. They were arrested the following year after a failed revolt by junior officers.[11] Despite an international campaign, the Brazilian government extradited Olga, who was pregnant, to Nazi Germany. After she gave birth to a daughter, she was sent to the Ravensbrück women's concentration camp. In 1942, she was

---

10   According to Litten, senior KPD intelligence agents planned the escape. See Frederick Litten, 'Otto Braun's Curriculum Vitae – Translation and Commentary', *Twentieth Century China*, Vol. 23, No. 1 (1997), 31–62.

11   The November 1935 revolt against the dictatorial regime of Getúlio Vargas was carried out in the name of the Aliança Nacional Libertadora. Actions took place in only three cities – Natal, Recife, and Rio de Janeiro – and were easily suppressed. Prestes was tortured and jailed until 1945. He remained leader of the Brazilian Communist Party for most of his life, guiding it in a reformist direction, but left the party in the 1980s after spending ten years in exile in Moscow.

murdered by the Nazis at the Bernberg Euthanasia Centre. By the time
Braun returned to Germany in the mid-1950s, his former girlfriend was
an icon of the German Democratic Republic.

Braun graduated from the Frunze Academy in the spring of 1932 and
was sent to Harbin in northwest China, then part of the Japanese puppet
state of Manzhouguo.[12] Disguised as an Austrian businessman, he made
'several investigatory trips' – in plain language he was spying – around
China. One was to Shanghai, where he delivered funds to the Soviet
master spy Richard Sorge to save the Noulens from death sentences by
bribing their trial judge. In the autumn of 1932, Braun relocated from
Harbin to Shanghai to advise the Comintern's China chief, Arthur
Ewert, on military matters.

Coincidentally, it was Ewert, a veteran of the Comintern underground,
who, in 1931, had recruited Luís Carlos Prestes to the Communist movement. Born into a poor farming family in East Prussia in 1890, he moved
to Berlin in his teens to find work. After training as a saddle maker, which
he correctly perceived as a dying trade, he took a job in a steel plant. In
1908, he joined the Social Democratic Party of Germany (SPD) and met
the Polish Marxist who would become his lifelong companion, Elise
Szaborowski. Known as Szabo, she was four years older than Ewert and
became his mentor in the labour movement. Under her guidance, he was
soon regarded as having leadership potential. In May 1914, now well
connected in the socialist movement, the couple emigrated to Canada.
When war broke out, they risked internment as enemy aliens but went
underground with the help of internationalist comrades, remaining active
in the revolutionary anti-war movement until they were arrested in 1919.
Ewert was deported immediately and Szabo the following year, after a
spell in an internment camp. Back in Germany, they joined the KPD,
where Ewert rose to become one of the party's top leaders, second only to
Ernst Thälmann, but in 1928, he was sidelined for opposing the 'Third
Period' policy of extreme hostility to the SPD. However, he continued to
carry out missions on behalf of the Comintern.

In September 1933, after a year in Shanghai, Otto Braun left for the
Jiangxi Soviet. Ewert's final order to him before he left was to reconcile

---

12   In his memoirs Braun says he was sent by the Executive Committee of the
Comintern. In a 1969 curriculum vitae he says it was the GRU. Perhaps he was given
assignments by both.

Zhou Enlai and Mao Zedong, who were at odds over military strategy. Transporting a tall, blond-haired, blue-eyed German into the Soviet area was not a simple matter. Braun took a passenger steamer to Shantou, but during the journey upriver he had to spend forty-eight hours lying down under the decking of a small boat before trekking through devastated contested areas to the CCP capital, Ruijin.[13] The CCP security chief, Deng Fa, greeted Braun. That evening, he met with Bo Gu and Luo Fu (Zhang Wentian). A few days later they all attended a meeting of the Revolutionary Military Committee in Braun's quarters, along with Mao Zedong.

Two years before Braun arrived in Jiangxi, the CCP had proclaimed a provisional government as a rival to the KMT government in Nanjing. On 7 November 1931, the anniversary of the October Revolution, a 600-strong delegate conference announced the formation of a Chinese Soviet Republic. The state structure was modelled on the Soviet Union, with Mao Zedong as chairman of the Central Executive Committee and the Council of People's Commissars. However, the new republic was remote and, in Chinese terms, tiny. Its capital, Ruijin, a small mountain city on the Jiangxi side of the border with Fujian, controlled sixty square kilometres of territory straddling the two provinces, with a population of around five million. This Central Soviet Area was the largest, and best armed, of six non-contiguous areas that together made up the republic. The other five areas included parts of Zhejiang, Anhui, Hunan, Hubei, and Henan Provinces. In total, the Soviet Republic controlled around 150,000 square kilometres with a population of around eight million.[14]

---

13   Pantsov and Levine, citing Braun, say it was Mao's forces that plundered and laid waste to these areas, but Braun makes no mention of Mao. See Alexander Pantsov and Steven Levine, *Mao: The Real Story*, New York: Simon & Schuster, 2013, 260.

14   Braun described the 1932 situation of the six bases as follows: Central Soviet Area – East Jiangxi and West Fujian: 60,000 square kilometres, 25,000 troops, around 5 million inhabitants. Jiangxi-Zhejiang-Anhui border triangle: 15,000 square kilometres, 1 million inhabitants, around 5,000 troops. Hunan-Jiangxi border: 15,000 square kilometres, 1.5 million people, 10,000 troops commanded by Xiao Ke. Hunan-Jiangxi-Hubei: 12,000 square kilometres and 500,000 inhabitants. The area had one division of troops (number unspecified), but it was unstable and collapsed. The Henan-Hubei-Anhui border triangle was the second-largest area with 40,000 square kilometres, 3 million inhabitants, and 15,000 men of the Fourth Army, commanded by Zhang Guotao, and an additional 5,000 independent troops. Finally, the Hubei-Hunan border area comprised 20,000 square kilometres with 2 million people and 10,000 troops. According to Braun these were Central Committee figures. Braun, *A Comintern Agent in China*, 14–16.

In spite of its small size, the Chinese Soviet Republic posed a challenge to Chiang Kai-shek's authority that he could not tolerate. But Nationalist China faced other pressing problems. Two months before the Soviet was formed, the Japanese had faked an attack on a railway line near Mukden (now Shenyang) as a pretext to occupy Manchuria. Despite outnumbering the Japanese, the forces of the Manchurian warlord Zhang Xueliang crumbled. Chiang Kai-shek did little apart from protesting to the League of Nations. Facing public outrage, he was forced to call off operations against the Communists and temporarily resign from the government.[15]

Chiang had already launched three 'encirclement campaigns' to wipe out the Red Army. Mao's forces had defeated two. The third was curtailed by the Mukden crisis. For his fourth campaign, begun in January 1933, Chiang assembled half a million troops. Once again, he was defeated, and once more, Japanese aggression played a role, when imperial troops invaded Jehol (Rehe) Province. This time, Chiang signed the humiliating Tanggu Truce and agreed to evacuate a demilitarised zone across northern China, leaving the Japanese in control of the Great Wall but freeing his hands for a further encirclement campaign. Ominously for the soviet, his troops had only retreated as far as its borders. In September 1933, as Braun set off from Shanghai, Chiang launched his fifth, ultimately successful, encirclement campaign.

Mao was head of state of the Soviet Republic, but leadership positions in the party carried more weight, and his authority was limited and dwindling. A new generation of young cadres, returning from studying at Moscow's Sun Yat-sen University of the Toilers of China (UTK), had taken over the party leadership. Protégés of UTK's dogmatic and ambitious rector, Pavel Mif,[16] their leaders were his assistant Wang Ming

---

15   Chiang was accused of prioritising action against the Communists over resisting Japan. According to Theodore H. White, in Chongqing in 1941, at the height of Japanese bombing, Chiang told him that the Communists were like a disease of the heart, the Japanese like a disease of the skin. White agreed with the comparison. See the documentary *China: The Roots of Madness*, available on YouTube.

16   Mif succeeded the oppositionist Karl Radek at UTK and led a campaign to wipe out a strong Trotskyist faction among its Chinese students. In late 1930 he travelled to Shanghai and packed the CCP Central Committee with his supporters. The former party leader Li Lisan was sent to Moscow for re-education. See Pantsov and Levine, *Mao*, 235–6; and Alexander Pantsov, 'From Students to Dissidents: The Chinese Trotskyists in Soviet Russia', *Marxist Monthly*, Vol. 5, Nos. 8–11 (1994–95), available at marxists.org.

(Chen Shaoyu), and Bo Gu, who was appointed CCP general secretary in 1932. They had radical plans to expand the Soviet Republic by seizing several cities.[17] In their eyes, Mao's guerrilla-style military policy of giving ground and luring the enemy into traps was overcautious and conservative – a 'right-opportunist' deviation. The young Muscovites were supported at this time by Zhou Enlai, the Red Army's chief political commissar.

When Braun arrived in Jiangxi, the Soviet was not only beleaguered but was also a house divided against itself. Mao faced an array of internal opponents – not only Bo Gu and Zhou Enlai but other heavyweights, including Ren Bishi and Xiang Ying, a future leader of the New Fourth Army.[18] What is more, Mao's opponents were now on the spot in Jiangxi, the Central Committee having relocated from Shanghai earlier in 1933 as increasing KMT repression was making work there impossible.

Perhaps understandably, as an outsider, a foreigner and, after all, a mere advisor, Braun sided with the official party leadership. In his memoirs, Braun relates that Bo Gu was his consistent ally. He acknowledged that Bo Gu and Zhou Enlai briefed him before Military Council meetings and generally supported his suggestions. This, he admits, 'created the false impression that I possessed absolute authority'. However, he repeatedly stressed 'the purely advisory nature' of his role.[19] Advisors cannot be absolved of responsibility, but if Mao was shut out of military decision making, who was shutting him out? Surely not the advisor Braun, but his factional rivals in the Party, Bo Gu and Zhou Enlai.

Another fact often omitted from the official narrative is that Braun was not the Comintern's chief military advisor in China. That was his superior officer, Manfred Stern, who never set foot in the Soviet area but operated by remote control from Shanghai.[20] Stern was four years older than Braun and a far more experienced soldier. He was drafted into the

---

17   Pantsov and Levine, *Mao*, 254.

18   Frederick Litten, 'The Myth of the "Turning Point": Towards a New Understanding of the Long March', *Bochumer Jahrbuch zur Ostasienforschung*, No. 25 (December 2001), 3–44, 5.

19   Braun, *A Comintern Agent in China*, 35.

20   Stern arrived in China from the United States, where he had been operating an underground network, several months after Braun. He missed the pre-arranged meetings that were to put him in touch with the underground in Shanghai and only managed to make contact after running into Braun in the street.

Austro-Hungarian army at the start of World War I. Taken prisoner, he was released after the October Revolution and joined the Bolsheviks. During the civil war, he commanded a unit of Siberian partisans against Admiral Alexander Kolchak, the self-styled Supreme Ruler of Russia, and was elected to the parliament of the Far Eastern Republic. He later studied at the Frunze Military Academy and, like Braun, was recruited by the GRU. The two agents knew each other well and were on good terms, but Stern made it clear who was in charge. When Braun left for Jiangxi, he impressed on him that he must follow his orders to the letter.

Stern agreed with Wang Ming and Bo Gu about the prospects for expanding the Soviet area. Indeed, he was even more optimistic than the young Muscovites. Soon after arriving, he proposed an offensive against the Nineteenth Route Army in Fujian Province. Braun, Arthur Ewert, and even Bo Gu opposed the plan. The Nineteenth Army had battled bravely against the Japanese attack on Shanghai in 1932, and its commander, Cai Tingkai, was seen as a potential ally against Chiang Kai-shek.[21] But Stern dismissed Cai as a 'waverer' who should be given a demonstration of the Red Army's strength and then called to order. The policy towards him, Stern said, should be 'strike first, talk later'. The majority of the CCP leadership in both Shanghai and Ruijin, including Mao, supported Stern; his plan therefore went ahead and was, in military terms, a success. But Chiang's forces took the opportunity to seize Ruijin, and a forced march and counter-offensive were required to retake the Soviet capital.[22]

Expecting the Soviet Union to ship military aid to the Chinese Soviet Republic, Stern ordered Braun to build an airfield in Ruijin to receive it. Rearmed, the Soviet Republic would be able to push north as far as the Yangzi, taking Nanchang, capital of Jiangxi, on the way. Both Braun and Ewert thought the idea that the Soviet Union was about to start shipping arms to the Red Army was a fantasy, not least because Stalin had recently restored diplomatic relations with Chiang's regime. It followed that Stern's proposed offensive was also a flight of fancy. Ewert told Stern to leave operational decisions to the CCP leadership on the ground.[23] But when Braun

---

21 On 28 January 1932, Japan launched a sustained assault on Shanghai after an ultra-nationalist Japanese monk was killed by an enraged Chinese crowd. Tens of thousands of soldiers and civilians were killed in more than a month of fighting.

22 Ibid., 26–8.

23 Ibid., 29. Whether Stern had grounds for believing in the arms shipments requires research.

raised his own doubts, Stern reminded him that he was Braun's commander. Braun had the airfield built, but the aid never arrived. He also 'dutifully' obeyed Stern's instructions to build fortifications north of Ruijin, even though he was 'aware of the impracticability of this type of positional warfare'.[24] Given that his espousal of positional warfare was one of the main items on the charge sheet against Braun, his reluctance to carry out Stern's wishes is significant. Indeed, Braun did not advocate 'positional warfare'; he argued for 'short, swift thrusts' (duancu tuji), which are self-evidently mobile tactics – albeit not those advocated by Mao. The chief advocate of positional warfare was Zhou Enlai, who declared: 'Defending and enlarging the soviet territory and refusing to let the enemy ravage an inch of the soviet territory have become our central task.'[25]

In late November 1933, the Nineteenth Route Army rebelled against Chiang Kai-shek and declared a People's Government along with some Left KMT figures – including Eugene Chen. Though the CCP had made its peace with the Nineteenth, it was divided on how to react – whether to ally with Fujian against Nanjing, or exploit the conflict in the ranks of the enemy to go on the offensive. Mistrust of the Left KMT was understandable given the experience of 1927; according to Braun, only Bo Gu pushed for an alliance. The majority of the Central Committee were opposed; an article in the CCP magazine Struggle denounced the rebels as 'neither for the people nor revolutionary'.[26] Mao, for his part, dismissed the revolt as 'a new deception of the masses', while Stern repeated his call for a northern offensive to the Yangzi and proposed to take Nanchang and Changsha. According to Braun, the plan was so 'reckless and out of keeping with reality' that the Politburo rejected it out of hand. For the first time, Braun disobeyed Stern and proposed a flanking attack on the Nanjing forces as they advanced south through Fujian. He said later that his plan was not implemented due to 'indecisiveness'.[27] In any case, arguments over tactics towards the Fujian

24   Ibid., 47.

25   'For Land for Freedom for the Soviet Regime Fight to the End!', Hong xing, No. 39 (29 April 1934), 1. Cited in Jerome Ch'en, 'Resolutions of the Tsunyi Conference', China Quarterly, No. 40 (1969), 1–38, 25.

26   Anthony Garavente, 'The Long March', China Quarterly, No. 22 (1965), 89–124, 97.

27   See Braun's 1939 confession. M. L. Titarenko et.al., eds., VKP(b), Komintern i Kitai: Dokumenty [The CPSU, the Comintern, and China: Documents], 5 Vols., Moscow: ROSSPEN, 1994–2007, Vol. 4, Part 2, 1144-1151,1148.

government quickly became irrelevant as it crumbled in a matter of weeks.[28]

One of Mao's charges against Bo Gu at Zunyi was that he failed to understand the importance of the Fujian revolt. In his words,

> The crux to our defeating the enemy's 5th 'Encirclement' was the mutiny of the 19th Route Army in Fukien. The Party Centre then adopted the correct political line to exploit this internal contradiction of the KMT by concluding a truce with the 19th Route Army. However Comrade XX [i.e., Bo Gu] and others took a contrary strategic stand . . . Thus [we] lost this golden opportunity [because they] did not appreciate that the existence of the People's Government . . . was valuable to us.[29]

This was, according to Braun, Mao's 'most extravagant falsification of historical truth' at Zunyi, in which he 'simply inverted the facts'.[30] Mao had dismissed the rebels as reactionary, while Bo Gu had proposed allying with them. Mao effectively accused Bo Gu of supporting views that Mao had held and which, hedging his bets, he reaffirmed a few sentences later:[31]

> This was not to say that the 19th Route Army was a revolutionary army. No, it was merely a clique of reactionaries. It attempted to preserve the regime of the landlords and capitalists by using the worst kind of deception.[32]

Having defeated the rebels, Chiang Kai-shek restarted his fifth encirclement campaign against the Red Army. This time, the strategy was different. Chiang had learned from the previous campaigns that

---

28   Frederick Litten described the rebellion as a sham. See Litten, 'The Myth of the Turning Point', 12.

29   From the Zunyi Resolution as translated by Ch'en, 'Resolutions of the Tsunyi Conference', 10.

30   Braun, *A Comintern Agent in China*, 101.

31   Braun's translator, Wu Xiuquan, was persecuted during the Cultural Revolution for 'faithfully translating' the 'great renegade' Braun's attacks on Mao Zedong, even though he supported Mao and opposed Braun. He was jailed for eight years. After being released he presided over the trial of the Gang of Four.

32   From the Zunyi Resolution. Ch'en, 'Resolutions of the Tsunyi Conference', 10.

forays into Soviet territory turned into costly defeats. Both sides now relied on German military advisors. Chiang's advisors, Generals Hans von Seeckt and Alexander von Falkenhausen, prescribed a policy of slow strangulation, surrounding the Soviet area with fortifications and gradually tightening the noose. Chiang's forces, armed with heavy weapons and counting on air support, outnumbered the Red Army five to one. Combined with an economic blockade, the campaign wore the defenders down.

At the Zunyi Conference, Mao insisted that, despite the fearsome odds, with a correct approach the Red Army could have defeated the campaign and successfully defended the Soviet:

> During the 5th 'Encirclement we [were] having even better conditions to achieve a decisive victory . . . Comrade XX [Bo Gu] . . . over-estimates the objective difficulties . . . The *essential* reason for our failure [was that] our military leadership could not adopt correct strategy and tactics.[33]

The correct strategy and tactics were, according to Mao, 'decisive battles for defence (an offensive type of defence) – concentrating superior forces, selecting the enemy's weaknesses, using mobile warfare to destroy a part, or a great part, of enemy strength'. Instead, the leadership – that is to say, Bo Gu, Zhou Enlai, and Braun – adopted 'a pure defence line (or a defence of positions only) . . . combined with the so-called tactic of "short, swift, thrusts" '.

It is not clear where Mao thought these decisive battles should take place. If inside Soviet territory, that would require the KMT forces to leave the safety of their fortifications and make the kind of reckless advances that had led them to disaster in the past. But Chiang and his advisors had precisely ruled this out and were determined to stick to their cautious strategy, never straying too far from their fortified lines. If, on the other hand, the battles were to take place outside Soviet territory, that implied a breakout by the Red Army. If we are to believe Braun, in March 1934, he proposed a breakout to either the southwest or southeast to attack behind the blockhouse lines. He was opposed by everyone, 'no one more vigorously than Mao Tse-Tung', who argued that 'a

33   Ibid., 1–2.

decisive victory in the interior' was still possible.[34] The difference between Mao and Braun was not over mobile versus positional warfare but whether the Red Army could inflict a crushing defeat on the enemy inside the Soviet area.

A decisive battle did take place inside the Soviet area – at Guangchang in April 1934[35]—but the Red Army was defeated. Zhu De's Third Corps was badly mauled by KMT air power and artillery. According to Braun, Mao approved the battle plans at two meetings of the Military Council.[36] Later, at Zunyi, Mao reversed his position, saying that Guangchang was one of several 'dare to die' battles that should never have been fought: '[We] should have avoided unnecessary battles and battles against undefeatable enemies but should not have avoided necessary ones and the ones against defeatable enemies.'[37] However, this is little more than a tautology. Deciding which were the right and wrong battles is easy in hindsight, but, as Braun pointed out to Lin Biao, victory is never certain before a battle. The leadership decided to defend Guangchang, according to Braun, because if it fell, it would open the road to Ruijin, but also because it was considered 'politically indefensible' to surrender it without a fight.[38] Arguably, the *political* decision to declare the Soviet Republic in 1931 implied a commitment to defend its territory and people and, in turn, implied a commitment to positional warfare. The other choices boiled down to two: revert to guerrilla warfare in the mountains, or break out of the Soviet Area and move elsewhere.

The fall of Guangchang made retreat inevitable, and a troika of Bo Gu, Zhou Enlai, and Braun was set up to formulate a plan.[39] By July 1934, the decision had been taken for a 'strategic transfer'. At the end of September, an article in *Red China* announced that the soviet was to be abandoned, and in mid-October 85,000 men left carrying whatever they could. Thirty thousand troops were left behind.[40]

---

34   Braun, *A Comintern Agent in China*, 68.
35   See Ch'en, 'Resolutions of the Tsunyi Conference', 21.
36   Braun, *A Comintern Agent in China*, 68–9.
37   Ch'en, 'Resolutions of the Tsunyi Conference', 13.
38   Braun, *A Comintern Agent in China*, 68.
39   Litten, 'The Myth of the Turning Point', 10–15.
40   The story of those who were left behind is told in Gregor Benton's 1992 book *Mountain Fires*.

The first period of the retreat was, on the face of it, disastrous. Mao characterised it as a disorderly retreat in blind panic. The Red Army lost about half its strength as it crossed the Xiang River:

> The first major battle was crossing the Xiang River. It was fought for a week – November 25th to December 3rd. By most accounts, it was a disaster. By the time they reached Zunyi, a month later, the Red Army had about 30,000 troops left . . . Things were not going well for the leadership of Li De (Otto Braun) and discontent was spreading.[41]

Many of the losses were planned, for ancillary troops were deliberately left behind.[42] But even if we accept that the breakout was badly planned and the losses were excessive, it is legitimate to ask whether things improved after Zunyi. According to Braun, they did not. As the marchers passed from Guizhou into Yunnan, they were mercilessly strafed and bombed by the KMT air force. Food was scarce, and the troops were reduced to eating their horses. The Red Army confiscated opium to use as currency to buy supplies. Retreat 'degenerated into outright flight'. Mao's formerly close allies Lin Biao and Luo Fu accused him of 'military bankruptcy'.[43] Again, the picture is far less clear cut than in the accepted narrative.

Another problem for the accepted narrative is that the Long March turned into a great triumph in official propaganda and became one of the founding myths of the CCP. The fact that Braun initiated it presents a dilemma for the official account; one historian, Ling Buji, admitted that 'it was Braun who came up with the evacuation idea that was later called the Long March. That was a wise decision, which should be recognized. Chinese historians have reached consensus on the point.'[44] The respected historian Yang Kuisong portrayed the breakout from the Soviet area as well planned and preceded by diversionary manoeuvres to wrong-foot the KMT forces. But Yang played down Braun's role, attributing the planning to Manfred Stern, or even Moscow:

---

41   State Council website, china.org.cn.

42   Litten, 'The Myth of the Turning Point', 18.

43   Braun, *A Comintern Agent in China*, 113–14.

44   'Otto Braun's "Solitary House" Visited', State Council Information Office, English-language website, china.org.cn.

Following instructions from Moscow, General Manfred Stern first ordered the Seventh Corps of the Red Army to march . . . to Fuzhou and then to northeast Jiangxi . . . Its task was to distract the Nationalist Party troops . . . Later . . . Stern ordered the Sixth Corps of the Red Army . . . to break the siege by moving westward [to] southern Hunan. This was done to prepare for the Central Red Army to break the siege, to settle down in the mountainous area of Hunan, and finally connect with the bases in Sichuan and Shanxi.[45]

Either way, Yang's account diminishes Braun's culpability. We can summarise the case for the defence of Braun as follows: there was a political imperative to defend the Soviet Republic that implied positional warfare. Braun was not solely, perhaps not even mainly, responsible for military policy – he shared it with Zhou Enlai, Bo Gu, and others in Jiangxi, and he reported to Manfred Stern in Shanghai. Furthermore, the military odds were so stacked against the Soviet that probably no strategy could have saved it. This is not to absolve Braun of mistakes. He undoubtedly made many. But he was not alone. The Maoist narrative of 'two lines' is an oversimplification of the debates within the leadership faced with Chiang's fifth encirclement.[46] The case against Braun is not proven.

After returning to the Soviet Union in 1939, Braun wrote a lengthy self-criticism which has been taken as evidence of his 'guilt'. He essentially recited the charge sheet laid against him by Mao Zedong:

My mistakes all concerned the strategy and tactics of the Chinese Red Army . . . they were all in the area of military work . . . but I clearly understand that they were not mistakes of a technical nature but were (in the words of the resolution of the enlarged meeting of the Politburo of the Central Committee of the Chinese Communist Party on 8 January, 1935) 'mistakes in part related to the entire political line of the Party', and flowed from a right opportunist view of the situation in China at the time.

After disagreements and criticisms of the actions of the Red Army in 1932, the main leader of the Soviet movement and the Red Army,

---

45   Shen, *A Short History of Sino-Soviet Relations*, 52–3.
46   Litten, 'The Myth of the Turning Point', 4.

Comrade Mao Zedong, took little part in the military leadership and responsibility for this work passed to Bo Gu in the central committee and Zhou Enlai in the army.

Having arrived at the invitation of the Central Committee and having worked closely with Bo Gu in my work in Shanghai, I one-sidedly maintained relations with him and factually took over decision making regarding the actions of the Red Army. In this I went far beyond my remit and objectively usurped the command of the Red Army for a period of a year.

I defended my views extremely stubbornly and forcefully, with the result that, it is true with the support of the Secretary of the Central Committee Comrade Bo Gu, other opinions were suppressed and initiatives of commanders at the front were ignored. In particular, faced with severe criticism from Comrades Mao Zedong and Luo Fu, I defended my views without a hint of self-criticism and moreover considered that in the new situation of the 5th Encirclement Campaign, the rich experience of the Red Army was no longer of any use.[47]

Braun faced several daylong sessions during which Zhou Enlai and Mao Zedong's brother Mao Zemin levelled charges against him. He had heard rumours that Mao Zedong had ordered Zhou Enlai and his brother to have Braun 'expelled from the Party . . . as an "enemy of the people" and, if possible, to have me liquidated'.[48] Pavel Mif, the arch-Stalinist who had also backed Wang Ming and Bo Gu, had not kept pace with the ever-changing party line and was executed on 10 September 1939. Mif had been under arrest since 1937, meaning that during his interrogation, Braun almost certainly knew of Mif's likely fate.[49] Indeed, Wang Ming had 'urgently advised' Braun not to return to Moscow, saying he risked being exiled or shot.[50] A close reading of Braun's self-criticism shows that he prudently admitted all the faults attributed to him in the Zunyi resolution while deflecting blame onto Bo Gu and

47 Titarenko, *CPSU*, Vol. 5, 1145–6, translation by the author.
48 Braun, *A Comintern Agent in China*, 263. We only have Braun's word for this, but such intrigues were not uncommon at the time.
49 Mif was shot on 10 September 1939. Braun's confession was dated 22 September 1939.
50 Braun, *A Comintern Agent in China*, 248.

Zhou Enlai. There can be little doubt that Braun was simply trying to save his own life. No impartial tribunal would admit his 1939 self-criticism as evidence.

Braun's memoirs, published in East Germany in 1973, represent his views more accurately. Written at the height of the Sino-Soviet conflict, they are openly partisan and stridently critical of Mao. In his afterword, Braun declared his loyalties:

> Mao Tse-tung [has] long since unveiled himself as the enemy of the working class . . . I regard these memoirs as a weapon in the political struggle against Maoism which ought to help unmask the Maoist distortion of history. It is in this sense that I should like them to be understood.[51]

Braun criticises the complete lack of democracy in Yan'an, and the militarisation of the party and all aspects of life: 'Never once did I experience an election. Civil officials, educational facilities, and institutions were all subject to strict military regimentation. Functionaries, teachers, students, even the artists, were actually quartered in barracks.'[52]

According to Braun, the social composition of the base areas favoured the institutionalisation of army-style command structures. There was neither a working class nor a bourgeoisie; rather, the population consisted of poor peasants and a thin layer of gentry. The much-trumpeted 'mass line' was simply a way of 'drumming into the mostly illiterate populace simple and catchy slogans [made] comprehensible through theatre, song and dance performances'. It would be a simple matter, when necessary, to use such people as a stick to beat political opponents in the Party. All this was no doubt true, if somewhat disingenuous coming from an official in the GDR.

However slanted, Braun's memoirs contain useful information. He wrote that Zhang Xueliang's detention of Chiang Kai-shek was greeted in the Red base with 'genuine rapture'. Braun, who had fought against Chiang's troops, does not say if he shared the elation at the time but it is highly likely. His memoirs also confirm that, during the first phase of anti-Japanese war from 1937 to 1941, while Stalin sent thousands of

---

51   Ibid., 265.
52   Ibid., 258–9.

artillery pieces, tanks, warplanes, advisors, and pilots to support the Nationalists, military aid to CCP forces was minuscule. Soviet shipments to Yan'an consisted mainly of Marxist literature. A bitter joke circulated that the Soviet Union sent 'weapons to the bourgeoisie, books to the proletariat'. However, writing later in East Germany, Braun dismissed such complaints as carping. It was once the orthodox view that Chiang Kai-shek kept his best troops in reserve to fight the Communists. Recently, it has become fashionable among historians to praise the Nationalist war effort and criticise Mao for not fighting Japan. Braun's memoirs hint at a possible explanation for Mao's supposedly culpable inaction: that Mao was deliberately starved of weapons by Stalin because, if armed, he might have marched to Manchuria and embroiled the Soviets in a war with Japan, whereas Stalin's aim in arming Republican China was to keep Japan occupied in south and central China, far away from the Soviet borderlands.

The memoirs also confirm that Yan'an was repeatedly bombed by the Japanese. Beginning in September 1937, the Japanese bombed the city almost daily, sometimes several times a day, to the point of destruction. The air raids on the city and its surroundings continued for years. Braun himself was nearly killed by a bomb that vaporised his interpreter.[53] He recalled that among the few weapons delivered by the Soviet Union were anti-aircraft machine guns that turned out to be entirely ineffective.

Unsurprisingly, Braun's memoirs are entirely uncritical of Soviet policy towards China during the anti-Japanese war. After the 1937 Japanese invasion, he said, the CCP should have immediately acknowledged Chiang Kai-shek's wartime leadership and subordinated itself unconditionally to the KMT. Instead, Mao pursued a 'sectarian' and 'nationalist' political line that was responsible for all clashes with the KMT and the eventual breakdown of the United Front. For those responsible for this new line, it was as if the massacres of 1927 had never taken place. What Braun described as sectarianism could be viewed as prudence in dealing with an ally that had once before turned into a deadly enemy. Braun goes so far as to hint that the existence of extreme anti-Communists within the KMT, even those prepared to collaborate with Japan, was the result of Mao's 'unmitigated striving for hegemony'.[54]

---

53   Ibid., 219.
54   Ibid., 240.

The inescapable conclusion is that Braun's political line amounted to supporting everything the Soviet Union did and calling it proletarian internationalism.

Braun also accuses Mao of the opposite sin: capitulation to Chiang Kai-shek through an offer to provide a list of names should CCP members ever be allowed to join the KMT. According to Braun, this 'surpassed even Chen Duxiu's right-opportunism.'[55] However, his historical knowledge lets him down here. A list of names of CCP members *actually* in the KMT is precisely what Soviet advisors (not Chen Duxiu) gave to Chiang Kai-shek after his March 1926 coup in Canton – a list that was later used to deadly effect. But Braun confessed he could make no sense of Mao's intentions as he seemed to be ' "overtaking on the right" the Marxist Leninists led by Wang Ming'.

What of the criticisms of Braun's personal behaviour? The charge that he enjoyed special privileges is easily dismissed. Indeed, his privileged position was normal for foreigners in base areas, as all foreigners in the service of the CCP received special treatment. Guests were given accommodation, rations, and so on equal to or exceeding those of the CCP leadership. It is, of course, well documented that the leadership enjoyed much-better living conditions than the rank and file. Even Japanese prisoners of war lived better than rank-and-file Red Army soldiers. Since he was a military advisor, Braun also had assistants and interpreters, but there is no evidence he was treated better than other foreigners.

Braun is also excoriated on government websites for his womanising. After the embarrassing incident with the married woman, Braun became friendly with a woman called Lai Shuidi, who agreed to marry him, but the party refused to sanction the relationship after it emerged that Lai was already married and that her husband was a member of a reactionary militia. Extraordinary and sinister events followed. Bo Gu instructed the head of the Women's Committee, Li Jianzhen, to find a politically suitable companion for Braun. Ultimately, Li persuaded a woman called Xiao Yuehua that it was her revolutionary duty to the party to marry this foreigner, ten years her senior. Xiao, described as coming from a poor background and having little education, agreed to sacrifice herself for

---

55   Stalin made Chen Duxiu, who opposed the policy of collaboration with the KMT, a scapegoat for its consequences.

the revolution. Bo Gu officiated at the wedding with Li Jianzhen acting as maid of honour. If we assume, for the sake of argument, that there is more to this story than a rumour, and that it was not simply fabricated to discredit Bo Gu, then it disgraces the CCP and its so-called Women's Committee rather than Braun, who was presumably not told of the intrigue.

As might be expected, the marriage was unhappy, not least because Braun never mastered Chinese and Xiao could speak no other language. They quarrelled often and spent long periods apart. They had a brief spell of happiness in Yan'an after Xiao gave birth to a son but soon began arguing again and parted. Braun then took up with an actress called Li Lilian who had arrived in Yan'an together with Jiang Qing. Once again, it turned out that his love interest was already married; according to George Hatem's wife, Su Fei, Li's husband turned up to confront Braun at the house he shared with Hatem. Braun emerged brandishing a gun and chased the husband away. This was reprehensible behaviour indeed. And one can, at the very least, question the judgement of the twenty-four-year-old Braun who divorced his wife to take up with Olga Benário who, although self-willed and independent, was still a sixteen-year-old schoolgirl.

Braun, then, was a flawed character, at the same time that as a young man, he was also a revolutionary who risked his life many times for the cause of international socialism. Like many others, he later transferred his loyalty from an ideal to a country he believed embodied the ideal. In his words, 'All my life I have considered the touchstone of every Communist, regardless of nationality or situation, to be his posture towards the Soviet Union.'[56] Braun's faults do not alter the obvious conclusion that Mao used him as an 'ideal scapegoat' for the collapse of the Jiangxi Soviet.[57] By pinning all or most of the blame on a foreigner, he left the door open for reconciliation with Bo Gu and Zhou Enlai, who soon joined his camp.

In the late summer of 1939, Braun was peremptorily summoned back to Moscow. A note delivered before dawn told him to go immediately to the airport. He left in haste, saying only the briefest of goodbyes to Li Lilian and rode off on horseback. Since Zhou Enlai was leaving on the

---

56 Braun, *A Comintern Agent in China*, 264.
57 Litten, 'The Myth of the Turning Point', 25.

same plane, there was a farewell ceremony attended by Mao and others, and Li Lilian had time to reach the airport before the plane left. She asked to be allowed to accompany her husband. Braun says that he also asked Mao to let her board the plane but was told that, without a visa, she would not be allowed into the Soviet Union. Zhou Enlai promised to arrange for her to follow on later. In his memoirs, Braun remarks laconically that he never saw her again.

Back in the Soviet Union, Braun rejoined the Red Army. During the Great Patriotic War, he was assigned to win over German prisoners of war. After Stalin's death, he was repatriated to East Germany, where he worked on various literary projects including the German edition of Lenin's complete works. By the early 1960s, he was head of the GDR writers' association. In the mid-1960s, with Sino-Soviet polemics escalating, no doubt with official encouragement, he began work on his memoirs, which were published in 1973. In a photograph probably taken in the late 1960s or early 1970s, he looks like a well-to-do businessman in smart-casual clothes. He died in 1974 while on holiday in Bulgaria.

Arthur Ewert and Szabo left China in July 1934 and returned to Brazil at the same time as Luís Carlos Prestes and Olga Benário. There, they were arrested following the failed Communist insurrection of 1935 and brutally tortured to force them to reveal Prestes' whereabouts. Neither of them broke despite being starved, deprived of sleep, and mercilessly beaten. A United States consular official who took on the role of 'good cop' after the beatings related how the chief jailer, 'an experienced connoisseur of torture techniques . . . took off his hat to them.'[58] Soon afterwards, however, Ewert began to hallucinate and eventually went completely mad. Szabo was deported to Nazi Germany along with Benário and sent to the Ravensbrück concentration camp, where she died of exhaustion in 1939. Ewert was jailed in Brazil until 1945, when he returned to Germany. He spent the rest of his life in an East German sanatorium for the insane. In 1981, the government of the GDR issued a postage stamp in his honour.

Manfred Stern fought with distinction in the Spanish Civil War. In November 1936, under the *nom de guerre* General Kléber, he led the

---

58   David Hornstein, *Arthur Ewert: A Life for the Comintern*, Lanham: University Press of America, 1993, 252–3.

Eleventh International Brigade into battle against Fascist forces that had penetrated Madrid as far as the city centre. The Republican government of Largo Caballero had already fled, and the victory of the International Brigade, after fierce street battles, retrieved what had seemed a hopeless situation. General Kléber was hailed as the saviour of Madrid. The *New York Times* journalist Herbert Matthews, later famous for his interviews with Fidel Castro, wrote: 'Listening to General Kléber, one gets the impression of great dynamic force. He is a character possibly destined to play a great part in the troubled years that face the world.'

Unfortunately, that is not how things turned out. Stern's hero status did not save him from Stalin's terror. When he returned to the Soviet Union in 1939, he was sentenced to fifteen years hard labour and died in a camp in 1954.[59] Although Braun had differences with Stern over military and political tactics in China, there is little doubt that he would have included him among those 'for whose unyielding loyalty to the Party I would have put my hand in the fire'.[60]

---

59   Ludwik Kowalski, *Hell on Earth: Brutality and Violence under the Stalinist regime*, Shelbyville, KY: Wasteland Press, 2008, 15.

60   Braun, *A Comintern Agent in China*, 248.

7

Faith and an Act of Contrition

In September 2019, Isabel Crook was awarded a gold Friendship Medal by PRC chairman Xi Jinping as a reward for a lifetime of service and loyalty to China. As she is the oldest and one of the few remaining survivors of the group of 'old foreign experts', Isabel Crook is occasionally feted in the Chinese media. In 2014, on her one hundredth birthday, the front page of the English-language newspaper *China Daily* carried a picture of her with Premier Li Keqiang. She lives in a modest apartment on the campus of Beijing Foreign Studies University where she and her husband, David Crook, taught English from 1949 until their retirement, and where they brought up their three sons. A short walk away, in a dusty garden, there is a memorial to her husband – a small stone slab inscribed, in English, *In memory of David Crook 1910–2000*, and, in Chinese, *Eternal rest to Comrade Crook.*

Isabel Brown was born in Chengdu, Sichuan Province, in 1915 to a Canadian missionary couple, Homer Brown and Muriel Hockey, who had met and married in China. They were energetic and talented educators. Muriel set up Montessori kindergartens and schools for handicapped children, and Homer was one of the founders of West China University, which is now a medical school. As well as Isabel, Homer and Muriel gave birth to her younger sister Julia; two other children died in infancy. However, Isabel did not follow her parents into missionary work. As she later recalled, 'You had to have the call you see. And I didn't have it.'[1]

---

1   Isabel Crook, conversation with the author, Beijing 2018.

Nevertheless, she remained a devout Christian well into her twenties. After studying anthropology at the University of Toronto, she returned to Sichuan to work on a rural reconstruction project for the National Christian Council. Her thesis on the social structure of the small township of Xinglongchang (Prosperous Fields) was eventually published in 2013.[2] She also taught in the mission school. On 3 November 1940, when she wrote to her parents, she was experiencing a kind of religious elation:

> If we can't do something with the kids it will be all our fault. They are virgin territory . . . I'm afraid I have a bad case of euphoria. I don't know when I've ever stayed at such a high pitch of happiness for such a duration. My spirits are absolutely incorrigible . . . To give you an idea of my state of mind here are the sentences I underline in Baillie's Diary of Private Prayer.[3]

The township's name was ironic: the overwhelming majority of its 1,500 families were desperately poor. Isabel realised that opening schools in big cities only helped a wafer-thin layer of Chinese society. On 5 December 1940, she urged her parents to get out of the city and experience life in the countryside 'for a month at least. Living in this type of situation I hear the criticism . . . the foreigners don't get out long enough . . . but stay settled in Chungking'. Poverty was not the villagers' only enemy. Banditry was endemic, and even more dangerous than the bandits were the press gangs and grain requisitioning parties of warlord armies. The day before Isabel's twenty-fifth birthday, two hundred soldiers turned up, foraging for rice. They stored their loot in a farmhouse while the family was out working in the fields. When their commander discovered the rice, he beat the farmer to death, without bothering to find out how it got there.[4] It is easy to see how this event would arouse righteous anger as much as Christian compassion.

Reflecting on her decades of Communist activism, Isabel said that the anti-colonial revolution had triumphed while the socialist

---

2   Isabel Crook, Christina Gilmartin, Xiji Yu et al., *Prosperity's Predicament: Identity, Reform, and Resistance in Rural Wartime China*, Lanham: Rowan & Littlefield, 2015.

3   Letter from Isabel Brown (Crook), Xinglongchang, 3 November 1940, Carl Crook collection.

4   Letter from Isabel Brown (Crook), Xinglongchang, 17 December 1940, Carl Crook collection.

revolution had faltered because it had taken longer than expected to change people.[5] Her socialism, it seems, owed something to the evangelical notion that people must change or even be born again: while the revolutionary aims to change society, the missionary aims to change people. These aims are blurred not only in Isabel's creed but also in Mao's. Indeed, Chinese Communism, in its heroic phase, had a moralistic aspect, reflected in the rectification campaigns and self-criticism sessions. One could be labelled 'bourgeois' despite being penniless. The *Daily Worker* journalist Alan Winnington, who went to China in the late 1940s, once remarked to David Crook that Maoism had more in common with Moral Re-armament than Marxism

Isabel met David Crook in Chengdu, where, after two years in Shanghai, he had taken a job at the wartime campus of Nanjing University. He had travelled via Hong Kong, Haiphong, Hanoi, along the narrow-gauge French-built railway to Kunming and from there by bus to Chengdu. The journey through the mountains from Kunming was hair raising, and the flop-houses were infested with fleas and bedbugs. When he arrived in Chengdu, however, he lodged with Methodist missionaries and was given a manservant. A Communist and atheist, he found that some missionaries were Christian Socialists and were being watched by the KMT secret police. A few became lifelong friends.[6]

One of his colleagues at the university was Julia, Isabel's sister; when she was ill one day, Isabel took her place. David remarked absent mindedly that she had changed her hairstyle. Soon afterwards, he began to take an interest in Isabel, who was, by male consensus, the most striking woman on the campus. He discovered Isabel liked cycling and began inviting her out on bicycle trips. The daredevil war correspondent Jack Belden was in Chengdu and was also attracted to Isabel but found her too intense and conceited, saying she scared the hell out of him. On the cycling trips, David, a member of the British Communist Party,

---

5   Isabel Crook, conversation with the author.

6   For example, James Endicott (1898–1993), who was, like Isabel Crook, born in Sichuan to missionary parents. He joined the ministry and was initially a KMT supporter but switched his allegiance to the CCP after meeting Zhou Enlai and supported the CCP in the civil war. Thereafter, he remained a loyal supporter of the PRC until his death. Initially sympathetic to the 1989 student protests, he came to believe they had been manipulated by 'capitalist roaders'.

challenged Isabel's religious beliefs. Her experiences in Xinglongchang had already led her to question the privileges enjoyed by the missionaries. David clearly made an impression because, not long afterwards, he proposed marriage; Isabel accepted. Isabel's Protestant teetotal parents had some misgivings about their daughter's marriage to a Jewish Communist who had a well-deserved reputation as a bon viveur. Had they known more about him, they may well not have approved the engagement. Indeed, David Crook was a man with a past.

Crook was born into a well-to-do family in London. His father was in the fur trade, and his mother had a clothes shop on Bond Street. They lived in a Hampstead house with servants, including a young Frenchwoman hired as a language tutor. Crook was sent to a typical English public school in Cheltenham. In his late teens, after spending time in Paris, he was packed off to New York to set up in the fur trade and, with luck, become a millionaire. After the Great Depression scotched those plans, he moved in to the YMCA where, to his dismay, he became a favourite of the gay residents. However, he had been introduced to a smart set who frequented country clubs and organised dinner parties. A handsome young man with a fashionable English accent, Crook was popular with the ladies, who regarded him as their 'lion cub'. His business plans on hold, he found a new direction when a rare liberal-minded fur trader advised him to enrol at Columbia University and offered to help with his tuition fees.

At Columbia, Crook joined a generation of students radicalised by the Depression and the rise of fascism. He became active in student politics and went on a trip to support striking miners in the coalfields of Harlan County, Kentucky, site of a ten-year war between miners and bosses. It was an eye-opening experience. The seventy-odd students were met by 'welcoming parties' of gun-toting, drunken sheriff's deputies and followed wherever they went. They were taken to a courthouse where the district attorney harangued them as foreign agitators, and Jews to boot, and sent them over the state line into Tennessee. Back at Columbia, Crook joined the Communist-led National Student League and began reading Marxist literature. In November 1933, he organised a demonstration against the German Nazi ambassador who had been invited to speak on campus. Despite freezing weather, more than a thousand turned up.

Crook became one of the leading campus radicals and, after graduating, he was given a job lecturing on the dangers of fascism and war with the Intercollegiate Council on Public Affairs. In 1936, he returned to the UK, joined the Communist Party, and took part in the Battle of Cable Street. While writing for a left-wing student paper *University Forward*, he met the Communist poet John Cornford, who had just returned from fighting for the Workers' Party of Marxist Unification (POUM) militia in Spain.[7] An article by H. N. Brailsford describing a disciplined formation of German anti-Nazis marching into Madrid to reinforce the ragtag Spanish resistance tipped the balance, and he headed to Communist headquarters in King Street to volunteer. He was immediately accepted because of his public school military training and arrived in Spain on 2 January 1937, along with a group of overwhelmingly working-class volunteers. On his enlistment papers, he described his background as 'impoverished middle class'.

They were sent to the Albacete headquarters of the International Brigades – where the political commissar, the Scottish Communist Peter Kerrigan, gave a welcoming speech in a bullring – then for training to the poor village of Madrigueras, where the villagers had recently suppressed a fascist revolt led by the local priest. Crook was assigned to a machine gun squad equipped with a World War I–era Lewis gun captured from the British during the Russian civil war. Fred Copeman, a huge ill-tempered ex-sailor who had taken part in the 1931 Invergordon Mutiny, showed them how to operate it.[8] Crook wrote for the battalion newssheet, which was edited by the Marxist writer Christopher Caudwell.[9] The village girls were in tears when they were sent to the front a month later. When they arrived, Crook's squad was ordered to hand over the Lewis gun to a French battalion. Given a rifle, he was thrown into the Battle of Jarama.

Jarama was one of the bloodiest battles of the civil war, in which tens of thousands died in three weeks of fighting. Crook barely escaped with his life. He was saved by his friend Sam Wild, a tough merchant seaman, after they came under fire during a chaotic advance up what the

---

7 Cornford joined the quasi-Trotskyist POUM at the start of the war. After a trip home to England, he returned to Spain and joined the International Brigade. He was killed in action in December 1936.

8 According to the memoirs of the British sculptor Jason Gurney, *Crusade in Spain*, Copeman challenged almost everyone he met to a fight. Quoted in 'Jason Gurney', Spartacus Educational website, spartacus-educational.com.

9 Caudwell was killed soon afterwards.

Republican troops called suicide hill. While Crook, according to his own account, responded with random shots, Wild built a barricade out of stones. They were both wounded, Crook with two bullets in his thigh, Wild more seriously, but it was Wild who crawled back to the lines and directed stretcher-bearers to where Crook lay. He was shipped to a hospital in Madrid. Believing Wild had died of his wounds, Crook was troubled by a mix of guilt and gratitude that could never be expressed. In reality, Wild recovered, and they eventually ran into each other again.

Compared to the front, Madrid was a different world. In the bar at the Hotel Gran Via, Crook met celebrity supporters of the Republican cause – Ernest Hemingway, Martha Gellhorn, Mulk Raj Anand, Stephen Spender, and others. He had an affair with a Canadian journalist called Jean who was working in a blood transfusion centre set up by Norman Bethune. Crook disliked Bethune – describing him as a 'colossal egotist – certainly no Communist', but a discussion about 'Trotskyism' at Bethune's centre changed his life. He was taken aside by Georges Soria, a hyper-Stalinist correspondent for the French daily *L'Humanité* who was notorious for hysterical articles slandering the POUM as agents of Hitler. Soria asked Crook if he would consider carrying out special assignments. Crook readily agreed, and Soria introduced him to two Soviet agents who told him to return to his battalion and wait for orders. After a short time back at the front, he was summoned to Valencia to meet the Soviet consul. In short, he had been recruited, most probably by the People's Commissariat for Internal Affairs (NKVD).[10]

Crook was deployed against dissident leftists as Stalin exported his campaign of terror against the Opposition. During a short course in

---

10   Crook's sons believe that he was an agent of the Comintern rather than the NKVD. But Crook's online autobiography is explicit that he was recruited by the KGB, as he anachronistically put it. The only mention of Crook I could find in the Comintern archive is in a Russian translation of ILP leader Fenner Brockway's *Spanish Diary* in which he describes having breakfast with Crook. Brockway's diary was critical of the Comintern and intended for distribution to 'a limited number of Socialist comrades.' He published it only after the CPGB obtained a copy and printed 'revelations' from it in the *Daily Worker*. Although absence of evidence is not evidence of absence, the lack of other references to Crook in the Comintern archive indicates that he was probably not a Comintern agent. Since the NKVD directed the operation against the POUM, in all probability he was being directed by that agency. Crook never, however, held any formal rank in the NKVD but was a part-time, freelance agent. For his meeting with Crook, see Fenner Brockway, *Spanish Diary, 23rd June to 12th July 1937: Personal Report of a Visit to Spain*, available at Warwick Digital Collections, cdm21047.contentdm.oclc.org.

undercover work, Crook's instructor was none other than Trotsky's later assassin, Ramón Mercader. After completing his training, he was sent to Barcelona to spy on the POUM, the anarchists, and the Independent Labour Party (ILP). His controller was a Communist called Hugh O'Donnell who used the pseudonym Sean O'Brien. Posing as a freelance journalist, Crook began hanging around the bar in the Continental Hotel where ILP and POUM supporters drank. He soon got to know George Orwell, Orwell's wife Eileen, and POUM leaders, including the Belgian Georges Kopp. Having befriended their members, he took advantage of lax security at POUM and ILP headquarters (the two organisations shared the same building) to remove documents during siesta time. He had them photographed at a nearby Soviet safe house and returned them the same day. So completely did he win the confidence of his new friends that some of them entrusted him with letters home to be delivered via the British consul. He delivered them to the Soviet consul instead.

Since July 1936, when the Francoist revolt in Barcelona was crushed by the working-class action, the city's main public buildings, including the Telephone Exchange, had been controlled by anarchists and other leftist groups. The following May, supported by the Communists, Republican troops seized control of the buildings. To preserve Crook's cover, he was jailed along with the other dissidents but released soon afterwards. Ironically, he recalled that Kopp, one of his main targets, was particularly kind to him during his brief imprisonment.[11]

Rifling through the ILP desk drawers and reporting on the Blairs' marital problems was small beer, but Crook was soon involved in a more serious affair: the September 1937 case of the Austrian Left Oppositionist Kurt Landau. In his autobiography, Crook refers to Landau as an anarchist. In fact, Landau was a dissident Communist. He joined the Austrian Communist Party in 1921, was a branch chairman in Vienna, and remained a member until he was expelled in 1927 for 'Trotskyism'. Arriving in Spain in 1936 with his wife Katia, he joined the POUM. After the Stalinists launched a full-scale assault on the POUM and murdered its leader, Andreu Nin, Landau went on the run, taking refuge in the home of Carlota Durany, also a POUM member. Crook was part

---

11   The interrogator's report states that Crook was arrested at the request of 'the friends' – a form of words that probably refers to a secret agency of the Soviet state.

of an NKVD squad assigned to track him down. Landau had made the mistake of keeping in touch with comrades by telephone, and Crook obtained Durany's number from an American anarchist, Abe Bluestein.[12] Since the Communists now controlled the Telephone Exchange, it was a simple matter for the NKVD to trace Landau's whereabouts. Crook, the only member of the squad to have met Landau, was tasked with identifying him. Strolling arm in arm with a female agent, he pointed out Landau, who was sitting in Durany's garden. That evening, three agents posing as police raided the house and abducted Landau. O'Donnell later told Crook that Landau was put in a crate and taken on a Soviet freighter to Russia, where he was killed.[13]

Crook probably did not know Landau's likely fate when he fingered him, but his reaction to O'Donnell's disclosure was that what he had done was justified in the context of a life-and-death struggle against fascism. There is no doubt that he sincerely believed that Landau was aiding the enemy, but one is entitled to ask if the belief was reasonable. Membership of a political movement does not absolve one of the responsibility to think critically. After all, Crook discovered nothing incriminating in the POUM and ILP offices; his most interesting report was the rumour that Georges Kopp and Eileen Blair were having an affair. This is unsurprising, since the allegations of treachery levelled against the POUM were entirely groundless. Jesús Hernández, a Communist minister in the Republican government, described how NKVD agents, including Abram Slutsky and Alexander Orlov, concocted evidence including a risibly forged letter in invisible ink supposedly from Nin to Franco. At a meeting called to try to draw him into the plot, Hernández told the Soviet Ambassador, Marcel Rosenberg, that no one in Spain would believe the lie that the POUM was in league with the Fascists. Nevertheless, the NKVD used Communist Party members in the state apparatus, in particular the director-general of security, Colonel Antonio Ortega, to issue warrants for the arrest of Nin and other POUM

---

12   Abe Bluestein, although also an NKVD target (albeit a minor one), managed to return to the US unscathed. See Rebecca Dewitt, 'Abe Bluestein: An Anarchist Life', *Perspectives on Anarchist Theory*, Vol. 2, No. 1 (Spring 1998).

13   Carlota Durany, at great personal risk, reported Landau's abduction to the authorities, who denied any knowledge of the arrest. She was subsequently detained three times, the last time just before the fascists took Barcelona. Fortunately, a sympathetic prison guard released her before they arrived.

militants without the knowledge or approval of government ministers. Rosenberg and Slutsky were later recalled to the USSR, where they were killed by Stalin. Orlov avoided their fate by defecting to the United States, where he wrote *The Secret History of Stalin's Crimes*. Ortega, who was browbeaten by Italian Communist Party leader Palmiro Togliatti and Dolores Ibárruri (known as La Pasionaria) into issuing the warrants, was shot by the Fascists after the fall of the republic.[14]

Katia Landau, who was already in prison when her husband was abducted, went on a hunger strike after hearing of his disappearance. Thereafter, she campaigned continually to find out what happened to him until her death in 1984.

By 1938, despite Crook's confidence that, with the anarchists and POUM beaten, the disciplined armies of the republic would prevail, the Fascists were getting the upper hand. He was taken for a drive by two NKVD agents who asked him whether he would consider continuing his work in Shanghai. Eager to see China, he accepted without hesitation. He was sent to renew his passport in Paris, where he dutifully contacted the Trotskyists and marched on a demonstration under the banner of the Fourth International but took time out to listen to a 'stirring' speech by Maurice Thorez at a Popular Front rally. He also managed to fit in a visit to his family, now living in slightly straitened circumstances in Yorkshire. After what had happened to Kurt Landau, Crook must have known the possible fate of his targets, but he was undeterred, excited to be told he would be travelling via Moscow, where Stalin's show trials were in full swing. When he told an NKVD man that he looked forward to seeing him again, the agent replied pointedly, 'If I am still alive.' Perhaps the NKVD man, as some were, was an Oppositionist. It does not seem to have occurred to Crook.

In the end, he did not get to see Moscow. He travelled to Shanghai by ship from Marseilles. In Shanghai, he ran up a bill at a fashionable hotel near the racecourse while waiting for his next NKVD pay check. But, when a Russian woman handed him his cash, she told him to move in to the YMCA to preserve his cover. A Soviet vice-consul told him his task was to spy on Frank Glass, a South African who was one of the founder

---

14   Jesús Hernández, 'How the NKVD framed the POUM', excerpt from *Yo fui un ministro de Stalin* [I was a minister of Stalin] (Mexico City: Editorial America, 1953), translated and serialised in *Labor Action* and reproduced at marxists.org.

members of the South African Communist Party (SACP) but was now helping to organise the Trotskyist movement in China. At the time, the Chinese Trotskyists were a tiny political force that, however, included several former leaders of the CCP, including its founder and first leader, Chen Duxiu.

Crook took a job at St John's Mission University as a cover and eventually moved to the same apartment block as Glass near the Bund. It was a rough area, full of gambling houses and brothels. In a pub in so-called Blood Alley, Crook fell in with the journalist crowd using his International Brigade experience as an entrance ticket. There, he met Glass, the American journalist Jack Belden, and others. He read up on Chinese politics to learn about Chen Duxiu. He told Frank Glass he had become disillusioned with the Communists in Spain. Glass gave him Harold Isaacs's book *The Tragedy of the Chinese Revolution* to read as well as other material, including his own articles in the *China Weekly Review*. The writings were convincing and, for a time, it seemed that the spy might be won over to the cause. But Crook continued to report to the Russians at their designated safe house until one night in 1940 he arrived to find nobody there. Trotsky had been assassinated, and Stalin had called off his dogs.

That, as far as we know, was the end of David Crook's career as a Soviet spy. Britain was at war with Germany, but since Stalin, having failed to coax the Western powers into an anti-fascist alliance, had made a deal with Hitler, Crook felt no compulsion to join the war effort. According to the CPGB and the Comintern, the war was an imperialist conflict that the working class should stay out of. That line would change when Hitler invaded the Soviet Union in 1941, but for the time being, with no other particular plans, Crook decided to explore China and travelled to Sichuan where, as we have seen, he met Isabel.

In principle, there is nothing wrong with underground work. It was forced on the Bolsheviks by the tsarist autocracy. The Comintern had to work clandestinely because of the civil war, intervention and blockade, and anti-communist laws in all capitalist countries. But by the time Crook joined the game, underground work had been perverted into a quest to hunt down and exterminate all opposition to Stalin's dictatorship within the Communist movement. Crook went along with it. No doubt, he rationalised his activities on the grounds that revolutionaries must obey orders from a central organisation, but his motives, by his own admission, were various. They included anti-fascism but also glamour, excitement, and even money.

When Germany invaded the Soviet Union, the party line changed, and, as a loyal CPGB member, David Crook returned to Britain to enlist. Isabel also went, but they travelled separately. Isabel flew over the Hump (as pilots nicknamed the Himalayas) to India, crossed the subcontinent, and took a ship around the Cape of Good Hope (then infested with German U-boats). David Crook returned to Britain via Hong Kong and the United States. On a liner, he fell in with members of the International Seamen's Union who were pro-Stalin and anti-Trotsky. They reinforced his orthodox views, and he threw the books Frank Glass had given him into the sea. While he was on the way to San Francisco, the Japanese attacked Pearl Harbor, and the ship stopped at Honolulu to pick up some of the wounded, some of whom looked like 'human cinders'.

In San Francisco, he found a letter at the American Express office informing him that his mother had died. With both the United States and Britain now in the war, he had little chance of getting a passage home, so he looked up Edgar Snow, who gave him a job fundraising for the Chinese Industrial Cooperatives Association (Indusco).[15] However, after a chance meeting with a ship's captain, who suggested he might be able to work his passage home, he enlisted on a Norwegian oil tanker and returned to the UK in a convoy. He was reunited with Isabel and they married in a registry office. They visited the family in Yorkshire, where David's father tried to convince Isabel to convert to Judaism. They were at a loss as to how to refuse without hurting the family's feelings but managed to get the chief rabbi to suggest that conversion was not a good idea.

David enlisted in the Royal Air Force, was assigned to intelligence work, and was sent for training at a stately home near Rugby. Meanwhile, Isabel worked in a munitions factory in north London. They saw each other at weekends. When it was discovered that David knew a little Chinese, it was decided that he should be trained in transcribing Japanese, and he was sent to the School of Oriental and African Studies (SOAS) in London to study phonetics. He was promoted to sergeant but soon became obsolete as a transcriber after the invention of tape recorders.

---

15   While in Shanghai, David had got to know Snow's wife, Nym Wales, who had helped set up Indusco.

However, someone decided he was officer material, and he was sent back to the stately home, where he was transferred to officers' quarters. He spent his last leave before being sent overseas in the Lake District with Isabel. Just before leaving the country, he contacted Robbie Robson, a Communist Party Central Committee member, to ask for instructions, but Robson simply told him to be a good officer and defeat fascism. The congruence of party line with patriotic duty settled any lingering doubts he had about Stalinism. 'I was comfortable once more in the arms of Uncle Joe. Trotsky was once more the embodiment of evil.'

In 1942, Crook was posted to India, beginning three years in the Far East that, as he put it, were 'more like a pleasure trip than a tour of duty in a bloody war against fascism'. In the officers' quarters on board ship, they were served ice cream dipped in liqueur and had 400 'irresistible' nurses to dance and flirt with. Meanwhile, the other ranks languished below decks in squalid conditions. After landing in Bombay, he was sent to Abbottabad, near the Soviet border, where he found a caricature of colonial life. There was a club so exclusive that not even all the local white men were allowed to join, but officers were welcome. He tried, in a small way, to combat the prevailing racism by giving lectures on India's ancient civilisation but was forced to recognise his own unconscious bias when he was surprised to hear a white officer address his Sikh superior as 'Sir'. After a year, he was given leave and took trips to Calcutta where he saw the after-effects of the Bengal famine, and to Gangtok, a centre of Tibetan Buddhism in the Himalayas.

Crook's unit was reassigned to a base in Colombo where, as a guest of the Royal Navy Fleet Air Arm, he was promoted to the rank of flying officer, with all the attendant privileges. His unit had little to do, and his fellow officers took up smuggling. He tried to join a Singhalese tennis club but was told by a member that whites were not allowed. Impressed by this, he befriended the club member, who turned out to be a well-to-do anti-colonialist lawyer who put him in touch with the leader of the Sri Lankan Communist Party, Peter Keuneman, who had also fought in Spain. Crook visited rubber plantations where the workers were being driven hard to meet wartime demand. The British plantation owners told him the workers were all Tamils because the Singhalese were 'too damned lazy'.

From Sri Lanka, his unit was transferred to Rangoon, where David's life once again appeared to be that of a care-free fun-lover. He was appointed mess officer, 'liberated' a piano from an abandoned colonial house, and employed some Indians to lay out a dance floor. But he also found time for politics. He contacted the Anti-fascist People's Freedom League and, through the leader of the Communist Party, Thakin Than Tun, he met famed nationalist leader Aung San. He arranged for Thakin Than Tun to speak to his Air Force Wing. Following the Labour election victory in July 1945, there had been an upsurge of political activity in the armed forces. A Forces Parliament had been set up in Cairo and an East and West Association in Rangoon. David helped organise fortnightly meetings. At one of them, Aung San addressed a crowd of 1,300 locals and Westerners. The Labour member of Parliament Tom Driberg spoke at another.

The last legs of Crook's tour of duty were spent in Hong Kong and Singapore. In Singapore, after Churchill made his Iron Curtain speech, David was called in and told he was being removed from intelligence work. His last job in the Royal Air Force was as a 'glorified bartender' at Allied headquarters.

Meanwhile, back in England, Isabel Crook had joined the Canadian Army and was given the rank of lieutenant. After officer training in Windsor, she was assigned to study shell shock. When the couple were reunited in London, they took advantage of ex–service personnel grants to sign up for university courses, Isabel at the London School of Economics and David at SOAS, where he studied Chinese but not very seriously. Sitting in on some of Isabel's anthropology seminars, he bombastically denounced it as a subject in the service of colonialism. They lived in fashionable Bloomsbury and sold the *Daily Worker* around St Pancras railway station. Always well connected, David got to know the Labour chancellor of the exchequer, Stafford Cripps, who suggested he look for a job in the Foreign Office. But, at the interview, he ruled himself out by enthusing about Mao Zedong and dismissing Chiang Kai-shek as a dictator. It was, he later reflected, a lucky escape that saved him from sharing 'the same fate as Kim Philby and his kind'.

Their stay in England was cut short when they found out they were entitled to a repatriation grant that would give them a free passage back to China. Isabel was keen to return, even though her parents had left China in 1942 after thirty years, the maximum term according to the rules of their missionary society. When they boarded the liner in Liverpool, they intended to stay in China for only around eighteen months. Isabel was planning to complete a PhD in London, while David planned to use the time in China to send back dispatches from the liberated areas and, on the strength of this, had managed to get stringer's credentials from Reuters and the *Times*. In Hong Kong, they presented letters of introduction to Qiao Guanhua, who would later serve as PRC foreign minister, and his wife, Gong Peng, who had been the wartime spokesperson of the CCP. Having been vetted by the Chinese Communists, they continued via Shanghai to Tianjin and then Beiping, where they were given a tour of the city in a British Council limousine flying the Union Jack. (Beiping which means Northern Peace was the name of Beijing while Nanjing – Southern Capital – was the capital of China.)

Back in Tianjin, they hitched a ride on a United Nations Relief and Rehabilitation Administration (UNRRA) convoy to the JinJiLuYu (Shanxi-Hebei-Shandong-Henan) Border Region, where they spent eight months in the village of Ten Mile Inn, located at the conjunction of the four provinces near the foot of the Taihang mountain range. Although they were both used to scenes of hardship in China, they were astonished by the extreme poverty of the area, where a shortage of water meant people rarely washed and, for most families, household furniture consisted of tiny stools and tables barely four inches high. Women suffered especially, prematurely aged in their forties from back-breaking work and continual childbearing. From February to April 1948, with the agreement and assistance of local cadres, they observed a land reform work team, which consisted mainly of *People's Daily* journalists, as it carried out the 'Campaign to Adjust Land Holdings and the Purification and Reorganisation of the Party'. The material they collected before, during, and after the campaign formed the basis of their book *Revolution in a Chinese Village*. When they left Ten Mile Inn, they were sent to Shijiazhuang to teach at a training school for foreign affairs officials in the nearby village of Nanhaishan. They did not know it at the time, but they would continue to work as teachers in China until their retirement four decades later.

The Nanhaishan school was regularly strafed by KMT warplanes, and they were forced to teach in the fields and on mountainsides. But the Nationalist collapse came sooner than expected, and by the end of January 1949, Beijing was in Communist hands. Isabel, who was pregnant, arrived in the city in time to watch the victory parade. The Lebanese

American doctor George Hatem drove her by jeep to Qianmen, one of the battlemented gates to the Forbidden City, where she stood alongside Lin Biao. David Crook arrived in Beijing in time to hear Mao speak at the Temple of Heaven, and both he and Isabel saw Mao announce the foundation of the People's Republic at Tiananmen Square. The first of their three sons, Carl, had just been born, and they registered him at the British Consulate as a British subject.

David's faith in Stalin was shaken when Yugoslavia was expelled from the Cominform. When informed of the split, he could hardly believe his ears. After all, Tito's partisans had fought ferociously against the Nazis and their local proxies the Ustashe. Now it seemed Titoism was the new Trotskyism. But, as before, when his target Frank Glass had nearly won him over, David put the issue from his mind and remained loyal to mainstream Communism.

In 1952, because he knew some Spanish, David had been asked to translate at the Peace Conference of Asia and the Pacific Regions. He revised his rusty skills by reading the Spanish edition of *For a Lasting Peace and People's Democracy*, a Cominform magazine with content as soporific as its title. He took the opportunity to spend time with old comrades from the British delegation but was taken aback when one of them remarked: 'David, you've lost your identity.' Indeed, several years in the Spartan atmosphere of Mao's China had effaced much of his formerly urbane demeanour. When he and Isabel had arrived in Beijing wearing military-style fatigues, a former student had exclaimed: 'What on earth has happened to Mr Crook! In Shanghai, he used to dress so smartly, in a white sharkskin suit.'

In 1953, they moved to the newly founded Beijing Foreign Studies University, where they would remain for the rest of their working lives. In China's still patriarchal society, David Crook was appointed to a senior position in the English department, although Isabel was more academically qualified. His role gave him some authority to prescribe teaching methods, and he tried to combat the Chinese emphasis on rote learning and literary English. They were, he wrote, able to turn out students who could actually speak the language rather than simply quote a few lines from Shakespeare. But what he called Confucianism, academic snobbery, and pedantry were never far from the surface.

The following several years were a period of relatively normal family life for the Crooks. As foreigners, of course, they lived privileged lives.

During the Great Leap Forward, when a minimum of several million starved to death, they were able to supplement sparse canteen food with purchases from the Beijing Friendship store. They raised three sons; Carl was born in 1949, Michael in 1951, and Paul in 1953. The boys went to a Chinese kindergarten and grew up speaking Chinese as their native language. When Carl was three and Michael one, Isabel's missionary parents returned to China for a visit, and David even managed to take them to church on Sunday. Although both David and Isabel Crook found the constant political campaigning in China irksome, they remained committed Communists. The Beijing branch of the British Communist Party met in their front room. David Crook never abandoned the hope that he would, one day, be able to return to the UK to take part in the British revolution. Even in periods when it was politically suspect and dangerous to do so, they would tune in to the BBC World Service news, taking care to turn the sound down for the Lilliburlero theme tune. Although they agreed with the ideological content of the Chinese press, they believed revolutionaries needed to keep up to date with the real news, even from imperialist sources – critically digested of course.

The children took part in the family political discussions. So it was, Michael Crook later recalled, that 'when the Cultural Revolution came, we were primed'.[16] Michael, who was studying at the middle school affiliated with Peking University, joined the Red Flag faction of the Red Guards. His parents were critical of many aspects of Chinese society, including the leaden bureaucracy and the 'Confucian contempt for manual labour' shared by many intellectuals, so were enthusiastic about the opportunity to speak out. They joined a university campus group, also called the Red Flag faction, largely because they knew and trusted the group's leaders as 'honest, able and devoted comrades'. When the Cultural Revolution began, the family were on paid leave in Canada and Britain. David Crook later wrote that he made two 'colossal blunders'. The first was leaving China at the outset of the Cultural Revolution; the second was returning to China. Less than a year after he returned, he was seized by a rival campus group – the Rebel Regiment – and accused of spying. He did not see his family again for five years.

The Rebel Regiment hawked their 'British spy' around several government agencies. The Public Security Bureau refused to take him off their

---

16   Michael Crook, interview with the author, May 2018.

hands without evidence, but the Beijing Garrison of the People's Liberation Army (PLA) agreed to lock him up at their headquarters. Michael, who, at sixteen, had found a job in a woodworking factory, was politely thanked for his work, presented with a portrait of Chairman Mao, and asked to leave by managers who were embarrassed to have employed the son of a spy.[17] David Crook was held for six months by the army, during which time he noticed that even his guards were divided into rival factions; one group treated him significantly better than the other. He was then transferred to a high-security prison where he remained until his release in 1973. He was urged to confess in lengthy interrogation sessions during which the innocuous details of how he had come to China on a government repatriation grant, his stringer credentials from Reuters, the British consul's agreement to forward his articles to London and so on, were taken as absolute proof of guilt.

Meanwhile, Michael was 'not in a panic, but in a rage' about his father's imprisonment and rode his bike around government offices where he 'screamed outrage' at officials who claimed to know nothing about the case. He and his mother took sleeping bags and blankets to one government office, planning to stage a sleep-in until he was released. Eventually, they found out where David was being held and Isabel was allowed to send him some books, a radio, and other small comforts. The children were still in their teens. Carl, the eldest, took refuge in books while Paul, the youngest, drew comfort from his parents' often-repeated assurances that revolution had its ups and downs, but things would turn out alright in the end.[18] But things got worse before they got better. At the end of 1968, Isabel Crook was seized by Red Guards. Unlike her husband, she was not put in prison but was held captive by the rival faction in a room on campus. Eventually, the boys located the building she was being held in and were allowed occasional visits, but she was held for more than three years.

With both parents imprisoned, Michael's anger grew into a determination to leave China as soon as possible. He continued making trouble, this time with demands for an exit visa, which were always refused. However, by early 1972, around the time of Nixon's visit to China, conditions for some political prisoners improved. In May, David was driven

---

17   Ibid.
18   Paul Crook, interview with the author, May 2018.

from prison to meet Isabel and his now grown-up sons. The meetings then took place monthly until David was released at the end of January 1973. In line with a common practice of the Chinese Communist Party, released political prisoners, allegedly former spies or enemies of the state, were given a profuse apology and welcomed back into the ranks of the revolution. On 8 March 1973, International Women's Day, Premier Zhou Enlai presided over a formal ceremony in the Great Hall of the People where he apologised to eighty or so families who had been affected by the detentions. Showing characteristic attention to detail, he picked out Michael and told him he would be allowed to leave China.

All three sons left China soon after David Crook's release. This caused friction with their father. For their part, they could not understand why their parents did not leave. According to Paul, after being released from prison, his father became much more positive about people like George Orwell, whom he had previously seen as enemies. While on 'the big picture he didn't really waver ... beyond that, which branch of the Communist ideal whether it was the Trotskyists or the Stalinists or whoever' was the right one, he was far less sure.[19] Michael described his father's political evolution as follows: 'He started as a Stalinist, he moved to be more of a Leninist, then later he started questioning Lenin and [eventually] the picture by his bedside was [of] Rosa Luxemburg'.[20] David Crook also began, gradually and tentatively, to confess his NKVD past to his family. He had never hidden the fact that he had done underground work, but he was now prepared to give details.

The change in David Crook's political views was gradual. Bizarrely, just eighteen months after his release, he and Isabel spent three months touring the world speaking in defence of the Cultural Revolution. They especially praised Mao's educational policy, which, they said, aimed to produce socialist, educated working people, not intellectual aristocrats. The 'anti-Mao line', they said, 'derived straight from Confucius'. Carl, exasperated with his father's continued faith in the system, wrote in a note: 'He doesn't even know how to read between the lines of the newspaper. Simply takes it at face value. It's pathetic.' By the 1980s, however, David Crook was more critical. When George Hatem organised a celebration for veteran experts hosted by Premier Zhao Ziyang, David

19   Ibid.
20   Michael Crook, interview.

complained that per capita spending on education in China was among the lowest in the world and teachers' salaries were lower than those of manual workers. Both he and Isabel persisted in attacking Confucian-style rote learning, and in their history lessons they 'cut kings and queens down to size and played up people's heroes' like Spartacus and Toussaint L'Ouverture.

Trips to ethnic minority areas of China opened David Crook's eyes to Han chauvinism. After a trip to Inner Mongolia, where, during the Cultural Revolution, Kang Sheng had whipped up a witch hunt against former members of the Inner Mongolia People's Party, he wrote an article called 'Frameup of a Nation'. It was published in Hong Kong but not on the mainland. In Xinjiang, ordinary people told them that the Han did not want to be there and the minorities did not want them here. When they visited a mosque, their Han companions were refused entry. They were refused permission to go to Kashgar, undoubtedly because of unrest there. They noticed that minorities were losing command of their languages because they had to study in Chinese at secondary school. In Tibet, they were horrified to see a Han bus driver order a poor Tibetan around like a slave. On the other hand, David had no time for Western backpackers who idealised ancient Tibetan society. He was repelled by Tibetan religiosity, their exhausting prostrations, and the packs of dogs left unmolested like sacred cows. He asked 'an enlightened Tibetan' how long it would take for 'superstitions' to fade. 'More than a century' was the reply.

When *China Daily* appeared in 1980, David Crook began writing letters to the editor that were regularly published. Most were written in a mildly critical tone that the party could accept. He decried the preference for rich tourists, the idea (then just a suggestion) that cars should replace bicycles, the import of trashy films like *Rambo*, and so on. He even managed to get a letter printed criticising overgrazing in Inner Mongolia. Another letter complained about the *China Daily* headline 'UK Print Unions Foiled' and the accompanying article, about the 1986–87 Wapping print strike, that 'rejoiced with Murdoch'. When he set his students the discussion topic 'Black is Beautiful' and not a single student agreed, he wrote an angry letter decrying the widespread racism in Chinese society, but *China Daily* refused to print it.

Crook began exploring ideas and concerns that, as a hard-line Stalinist, he had once dismissed as petty bourgeois. Though he had long downplayed his Jewish heritage, now he began to take an interest in his background. While he had always, in theory, been in favour of women's liberation, his personal life had lagged far behind. Even Isabel had, in line with the thinking of many Communists at the time, rejected the idea of an autonomous women's movement. Later, however, she joined the campus women's group and became one of its leading lights. Gay liberation presented a particular problem for David when his youngest son came out. It had been common currency among old-style leftists to regard homosexuality as a disorder of an effete ruling-class or fascist paramilitary organisations. Like many others, including Orwell, David's homophobia was strong. It took some time for him to overcome it.

Gradually David began to cast off his 'ossified thinking'. He read Orwell's *Burmese Days, 1984,* and even *Homage to Catalonia,* with its denunciation of the role of the Stalinists. He realised that Orwell's descriptions of the mangling of language, rewriting of history, and 'bestial bureaucrats' 'applied only too aptly to China'. The jailing of the Democracy Wall activist Wei Jingsheng and the sacking of the liberal party secretary Hu Yaobang opened his eyes to the ugliness of bureaucratic rule in China. When the students marched to Tiananmen Square after Hu Yaobang's death in April 1989, David and Isabel Crook took them mineral water. And when martial law was declared they posted a letter on their university campus gate and sent a copy to the *People's Daily*:

> [We] fervently hope that no attempt will be made by China's leaders to settle the present crisis by force. We believe the use of force would not bring about unity between the People's Government and the Chinese people but would widen the rift between them. We believe it would not establish stability but would create chaos. We believe that unity must rest on mutual respect, that stability can be based only on democracy, not on repression.

According to Michael, his father's 'sympathies were totally with the students. In May of 89, he wrote a letter for the central leaders and asked me to deliver it.' Isabel, however, was conflicted. When it came to the 4 June crackdown, 'Dad thought it was a crime, Mum thought it was a bit more like an unfortunate situation'. David wrote in his autobiography that support for the students was almost universal in the university. 'The whole campus, except for a handful of teachers and functionaries . . . was united against the massacre, the cover-up, the lying and the repression'. Former rivals from the Cultural Revolution had long since let bygones be bygones and renewed old friendships. Whether from the Red Flag or the Rebel Regiment, they supported the demonstrations. Quoting the prophet Amos, 'Crook wrote:

> When will be the time for 'feasts and smelling incense?' When it is officially proclaimed that June 4 was a massacre – a killing of civilians by soldiers for the sake of those in power . . . When it is officially proclaimed that the movement of the spring of 1989 was not a 'counter-revolutionary rebellion' but, in the main a demand for democratic rights and against the abuse of office for self-enrichment, against nepotism and corruption.

In the mid-1990s, David and Isabel Crook travelled to Leeds to visit Wang Fanxi, one of the leaders of the Chinese Trotskyists he had spied on in Shanghai. Wang had moved to Leeds in 1975 from Macau after Maoists threatened to abduct him to mainland China. David apologised to Wang, and Wang accepted his apology. He said afterwards that Crook was an old man and that it was a good thing that he had finally accepted that he had been in the wrong. It would be tempting to think that Crook's apology was less than sincere – an attempt, perhaps, to save his reputation. But Wang Fanxi believed the apology was genuine and that Crook had had a real change of heart.[21] Around the same time, according to Michael Crook, his father also went to the US West Coast to apologise to another Trotskyist. This was almost certainly Alexander Buchman, who had spent six years in China before serving as one of Trotsky's bodyguards in Mexico. David Crook had finally abandoned his faith in Stalin.

---

21   Gregor Benton, interview with the author, February 2019.

8

Trotskyists

David Crook's first target among the Trotskyists in Shanghai was Frank Glass, a South African who had arrived in China in 1931 at the age of thirty.[1] Although now largely forgotten, Glass was one of the pioneers of the South African labour movement.[2] After leaving school at fifteen, he took a series of low-level white-collar jobs, beginning as a clerk in a Cape Town brewery. During the First World War, he encountered social-ist ideas, sided with the internationalists, and campaigned against the war. By 1918, he had joined the syndicalist Industrial Socialist League and was writing articles for its newspaper, the *International*. In April 1921, responding to Comintern appeals, the league relaunched itself as the Communist Propaganda Group. Some weeks later, near the town of Bulhoek, police massacred 200 members of a black millenarian sect called the Israelites, who had set up a farming commune and declared their independence from the state. While respectable commentators, seeking to excuse the government, criticised the Israelites as provoca-tive, Glass wrote an impassioned denunciation of the atrocity. It could

---

1   Like everyone in the Shanghai underground, Glass was risking his life. In his case, the threat was not just from the KMT and the Settlement police but also the Stalinists. Crook's work in Spain had already claimed the life of at least one dissident Communist; it was only Stalin's perception that the threat from Trotskyism was receding that led to him being called off. We have Crook's testimony to Glass's persuasiveness and lucidity.

2   Baruch Hirson, *The Restless Revolutionary*, London: Porcupine Press, 2003, xv.

not be printed in South Africa, but Sylvia Pankhurst, the most radical of the famous suffragette family, published it in her *Workers' Dreadnought*.

> Oh, what an act of heroism my countrymen – machine-guns against sticks and assegais. Throw up your hats ye freedom-loving Britishers and sing 'Britons never shall be slaves'. But, listen! The Johannesburg *Star* thinks that less expense would have been incurred if one or two bombing aeroplanes had been employed'. Ye Gods, and this in the year of our Lord 1921!
>
> This brutal act of savagery is indicative of the brutal methods of suppression to which the capitalist class will resort in order to preserve their system intact. If ever proof were required of the cheapness of human life in the interests of private property . . . [it is] the cold-blooded butchery of those 200 natives at Bulhoek.[3]

The Bulhoek massacre galvanised the various groups sympathetic to the Comintern to form a party, and on 30 July 1921, the South African Communist Party was launched. Twenty-year-old Glass was the youngest delegate at the founding conference.

In 1927, Glass married a fellow activist, Fanny Kellerman, and together they opened a left-wing bookshop in Johannesburg. For the next decade, Glass, like his comrades in the SACP, struggled to reconcile the interests of the white working class – which was organised in trade unions, militant on economic issues, and intermittently anti-capitalist – with those of the impoverished black majority whose working conditions and wages, when they were employed at all, were a world apart. Indeed, squaring that circle ultimately proved impossible. Patient work in the labour movement brought only incremental gains, and Glass began to look overseas for inspiration. Energised by the 1925–27 upsurge in China, he inevitably became aware of the debate over strategy within the Comintern. In 1928, convinced by the arguments set out in the American Trotskyist paper the *Militant*, he joined the Left Opposition.

Glass left South Africa for China in 1931. Fanny Kellerman stayed behind and relaunched their bookshop as Vanguard Books. Over subsequent decades, she turned it into one of the main focal points for South African leftists. Whether problems in their marriage contributed to

---

3   Quoted in ibid., 30.

Glass's decision to leave is unclear (he was also heavily in debt). He left behind few personal details in his writings, but his actions and life decisions suggest he shared his father's impulsive and restless nature. In 1911, when Frank was eight years old, Ernest Glass had taken his wife and three children from England to South Africa. A draper by trade, Ernest had detested his work. He had dreamed of becoming an actor, but a career in the theatre was ruled out by his father, a congregationalist minister. Frank's mother Gertrude was also a devout Christian, and her marriage to Ernest seems to have been unhappy. When Frank was nineteen, Ernest had disappeared from the family home, apparently intending to walk the 700 miles from Cape Town to Durban and a new life, but he caught pneumonia, turned back, and died a few days later.[4]

When Glass arrived in China in 1931, oppositionists still regarded themselves as a faction within the Comintern and worked, albeit often clandestinely, within the official Communist parties. Glass introduced himself to Agnes Smedley and worked with her in the campaign to free the Noulens, who, it was rumoured, were also opposition supporters. In 1932, he even took a job with TASS, the Soviet news agency. At this stage, he may not have been planning a long stay in China. In his recollection, he was thinking of moving to Australia when he ran into Harold Isaacs at Agnes Smedley's apartment.

Isaacs, who later wrote the *Tragedy of the Chinese Revolution*, one of the classics of the Trotskyist canon, arrived in Shanghai a few months before Glass. He was, at the time, by his own admission 'a twenty-year-old tyro journalist' with only 'the dimmest flickers of political ideas'.[5] In contrast to Glass's working-class background, Isaacs's parents were wealthy New Yorkers. After graduating from Columbia, he worked briefly for the *New York Times* before heading to East Asia on what was part career move, part adventure trip. While working as a stringer for local English-language newspapers, he was 'discovered' by the ubiquitous Smedley. He recalled her as an 'intense jumpy woman', who 'often failed to distinguish fact from fiction', but he admired her

---

4   Frank's brother, Norman, compounded the bleak family story when he was deported from South Africa for minor teenage hooliganism. He moved to Australia, where he lived a lonely life and died in his fifties. Frank's sister, Madge, fared better, becoming a teacher.

5   Harold Isaacs, *Re-encounters in China: Notes of a Journey in a Time Capsule*, Florence: Taylor & Francis, 2016, 4.

commitment.[6] Smedley, for her part, was immensely impressed by Isaacs; she told the African American poet Langston Hughes that Isaacs was the 'brightest young American journalist in the Orient'.[7]

Smedley lost no time in showing off Isaacs, her 'prize find', to Song Qingling. Seventeen years younger than Song, Isaacs was nevertheless immediately overwhelmed by a kind of schoolboy crush. Song was, unlike Smedley, nuanced, charming, and beautiful. She 'was soft and she was hard', 'cool yet warm', and 'always correct'. Although she was 'gracious and polite', no one, not even Smedley, who tried her best, could dominate her. He later confessed that in awe of 'her beauty, her courage, her queenly espousal of just causes, I came to love her as a young knight pure in heart'.[8] As the widow of Sun Yat-sen, she was officially – and, Isaac believed, truly – celibate. But it seems he even had vague hopes of an affair. When his fiancée Viola arrived in Shanghai in 1932, he found he had divided loyalties.[9] He nevertheless married Viola in the US consulate in a five-minute ceremony, with Frank Glass as their witness.

Song Qingling was suitably impressed by Isaacs, as were her Comintern colleagues. They decided to find a use for him as editor of an English-language newspaper to be published out of reach of the KMT censors in Shanghai's concession areas. That would be some time in the future, however. In the meantime, Isaacs was influenced by Glass who, in contrast to Smedley, was 'measured and factual in the way he talked'. In 1931, he and Glass took a steamer up the Yangzi River to Chongqing. The constant patrols by American and other foreign gunboats were a stark demonstration of China's subjection to the imperialist powers.[10] Isaacs's political ideas were as yet unformed, and Glass simultaneously won him over to Communism and the Opposition. This was all the easier since the split between the factions was not yet definitive. Glass and Smedley were on friendly terms. The leftist Zeitgeist bookstore, run by Ursula Kuczynski and the thoroughly loyal Irene Weidemeyer, still

---

6 Ibid., 28.
7 Etsuko Taketani, 'Spies and Spiders: Langston Hughes and Transpacific Intelligence Dragnets', *Japanese Journal of American Studies*, No. 25 (2014), 30.
8 Isaacs, *Re-encounters*, 64.
9 Ibid., 65.
10 The United States Yangzi River Patrol Force sailed the Yangzi and coastal waters from 1854 to 1949.

stocked books by Trotsky.[11] Having continued to Chengdu, leaving Glass in Chongqing, Isaacs returned downriver alone during the Great Yangzi Flood of August 1931 and saw corpses and wreckage floating everywhere.[12] Weeks later, Japan's brazen seizure of Manchuria confirmed his conversion to Communism – albeit, thanks to Glass, with an inoculation against Stalinism.

The first issue of *China Forum*, Isaacs's Comintern-backed newspaper, appeared on 13 January 1932. Smedley and Glass were regular contributors. A fortnight after the launch, Japan launched a brutal assault on Shanghai. China's Nineteenth Route Army fiercely resisted the attack, and Isaacs reported from the thick of the fighting. He even joined in by throwing a grenade and taking a rifle shot at Japanese troops.[13] Regarding his reports as provocative, the KMT government demanded his extradition from the International Settlement on several charges, some of them capital offences under China's draconian penal code. The *New York Times* printed a story headlined 'American Editor Warned of Trial by China— Death Penalty Possible'. Isaacs was covered by extraterritoriality, and the American consulate reluctantly protected him, but no printers would touch his paper afterwards, and he set up a printing press of his own. In the following weeks, Isaacs and Smedley co-wrote a short book, *Five Years of Kuomintang Reaction*, publishing it under the *China Forum* imprint.

Isaacs was the originator and driving force behind the creation of the China League for Civil Rights, one of the most prominent of the front organisations established by the Comintern in China. He drew up a plan to attract the support of intellectuals and public figures at home and abroad. Its sponsors in China included not only leftists like Song Qingling and Lu Xun but also liberal intellectuals like Hu Shi and Cai Yuanpei.[14] The league had some successes   including helping save the Noulens from execution – but despite a vigorous campaign, it could not save the labour leader Luo Dengxian, who was shot in August 1933. Isaacs was also a Comintern bagman and delivered a modest regular

---

11   Kuczynski later became famous as Ruth Werner, aka 'Red Sonja', the Soviet spy.

12   More than 2 million people died as a result of the flood. See Chris Courtney, *The Nature of Disaster in China*, Cambridge, UK: Cambridge University Press, 2018.

13   Isaacs, *Re-encounters in China*, 14.

14   Chen Jinxing, 'The Rise and Fall of the China League for Civil Rights', *China Review*, Vol. 6, No. 2 (2006), 121–47, 124.

stipend to Ho Chi Minh, then living precariously in Shanghai. Isaacs suggested to a TASS correspondent that it would be a simple matter to ship Ho to the Soviet Union on a freighter, but was given to understand that the Soviets would not risk their trade links for the sake of Ho's security. It was, he later concluded, how the Russians regarded their relations with other revolutionary movements . . . their immediate interests were paramount'.[15] Although Isaacs later broke with the Communist movement, he never lost his admiration for Ho Chi Minh, who 'was obviously, even then, a man of considerable force and unique personality. He was quizzical, he was always quiet and calm. He, obviously, conveyed force. I don't think I ever saw him agitated.'[16]

By 1933, strains between the official Communist movement and the Opposition were reaching breaking point. Internationally, the main reason was Hitler's rise to power in Germany, unintentionally facilitated by the criminally stupid policy of the Comintern and the KPD. In China, the hostile and sectarian attitude of the CCP to the 1933–34 Fujian revolt against Chiang Kai-shek was a secondary factor. After Isaacs travelled to Fuzhou to cover the rebellion, the CCP demanded that he write an article linking the Left Opposition with the short-lived Fuzhou regime. Isaacs resisted this attempt at outright falsification; it was not the first time he had clashed with his sponsors. In 1932, he had refused to print a criticism of Chen Duxiu after he was arrested by the KMT. He was also taken to task for not mentioning Stalin in an article on the sixteenth anniversary of the Russian Revolution.

After Isaacs innocently told Song Qingling about his exasperation with the continual editorial interference, she immediately informed Soviet agents of his heretical tendencies, and the Comintern cut off subsidies to *China Forum*. Since Isaacs could not support the paper out of his own pocket, he was forced to close it down. Isaacs never found out about Song Qingling's betrayal and revered her for the rest of his life.[17] He wrote to the CCP Central Committee to complain that, in return for 'slight financial support', it had demanded that he uncritically print

15   Harold Robert Isaacs, 'Vietnam: A Television History', interview, 14 July 1981, GBH Archives, openvault.wgbh.org.

16   Ibid. Isaacs met Ho Chi Minh again in Hanoi in 1945 while working for *Newsweek*.

17   Gregor Benton, *Prophets Unarmed: Chinese Trotskyists in Revolution, War, Jail, and the Return from Limbo*, Leiden: Brill, 2017, 395, 920–1.

Comintern propaganda. The last issue of the paper appeared on 13 January 1934. Isaacs gave its printing press to Frank Glass, and soon afterwards he and Viola left for Beijing, where he began work on the *Tragedy of the Chinese Revolution*. Just before he left, Song Qingling, whether disingenuously to preserve her cover, or out of genuine affection, told him to be wary of the Communists, saying, 'You don't really know these people. They are capable of anything.'[18]

Lu Xun organised a farewell dinner in Isaacs's honour. According to CCP myth-making, Lu Xun was a CCP loyalist and a steadfast opponent of 'Trotskyism'. But Isaacs believed the dinner had political significance as a gesture on Lu Xun's part against CCP sectarianism.[19] When he declared for the Opposition, Isaacs and his wife were translating a volume of Chinese short stories with Lu Xun and Mao Dun.[20] Lu Xun continued to work with them on it after the break – further evidence that he was not an uncritical CCP supporter. When Isaacs sent the collection to publishers in New York, they rejected it, fearing a boycott by the CPUSA.[21] It was eventually published, as *Straw Sandals*, in 1974 by MIT press.

In 1933, a twenty-two-year-old American, Alex Buchman, arrived in Shanghai after being expelled from Japan. The Shanghai Special Branch logged his arrival on 25 August. Buchman had recently graduated as an aircraft engineer but, with unemployment in the United States at its highest-ever level of 25 per cent, he had decided not to waste his time looking for work and set off for East Asia. His original plan had been to return via the Soviet Union on the Trans-Siberian Railway, but he ended up staying in China until 1939. Buchman, who came from a wealthy family of intellectuals, was already a Communist sympathiser. In Japan, he had looked up the African American poet Langston Hughes, a fellow Clevelander, who had recently arrived there after a trip to the Soviet Union. It had been his association with Hughes and other leftists that had brought him to the attention of the Japanese police, leading to his deportation on charges of 'dangerous thoughts'.[22]

18   Isaacs, *Re-encounters in China*, 66.

19   Benton, *Prophets Unarmed*, 1041.

20   The collection included Lu Xun's *Diary of a Madman* and Ding Ling's *Diary of Miss Sophia*.

21   Isaacs, *Re-encounters in China*, 39.

22   Langston Hughes went to the Soviet Union with several dozen black writers, artists, and musicians to make a film about the oppression of black people in the United

Buchman was won to Trotskyism by Frank Glass and afterwards never wavered in his commitment to the causes of anti-Stalinism and world revolution. Those who knew him described him as modest, correct, and courageous, 'a *caballero* in the finest sense of the word, generous to a fault ... clear-sighted, committed and elegant'.[23] He worked as a photojournalist with *China Review*, TASS, Havas (the forerunner of AFP), and the Trans-Pacific News Agency but never regarded himself as anything more than an amateur photographer. In fact, his huge collection of photos of wartime Shanghai lay in his cellar for sixty years until a professional photographer persuaded him to exhibit them. They fetched hundreds of dollars each. Characteristically, Buchman donated the money to Amnesty International.

When a print worker stole the Trotskyist's printing press, Glass and Buchman disguised themselves as police officers and staged a 'raid' to seize it back. Buchman, who was extraordinarily generous in his support for the Chinese Trotskyists, financed and published a journal *Tongxiang* (Tendency), edited by Wang Fanxi, that sold two thousand copies per issue. Frank Glass's earnings were intermittent, and what little money he made he donated to the Trotskyists. But Buchman gave him a rent-free room in his apartment and also subsidised his living expenses, so, via Glass, Buchman was also indirectly financing the movement.

Unfortunately, an ability to recognise the crimes and blunders of Stalin and his coterie of mediocrities does not confer political infallibility. In 1934, both Glass and Isaacs recklessly took sides in a factional battle within the Chinese Left Opposition. Some context is necessary to understand the dispute. The Chinese Trotskyist movement was born in Moscow at the Communist University of the Toilers of the East and Sun Yat-sen University among several hundred young militants who, after fleeing the defeat of 1927, arrived angry, disillusioned, and searching for answers. No longer willing to follow the political line of the leadership, they were influenced by Russian oppositionists, including Karl Radek, rector of Sun Yat-sen University, who had joined the Opposition after Chiang Kai-shek's March 1926 coup. According to Radek,

---

States, but the production was cancelled as Stalin sought to improve relations with Washington.

23   Susan Weissman, 'Alex Buchman, the last Survivor of Trotsky', *Critique*, Vol. 32, No. 1 (2004), 151–62, 161.

Chiang Kai-shek . . . allows [his troops] to shoot workers . . . under the Guomindang banner but . . . the Communists do not speak out before the broad masses as an independent Communist party . . . In his theses to the Second Comintern Congress Lenin . . . states: 'We shall support a national-bourgeois movement only when it will not hinder our organization of workers and peasants.' But when one smashes peasants' organizations, when one shoots workers, does it hinder our organization of workers and peasants? It seems to me that it does a little.[24]

In his lectures, Radek was formally obliged to toe the official line, but he made sure the opposition message got through to his students.[25] His influence helped the Trotskyists win several hundred sympathisers among the Chinese in Moscow. One was Liu Renjing, a founder member of the CCP, one of the twelve delegates to its first congress, and a former general secretary of its youth league. Liu was a maverick among the Oppositionists. While the majority voted to work within the CCP, Liu announced that he planned to set up an independent organisation. On his way back to China, he passed through Turkey to meet Trotsky, then exiled on the island of Prinkipo. Trotsky wrote a 'Draft Programme of the Chinese Bolshevik-Leninists' for Liu to take back to China, and thereafter, Liu presented himself as the privileged conduit of Trotsky's ideas to the Chinese Opposition.

Meanwhile back in China, in the autumn of 1929, Chen Duxiu, the grand old man of the Chinese Revolution, inspirer, and leader of the May Fourth Movement, founder of the CCP and its leader from 1921 to 1927, declared his support for Trotsky. Chen, who had instinctively opposed the Comintern line but reluctantly agreed to implement it, found theoretical support for his misgivings in Trotsky's writings. Trotsky's theory of Permanent Revolution resembled ideas that he, Li Dazhao, and Liu Renjing had previously sketched.[26] When Liu arrived

24 Karl Radek, speech, 27 March 1927, quoted in Alexander Pantsov, *The Bolsheviks and the Chinese Revolution*, Honolulu: Hawaii University Press, 2000, 130. Radek gave this speech two weeks before Chiang's Shanghai coup.

25 See Alexander Pantsov, 'From Students to Dissidents: The Chinese Trotskyists in Soviet Russia', *Marxist Monthly*, Vol. 5, Nos. 8–11 (1994–95), available at marxists.org.

26 Arif Dirlik, *The Origins of Chinese Communism*, Oxford: Oxford University Press, 1989, 232.

back in China, he initially welcomed Chen's adherence to the opposition and made overtures to him and his supporters, who included another former senior CCP leader, Peng Shuzhi. But, at the end of 1930, Liu set up his own separate organisation called *Shiyue* (October), citing Chen's supposed concessions to the concept of a democratic dictatorship of the workers and peasants. Trotsky, who heard of these developments from afar, was exasperated by what he saw as squabbles over words. He wanted both Chen and Liu within the anti-Stalinist opposition and insisted that the different groups, which by then numbered four, unite.[27] This was, at least on paper, achieved at a Unification Congress held in May 1931.

KMT repression soon made the internal disputes in the Trotskyist movement irrelevant. Shortly after the Unification Congress, most of the leaders were jailed. Chen Duxiu temporarily evaded capture but was arrested in 1932. With its leaders in jail, the Chinese Trotskyist movement had virtually expired when, in 1934, Frank Glass and Harold Isaacs set out to revive it. One of the few leaders who remained free was Liu Renjing, and Glass and Isaacs managed to track him down. But Liu's hostility to Chen Duxiu had grown. Twenty years younger than Chen, he saw himself as the leader of a new generation destined to sweep away all traces of opportunism. He was supported by younger Oppositionists who saw Chen as one of the old guard who had led the revolution to disaster. In 1934, Liu wrote: 'Comrade Chen Tu-hsui's role as a revolutionary leader is finished ... Chen Tu-hsuism a variety of Menshevism [we must carry out] merciless criticism of Comrade Chen's zigzags and inconsistencies.'[28]

Liu Renjing had qualities apart from factionalism. He was well read, had a grasp of theory, and was a persuasive speaker. He impressed both Glass and Isaacs, providing and translating the bulk of the material that Isaacs used to write *The Tragedy of the Chinese Revolution*. In a letter to the International Secretariat of the Opposition, Glass called him 'the voice of Marxism in China' and appeared to endorse Liu's view that the Chinese opposition was mired in passivity and would either 'get out of the swamp or, if not, it would be better to die rapidly'.[29] The stage was set

---

27   Chen Duxiu's Proletarian group; Liu Renjing's October; Our Word, which included Wang Fanxi; and Struggle, the smallest of the groups.

28   Quoted in Gregor Benton, *China's Urban Revolutionaries: Explorations in the History of Chinese Trotskyism, 1921–1952*, New Jersey: Humanities Press, 1996.

29   Letter to the International Secretariat, reprinted in Benton, *Prophets Unarmed*, 921–3.

for what Wang Fanxi called the 'tragi-comedy' of Glass and Isaacs conspiring with Liu Renjing to expel Chen Duxiu, arguably China's most renowned revolutionary, from the Chinese Left Opposition.

The naivety of Isaacs, at twenty-four years old a decade younger than Glass and a newcomer to the movement, can perhaps be forgiven. It is harder to understand how someone as experienced as Glass failed to exercise elementary caution. Indeed, his reckless backing of Liu perhaps reflects an impulsiveness in his character. He did not speak Chinese, and his knowledge of the Chinese revolutionary movement, let alone the country as a whole, could not have been much more than elementary. When Chen, in prison, heard what had happened, he was enraged. From Chen's point of view, as Wang Fanxi put it,

Li [Glass] and Isaacs had suddenly turned up from nowhere and joined forces with a handful of youngsters barely out of school to make a long list of all his mistakes, demand a recantation, and – when this failed – pass a resolution expelling him from the organization![30]

Chen saw Glass as just another meddling foreigner, like the Comintern agents who had forced an unworkable strategy on the Chinese Communists and then made him carry the can. He even suggested Glass was a police agent. When, later, at Wang Fanxi's prompting, Glass admitted his mistake and helped reconstruct the Trotskyist group, the main obstacle was Chen's 'burning hatred' for Glass. He 'wrote letter after letter urging us never again to co-operate with the Mao-tzu [hairy foreigner].'[31] Liu Renjing made the dispute worse by claiming that Glass was a representative of the International Secretariat, bringing back memories of Henk Sneevliet, who, in 1922, had waved his Comintern order at recalcitrant CCP leaders to bring them into line. In fact, Glass was not, and had made no claim to be, a representative of anyone but himself. He was horrified when Wang Fanxi told him that Liu Renjing had misrepresented him as some kind of envoy.

---

30   Wang Fanxi, *Memoirs of a Chinese Revolutionary*, New York: Columbia University Press, 1991, 174.

31   Ibid. *Mao-tzu* (Pinyin *maozi*) is a derogatory term that was mainly applied to Russians but by extension to all foreigners.

Trotsky again intervened to end the dispute. When Isaacs visited Trotsky in Oslo to discuss and revise the first draft of *Tragedy of the Chinese Revolution*, Trotsky impressed on him the importance of Chen Duxiu to the movement and made sure the message reached Glass in China. Chen was eventually reconciled to working with the 'hairy foreigner' again, and, in part thanks to Glass's efforts, a unified Central Committee was reconstituted in 1936.[32] However, serious damage had been done to the Trotskyist movement. Thereafter, although 'superficially reconciled to his comrades, in practice Chen remained aloof from the organisation he had helped to found.'[33] In Glass's defence, it should be said that the primary responsibility lay with the erratic and ambitious Liu Renjing. Despite their mistakes, Wang Fanxi's assessment of Glass and Isaacs was generous:

> Both Li Fu-jen[34] and Isaacs were sincere revolutionaries . . . but they were unfamiliar with the Chinese Opposition, and therefore fell foul of Liu Jen-ching's demagogy . . . [Glass] was an honest and sincere comrade, and was neither a bureaucrat, as I had previously suspected, nor an adventurer, of which there were many in Shanghai at that time.[35]

After Glass's death in 1988, Wang would pay tribute to his political principles and character:

> Frank Glass was a true internationalist and a revolutionary Communist. During his long life he played important roles at different times in various countries – South Africa, China, and the US – and in the Fourth International. Frank hardly ever spoke of himself. He was too modest to talk about his contributions and too honest to exaggerate his own importance.[36]

---

32   Robert Alexander, *International Trotskyism 1929–1985: A Documented Analysis of the Movement*, Durham, NC: Duke University Press, 1991, 211. By this time, Liu Renjing was in jail. He was arrested when leaving Beijing after finishing work on Isaacs's book. According to Wang Fanxi and Zheng Chaolin, Liu defected to the KMT. After the CCP took power, he immediately issued a statement denouncing Trotskyism. Wang Fanxi, *Memoirs*, 140–1.

33   Greg Benton, introduction to Baruch Hirson's biography of Frank Glass, *The Restless Revolutionary*, London: Porcupine Press, 2003.

34   Li Fu-jen (Pinyin Li Furen) was Glass's Chinese pseudonym.

35   Wang Fanxi, *Memoirs*, 172–5.

36   From Wang Fanxi's obituary of Frank Glass, quoted in Benton, *Prophets Unarmed*, 1173–6.

While in Shanghai, Glass met Grace Simons, Rayna Prohme's younger sister who had arrived with her husband, Wilbur Burton – a journalist who wrote for Edgar Snow's *China Weekly Review*.[37] She had married Burton despite Rayna's warning that he was 'a coarse, utterly insensitive conceited young puppy, imagining himself a veritable Don Juan'.[38] There may have been some truth in Rayna's assessment of Burton. For whatever reason, Grace tired of him and moved in with Glass. It seems there were no hard feelings between the two men, who remained friends despite their personal entanglement and political differences.[39]

Glass visited Trotsky in Mexico in 1937, and he and Grace moved to the United States where they married. They both joined the Socialist Workers Party. During the Chinese civil war, Glass stuck to the orthodox Trotskyist view that the CCP had degenerated into a petty-bourgeois party that would inevitably compromise with the KMT. However, along with the entire Trotskyist movement, he was confounded when Mao's peasant army drove Chiang Kai-shek into exile. He concluded that the CCP could no longer be considered Stalinist. It had, albeit after 'many hesitations and opportunistic twists, led the workers and peasants to victory'.[40] He criticised the leadership of the Socialist Workers' Party for failing to look reality in the face. When Mao launched the Great Leap Forward, Glass and Grace, along with Arne Swabeck, a founder member of both the CPUSA and the SWP, became cheerleaders for the People's Communes. According to Swabeck, who eventually left the SWP and joined the Maoist Progressive Labour Party, China was implementing 'the greatest leap forward in the history of mankind'.[41]

That Glass did not follow Swabeck was probably because he kept in touch with his old friend and comrade Wang Fanxi. Wang agreed with Glass on many points but refused to withdraw the charge of Stalinism

---

37   As a journalist, Burton was highly regarded. His articles included 'The French Stranglehold on Yunnan', a long feature on China's southwest border region.

38   Letter from Rayna Prohme to Grace Simons. Baruch Hirson, Arthur Knodel, and Gregor Benton, *Reporting the Chinese Revolution: The Letters of Rayna Prohme*, London: Pluto Press, 2007, 84.

39   Hirson, *The Restless Revolutionary*, 121. Burton was anti-Stalinist but not a Trotskyist.

40   Ibid., 194, extract from May 1962 letter from Glass to Wang Fanxi.

41   The disasters, including famine, caused by the Great Leap Forward were not fully understood until later. Glass dismissed critical reports from Chinese comrades as 'Petit bourgeois sarcasm'. Ibid., 191.

from Mao's regime. In particular, he was appalled by Glass's contention that the Chinese Trotskyists imprisoned by Mao in 1952 had only themselves to blame as 'blinded by anti-Stalinist factionalism [they] failed to recognise the revolution'. Glass thought they should renounce their political views to obtain release. Wang countered that Mao imprisoned even those who recanted.[42] The two old friends continued to disagree, and although he did not leave, Glass became increasingly isolated within the Trotskyist movement. It had, he said, degenerated into a cult of its founder, leaving it unable to intervene in a wave of revolutions throughout the colonial world. Over time, however, his views on China changed again. When Mao launched the Cultural Revolution, Glass characterised it as a Stalinist-style purge and denounced the Red Guards as hooligans. He finally began a campaign, both inside and outside the Fourth International, for the release of the Trotskyist prisoners from Mao's jails.

In old age, Glass's health deteriorated. He became housebound, and his political activity was reduced to exchanging letters with Wang Fanxi and other old comrades. After Grace died in 1985, Glass moved in to a nursing home, where Alex Buchman visited him every day until his death in 1988. Grace had remained active long after Frank, especially on conservation projects. Both Simons sisters have public memorials; Rayna's, in Moscow, records her part in a great revolution, while Grace Simons Lodge in Elysian Park is a memorial to Grace's successful campaign to save that Los Angeles green space from property developers.

Isaacs, despite writing one of its best-known works, did not stay in the Trotskyist movement. After returning to the United States in 1935, he was, for a time, a mainstay of the Trotskyist newspaper *Socialist Appeal*, but he quit in 1940 during the dark days of the Hitler-Stalin Pact, the start of the war in Europe, and Trotsky's murder. From 1943 until 1949, he worked for *Newsweek* in East Asia. In Chongqing, he sided with General Stilwell against the 'racketeer, extortionist and executioner' Chiang Kai-shek and his American supporters Patrick Hurley and Claire Chennault.[43] In Vietnam, he saw the British rearm Japanese

---

42   It seems that Liu Renjing, despite renouncing the movement, was imprisoned in 1952 along with the other Trotskyists.

43   Robert Vitalis, *White World Order, Black Power Politics: The Birth of American International Relations*, Ithaca: Cornell University Press, 2017, 146.

prisoners to fight the Viet Minh and restore French colonial rule.[44] Ho Chi Minh, who remembered him from Shanghai, told him he had been abandoned by his supposed allies – the French Communists, the Russians, and the Americans.[45]

In the 1950s, Isaacs migrated from journalism to academia and eventually became a professor of political science at MIT. He came to see political movements based on ethnic identity rather than class as the decisive factor in politics, linking the anti-colonial struggle with the battle against Jim Crow. Group pride would break 'the rule of the empires' as, according to Isaacs's over-optimistic assessment, it had already broken 'the system of white supremacy in the United States'.[46] His mature work, *Idols of the Tribe*, written in 1975, was a paean to American pluralism. Taking his cue from the civil rights movement, he argued, presciently, that ethnic and other group identities would play an increasing role in United States domestic politics. But it was a vision of the future, as group squabbles over the spoils generated by capitalism, that he embraced with resignation rather than enthusiasm:

> The internationalist socialist dream was destroyed twice – at the outbreak of the First World War – and when Bolshevism degenerated into Stalin's National Communism. The Russian version was then joined by Mao's rival National Communism which hurled racist abuse at each other.[47]

China had been, for him, a 'political puberty rite ending in the loss of my political youth if not yet quite all my illusions'. His early commitment was replaced by 'a haunted vacancy of confusion and unsolved riddles'. His hopes for a 'more humane' society having faded, he took comfort in his personal life, which was a consolation amid the 'bleakness of the human condition'.[48]

By contrast, Isaacs's MIT colleague Lucian Pye, who wrote the preface to *Idols of the Tribe*, was delighted by Isaacs's conclusions. A CIA-linked

---

44   Isaacs, interview.

45   Ibid.

46   Harold Isaacs, *Idols of the Tribe*, Cambridge, MA: Harvard University Press, 1975, 44.

47   Ibid., 18.

48   Isaacs, *Re-encounters in China*, 47, 219.

pioneer of collaboration between academia, the State Department, and the Pentagon, Pye celebrated Isaacs's vision of endless ethnic and group conflict as a triumph over the wishful thinking of Marxists and liberals. Isaacs's vision was indeed, in some respects, conservative. He saw the battle for African American rights as essentially won. Martin Luther King would be seen as a world-historical personality, Malcolm X as a marginal figure. Rivalries among interest groups based on ethnicity, gender, and other identifiers would remain peaceful because the size of the cake to be shared out would continue to grow. One wonders what he would have made of the 2008–9 financial crisis, the rise of Donald Trump, and the recrudescence of white supremacism. From his essentially centre-left perspective, he would no doubt have welcomed the 2020 election of Joe Biden.

In 1980, Isaacs and his wife returned to Beijing and were invited to dinner by Song Qingling, who by then held the honorific post of vice-chair of the People's Republic. Presumptuously, Isaacs greeted Song with a kiss, telling her, 'Suzie, the one thing I do carry with me as precious from that time in Shanghai was the love I had for you.' Song replied stiffly, 'I am honoured,' with an expression he 'could not read'.[49] It was not the welcome Isaacs had hoped for. When Ding Ling and Mao Dun joined them, Song greeted them effusively. Already seriously ill, Song was practically carried to the dining table. Over dinner, Isaacs tried to probe his old comrades about conditions in the PRC, but, whether out of loyalty, prudence, or both, they replied in bland and general terms.[50] Song died a few months later. On a side trip to Canton, Isaacs visited the memorial to the dead of the Canton Commune. Although he was by then a liberal, he bemused his tour guides by reprising the argument of his 1938 Trotskyist text. The martyrs, he told them, were victims of Stalin's stupid policies.[51]

In 1952, to the fury of his former comrades, Isaacs published a new edition of the *Tragedy of the Chinese Revolution*, leaving out Trotsky's introduction and adding a conclusion on 'The Blind Alley of Totalitarianism'. He had also substantially rewritten several chapters, blunting the message of the original text. Isaacs, as the author, was

---

49   Ibid., 71.
50   Ibid., 177–9.
51   Ibid., 185–6.

entitled to revise his work, but the Trotskyists had come to see the book as their property and, to Isaacs's irritation, had republished it in samizdat form around the world. They argued that Isaacs had no moral right to revise the book, since it was a collective work written in close collaboration with others, above all Trotsky. *Fourth International* magazine called Isaacs's 'defacement' of the book 'a minor crime of our times':

> The *Tragedy* is nothing more than the popularization of Trotsky's *Problems of the Chinese Revolution* . . . [Isaacs] applied his journalistic skills to tools which had been fashioned and along a pattern that had already been drafted . . . It was an important, even a brilliant work, but in no sense original. Isaacs provided the 'manual' labor for Trotsky's intellectual creation.[52]

Isaacs's motive for revising *Tragedy* is not clear. Perhaps it was no more than a desire to express his current views. But there may have been other reasons. Although he had broken with the Trotskyists in 1940, the FBI kept him under investigation until 1954; the State Department refused to grant him a passport in 1947 and delayed a further application in 1950. He may have felt the need to make a more substantial demonstration of loyalty. In 1961, when the pressure was off, he published another edition of *Tragedy*, leaving out the conclusion on totalitarianism and reversing some of his earlier revisions.[53]

Whatever his reasons, neither revised edition could have been expected to have the impact of the original. Nor did any of his other works. When Isaacs died in 1986, the obituaries referred to him as the author of the *Tragedy of the Chinese Revolution*. He will be remembered for the book he wrote as a twenty-eight-year-old revolutionary. His son Arnold, a foreign correspondent like his father, seemed to draw a line under the controversy over the revisions when he wrote a preface for a 2009 reprint of the 1938 edition.

After leaving China in 1939, Alex Buchman visited Trotsky in his fortified house in Coyoacán, Mexico City. His original purpose was to show Trotsky his photographs of China, but he joined Trotsky's team of

---

52   George Clarke, 'The Tragedy of Harold Isaacs', *Fourth International*, Vol. 13, No. 1 (January–February 1952), available at marxists.org.

53   Vitalis, *Black Power Politics*, 146–7.

bodyguards and stayed for five months, leaving just before the attack led by the Stalinist muralist David Siqueiros; he was replaced by Robert Sheldon Harte, who was killed by the Siqueiros gang. Buchman was suspicious of Ramón Mercader, who had already infiltrated the household. To the modest and loyal Buchman, Mercader seemed shallow and superficial – a bit 'off' – and he recalled that Mercader refused to have his picture taken.[54] Using a home movie camera, Buchman took the only surviving colour film of Trotsky. A 1990 documentary, *Trotsky's Home Movies*, produced by Tariq Ali, intersperses interviews with Buchman with excerpts from his footage.

After Mexico, Buchman moved to Los Angeles, where he worked as an aircraft engineer. He met his half-Japanese, half-English wife, Debbie Bloomfield, in 1930 on the boat from Japan to Shanghai. She and Buchman lived together in Shanghai but did not marry until after they moved to the United States. They had to leave California for the wedding because of its racist anti-miscegenation laws. Buchman was investigated by the FBI after trying to set up a union but was cleared after his defence lawyer proved that he had nothing to do with the official Communists. Buchman remained a Trotskyist until his death in 2003 at the age of ninety-one. He helped Wang Fanxi publish his memoirs in the United States and paid for them to be translated into Spanish. After being put in touch with Baruch Hirson by Suzi Weissman, he helped Hirson with his biography of Frank Glass. Hirson, who was jailed for nine years from 1964–73 by the apartheid regime, had been won to Trotskyism by Fanny Kellerman, Glass's first wife.[55]

---

54   Weissman, 'Alex Buchman', 159.
55   In 2011, Sierra Leone issued a postage stamp honouring Hirson as a Legendary Hero of Africa.

9

Red Star and Paper Tiger

A recent study of global Maoism attributes almost-miraculous properties to Edgar Snow's 1937 book *Red Star over China*. Part inspirational text, part practical manual, but above all an instrument of conversion, it was the movement's bible. If this narrative is to be believed, Maoism was created less by the shock waves from a revolution in a country of half a billion than by a book written by a 'former frat boy from Missouri'. And *Red Star* not only spread Maoism internationally but also 'fashioned' it inside China. It was not so much the kidnapping of Chiang Kai-shek, or the fall of Beiping with hardly a shot fired,[1] that sent patriotic youth flocking to the CCP's remote headquarters, but the hand-cranked Chinese editions of *Red Star* that appeared months later. In the beginning was the word, as it were, and as St Paul created Christianity, so Edgar Snow created Maoism. There are even suggestions that he outdid Paul in a spectacular example of life imitating art by converting Mao himself, who so fell in love with the Yan'an myth Snow spun that he wreaked devastation trying to recreate it throughout China.[2] Giving Mao's amanuensis such a starring role is, at first sight, startling. But we are on familiar territory – the perennial whodunnit – the hunt for who

---

1 Not to mention Red Wuhan, the three Shanghai insurrections, the Canton Commune, and the captures of Nanchang in 1927 and Changsha in 1930. The Chinese Communist Party was not a secret uncovered by Snow.

2 Julia Lovell, *Maoism: A Global History*, London: Vintage, 2020, 86.

lost China.[3] Snow is the star of a cast that includes George C. Marshall, who leaked 'substantial intelligence' to Zhou Enlai and Richard Nixon – who was 'infatuated' with Zhou and presumably abandoned the fight to win China back. On this view, Snow was the most magical of the CCP's 'magic weapons', to use a phrase that has recently become fashionable among China watchers.[4] No wonder Snow, whose 'murkier motivations' included 'left-wing leanings', sought refuge in Switzerland.[5] According to this line of thinking, which had more than academic consequences in Snow's time, the United States 'lost' China, and perhaps nearly the world, because of him.[6]

If this is a case of words sprinting ahead of an idea, we can nevertheless admit that *Red Star* was an extraordinarily influential book. Snow's great friend John King Fairbank called it 'an event in Chinese history'. Quantifying the impact of that event is not a simple matter and rather depends on one's philosophy of history. A question that can be explored more fruitfully is whether the frat boy who did so much to inspire Maoism was a Maoist himself. Snow was certainly sympathetic to the CCP and the Comintern, but his exact political stance was, and remains, ambiguous. Stalinists called him a Trotskyist, and Trotskyists called him a liberal. Liberals initially lauded his work, but many, if not most, later came round to a semi-McCarthyite view that he was a traitor, if not to the United States, then to 'democratic values'.

As with everyone, Snow's views evolved, but we can be fairly sure that, in 1928, when he joined tens of thousands of adventurers in the free port of Shanghai, the liberal tag was accurate. Snow came from a well-to-do family in America's Midwest. His father owned a publishing business in Kansas City, and Snow, following the family trade, enrolled at Missouri's Columbia School of Journalism. In booming 1920s America, advertising was the place to be for bright young men with a talent for crafting a slogan; in 1926, Snow found a job with a New York agency, mixed with the smart set, and made a modest killing on the

---

3 Lovell, *Maoism*, 79.

4 The Chinese word *fabao* originated in Buddhist and Daoist traditions and is in everyday use in China signifying a useful tool or method. The CCP uses it precisely because it is a commonplace term, but of course the 'magic weapon' translation sounds both menacing and weird to Westerners.

5 Lovell, *Maoism*, 87.

6 See Lovell, *Maoism*, 62–3, 77, 82–7.

stock exchange. With money in his pocket and bored with routine, he took up an offer from Kermit Roosevelt, one of his high-society friends, to work his way east as a deckhand on one of the Roosevelt family's ships. When his ship's engines broke down in Honolulu, he abandoned it, but soon ran into a pal from Princeton. The friend hid him in his first-class cabin on a liner to Yokohama, where he bluffed his way ashore by mingling with the welcoming paparazzi. Snow's stowaway escapade made him a minor hero in the press club, and *Harper's Bazaar* paid him the fabulous sum of 500 dollars for an article. He was, as he put it, 'treading on winged sandals on clouds of pink bliss'. His serendipitous rise continued in Shanghai, where fellow Missourian J. B. Powell offered him 'one of the prize jobs of the year' as advertising manager of the pro-KMT journal *China Weekly Review*.

Snow made a success of the sales job, and Powell promoted him to assistant editor. Although he annoyed American expatriates by writing satirical articles about their shallow lives in Shanghai, 'where a bank clerk could afford to keep a mistress', Snow still had no well-defined political views. But, by 1930, the world economy was collapsing, and there was famine in northern China. A chance meeting with Rewi Alley, ironically while researching a feature to promote China as a tourist destination, diverted him to the fringe of the Gobi Desert, where he saw a town starving to death. He began mixing with Shanghai's leftists and, when Consolidated Press hired him to report on India, Agnes Smedley gave him a letter of introduction to Nehru. Passing through Burma, he reported on a peasant rebellion led by the Buddhist mystic Saya San. The uprising, sparked by the collapse of rice prices in the Great Depression, was crushed by the British imperialists, who hanged Saya San after a sham trial and slaughtered thousands of his followers. In India, Snow interviewed Nehru and met Gandhi; he was not greatly impressed by either. More importantly for his political development, he reported on the Meerut conspiracy trial of thirty-three Communists and trade unionists and met Suhasini Chattopadhyaya, a younger sister of Smedley's ex-husband. Suhasini gave him a crash course in Marxism – or what passed for Marxism in the 'bolshevised' Comintern. He learned the difference between a bourgeois nationalist revolution and a proletarian socialist revolution and was no doubt told that the former must be completed before the second could begin, since deviation from this orthodoxy was anathemised as 'Trotskyism'.

When Snow returned to Shanghai, China was in crisis. Floods on the Yangzi had drowned and starved hundreds of thousands, perhaps several million, people.[7] While Chiang Kai-shek was preoccupied with crushing the Communists in the south, Japan seized Manchuria and used the pretext of a clash between ultra-nationalist Japanese Buddhists and Chinese civilians to attack Shanghai. Snow reported on the prolonged and determined resistance of the Nineteenth Route Army led by General Cai Tingkai, who later joined the Communists.[8] An accumulation of events had influenced Snow's thinking, and he was by now integrated into the left-wing circle around Song Qingling. He married fellow journalist Helen Foster and, in 1933, the couple moved to Beiping, where they met Fairbank and other China experts, including Karl Wittfogel (who was then still a Communist). Snow translated short stories by Lu Xun, Ding Ling, Mao Dun, Ba Jin, and others, publishing them in a volume dedicated to Song Qingling's 'incorruptible integrity, courage, loyalty, and beauty of spirit'. Both Snow and Foster taught journalism at Yangjing University, whose liberal principal John Leighton Stuart had allowed it to become a centre of political dissent and a safe haven for underground activists. In late 1935, when thousands of Beiping students demonstrated against Japanese plans to establish a puppet government in North China, Snow and Foster actively supported them.[9] According to Snow, who was not one to play down his role in history, the December Ninth Movement, as it became known, was planned by Christian students 'in our living room'. Right wingers charged that it was stirred up by Communist agitators, and Snow later reported that the Christian activists all joined the CCP.[10] Whatever the extent of the CCP's role, Snow's open association with left-wing causes and leftists led to accusations that he was a Comintern agent, and he asked the US ambassador for protection.[11]

---

7   The official government report recorded 140,000 deaths from drowning alone.

8   Cai Tingkai supported the 1933 Fujian Rebellion against Chiang Kai-shek, defected to the Communists during the Civil War, and signed the Proclamation of the People's Republic.

9   The December Ninth Movement spread to several Chinese cities and forced the Japanese into a temporary retreat.

10   Edgar Snow, *Journey to the Beginning*, London: Lowe & Brydone, 1958, 139.

11   Wittfogel was researching Chinese history in Beiping. Snow was considered as highly suspect in Moscow. On 19 August 1939, GPU agent G. I. Mordvinov wrote to Comintern head Georgi Dimitrov that Snow was a Trotskyist, implying that he should be liquidated. RGASPI 495.74.295.7-40.

Snow had tried and failed to get to the Soviet areas in southern China during Chiang Kai-shek's encirclement campaigns. By 1936, however, an informal ceasefire between Zhang Xueliang's troops and the Red Army had opened up the possibility of travel to the CCP's new bases in the north. With an invitation arranged by Liu Shaoqi and Song Qingling, Snow travelled to Xi'an, where he joined George Hatem – the CCP leadership had asked Shanghai to send a doctor and a friendly but credibly independent journalist. Zhou Enlai met them outside the city and escorted them to the CCP headquarters in Bao'an, where Snow, in interviews with Mao Zedong over a period of ten days, collected the core material for *Red Star over China*.

The first edition of *Red Star over China*, published in Britain by the Left Book Club in 1937, was an instant bestseller. Simultaneously, pirate translations circulated throughout China, especially among radicalised youth. Snow became an international celebrity overnight. The book also became a bestseller in the United States when it was published by Random House the following year, but it was not universally welcomed. The CPUSA called it 'vicious Trotskyist propaganda' and refused to stock it in its bookshops. The reason was that, referring to the defeat of 1927, Snow had written that 'the Comintern could be held responsible for serious reverses suffered by the Chinese Communists'.[12] To be sure, he added that although Comintern policy 'ended in catastrophe', Trotsky's 'Jacobin' alternative 'would have ended in a much earlier and more complete catastrophe',[13] a conclusion that reflected Snow's own cautious, moderate views (and ignored the fact that it was the Comintern that ordered suicidal Jacobin-style uprisings after the defeat). However, even heavily qualified criticism of the Soviet line was unacceptable to slavish Stalinists, who also deduced from Snow's evident familiarity with Opposition arguments that he had heard them from Trotskyists in Shanghai.[14] Snow, taken aback by the vehemence of the attack and no doubt worried that a boycott would affect sales, wrote to the CPUSA leader Earl Browder offering to 'excise certain

---

12 Edgar Snow, *Red Star over China*, London: Grove Press, 2018, 410.

13 Ibid., 413.

14 Snow wrote in some detail about Zinoviev's shifting positions on China, although he was not indelicate enough to mention that the former Comintern head had been shot in August 1936 while Snow was interviewing Mao in Bao'an.

sentences'. A revised edition, with the criticisms of the Comintern blunted, appeared a few months later.[15]

The ambivalent politics of *Red Star*, especially its first edition, reflected Mao Zedong's thinking as much as Snow's. Mao was fully aware that the defeat of 1927 was the result of the Soviet-Comintern policy of trusting and arming militarists like Chiang Kai-shek and Feng Yuxiang. He had famously concluded that political power grows out of the barrel of a gun, and that the party must command the gun but, for factional reasons, he followed the official line and placed the blame for the 1927 defeat on Chen Duxiu's 'wavering opportunism'. He knew that his Kremlin-backed rival for the party leadership, Wang Ming, was only too willing to level the charge of Trotskyism against him should he absolve the former leader. But elsewhere in his conversations with Snow, he described Chen Duxiu as 'among the most brilliant intellectuals of China', and he also told Snow that the chief Soviet advisor, Borodin, 'stood a little to the right of Chen'. This was confusing enough for Snow, who was, we should remember, only just past thirty when he met Mao. In the first edition of *Red Star*, Snow even quoted Trotsky approvingly – likening his characterisation of the Chinese revolution as 'a drawing together of . . . a peasant war . . . and a proletarian insurrection' to Mao's 1934 statement that the Chinese Soviet's task was 'to bring the bourgeois democratic revolution to fruition and . . . turn [it] into a higher stage of Socialist revolution'. This was perilously close to the doctrine of Permanent Revolution and disappeared from later editions.

Of course, Snow was no Trotskyist. Simply writing down what Mao and others told him, he also repeated the boilerplate Stalinist slanders that Trotskyists were 'spies and traitors . . . led by the logic of their position to join the Blueshirts'. This provoked a furious response from Frank Glass, who admitted that a handful of Trotskyists had turned traitor but were eclipsed by 'scores and hundreds' of defectors from the CCP to the KMT, including former Red Army commander Zhang Guotao, who, until his apostasy, was celebrated as a revolutionary hero. Having rejected Comintern policy as bad and Opposition policy as worse, Snow offered no alternative but concluded that, since Stalin had triumphed, it was 'tedious' to prolong the discussion. He quoted Stalin to the effect

---

15   See Harvey Klehr, John Earl Haynes, and Kyrill Anderson, *The Soviet World of American Communism*, New Haven: Yale University Press, 1998, 336–8, 343–4.

that those who, like Kamenev, insisted that 'tactics' rather than the 'relation of class forces' caused the defeat of 1927 had 'abandoned Marxism' (without mentioning that, to reinforce his argument, Stalin had Kamenev shot). Glass did not dismiss Snow as a simple Stalinist.[16] Rather, he was a 'dull empiricist' liberal who had, despite his superficial analysis, produced 'the first really factual piece of writing about the Chinese Soviets'.

As the World War turned into Cold War and Chiang Kai-shek lost his grip on China, Snow became a target in the hunt for scapegoats. The principal charge was that he and other journalists had misrepresented the CCP as not real Communists at all, but 'agrarian reformers'. CIA director Allen Dulles called it 'one of the most successful long-range political deceptions . . . planted through Communist-influenced journalists'.[17] Some of the most vehement peddlers of this criticism were disillusioned former Communists and Snow's former colleagues in China. Freda Utley, for one, wrote that he was among 'the cleverest, smoothest and most subtle advocates the Kremlin ever had'.[18] Ironically, Utley was one of a small number of journalists who had previously written that the Chinese Communists were quite unlike their Russian counterparts and had transformed themselves into patriotic social reformers. Snow, on the other hand, could defend himself by pointing to passages in *Red Star* in which Mao and other leaders repudiated any suggestion that they had abandoned socialism or communism. The wartime programme of the CCP, which suspended radical land reform and called for the nation to unite behind the national government, was a temporary, tactical retreat of the type prescribed by Lenin and entirely compatible with 'the strictest loyalty to the ideas of Communism'. All editions of *Red Star* contained the following quote from Mao:

> The Communist Party retains the leadership on problems in the Soviet districts and the Red Army and retains its independence and

---

16 Some other Trotskyists did, of course. See, for example, George Stern, 'An Apologist for Chinese Stalinism', *Fourth International*, Vol. 2, No. 6 (July 1941), 190–1, available at marxists.org.

17 Kenneth E. Shewmaker, 'The "Agrarian Reformer" Myth', *China Quarterly*, No. 34 (1968), 66–81, 66.

18 Newspaper article cited in John Maxwell Hamilton, *Edgar Snow: A Biography*, Bloomington: Indiana University Press, 1988, 179.

freedom of criticism in its relations with the Kuomintang. On these
points no concessions can be made ... The Communist Party will
never abandon its aims of Socialism and Communism, it will still pass
through the stage of democratic revolution of the bourgeoisie to
attain the stages of Socialism and Communism.[19]

But the relationship between the bourgeois and proletarian revolutions – in particular the formula of the 'democratic dictatorship of the
proletariat and the peasantry' that the CCP inherited from the Old
Bolsheviks – allowed for almost infinite flexibility regarding tactics and
timing.[20] Moreover, Snow's 1936 interviews with Mao took place during
the Comintern's Popular Front period, when the CCP was calling for a
National United Front against Japan. There were certainly passages in
Red Star that right-wing critics could seize on to charge Snow with lull-
ing CCP opponents into thinking it was a benign force. 'Every
pronouncement of the Communists has shown clearly', Snow wrote,
'that they recognize the "bourgeois character" of the present revolution.'[21]
In the 1936 interviews, Mao pointedly avoided calling Britain and
America imperialist, preferring the label 'democratic capitalist powers',
and implied that the former concessionaires would be welcomed with
open arms to take part in China's economic reconstruction. But, if
accused of prettifying the CCP's foreign policy, Snow could point to a
1939 interview, after Stalin had abandoned the Popular Front and signed
a non-aggression pact with Hitler, when Mao told him that the world
war had become a war between imperialists among whom the British
were the most perfidious.[22]

To find a consistent presentation of the CCP's political line in *Red
Star* is an impossible task. Mao was an independent thinker and politician, but, at least during the 1930s, he operated within parameters set by
the Comintern. Snow reproduced Mao's views from the Comintern's
Third Period – before he interviewed him, the Popular Front period,

---

19   Quoted in Snow, *Red Star*, 488.

20   Even the strictest Stalinist could be caught out if he strayed beyond what was
acceptable or was slow to adjust to changes in emphasis – as happened with Pavel Mif,
Karl Radek's successor as rector of Sun Yat-sen University. Mif was shot in 1938. Radek
died in a labour camp the following year.

21   Snow, *Red Star*, 479–80.

22   See Shewmaker, 'Agrarian Reformer Myth', 74.

and 1939 when the Popular Front was (temporarily) abandoned.[23] It was possible to find both a conciliatory and a hard-line Mao in Snow's writings, depending on which one cared to emphasise. And, of course, Mao did not simply adjust to changes in Comintern policy; rather, he changed his mind in line with circumstances. We should remember that not even Mao had a crystal ball; until the atom bomb was dropped, everyone expected the war against Japan to continue for several more years. Furthermore, the final outcome remained uncertain – as illustrated by the 1944 Ichigo offensive, which steamrollered over KMT forces in southern China, forcing Chiang Kai-shek to relocate troops that had been blockading CCP-controlled areas. In recording Mao's changing lines, Snow was, as Frank Glass charged, an empiricist. Snow, however, would have maintained that he was just doing his job as a journalist.

Snow was not, of course, apolitical. He held the anti-fascist views that became a wartime consensus encompassing a political spectrum from far left to right-wing conservatives. Reporting from the Soviet Union during the Second World War, he expressed the view of countless of his generation who, while having no love for Stalin's regime, knew which side they were on:

In this international cataclysm brought on by fascists it is no more possible for any people to remain neutral than it is for a man surrounded by bubonic plague to remain 'neutral' toward the rat population. Whether you like it or not, your life, your life as a force is bound either to help the rats or hinder them. Nobody can be immunized against the germs of history.[24]

Unlike many others, Snow was not forced to testify to the House Un-American Activities Committee during the McCarthyite witch hunt. Indeed, one of the committee's most prolific informers, Louis Budenz, testified that Snow was not a Communist.[25] Nevertheless, he was

23   Snow quoted some of Mao's views from 1934. If he had looked further back, to 1931, he would have found Mao expressing views that would horrify today's party leaders – acknowledging the right of Tibet and Xinjiang to secede, for example.

24   Quoted in Hamilton, *Edgar Snow*, 229.

25   Robert Newman, *Owen Lattimore and the "Loss" of China*, Berkeley: University of California Press, 1992, 267.

questioned by the FBI, and his reputation as a fellow traveller made it difficult for him to find work in the United States. In 1959, Snow went into self-imposed exile in Switzerland with his second wife, the actress Lois Wheeler. His views remained eclectic. In his 1958 autobiography, he described Marxism as a 'heretical' descendant of Western Judeo-Christianity that was an imperfect fit as an ideology for anti-colonial revolutions in Asia. The old empires were crumbling but were being replaced by neo-imperialisms. Stalin had squeezed Eastern Europe dry with swingeing reparations, while the expansive foreign policy of the United States was quite unlike that of the old European empires; it was not a quest for markets or raw materials, but a kind of 'auto-imperialism' designed to subsidise its domestic arms industry.[26] Snow had witnessed the rearming of Japanese POWs by the British to restore French authority in Vietnam. In an interview with Douglas MacArthur, he discovered, to his surprise, that the general agreed with him that the British were guilty of 'an ignoble betrayal'.[27] Here, again, Snow sounds far more like an 'empiricist' journalist than an ideological opponent of the United States. In a 1970 letter to the eminent China expert Owen Lattimore, he gave what may be a reasonably accurate account of his political evolution. He told Lattimore that he had studied the entire Marxist canon but retained his faith in American 'exceptionalism' throughout the 1950s. Even McCarthyism did not shake his belief that there was an essential difference between the United States and the old European colonial empires. It was not until Kennedy sent troops to Vietnam that he decided that American imperialism, precisely because it disguised itself as a mission to spread freedom, was 'the most vicious and dangerous kind yet seen'.[28]

Snow returned to China three times after the CCP took power, in 1960, 1965, and 1970. His final trip was one of the first diplomatic overtures towards Nixon's visit. In 1965, he interviewed the 'old warrior' Mao, who treated him to a discursive tour of world affairs. His 1960 visit during the Great Leap Forward was the most controversial. Despite reports of famine and refugees fleeing the mainland to Hong Kong,

26   Snow, *Journey to the Beginning*, 385–8.
27   Ibid., 389.
28   Newman, *Owen Lattimore*, 531–2. Lattimore, a China expert who served as an advisor to Chiang Kai-shek in World War 2, was later witch hunted by Senator Joseph McCarthy for 'losing China.'

Snow insisted that, while there were serious food shortages, no one was starving to death. With the benefit of hindsight, Snow's critics have accused him of covering up the worst famine in Chinese history. Just as during what we should now perhaps call the first Cold War, Snow's most fervent opponents included former Maoists who held Snow to higher standards than they held themselves. In 1972, the year Snow died and a full decade after the Great Leap Forward, journalist and historian Jonathan Mirsky – who would, in 1989, insist that Snow must have known what was happening in 1960 – praised the 'innovative and creative aspects' of the Cultural Revolution.[29] John King Fairbank defended his old friend against this particular attack, calling Snow a journalist of great integrity who had been 'set up by Mao and mugged by the Cold War'.[30] But Snow's critics were not to be appeased, and today, as the new cold war between the United States and China deepens, he has remained a target. His reputation is unlikely to be enhanced by *China Daily*'s recent announcement that it has set up an Edgar Snow newsroom. Indeed, the examples of Al Jazeera and RT have shown that authoritarian states can set up news organisations that attract talented journalists and worldwide audiences, but the CCP's unwillingness to permit even the most minimal editorial freedom means that, barring a dramatic change of tack, it has no chance of employing anyone approaching Snow's stature in the newsroom named after him.

In a 1946 interview with the American journalist Anna Louise Strong, Mao Zedong coined one of his most famous aphorisms: 'All reactionaries are paper tigers.' He repeated the metaphor several times, and the quotes were collected in the little red book under the heading 'Imperialism and all reactionaries are paper tigers'. Originally a response to Strong's suggestion that the A-bomb was an unbeatable weapon in the hands of the United States, Mao's dictum combined absolute self confi dence with an appealing image that, for non-Chinese, added a touch of the exotic. The imagery was nearly lost, however, as Strong originally rendered Mao's use of the ancient Chinese term as 'scarecrow'; however, George Hatem corrected her. If we are to believe that, as with Edgar

---

29   Jonathan Mirsky, 'China after Nixon', *Annals of the American Academy of Political and Social Science*, Vol. 402, No. 1 (1972), 83–96.

30   John King Fairbank, 'Mao and Snow', letter to the *New York Review*, 1989, nybooks.com.

Snow's *Red Star*, Maoism was all about image building, then Anna Louise Strong's contribution was substantial. The 'paper tiger' quotation became a propaganda weapon during the Sino-Soviet split when Mao denounced the Soviet Union's 'revisionist' quest for détente with the United States, before performing a U-turn, welcoming Nixon to Beijing and branding 'Soviet social-imperialism' the main enemy.

Unlike Snow, Strong was not from the anti-fascist, Popular Front generation but, like George Hardy and Agnes Smedley, a first-generation Communist defined by opposition to the First World War and support for the October Revolution. However, unlike Hardy and Smedley, she came from a middle-class family; her parents were socially conscious missionaries, and her path to socialism was via Christianity and social work. She worked at Jane Addams's Hull House in Chicago and supported her father's Christian activism in Seattle. A spell in bohemian Greenwich village exposed her to more radical ideas, leading to a job organising exhibitions for Florence Kelley's National Child Labor Committee. Invited to organise a child welfare exhibition in Ireland, she became a supporter of the Republican movement. Back in America, she joined the IWW after reporting on the 1916 trial of one of its members following the Everett massacre.[31] When Woodrow Wilson declared war in 1917, she wrote: 'Our America is dead. The people wanted peace, the profiteers wanted war – and got it.'[32] She worked for the IWW paper, the Seattle *Daily Call*, until it folded, and afterwards for the *Union Record*, which, although owned by the AFL, was radical enough to print one of Lenin's speeches. In an eponymous editorial, Strong called the 1919 Seattle General Strike a movement that would lead 'no one knows where', implying an open-ended assumption of power by the strikers. But the strike collapsed after less than a week and Strong was arrested along with the entire staff of the *Union Record*.

Like many radicals of the period, Strong visited Soviet Russia. In 1921, while working for a Quaker famine relief organisation in the Volga

---

31 On 5 November 1916, two hundred sheriff's deputies in the northwest port of Everett opened fire on IWW members demonstrating in support of striking woodworkers. A dozen IWW members were killed. Two deputies were also killed by friendly fire. Seventy-four Wobblies were arrested, and one, Thomas Tracy, was charged with murder but acquitted.

32 Tracy Strong and Helene Keyssar, *Right in Her Soul: The Life of Anna Louise Strong*, New York: Random House, 1983, 67.

region, she contracted typhus and nearly died. By 1922, as a correspondent for Randolph Hearst's International News Service, she was able to
interview Bolshevik leaders and formed a bond with Leon Trotsky, to
whom she gave English lessons. In a letter to her father, she described
how Trotsky had asked her to visit his office several times a week and
had given her the use of an official car.[33] Trotsky questioned Strong
closely on the prospects for the labour movement in the United States
but was especially appreciative of her commitment to Russia's post-
revolutionary reconstruction.[34] It was the era of the New Economic
Policy (NEP), and Trotsky saw her as an opinion former who could
encourage American businesses to invest. He encouraged her efforts,
together with Borodin, whom she had met in Seattle, to set up a Russian-
American Club in Moscow (a project that was, prophetically, suffocated
by bureaucracy). In Trotsky's preface to Strong's book *The First Time in
History*, he praised her for sticking the course with the new regime,
unlike other 'friends' who had lost interest once the 'tragic poetry' of
revolution and civil war was replaced by the 'prose of NEP'.[35] Strong left
Russia in 1923. When she returned in 1925, Trotsky, who had by then
been sidelined, advised her to go to China, the new epicentre of world
revolution.

Strong took Trotsky's advice and left for China, where, after speaking
to enthusiastic, mainly student, audiences in the Soviet embassy in
Beijing, she went on to Shanghai and Canton. On the way, she found
time to interview the warlord Feng Yuxiang and wrote him off as an
untrustworthy manipulator, showing herself a better judge of character
than the Soviet officials who formed an alliance with him. When she
arrived in Canton, the great strike and boycott was at its height, and she
was ferried into the city in a small motorboat by Fanny Borodin, techni-
cally breaking the strikers' blockade.

---

33   The lessons led to (almost certainly untrue) rumours that Trotsky and Strong
were having an affair.

34   Strong told Trotsky that 'revolution in the United States' was 'too remote to be
practical politics.' See Anna Louise Strong, "Letter to her Father Sydney Strong," 14
December 1922, available at https://digitalcollections.lib.washington.edu.

35   Anna Louise Strong, *The First Time in History: Two Years of Russia's New Life*,
New York: Boni & Liveright, 1925, available at marxists.org. Strong eventually
persuaded her father to go to Russia to carry on his Christian-socialist work but,
perhaps oddly for a Christian socialist, he was disillusioned by the NEP and left
before long.

When Strong returned to the Soviet Union in 1926, she was prevented from meeting Trotsky.[36] She was shrewd enough to gauge the political direction in Moscow, having, a few months earlier, written the some-what wistful article 'Stalin "The Voice of the Party" Breaks Trotsky: The Rubber-Stamp Secretary versus the Fiery Idealist'.[37] She wrote to the American pacifist Paul Kellogg about a growing anti-foreign trend in Russia associated with the slogan 'Socialism in One Country'.[38] Strong would eventually bend with the new political wind in the Soviet Union, but first, she returned to China, fleeing the country together with Borodin. When she arrived in Wuhan, Borodin remarked to Chen Duxiu, 'Miss Strong is unlucky in her revolutions. She came too late for the Russian Revolution and has now come too soon for China.'[39]

Back in the USSR, while working on *Moscow News* with Borodin, Strong married Joel Shubin, a deputy minister of agriculture and editor of the *Peasant Gazette*. In her 1931 book *The Soviets Conquer Wheat*, she described the deadly chaos of Stalin's forced collectivisation as a 'strug-gle of new life against the patriarchal society'.[40] Not everything was smooth sailing; she complained so loudly about the censorship and bureaucracy suffocating *Moscow News* that she was invited to the Kremlin to discuss her grievances with Stalin, Lazar Kaganovich, and Kliment Voroshilov. She was, it seems, entranced by Stalin. After the meeting, she felt she had understood how the Soviet Union worked. Stalin was 'the greatest committee man, a man who could bring diverse views into harmony with a speed that amounted to genius'. She told her husband that she would 'take orders from those men anywhere in the world'.[41]

When Strong wrote her autobiography, *I Change Worlds: The Remaking of an American*, and was unsure what to say about Trotsky, Borodin told her to leave him out altogether; her chapter on Stalin was

36   In 1925, Litvinov had raised trivial and carping objections to Trotsky's interview with Strong. Trotsky replied disdainfully, not to Litvinov but directly to Molotov, going over Litvinov's head.

37   Anna Louise Strong, 'Stalin "The Voice of the Party" Breaks Trotsky: The Rubber-Stamp Secretary versus the Fiery Idealist', *Getaway*, December 1925, 18–24, available at marxists.org.

38   Strong and Keyssar, *Right in Her Soul*, 120.

39   Ibid., 126.

40   Ibid., 148.

41   Ibid., 152.

corrected by Stalin himself.[42] However, when colleagues on *Moscow News* began to disappear, she complained to Borodin, who insisted the purges were necessary to preserve iron unity; doubters must be eliminated for the sake of the greater good. It must have soon become clear to Strong that protesting, even in private, was simply too dangerous. In 1937, the paper's foreign editor, Rose Cohen, a former British suffragette, was arrested and secretly executed on trumped up-charges despite frantic lobbying by her former lover, CPGB general secretary Harry Pollitt.[43] Fortunately for Strong, she was able to leave the Soviet Union that year; she went first to Spain and then to China, where she met with Zhu De and other generals of the Eighth Route Army in Yan'an and, in Hankou, with Zhou Enlai, who made a point of lecturing her on the perils of Trotskyism. The result of this trip was her 1938 book *One-Fifth of Mankind*.

During the wartime alliance against Hitler, when portrayals of a benevolent 'Uncle Joe' were commonplace, and indeed welcomed in the United States, Strong stepped up her praise for Stalin to ludicrous levels. She compared his role in the Soviet government to that of a Democratic Party chairman and predicted that 'the legend of the inscrutable dictator will die. We may even come to hear Stalin spoken of, as a Soviet writer once described him, as "the world's great democrat." ' Stalin's secret, she wrote, was that he was a great listener. She quoted an anonymous 'Soviet citizen' who told her that '[Stalin] listens even to the way the grass grows' – comically misunderstanding what was undoubtedly her interlocutor's real meaning.[44] After Khrushchev's secret speech, in *The Stalin Era*, she both endorsed Stalin's paranoia and absolved him of guilt with the farcical thesis that the mass repression was carried out by Nazis who had 'penetrated high in the GPU and arrested the wrong people'.[45] She even blamed ordinary Russians since ' "the cult of personality", now blamed for all past evils, is a flaw in the worshipper no less than in the

---

42   Ibid., 160.

43   Pollitt knew Cohen had been arrested but did not find out she had been executed until twenty years later.

44   Anna Louise Strong, 'Stalin', in *The Soviets Expected It*, New York: The Dial Press, 1941, 46–64, available at marxists.org.

45   Anna Louise Strong, *The Stalin Era*, Altadena, CA: Today's Press, 1956, 68. Her evidence was a conversation with an 'exiled friend'.

worshipped'.[46] Stalin was, she admitted, ruthless; he 'condoned, and even authorized outrageous acts of the political police against innocent people', but insisted that there was 'no evidence . . . that he consciously framed them'.[47] Her overall conclusion, shared by many – not all of whom were apologists – was that only a Stalin could have built an industrial and military machine capable of defeating Hitler. The alternatives – her former idol Trotsky, or the 'Old Bolsheviks' – whom she once believed Stalin, the perfect party man, represented – would have 'led towards destruction'.[48]

Strong had escaped the Great Purges but was finally caught in the Stalinist net in 1949 amid the crisis over Titoism.[49] Someone with a lower public profile might have been liquidated, but Strong was a famous journalist and a bestselling author who had been a friend of the Roosevelts. Stalin merely deported her. Although he allowed her to leave unharmed, in February 1949, he ordered Mikoyan, who was in China negotiating with the CCP leadership, to inform Mao that Strong was a long-standing American spy.[50] Whether they believed him or not, the Chinese took no action.

It would have been easy for either side in the Cold War to concoct spying charges against Strong. She had extraordinary access to world leaders, one consequence of which was that she was used by the Soviets and the Americans to pass messages to each other. In January 1939, before attending an 'intimate family dinner' with the Roosevelts, she was briefed by Soviet representative Konstantin Umansky and reported back to him. President Roosevelt clearly knew that what he said would be reported to the Soviets, and he also expected to receive information from her.[51] In Stalin's paranoid imagination, anyone involved in such

---

46   Ibid., 126.

47   Ibid., 125.

48   Ibid., 126.

49   Borodin was arrested with her. See Appendix C: Decimation of the China Hands.

50   Letter from Joseph Stalin to Anastas Mikoyan, 4 February, 1949, available at nsarchive.gwu.edu/rus.

51   Diary of the chargé d'affaires of the USSR in the United States, K. A. Umansky, 30 January, 1939, in Documents of Foreign Policy of the USSR, Vol. 22. Umansky was appointed ambassador to the United States in May 1939 and was subsequently ambassador to Mexico, where he repaired relations after the assassination of Trotsky. He was killed in a plane crash in Mexico in 1945.

commonplace channels of communication could be acting for the Americans. On the American side, a similar logic applied during the McCarthyite period, and Strong's passport was confiscated. When it was returned to her in 1958, she seized the opportunity to get out of the reach of the FBI, moving to China, where she remained for the rest of her life, as the éminence grise of the foreign experts in Beijing's Friendship Hotel.

It was probably easier for Strong to switch her principal allegiance from the Soviet Union to China than it had been to abandon Trotsky for Stalin. Despite growing differences between China and the Soviets, when the split came it was Khrushchev, not Stalin, who was denounced by the Chinese side. It is unlikely that she was ever told of Stalin's specific accusations against her. She continued to write, faithfully supporting the Chinese line on all domestic and foreign issues. In her final years, she interviewed Mao three more times, but despite her appeals to the authorities, including a personal letter to Mao, none of the interviews were published in her lifetime.[52] When her death came, it was somewhat undignified; sensing that the end was near, she refused food and medication and pulled a drip from her arm. But Zhou Enlai, whether for political or personal reasons, ordered doctors try to revive her for more than two hours after her heart stopped. She was buried in the Babaoshan Revolutionary Cemetery.

52 Strong's notes from the interviews were eventually published in the *China Quarterly*, No. 103 (1985) in an article by her great-nephew Professor Tracy B. Strong and his wife, Helen Keyssar.

10

Gung Ho

Chinese Industrial Cooperatives (CIC) – also known as Indusco and, informally, as Gung Ho – is now a tiny organisation. It has a small office in Beijing and a couple of demonstration projects in western China. Its sister organisation, the International Committee for the Promotion of Chinese Industrial Cooperatives (ICCIC), is even smaller. Its current chairman is Michael Crook, son of Isabel and David Crook. Insofar as either organisation has a role, it is educational – preaching the benefits of cooperation within the boundaries permitted by the party. But during the War of Resistance against Japan, CIC oversaw the creation of around two thousand cooperatives in the unoccupied areas of the country. The Japanese army had conquered China's eastern cities and, with them, ninety per cent of China's industrial plant. Fifty million refugees, including many industrial workers, fled the invaders. Relocating industry, replacing lost production, and finding employment for the displaced and destitute were critical tasks.

CIC was an organisation born out of necessity. But, in the chaos of retreat, the initiative to create it was taken not by the Chinese government but by foreign sympathisers. In 1938, British consul John Alexander invited Edgar Snow and his wife, Helen Foster – also a journalist, who used the pen name Nym Wales – to a dinner party in Shanghai's International Settlement.[1] Alexander, who, perhaps oddly for a man in

---

1 Before Pearl Harbor, the International Settlement survived, although it was surrounded by the occupied Chinese part of Shanghai.

his position, was an enthusiast for cooperatives, talked at length about how they were 'the solution to the world's ills'. Snow and Foster, both Communist sympathisers, were sceptical that cooperatives could save China – an idea associated with Fabians and Christian Socialists like R. H. Tawney.[2] Foster was especially vehement, and Alexander let the subject drop. But within days, Foster had changed her mind and set about selling the idea with a convert's zeal.[3] One of those she browbeat was Rewi Alley, a New Zealander who had been working as a factory inspector for the Shanghai Municipal Authority. Alley was also initially sceptical, but, having been won over, he became the movement's most energetic and effective organiser. Edgar Snow saw Alley as an ideal public face for the CIC and promoted his image in pamphlets aimed at raising funds from overseas. In a journalistic flourish he wrote that 'where [T. E.] Lawrence brought to the Arabs the destructive technique of guerrilla war, Alley was to bring China the constructive technique of guerrilla industry'.

The year 1938 was the high point of the Second United Front, and the CIC's founders pitched it as an initiative that the KMT and the CCP could agree on. The KMT had been experimenting with credit cooperatives in the countryside for some time,[4] while the CIC would be politically neutral, seeking support from the Red Cross, the League of Nations, and the Chinese government. Funding was an immediate and pressing problem. At a preliminary meeting, Xu Xinliu, general manager of the National Commercial Bank, was elected chairman and later flew to Hong Kong to arrange a loan of 200,000 dollars.[5] John Alexander was elected secretary, but, for diplomatic reasons, his appointment was not

2   Some missionaries and charities advocated cooperatives as a solution to hunger and as a third way between capitalism and communism.

3   Helen Foster split from Edgar Snow in 1945. She returned to China in 1972 and 1978. There is a Helen Foster Snow Society in Beijing and a Helen Foster Snow wing in the Eighth Route Army Museum in Xi'an.

4   Ian Cook and Jenny Clegg, 'Shared Visions of Co-operation at a Time of Crisis: The Gung Ho Story in China's Anti-Japanese Resistance', in Anthony Webster, The Hidden Alternative: Cooperative Values, Past Present and Future, Tokyo: United Nations University Press, 2012, 327–346, 330, available at un-ilibrary.org.

5   Xu was killed on his way back when Japanese fighters forced his civilian aircraft down and repeatedly strafed it, killing almost everyone on board. It was the first time in history that a commercial airliner was deliberately shot down. The intended target was probably Sun Yat-sen's son Sun Fo, who had taken another flight.

made public. Behind the scenes, his boss, the British ambassador Archibald Clark-Kerr, who was known as a maverick, lobbied Song Meiling – Madame Chiang Kai-shek – on behalf of the plan.[6] The United States was also sympathetic, and Snow and Foster were invited to the White House. Eleanor Roosevelt joined the board of the CIC's American support committee. In China, the backing of the Song sisters was crucial. That of Song Qingling was a given, and with Song Meiling and Song Ailing (married to China's richest man, H. H. Kung) on board, success was assured. The Chinese government allotted 2 million dollars to CIC, which was formally launched on 5 August 1938, with H. H. Kung as chairman and Rewi Alley as chief advisor. Government funding never covered CIC's expenses and, in 1939, Song Qingling set up an International Committee to raise money from overseas. Based in Hong Kong, with the 'pink bishop' Ronald Owen Hall as chairman, the ICCIC raised 5 million dollars.[7]

For the next several years, Alley travelled throughout China as the movement's principal animateur, educating, advocating, cajoling, and then establishing and inspecting cooperatives. CIC established its first cooperative – of seven blacksmiths – in Shaanxi province. At its peak in 1941, there were 1,857 CIC cooperatives employing around 30,000 people – with, it was claimed, a quarter of a million others associated with and benefiting from them.[8] One of their main products was textiles – including, importantly, blankets and uniforms for the army. Metalworking shops also produced weapons. Not all the coops were genuine; some were fig leaves for commercial firms run by local gentry who were not above hoarding commodities – especially fuel – and price gouging. Alley scorned them as 'kerosene coops'. One could argue that employing 30,000 workers in a country of 400 million was a drop in the ocean. However, the impact of the CIC was not only economic but also educational and cultural; in particular, it championed women's rights and set up women's cooperatives.

---

6   At this time, only the Soviet Union was sending military aid to China. The British government was under pressure at home to offer some sort of support and speaking up for the CIC was a cost-free gesture.

7   Ronald Owen Hall championed workers' causes and ordained the world's first woman priest in the Anglican Church. During the Cold War he was predictably targeted by right-wingers as a dupe of the Communists.

8   Cook and Clegg, 'Shared Visions of Co-operation', 334.

   Rewi Alley was, in some respects, an unlikely radical. He was awarded
the Military Medal for bravery on the Western Front. His elder brother
Eric was wounded at Gallipoli, returned to his regiment, and subsequently killed in action in France. Another brother, Geoff, played for the
All Blacks national rugby team. When Rewi moved to China in 1927,
having failed as a farmer in New Zealand, he planned to sign up as a
mercenary in China's civil wars, without a clear idea of which army he
would join. Arriving too late to join the fighting, he instead enlisted in
the Shanghai Municipal Fire Service. Even as leftists were being rounded
up and killed throughout China, there is no indication that Alley
objected. He was a stereotype of New Zealand athletic masculinity,
wearing shorts in all weathers and cracking walnuts with his fingers. But
there was a reason he would never fit in to New Zealand society of the
time: Alley was gay. His friend Courtney Archer suggested that Alley
moved to China because his first sexual experience might have been
with a member of the Chinese labour battalions in France.[9] Shanghai
was huge, anonymous, and had the advantage of being far from his
family, to whom Alley never revealed his sexuality. China, relatively
untouched by the Abrahamic religions, had traditionally been more
tolerant of homosexuality, and among the privileged foreigners, laissez-
faire attitudes were commonplace. In Shanghai, Alley was able to share
a house with another gay man, Alec Camplin, without attracting unwel-
come attention.
   Alley might easily have followed the foreign crowd into a nihilistic
lifestyle. After all, Shanghai's nightlife offered endless amusement,
including cheap and easily available sex to suit most tastes. Instead, he
studied Chinese, translated poetry, and collected antiquities. He might
also have led a quiet life as an aesthete had he been indifferent to the
poverty surrounding him. But, during the great famine of 1928–30, he
took leave from his job to help with relief work and adopted two orphans.
His job in the Fire Service included carrying out safety inspections of
Shanghai's sweatshops, and he later left to become a full-time factory
inspector. He saw not only extreme poverty but also savage exploitation
on a daily basis – problems that required a political solution. After
witnessing the KMT execute a group of young men who had tried to

---

   9   Anne-Marie Brady, *Friend of China: The Myth of Rewi Alley*. London and New
York: Routledge. 2003, 12–13. Archer said Alley dropped a hint that this was the case.

organise silk workers in Wuxi, he gave up on the idea of reform.[10] He joined the left-wing circle around Song Qingling and began helping out with the Comintern's clandestine activities.

The English term 'gung ho' originated as a contraction of CIC's Chinese name, Gongye Hezuoshe. It made its way into the English language thanks to one of the CCP's unlikeliest supporters – the US marine general Evans Carlson. Carlson became a wartime hero in the United States when, as a lieutenant colonel, he led his eponymous Raider battalion on a lightning raid that wiped out the Japanese garrison on Makin Island.[11] One of the United States' first successes in the Pacific war, it was dramatised in the 1943 Hollywood movie *Gung Ho*, starring Randolph Scott as Carlson.[12] Carlson attributed his victory to building an esprit de corps using what he called 'ethical indoctrination' – a method he adapted from the training programmes of the Eighth Route Army.

When he arrived in China for the first time in 1928, Carlson was a conventional army officer who thought it was necessary 'to teach these Chinese a lesson [otherwise they will] lose their respect for foreigners'.[13] After being transferred to intelligence work, he nuanced his views and made friends with Edgar Snow, but when he left China it was to fight a counterinsurgency campaign against Augusto Sandino in Nicaragua. This exposure to guerrilla warfare was the first time he saw action; although it taught him tactical lessons, his political views remained unchanged. When he returned to China as an intelligence officer in 1933, he was sent to Beiping, where he resumed his friendship with Edgar Snow. He was recalled to the United States in 1935 to serve in Roosevelt's guard unit, and when he was subsequently reassigned to China, he kept up a regular correspondence with the president.

Carlson and Snow observed the 1937 Battle of Shanghai from a water

10   Rewi Alley, *Yo Banfa! (We Have a Way)*, Shanghai: China Monthly Review, 1952, 15.

11   Carlson's Raiders was one of four Marine Raider battalions, early special forces units, formed in 1942. The Makin Island raid was not a complete success. One of its objectives was to take prisoners, but the Marines killed all the Japanese they encountered.

12   For security reasons, Carlson's character was renamed Thorwald, but Carlson was drafted in as an advisor to the production. At the time of writing, the movie was available on YouTube.

13   Michael Blankfort, *The Big Yankee: The Life of Carlson of the Raiders*, n.p.: Pickle Partners Publishing, 2015 [1947], 211–12.

tower in the French Concession.[14] On this conflict, they had no political differences. Although the United States was officially neutral, Carlson was firmly on the side of the Chinese. After discussions with Snow, and reading *Red Star over China*, he persuaded his boss in naval intelligence, Harvey Overesch,[15] to send him to the Eighth Route Army headquarters in Yan'an as a military observer. Snow gave him a letter of introduction to Mao Zedong.

In December 1937, Carlson began the first of two trips to northern China to observe the operations of the Eighth Route Army.[16] He was greeted by Zhu De, who he described reverentially as an amalgam of Robert E. Lee, Abraham Lincoln, and Ulysses S. Grant.[17] Zhu told him the CCP's guerrilla strategy against the heavily armed but overstretched Japanese forces was akin to hornets harassing an elephant.[18] Carlson also met 'gallant' Agnes Smedley, who initially dismissed him as a spy before becoming his close friend. Smedley urged him to see for himself the 'pure democracy' practised by the Border Region governments.[19] He was allowed to accompany a troop to the headquarters of Nie Rongzhen, military commander of the Shanxi-Chahar-Hebei region. Carlson was impressed by the pace of the march – faster than anything that could be accomplished by Western armies – and by an attack en route that killed fifteen Japanese cavalrymen.[20]

Nie Rongzhen's government held village and county elections, set up cooperatives, and banned opium smoking for the under-50s. Carlson saw it as 'a population of between ten and fifteen million who were conducting a gigantic experiment in cooperative living'.[21] He got on famously with Nie – a 'rascal' who took him to banquets six times a day.

14   According to Snow, Carlson climbed the ladder to the tower in full view of Japanese troops. The *Daily Telegraph* correspondent Philip Pembroke Stephens, who also climbed the tower, was killed by machine gun fire.

15   In the early 1950s, Overesch headed the CIA in East Asia.

16   On his way, Carlson met Soviet pilots and mechanics in a guesthouse in Xi'an. See Evans Carlson, *Twin Stars of China*, New York: Dodd & Mead, 1940, 56, available at Hathi Trust Digital Library: babel.hathitrust.org.

Some scholars have claimed that 'recent research' revealed the extent of Soviet aid to China during the War of Resistance. In fact, it was an open secret at the time.

17   Ibid., 66.

18   Ibid., 76, 101–2.

19   Ibid., 68, 74.

20   Ibid., 104.

21   Ibid., 224.

Writing for an American audience, Carlson compared Eighth Route Army commanders to familiar heroes – He Long was a swashbuckler with a social conscience, a Chinese Robin Hood – although his choice of hero was sometimes odd. He compared Xu Haidong to Nathan Bedford Forest, a Confederate general who massacred black Union soldiers and was the first grand wizard of the Ku Klux Klan.[22] By comparison with CCP commanders, the Shanxi warlord Yan Xishan was 'more of a merchant than a general', a tired old man whose benevolent intentions were frustrated by a corrupt bureaucracy.[23] His troops 'lacked the spirit and discipline' of the Eighth Route Army; their 'faces were listless and their feet dragged'.[24] Yan's subordinate Bo Yibo was a 'paternal autocrat'.[25] In fact, Bo, the father of Bo Xilai, was, unknown to Carlson, an undercover Communist.

When Carlson, on his second trip, finally met Mao Zedong, he was overwhelmed. 'Kindly eyes regarded me thoughtfully from a face that suggested the dreamer' . . . 'the man whose mind had provided the foundation for China's modern liberal thought'.[26] Mao assured him that Communism was a distant goal for the CCP and that he wanted to enter a post-war coalition government with the KMT. Mao was, Carlson wrote, a 'humble, kindly, lonely genius'.[27] The area of northern China controlled by the Border Region governments was, 'in its political aspects, close to being a pure democracy, while in its social and economic aspects it approaches the cooperative effort urged by Jesus of Nazareth'.[28]

Carlson came from a religious family – his father was a minister – and although he ran away from home in his teens to join the army, he remained a believer, albeit unorthodox, all his life. He was 'so impressed by the similarity between the doctrines being practised by the Eighth Route army and the people and the doctrines of Christ' that he took a New Testament with him on his second trip.[29] His writings seem extravagant, even risible today, but they were not out of step with the wartime

---

22   Ibid., 113, 118.
23   Ibid., 125.
24   Ibid., 120.
25   Ibid., 92.
26   Ibid., 167.
27   Ibid., 171.
28   Ibid., 231.
29   Ibid., 176.

propaganda of the epoch – in this case intended to draw the United States into a war it had not yet joined. To be fair to Carlson, the Red Army guerrillas, like the early Christians, were ideologues who preached equality and lived in poverty – although others, Helen Foster for example, preferred to compare them to the Spartans.

Carlson was also writing – in line with CCP policy – in the spirit of the United Front. After meeting Chiang Kai-shek and Song Meiling, he described Chiang Kai-shek as a sincere Christian who displayed 'intelligence, loyalty and stubborn determination', while Madame Chiang was 'an instrument of destiny' in the service of her people'.[30] After observing the Battle of Taierzhuang, China's first significant victory over the Japanese, he lauded the KMT general Li Zongren as a soldier whose commitment and integrity approached that of the Eighth Route Army commanders.[31] The Chinese artillery outgunned the Japanese, and Russian planes provided air support, but it was the fighting spirit Li Zongren inspired in his troops – another example of 'ethical indoctrination' – that was decisive.

Back in Hankou, Carlson was one of the self-styled 'Last Ditchers', along with famed photographer Robert Capa, Agnes Smedley, Freda Utley, and others. It was in Hankou that he met Rewi Alley and praised his 'phenomenal energy'. After Wuhan fell, Carlson resigned his commission to give himself the freedom to plead the Chinese cause in the United States. His book *Twin Stars of China* concluded with a flourish about Chiang Kai-shek's 'experience . . . devotion to the nation and . . . personal integrity' and the Communist Party's 'brilliant, self-effacing leaders', and how the CCP and KMT were united around 'the objectives set for the nation by the late Doctor Sun Yat-sen'.[32] It was an illusion. The border-region governments were in theory subordinate to the central government but in practice independent. As such, the formal integration of the Red Army into the government forces was no more than a rebadging

---

30   Ibid., 130. Carlson confessed that he found Chiang Kai-shek's Christianity hard to reconcile with his slaughter of Communists in 1927.

31   Li Zongren was a Nationalist general from southwest China who led successful campaigns during the Northern Expedition. After falling out with Chiang Kai-shek, he was recalled to service in 1937 and defeated the Japanese at the Battle of Taierzhuang. He was briefly vice-president of China in 1949 before going into exile. In 1965, he unexpectedly reconciled with the CCP and returned to mainland China.

32   Carlson, *Twin Stars of China*, 304.

exercise. If Chiang Kai-shek could not tolerate the existence of a rival army, the CCP leadership could not survive without it. (Chiang later told the American mediator General George C. Marshall that asking the Communists to disarm would be like negotiating with a tiger for its skin.) Within a year of the publication of *Twin Stars*, the New Fourth Army Incident, when Nationalist troops inflicted heavy casualties on the Communist-led New Fourth Army, effectively ended the United Front.[33]

One consequence of the collapse of the United Front was that Rewi Alley lost his job as chief advisor to the CIC. He turned to teaching, becoming deputy head, then headmaster of the Bailie School in Shandan. The school, named after the Protestant missionary turned agricultural reformer Joseph Bailie, had been established by George Hogg as an orphanage associated with CIC.[34] After Hogg tragically died in 1945 after a minor cut turned septic, Alley took over as headmaster and remained in charge until moving to Beijing in 1952.[35] The school was financed by foreign donations, initially from UNNRA and later from the New Zealand aid agency CORSO, some of whose grants were discreetly provided by the New Zealand government.[36] After 1949, the school's foreign funding and its missionary tag made it doubly suspect. Alley was criticised during the Three Antis (*sanfan*) Campaign,[37] and, in 1952, the school was transferred to Lanzhou and placed under the control of the Oil Ministry. While Alley lost his direct involvement, he retained the honorary title of headmaster and retained a strong family connection as one of his adopted sons became the real headmaster and the other worked for the Oil Ministry.

---

33   Carlson died of heart failure in 1947. Had he lived he would almost certainly have been witch-hunted during the McCarthy era.

34   Joseph Bailie (1860–1935) was born on a farm in Ireland, moved to the United States, and went to China as a Protestant missionary in 1890. He resigned the ministry after witnessing famine and thereafter devoted himself to land-reform schemes to aid landless peasants, with support from Sun Yat-sen, Henry Ford, and others. He also set up a College of Agriculture and Forestry in Nanjing.

35   After arriving in China in 1938, George Hogg helped smuggle medicines to Communist guerrillas and befriended Nie Rongzhen. He relocated the Bailie school to save the orphans from conscription into the KMT armies. He died of tetanus in 1945. A 2008 feature film, *The Children of Huang Shi*, recounts his trek across China with the orphans.

36   Brady, *Friend of China*, 43.

37   The 1951 Three Antis campaign was directed against corruption, waste and bureaucracy.

Alley lived comfortably in Beijing, collecting antiques and writing poetry and pro-China propaganda; his most famous book was *Yo Banfa*, a paean to the can-do spirit of New China. By bending with the wind of political campaigns and toeing the line in public statements, he managed to steer clear of serious trouble. During the Cultural Revolution, while some foreigners joined one faction or another, Alley stayed out of the fray and advised others to do the same. As a result, he escaped comparatively unscathed, despite ultra-nationalist radicals denouncing CIC as an imperialist plot. He was stripped of his honorary headship of the Bailie school, but it was given back in 1977, when both the school and CIC were officially rehabilitated. In the 1980s, both the CIC and ICCIC were revived as organisations.

Alley's work in China and his writings were known in New Zealand, albeit to a relatively small group, through the medium of the New Zealand China Friendship Society. During the period of reform and opening up, as China sought to improve relations with New Zealand, he became a symbol of friendship and was hailed as a 'bridge builder' in official statements by both sides. In 1985, two years before Alley died, Labour prime minister David Lange made him a companion of the Queen's Service Order, calling him one of New Zealand's greatest sons. In both countries, the image of a dynamic, practical humanitarian who had no discernible personal life prevailed until the publication, in 2003, of a critical biography by the New Zealand academic Anne Marie Brady. Although it was an open secret in China that Alley was gay,[38] Brady was the first to discuss his sexuality in print and did so, to some extent, sympathetically. It was, she wrote, understandable that a gay man sought refuge from New Zealand's 'hypermasculine' society and never came out to his family. She absolved Alley of charges of paedophilia spread by New Zealand diplomats but claimed it was 'undeniable' that he slept with his older students.[39] Elsewhere, Brady is less sympathetic. She suggests Alley was a kind of white saviour, citing Edgar Snow's comparison with Lawrence of Arabia, the archetypal 'Orientalist-as-agent'. But Snow was consciously manipulating his American audience's prejudices rather than expressing his own. He said as much in a letter to a Chinese

---

38   According to Isabel Crook, 'everybody knew Rewi was gay'. Isabel Crook, conversation with the author.

39   Brady *Friend of China*, 44, 133.

nationalist, as Brady reports.[40] Understood this way, Brady's charge that Snow saw Alley as someone who 'could help China in a way that no Chinese was capable of', misses the mark. It is simply not credible that either Snow or Alley believed the Chinese required foreign saviours. Brady is on stronger ground when detailing the personal and political compromises Alley made to stay safe in the People's Republic. The treatment of gay men by the puritan new order was at times harsher than back home in New Zealand.[41] In his old age, Alley was troubled by guilt for having acquiesced in the repression of comrades and friends. But Brady's characterisation of Alley's decision to remain in China after 1949 as a Faustian choice is not quite accurate. Although Alley may have privately described Mao as a 'prick', he remained absolutely loyal to the People's Republic and would never have agreed that the devil dwelt in Beijing.

40   Ibid., 33.
41   However, homosexuality was not decriminalised in New Zealand until 1986.

11

A Lord and a Bold Lady

Roosevelt's special envoy to Chiang Kai-shek, Patrick Hurley, the 'strange old man' who engineered General Joseph Stilwell's recall from China, believed all sorts of KMT propaganda.[1] He thought the Eighth Route Army's commander-in-chief, Zhu De, had agreed to a truce with the Japanese in return for supplies of radio equipment. But the truth was even stranger than that particular fiction. In fact, the Eighth Route Army's radio network was built by a young British university professor, Michael Lindsay, who later sat in Britain's House of Lords. While working at Yanjing University in Beiping, Lindsay smuggled radios to the Communist guerrillas who controlled the countryside west of the city. A tweedy, pipe-smoking Scot in the Richard Hannay mould, Lindsay's exploits had a *Boys' Own* quality. Bluffing his way through Japanese checkpoints with a pistol at the ready, he ferried resistance agents around Beiping on the back of his motorcycle. After the United States and Britain declared war on Japan in December 1941, Lindsay, accompanied by his Chinese wife and their young children, spent four years as the Eighth Route Army's chief radio technician.

Lindsay arrived in China in 1937 on the same ship as Norman Bethune. Yanjing's principal, the missionary and future United States

---

1 'Strange old man' was Harold Isaacs' description of Hurley. 'Eccentric' would not do justice to the man, a flamboyant Irish American and overconfident amateur diplomat.

ambassador to China John Leighton Stuart, had hired him on the recommendation of his father, the educational reformer Sandie Lindsay.[2]
Lindsay junior had recently graduated from Oxford, where his father
was master of Balliol College. To help Stuart wean his Chinese students
away from their attachment to traditional rote learning, he set up a tuto-
rial system. He also recreated an Oxford atmosphere at Yanjing by laying
on formal dinners with waiter service for his students.[3] When his
father died in 1952, Lindsay inherited his title, becoming Baron Lindsay
of Birker. His wife, Li Xiaoli, who had been one of his students, became
Lady Lindsay – a rare, possibly unique Chinese member of the British
aristocracy.

Beiping was occupied by the Japanese, but, until Pearl Harbor, Yanjing
University was able to continue functioning as a semi-autonomous
institution. Stuart cultivated the fig-leaf government of collaborator
Wang Kemin to keep Japanese interference to a minimum. He did not
permit overt political activity on campus but turned a blind eye to and
even encouraged underground activity. The university was in the northwest suburb of Haidian, not far from countryside controlled by
Communist guerrillas, and it became a haven for the resistance. Lindsay,
like Stuart, sympathised with the Chinese. In 1938, with two colleagues,
he twice bicycled across the Japanese lines near Baoding into territory
controlled by the Communist general, Lu Zhengcao.[4] Lu welcomed the
foreigners with brass bands and parades. On the second trip, they
reached the headquarters of the regional commander, General Nie
Rongzhen, where Lindsay met Norman Bethune again. They were
invited to observe a guerrilla attack on a railway line and came under
fire after stumbling into a Japanese patrol. In the 1939 summer vacation,
Lindsay and the seismologist Ralph Lapwood were trapped by floods in
guerrilla territory. It was November by the time Lindsay got back to
Yanjing University, by air, via Xi'an, Chongqing, and Hong Kong.

Desperately short of supplies, the guerrillas were only lightly armed,
and Lindsay saw it as his duty to assist them. Using his status as a neutral,
he could pass through Japanese checkpoints with relative ease. He used

2   Sandie Lindsay was ennobled by Clement Attlee in 1945.
3   Alfred Kuo-liang Ho, *China's Reforms and Reformers*, Westport: Praeger, 2004,
47.
4   Lu Zhengcao was a former aide to the 'young marshall' Zhang Xueliang. He
joined the Communist Party after the Xi'an Incident.

picnicking or sightseeing trips as pretexts to smuggle medicine. Having discovered the guerrillas lacked reliable radios, he began building sets from parts bought by mail order from Hong Kong and Shanghai. Sometimes he rode his motorbike; Stuart lent him his car for bulkier loads.

Like Lindsay, Li Xiaoli came from a well-to-do background, and her extended family included rich landowners and merchants. Her father, Li Wenxi, was a cavalry officer in the army of the Shanxi warlord Yan Xishan and rose to become head of a military school. Li Wenxi was relatively enlightened. He took part in the 1911–12 Xinhai Revolution, sent his daughters to school, and refused to let their feet be bound. While in high school, Li Xiaoli, like many of her contemporaries, bobbed her hair and got involved in radical politics. She did enough to attract the attention of the authorities, but her father packed her off to school in Beiping before she could be arrested. At Yanjing University, she joined Lindsay's class and began helping him translate labels on the medicine he was delivering to the guerrillas. She soon progressed from translating to accompanying Lindsay on his smuggling trips, riding pillion on his motorbike. Sometimes Japanese soldiers would make desultory attempts to pursue them on their slower bikes, and Lindsay would wave nonchalantly as he left them behind. Li Xiaoli fell in love with her derring-do teacher. When John Leighton Stuart married them in the university chapel, Li Wenxi came to the wedding to give his daughter away.

Lindsay converted a room in their apartment into a workshop and often worked through the night building radio sets for the guerrillas. Ever resourceful, he disconnected the workshop from the local electricity supply and connected it to the more reliable Beiping grid. In addition to his radio building, he carried out clandestine liaison tasks. He smuggled General Nie Rongzhen's head of intelligence into Beijing on his motorbike. Lindsay saw himself as a freelance British agent and took the opportunity to send a message to Nie, asking him if he would host a British military intelligence unit. According to Lindsay, Nie was happy to do so, but the British failed to follow it up. The Americans were more willing to cooperate. Stuart introduced the Lindsays to the US military attaché David Barrett and the Office of Strategic Services (OSS)[5] officer Charlie Stelle, both of whom later took part in the Dixie Mission to

5   The Office of Strategic Services was the forerunner of the CIA.

initiate military cooperation with the Communist forces in Yan'an. Between them, they hatched a plan to move Eighth Route Army radio equipment out of the British Concession in Tianjin before it was occupied by the Japanese. American Marines moved the radios to the US legation building, and Lindsay picked them up from there using Stuart's car. He and Li Xiaoli then drove them past Japanese checkpoints to the guerrillas in two trips. On the second trip, Li Xiaoli, sitting in the front seat, had a radio in virtually plain sight under her feet. They were beginning to take risks, in this case for little gain, as the radios were of such poor quality that they were only useful for spare parts.

During the autumn Moon Festival in 1941, Lindsay, Li Xiaoli, two other Yanjing professors, and a Chinese agent drove another delivery through Japanese checkpoints. They planned to tell the sentries they were going to celebrate the festival at a nearby temple. By this time, the situation was tense, and both Michael and the agent were carrying pistols, ready to shoot their way through if necessary. They passed a checkpoint without stopping because they saw no sentries but were called back, and a Japanese officer slapped the Chinese agent in the face. Somehow, they managed to talk their way out of the confrontation. They rendezvoused with the guerrillas and handed over the equipment, plus some mooncakes, then spent a nervous few hours at the temple to back up their cover story. Puppet troops searched their car on the way back but missed propaganda pamphlets the guerrillas had given them. The risks they were taking were becoming unacceptable. In any case, when war broke out with the allies, they knew they would be interned as enemy aliens. They prepared to flee to the guerrilla area.

With war between Japan and the United States imminent, Stuart called a staff meeting to explain that the only way to avoid internment was to leave for the guerrilla area. Most of the staff opted to stay in Beiping. On 8 December, when they heard on the radio that Japan and the United States were at war, the Lindsays scrambled to escape in Stuart's car. Only physics professor William Band and his wife Claire were ready in time to go with them. Michael was armed with a pistol and two revolvers given to him by a Chinese agent. As they sped off campus just ten minutes before the secret police arrived, he had his pistol drawn. It seems William Band was not impressed. His memoirs hint strongly that he viewed Lindsay as a daredevil who took risks without consulting or considering his companions.

John Leighton Stuart and the rest of the staff were interned until the end of the war. When Stuart left China after serving as ambassador, Mao Zedong wrote a scathing mock farewell accusing him of deceiving the Chinese people by pretending to love both China and the United States.[6] But, in Lindsay's account, Stuart comes across as an honourable man who stood by China against the Japanese and allowed his university to become a rendezvous point for Eighth Route Army agents. It is a view shared by many otherwise entirely loyal old friends of China.[7]

After escaping from Beiping, the Lindsays' first objective was to reach the headquarters of General Xiao Ke, commander of the Pingxi[8] military district. A guerrilla detachment led them in pitch darkness along narrow cliffside paths past Japanese blockhouses to a secure village. They trekked for three weeks, travelling at night in complete silence, resting in villages when they could. Everywhere, they found evidence of brutal punitive operations by the occupiers. In one village, the women had smeared themselves with faeces in a desperate attempt to avoid being raped by Japanese raiders. At Christmas, a family slaughtered a pig for them rather than let the Japanese steal it. Several times, they narrowly avoided Japanese patrols. On one occasion, they left a village minutes before a Japanese attack in which several civilians were killed. They escaped only because Li Xiaoli had thrown away a cup of boiled water that was too hot to drink.

The Lindsays spent most of January and February 1942 at Xiao Ke's headquarters. A veteran of the Northern Expedition, the Nanchang Uprising, and the Long March, Xiao was still only in his early thirties. He and Lindsay had much in common. They were young, idealistic but pragmatic, well educated, and cultured. Lindsay joined Xiao as he played volleyball with his troops, and Xiao loaned his fourteen-year-old servant, Tu Hongyou, to the Lindsays. Tu was one of the so-called little devils of the Eighth Route Army. He had joined the army at the age of twelve but was not yet allowed to fight.[9]

*   *   *

6   Mao Zedong, 'Farewell, Leighton Stuart!' 18 August 1949, available at marxists. org.

7   Isabel Crook, for example, petitioned the leadership to commemorate Stuart.

8   i.e., west of Beiping.

9   In June 1989, Xiao Ke was one of a handful of retired generals who opposed using force to disperse the demonstrators.

In May 1942, the Lindsays reached the regional headquarters of the Jin-Cha-Ji Border Region government which controlled an area with a population of around 25 million in the provinces of Shanxi, Chahar, and Hebei.[10] General Nie Rongzhen, the regional army commander, made Lindsay his chief wireless technology advisor. Lindsay established a training programme for radio technicians, and, under his direction, the entire region's radio equipment was systematically upgraded. The army's existing radio sets were bulky and faulty. The new sets built under Michael's direction were compact, easy to carry, and much more reliable. Some components were taken from captured Japanese radios, but most were bought at inflated prices from Chinese merchants who smuggled them from the Japanese-occupied cities.[11]

The war in the region had settled into a standoff. The Japanese controlled the railway lines, cities, and main towns, while the guerrillas controlled the villages. The Japanese strategy was to build networks of blockhouses to gradually extend their control into the countryside, but a lack of manpower meant many blockhouses were manned by poorly motivated puppet troops, who often came to local understandings with the guerrillas. The peasants supported the guerrillas and provided intelligence on enemy troop movements. Japanese intelligence was, by contrast, poor. Their agents were few and unreliable, and their knowledge of guerrilla movements and base locations was faulty or out of date. Village heads, ostensibly in their pay, were often double agents working for the Eighth Route Army.

In Lindsay's view, the regional government functioned well with minimal bureaucracy. Supplies were delivered efficiently, even during Japanese offensives. In the simple rural economy, people were paid in kind – in grain, clothing, and so on. Cash wages, where they existed, were pocket money to be spent on luxuries, so inflation never became the problem it was in the KMT areas. Troops paid for grain with certificates that the peasants could use to pay taxes, whereas previously they had to physically deliver grain to depots. To peasants used to the

---

10   Jin, Cha, and Ji are Chinese abbreviations for Shanxi, Chahar, and Hebei Provinces. Chahar Province was abolished in 1952. Most of its former territory is now part of Inner Mongolia. The Jin-Cha-Ji Border Region government was nominally subordinate to the KMT during the war against Japan.

11   This underground trade was perhaps the source of Hurley's radios-for-truce canard.

exactions of petty officials for personal gain, it was a fairer system. Of
course, the Lindsays lived privileged lives. Lindsay was a key military
asset, and he and Li Xiaoli were provided with the best rations,
comfortable housing, and servants. Military escorts accompanied
them when they travelled. They became close friends with Nie
Rongzhen.[12]

Even for the relatively privileged, life was hard and danger never far
away. Around this time, Li Xiaoli discovered she was pregnant. One
day, already several months pregnant, she was washing clothes in the
river when a Japanese plane attacked. Michael rushed her to shelter in
a nearby cave. Eight people were killed, including two of the women
who had been washing clothes. When Li Xiaoli was eight months pregnant, she was told the baby was in the wrong position and was sent to a
medical centre some miles away, where there were doctors qualified to
deal with a breech birth. But when they arrived, the centre was attacked
by a Japanese patrol, and she was carried up a mountain on a stretcher
until they reached a place too steep for the stretcher to pass. She was
forced to climb on foot over a peak called the King of Hell's nose to a
remote hamlet. On 15 October, a small and delicate female doctor
arrived, and Xiaoli gave birth to a girl. They named her Erica, after
Michael's mother.

Medical provision was primitive. It is an indication of the extent to
which the guerrillas were forced to improvise that Jiang Yizhen, head of
the army medical service, had no formal medical training. Jiang, who
became a close friend of the Lindsays, had joined the army at the age of
thirteen and was trained on the job, latterly by Norman Bethune. Despite
having no qualifications, he was considered the best surgeon in the area.
He was a Communist, but an independent thinker who refused to
blindly follow the party line. For example, he persuaded the leaders to
buy quinine to treat malaria instead of following the dogma of using
locally produced Chinese medicine. After the war, Jiang gave up practising medicine and worked as an agricultural official.

Lindsay spent most of 1943 replacing the radio equipment in the
frontline area and training technicians. Li Xiaoli was busy with the baby
but found the time to teach English and raise chickens. They were

---

12   Nie Rongzhen was later named one of the ten marshalls of the PRC and
commanded its nuclear weapons programme.

relatively safe, but there was always the threat of bombing raids. Xiaoli remembers shielding baby Erica under a rock as a bomber circled above and panicked bathers ran naked from the river to seek shelter.

In May 1943, a Frenchman and a Swede called Soderbom arrived at the base. Lindsay was still trying to persuade British intelligence to send agents to work with the Communists and gave Soderbom a letter to pass on when he left. When Soderbom got to Xi'an, the KMT found the letter and beat him up. Two White Russians, one of whom pretended to be British even though he could scarcely speak English, fared much worse. When the Japanese launched an offensive in September 1943, the guerrillas, suspecting they might be spies, shot them.

The offensive lasted two and a half months. The Lindsays fled with a group of young women from the drama group to a village called Mu Chang. They remained there for several weeks, and Lindsay was able to resume his training program for radio technicians. But, in November, the Japanese made a surprise attack on Mu Chang, and they abandoned their baggage and fled. A unit that covered their retreat lost ten of its twelve men in a firefight with Japanese cavalry. The Lindsays stumbled in pitch darkness along a dangerous path to a small village nearby. Wolves prowled along a nearby ridge as they walked through the snow. The next morning, that village was also attacked, and as they scrambled to escape, they left behind a radio instruction book. When the Japanese found it, they beat the village head to death. Another guerrilla unit that came to rescue the Lindsays and their companions was ambushed; its commander's wife and child were killed.

When they were finally able to return to the old central headquarters, they found it devastated. Their former neighbour Mrs Zheng was lying in bed, ill and emaciated. Her husband had been killed trying to escape, and her baby daughter had died of starvation. But, when Lindsays found the new headquarters, they were reunited with belongings they thought they had lost forever – including their diaries and photographs.

By early 1944, Lindsay decided he had done all he could in the Jin-Cha-Ji Border Region, having rebuilt all the radio sets and trained a team of radio engineers. He asked to be transferred to the Communist stronghold of Yan'an where, still hoping to involve British intelligence, he planned to ask the allies to supply the Eighth Route Army with heavy weapons in return for intelligence.

They travelled in a 400-strong party including a military escort led by a Captain Li,[13] a very able but strict officer. When they crossed a snow-covered mountain, he refused all requests to rest, so as to avoid hypothermia. Li Xiaoli nearly fell off her mule down a ravine and had to take benzedrine to stay awake. Captain Li outwitted the Japanese several times by taking his party through areas close to garrisons, where they were least expected. The Japanese had been tipped off about the presence of this large group but spent freezing nights on mountainsides waiting for them in the wrong places. They crossed the Taiyuan-Datong railway line under the noses of the Japanese, so close to the town of Ningwu that they were blinded by the headlamps of a train standing in the station.

They arrived in Yan'an in May 1944 and were greeted by Zhu De, who asked Michael to work on radio communications. Michael said the priority should be to build a radio station capable of transmitting to America so as to break the KMT's monopoly of propaganda and get Yan'an's message across to the outside world. He carried out his plan with his characteristic ingenuity. After working out the direction of San Francisco using spherical trigonometry mugged up from a textbook he found lying around, he laid a directional antenna across a valley. He borrowed a theodolite to position the posts to hold the antenna wires and powered the radio with an old truck engine.

While Michael was working on his long-range radio, Yan'an's isolation was ended by the arrival of a group of foreign correspondents. Yan'an was hurriedly decked out with United Front propaganda and portraits of Sun Yat-sen and Chiang Kai-shek for the arrival of the journalists. Lindsay already knew Gunther Stein of the *Guardian*, Jimmy Wei of the Chongqing press agency, and Israel Epstein, who later became a fixture in Communist China's media. He impressed on Zhu De, Zhou Enlai, and others that they should seize the opportunity to get their message across. One jaundiced correspondent remembered Lindsay as ubiquitous, well connected, and a great booster of the leadership. But, in part because of his efforts, the journalists left with a favourable impression of Yan'an.

The Dixie Mission arrived in Yan'an soon afterwards, on 2 July 1944. The Lindsays already knew its leader, Colonel David Barrett from their

---

13   Perhaps Liu. Michael Lindsay wrote the commander's name as Liu; Li Xiaoli wrote it as Li.

Yanjing days. Barrett was an old China hand who spoke the language fluently, and given that Mao and the other Communist leaders were eager to welcome the Americans, a honeymoon period followed. The Americans brought luxuries like colour magazines and chocolate. In the evenings, the GIs danced with young women, and George Hatem organised parties where the drink flowed freely. Americans and Chinese went pheasant hunting together. An English-language school was opened alongside the existing Russian and French schools, and Li Xiaoli was hired as a teacher.

Lindsay proposed to the Americans to exchange regular weather reports – essential for the US Air Force – in exchange for radio equipment. The Americans agreed, and the Chinese began to supply the reports. But, while the Chinese faithfully sent the weather reports, there were endless wrangles over the radios. The Americans offered sets that were meant to be carried in jeeps rather than by foot soldiers. Lindsay asked for components to build lighter sets, but they never arrived. He told Ye Jianying to send the Americans an ultimatum threatening to cut off the weather reports, but it was never sent. Instead, the Chinese began behaving pettily, delaying the reports and taking ages over translations. When the Americans finally sent some equipment, it was the wrong type. Lindsay wanted to send it back but was overruled.

Lindsay completed the long-range radio in August 1944 and began helping Xinhua transmit English-language news to the United States at 4:00 p.m. each day. He helped translate and edit the news bulletins and was able to influence the content and style of the news, but whenever he was away, it reverted to the standard wooden output. Exasperated, he repeatedly tried to explain to Xinhua head Bo Gu that they should give reasons for criticising the KMT, not just hurl abuse. On account of such problems, which were part of Lindsay's more general frustrations with bureaucracy, he gradually drifted away from working with Xinhua. Yan'an did not have the egalitarian and can-do spirit he had seen in the Jin-Cha-Ji region. His concerns were shared by some senior officials. Lu Zhengcao complained that the farther west he went, the more difficult it was to get things done. The response of Yan'an officials was to blame the backwardness of the area, but Lindsay pointed out that it was the newcomers, not the locals, who had introduced the red tape.

At the seventh party congress that took place from 23 April to 11 June 1945, and which he attended as an interpreter, Lindsay's frustrations with the Yan'an bureaucracy boiled over. Hundreds of people had arrived in Yan'an as delegates, including some of the Lindsays' old friends. However, they were unable to meet with several of them, including Jiang Yizhen, because of a new rule that people could not visit a compound without a letter of introduction. The excuse given was the need to combat spies, but its effect was to frustrate useful and perfectly harmless encounters. For example, delegates from an oilfield were not able to meet a foreign oil expert who was at the congress. Lindsay wrote a forty-page report attacking the bureaucracy. He complained that, unlike the frontline areas in the Jin-Cha-Ji region, where politics took second place, Yan'an was a strict one-party state. People were afraid to criticise their superiors or the party line. Instead, they grumbled in private. He later wrote that 'Party discipline prevented criticism even of mistakes which the leaders were perfectly willing to correct ... By its present standards, the Chinese Communist Party was 'revisionist' during the Yenan period.' [14] He finished the report a week or so before leaving Yan'an and presented it to Zhou Enlai. Zhou may have read it, but it is hard to imagine that the leadership would have accepted being lectured by a foreigner. It was a sign of Lindsay's Oxford-bred self-confidence that he expected them to.

After Japan surrendered, Hurley invited Mao to Chongqing for peace talks. According to Lindsay, who may have exaggerated his influence, Ye Jianying and Yang Shangkun asked for his advice on whether Mao should accept. Lindsay said it would look bad if Mao refused, but that he must insist on guarantees of his safety. He was unimpressed with Hurley, who, he thought, not only despised the Chinese in general but also underestimated the strength of the Communists and believed the KMT would easily win a civil war. When Mao returned from Chongqing, he announced that he would support a democratic government under the leadership of Chiang Kai-shek. But nothing had been agreed regarding a coalition and, furthermore, he had agreed to withdraw all Communist forces to positions north of the Yangzi River. For the first time, the Lindsays heard open criticism of Mao in Yan'an. They were told he had narrowly fought off a vote of no confidence at a top party meeting. People complained that while the Americans were

---

14   Michael Lindsay, 'The Great Cultural Revolution and the Red Guards', *World Affairs*, Vol. 129, No. 4 (1967), 225–32, 228.

helping the KMT, the Russians were doing nothing to support the Communists.[15]

Nie Rongzhen invited Michael to stay in China to help with a project to build a model city. Michael initially agreed, but as hopes of peace faded, he changed his mind. Shortly afterwards, the Dixie Mission invited the Lindsays to move to their residence, as it would be protected from bombing by the American flag painted on the roof but the Lindsays had decided to leave and flew to Chongqing on a Dixie Mission plane. There were now four of them. Li Xiaoli gave birth to their second child, James, in Yan'an in January 1945. Before leaving, Lindsay discussed his plans to influence British foreign policy with Zhou Enlai. Zhou gave him 3,000 US dollars, a substantial sum at the time, to finance his efforts.[16] Two days before they left, Chairman Mao and Jiang Qing visited them for a farewell dinner. Mao insisted that the Communists did not want civil war:

> The Chinese Communists, do not want any more fighting . . . We
> don't ask much. We want to be recognized by the central government
> as legitimate and given our share in the government of the country
> after so many of our men have sacrificed their lives.

Mao was animated and red in the face. Li Xiaoli thought he was speaking sincerely.[17]

Lindsay returned to the UK hoping to persuade the Labour government to use its influence to prevent the outbreak of civil war in China. His father had recently made a speech in the House of Lords calling on the government to establish relations with Yan'an to draw the Chinese Communists out of the Soviet orbit and Michael thought his own on-the-ground experience in China might carry some weight. The *Times* had published some of his dispatches; in 1944 the Popular Front–style China Campaign Committee had reprinted them in a booklet, *The North China Front*. He toured the country speaking to Workers' Educational Associations. But no one in authority was prepared to listen

15   Hsiao Li Lindsay, *Bold Plum, With the Guerrillas in China's War against Japan*, Morrisville: Lulu, 2007, 336–7.

16   Li Xiaoli called it travel expenses, but it was far too large a sum to make that plausible.

17   Hsiao Li Lindsay, *Bold Plum*, 343–4.

to him. Labour's deputy foreign minister, Kenneth Younger, told him that Foreign Office officials believed he was a member of the Chinese Communist Party.

In reality, Lindsay was not a member of any Communist Party, but a social democrat like his father. His decision to join the guerrillas of the Eighth Route Army was largely based on proximity. He was sympathetic to the Chinese Communists because they were starved of supplies and, having seen them in action, because he thought they were more pragmatic than the doctrinaire Russians. Despite the bureaucracy in Yan'an, they ran the areas they controlled relatively efficiently. The moderate land reform they carried out during the anti-Japanese war – combining rent reductions and progressive taxation with some redistribution – had improved conditions in the countryside. While on the run from the Japanese, the Lindsays befriended a landlord who complained he had been forced to sack his servants but was still relatively well off. He was even able to appeal to the authorities in a dispute with a tenant who was making 'unreasonable' demands. It was the sort of moderate reform that Lindsay approved of. He believed that, if the United States had followed an even-handed policy, the Chinese Communists might have broken with Stalin in 1946 instead of with Khrushchev in 1960 and would have evolved into quite a different party.

Lindsay and Li Xiaoli revisited China briefly in 1949, and in 1954 they returned as interpreters for a British Labour Party delegation led by Clement Attlee. But by 1955, Lindsay had decided that the doctrinaires in the Communist Party had taken over. His criticisms of the leadership led to them being refused Chinese visas in 1958. Lindsay saw the Great Leap Forward as a disaster but, oddly, thought it had taught the leadership the lesson that they had tried to change the economic base with too little ideological preparation. In his pragmatic, empirical way, he became a critical enthusiast for the Cultural Revolution, which, he said, directed fire at the 'superstructure'. (He was no Marxist and took great delight in noting that his analysis turned classical Marxism on its head.) He suggested Mao should have launched the Cultural Revolution earlier – in 1956, after the Hundred Flowers Campaign – and was sanguine about the mistreatment of party officials and intellectuals:

The attacks of the Red Guards against people in the Party are easy to understand. The typical Communist *apparatchik* is not an attractive

character . . . It is hard to feel any sympathy for the Party cadres now
under attack or for the intellectuals who now find themselves in trouble after years of . . . denouncing their colleagues who had greater
intellectual honesty.[18]

However, when the Lindsays were again allowed to visit China in 1973,
they were repelled by the excesses they discovered. It was time for
another change of direction. In his 1975 book *The Unknown War*,
Lindsay wrote that he had supported the Communists in the 1940s but
now believed the KMT were a better option for China.[19] He maintained
he had not changed his views – rather, the Communists had abandoned
their wartime moderation in favour of extremist policies like forced
collectivisation and the suppression of traditional culture.

Lindsay continued his academic career in the United States and
Australia – both places that Li Xiaoli had difficulty entering because of
racist immigration laws. Their third child, Mary, was born in the UK in
1951. In 1946–47, while Lindsay was lecturing at Harvard University, Li
Xiaoli used the diaries she had recovered after the 1943 Japanese offensive to write a memoir of their experiences in China, but, in the atmosphere of the Cold War, no publisher would touch it. It did not appear in
print until sixty years later. By that time, Michael Lindsay had died and
Li Xiaoli had returned to China to live in a Beijing apartment provided
by the government in recognition of her wartime service.

---

18   Lindsay, 'The Great Cultural Revolution and the Red Guards', 231.
19   Michael Lindsay, *The Unknown War: North China, 1937–1945*, Beijing: Foreign
Languages Press, 2003, 153.

12

Mao's Model Internationalist

In his home country of Canada, Norman Bethune, a surgeon by training, battled endemic tuberculosis after curing himself of the disease using unorthodox therapies. As a doctor, he was skilful and innovative, inventing a range of surgical instruments and operating on cases that others thought hopeless. After experience taught him that tuberculosis was a disease of poverty, he provided cheap or free treatment to his working-class patients and championed the cause of socialised medicine. He volunteered for the Republican side in the Spanish Civil War, pioneering mobile blood-transfusion units that saved the lives of wounded soldiers who would otherwise have died on the way to hospital. Courageous to the point of recklessness under fire, he witnessed Francoist atrocities, which he denounced in pamphlets and radio broadcasts. After Spain, he spent nearly two years as a surgeon and medical reformer with the Eighth Route Army in northern China. When he died of sepsis, exacerbated by exhaustion, in November 1939, Mao Zedong wrote a eulogy, praising Bethune's

> spirit of internationalism . . . the only way . . . to liberate our nation and people and to liberate the other nations and peoples of the world. This is our internationalism, the internationalism with which we oppose both narrow nationalism and narrow patriotism.[1]

---

1   Mao Zedong, 'In Memory of Norman Bethune', 21 December 1939, available at marxists.org.

During the Cultural Revolution, Mao's eulogy, *In Memory of Norman Bethune*, became one of the *lao san pian* – the three must-read articles by the chairman. Bethune's fame in China was assured by Mao's sponsorship, and today, every Chinese schoolchild learns about the famous internationalist fighter Doctor Bai Qiu'en. There are statues of Bethune throughout the country, and the many medical establishments named in his honour include the Bethune International Peace Hospital in Shijiazhuang and a medical school in Jilin.

A great deal of what the rest of the world knows, or thinks it knows, about Norman Bethune was written by Ted Allan, an Oscar-nominated and Golden Globe–winning screenwriter. Allan co-wrote the 1952 biography *The Scalpel, the Sword* and scripted the 1990 biopic *Bethune: The Making of a Hero*. The 1952 work, written when Allan was a member of the Canadian Communist Party, is a hagiography, based partly on a fictionalised account of Bethune's time in China written by a future PRC culture minister.[2] The feature film, at the time Canada's most expensive production, starred Donald Sutherland in the title role and portrayed Bethune as an overbearing, womanising drunk who, at the end of his life, found salvation by serving the Chinese people.

Bethune had befriended Allan, the younger man by twenty-five years, in 1936 and encouraged him to pursue writing as a career. Both men went to Spain as volunteers. Allan had been working for the Canadian Communist Party newspaper the *Daily Chronicle* and hoped to be sent to Spain as its correspondent. When that fell through, he joined the International Brigade. He expected to be sent to the front but, after learning that he knew Bethune, Peter Kerrigan, the political commissar of the British Battalion, sent him to Madrid to investigate unspecified rumours of misconduct among foreigners working in Bethune's blood-transfusion unit. Kerrigan told Allan to report his findings directly to Luigi Longo, the inspector-general of the International Brigades.[3]

---

2   Larry Hannant, *The Politics of Passion: Norman Bethune's Writing and Art*, Toronto: University of Toronto Press, 1998.

3   Kerrigan, a former boxer, was a hard-line disciplinarian whose bullying was widely feared by CPGB members. In Spain, he reported to André Marty, a French Communist notorious for ordering executions of International Brigade volunteers on dubious charges. In a 1976 interview with the Imperial War Museum, Kerrigan defended the controversial execution of Major Gaston Delasalle, who was scapegoated for the loss of the Battle of Lopera. Kerrigan was an uncompromising man who cut off all contact with his daughter when she joined a Trotskyist group. See Kevin Morgan et al.,

Allan, embarrassed, confessed to Bethune that he had been sent to spy on him. Bethune laughed it off, but in May 1937, six months after arriving in Spain, he was ordered back to Canada in disgrace after Allan and Henning Sorensen, a colleague in the transfusion unit, sent a letter to the Canadian Communist Party demanding his recall. A combination of professional rivalry between Bethune and Spanish doctors, resentment of foreigners taking leadership roles, Stalin's hunt for oppositionists, paranoia about 'fifth columnists', and Bethune's unreasonable behaviour undermined his position as head of the transfusion unit. Allan's 1990 film script implied that Bethune was sent home because of his heavy drinking. But documents in the Comintern archive show that, in addition to 'immorality', Bethune was also accused of misappropriating funds and, alarmingly, was suspected of spying for the fascists. An April 1937 report from the General Staff of the Spanish War Ministry states: 'A suspicious fact which should also be taken into account is that Mr Bethune openly takes detailed notes of the locations of bridges, crossroads, distances between locations, journey times, etc., writing it all down carefully.'[4]

Bethune's loyalty was questioned because he was having an affair with a Swedish woman, Kajsa von Rothman, who had, according to the General Staff document, worked as a nurse in the anarchist Iron Column.[5] Bethune and Von Rothman were arrested, along with the entire foreign staff of the transfusion unit, as well as some other foreign hangers-on who had socialised with them, including an Austrian commander, Hermann Hartung. Bethune was soon released, but Rothman and Hartung disappeared. The document suggests that Hartung was executed – he was, in fact, imprisoned and deported.

The spying charge was, in reality, preposterous. Bethune took notes and drew maps in order to determine the fastest routes for ambulances to take between hospitals and the front line. That he did so openly should have alerted any sensible person that the accusations against him were the product of paranoia, or simply malicious. Kajsa Rothman, no more an enemy agent than Bethune, had returned to Sweden to raise

---

Communists and British Society, 1920–1991, London: Rivers Oram Press, 2007, 115–16; and 'Kerrigan, Peter (Oral History)', Imperial War Museum, 1976, iwm.org.uk.

4   RGASPI 545.6.542.

5   The Columna de Ferro was a Catalan anarchist militia that had clashed with Communists.

funds and rally support for the Spanish loyalists. Back in Spain when the Republic fell in 1939, she was one of more than half a million who fled across the Pyrenees to France, where she worked in refugee camps before going on, with other fugitives, to Mexico, where she died in 1969.[6]

Bethune never found out that he was suspected of espionage;[7] by July 1937, he was planning to return to Spain as a volunteer in the International Brigades. This provoked another of his former colleagues in the transfusion unit, Hazen Sise, to write to the 'comrades of the Cheka' asking them to send a coded message to Tim Buck, the general secretary of the Canadian Communist Party, to block Bethune's return.[8] Sise's report repeated all the accusations in the General Staff document, including the spying slur, and added a new one: that Bethune had smuggled film footage out of Spain without passing it through censorship. It was another absurd charge; Bethune used the footage to create the documentary *Heart of Spain*, in collaboration with the radical filmmakers Herbert Kline and Charles Korvin.

Bethune's betrayal by Allan, Sorensen, and Sise took place in the context of the pervasive culture of snitching in the 'Bolshevised' Comintern. Having ceded the political terrain to the Nazis with its Third Period idiocy, Moscow now swung in the opposite direction –wooing the bourgeoisie in the hope of enticing the European empires into an alliance against Hitler. In Moscow, Stalin was shooting the Old Bolsheviks, and rooting out oppositionists became a primary duty of party members in all sections of the Comintern. Informing was institutionalised in the International Brigades; a pro forma asked officers and commissars whether the volunteer should be classed as 'a good anti-fascist', 'a good party member', 'an enemy (e.g. Trotskyist, agent provocateur etc.)', or a 'declassed element (e.g. deserter, disruptor etc.)'.[9] Being labelled an enemy or a declassed element, perhaps on the basis of gossip alone, had potentially fatal consequences. Years later, a former volunteer confronted Allan and accused him of nearly causing him to be shot by conniving in an accusation of 'Trotskyism'. It seems that Allan was

6   'Karin (Kajsa) Rothman', Svenskt kvinnobiografiskt lexikon, skbl.se.

7   In a sense, the transfusion unit was a nest of spies, but not for the fascists. It was there that David Crook was recruited to the Soviet secret police.

8   RGASPI 545.6.542.

9   RGASPI 545.6.542.

unconcerned about the man's fate and surprised he had survived.[10] Allan's motives in keeping the Bethune story alive are unclear; perhaps he felt a mixture of admiration and guilt, but money may also have been a factor. He was well paid for the film script and, after acquiring Bethune's papers, he restricted access to them in an attempt to monopolise Bethune studies.[11]

There was little to suggest Mao's model internationalist in the young Norman Bethune. Son of a protestant minister, he was, if anything, a keen empire patriot. As a twenty-four-year-old medical student, he was the eighth man in Toronto to enlist for the First World War. He served with distinction in a frontline ambulance unit, until he was wounded at Ypres and invalided out. Back in Toronto, he was impertinently white feathered, but, far from reacting with outrage, he joined the Royal Navy. Demobilised in London, he interned at the Great Ormond Street children's hospital. He was not quite finished with military life, however. After returning to Canada, he joined the newly created Air Force but quit within a year, returning to the mother country to work at the Edinburgh Royal Infirmary. In 1923, he married Frances Penney, a Scottish heiress whose modest fortune helped him set up a medical practice in downtown Detroit.

Despite Bethune often forgiving the bills of his poor, immigrant patients, the practice was successful, and the couple enjoyed a middle-class lifestyle; Bethune bought a car and joined a golf club.[12] But everything changed in late 1926, the year of Bethune's tuberculosis diagnosis. Expecting to die, he separated from Frances and checked into the famous Trudeau Sanatorium in New York State. At his insistence, the couple divorced soon afterwards. Against the odds, Bethune recovered after insisting on radical, risky therapy, and he and Frances remarried in 1929. In the meantime, Bethune had begun a medical crusade against tuberculosis as assistant to the distinguished surgeon Edward Archibald

---

10 The 'Trotskyist's' name was Harry Muskovitz, or Moskovitz. He spat on Ted Allan in the street and reviled him for betraying a fellow Jew. See the online biography of Ted Allan by his son: normanallan.com. During the filming of the Bethune biopic, Allan clashed with Donald Sutherland, who accused him of overemphasising the negative aspects of Bethune's character.

11 See Hannant, *Politics of Passion*, 373.

12 Roderick Stewart and Sharon Stewart, *Phoenix: The Life of Norman Bethune*, Montreal: McGill-Queen's University Press, 2011, Kindle.

at his chest clinic in Montreal. Archibald regarded Bethune as a talented but reckless surgeon who took too many risks with patients' lives and, consequently, had a higher mortality rate than his colleagues. Bethune countered that he operated on cases that more conservative doctors regarded as hopeless, and that he was actually saving lives. Their differences led to increasingly heated clashes and, eventually, Archibald sacked Bethune. He later complained that Bethune 'had a superiority complex and was entirely amoral'.[13]

Bethune took risks and sought confrontation in both his professional and personal life. He had many lovers, flirted outrageously – including with his colleagues' wives – and once brazenly asked a husband for permission to sleep with his wife. Some of his behaviour, such as pissing in a plant pot at a party, might be dismissed as a hangover from medical student horseplay. Other episodes were more obviously the result of his uncontrolled drinking. While working at the Sacré Coeur Catholic hospital in Montreal, he set fire to his lodgings and slept in the hospital grounds for several months until the scandalised nuns ordered him out for bringing women back to his tent. Frances could no longer tolerate his behaviour and, in 1933, divorced him for the second time. Charitably, one might attribute Bethune's compulsion to épater les bourgeois as characteristic of a generation traumatised by trench warfare.[14] After being demobilised in London, he mixed with its bohemian artistic set, wrote poetry, and showed some talent as a painter. While recovering at the Trudeau Sanatorium, he painted an impressive mural, *TB's Progress*, after Hogarth's *Rake's Progress*. Another of his paintings, *Night Operating Theatre*, was exhibited in the Montreal Museum of Fine Arts annual show in 1935.

Politically, Bethune had no firm moorings, but a war on tuberculosis entailed a battle against the social conditions that spread it disproportionately among the poor. His support for state health care provision attracted him to the Fabians of the Cooperative Commonwealth Federation (CCF) and the League for Social Reconstruction. In 1935, the year Sidney and Beatrice Webb published *Soviet Communism: A New Civilisation*, he attended the International Physiological Congress in Moscow. He was impressed by the Soviet system for treating

---

13   Letter from Edward Archibald to a colleague, citied in Stewart, *Phoenix*.
14   Stewart suggested he may have suffered from a bipolar or related disorder.

tuberculosis and, true to his impulsive nature, shortly after returning, he joined the Canadian Communist Party. However, he retained strong misgivings, communicated in a letter turning down an invitation to chair the Montreal Friends of the Soviet Union. He was 'a half-hearted convert' with 'a strong feeling of individualism' and 'dislike of crowds and regimentation' who, furthermore, despaired of the 'passivity of the oppressed workers'. But he also wrote to Marian Scott, a married painter with whom he had fallen in love, of his frustration with the CCF – a talking shop that, he believed, eschewed the violence necessary to dispossess the 'moneyed people'. Democracy would never accomplish radical social change, and, he warned, only 'after the course is set can it be permitted to guide the ship'. He signed off by reminding Scott, somewhat eerily, that he came from 'a race of men, violent, unstable, of passionate convictions and wrong-headedness, intolerant yet with . . . a vision of truth and a drive to carry them on . . . even though it leads . . . to their own destruction'.[15]

The initial steps to send him to Spain were made by the CCF, which organised the Committee to Aid Spanish Democracy to raise funds. In Madrid, having decided his most effective contribution would be a mobile blood-transfusion unit, Bethune set about organising it with enormous energy, travelling to France and Britain to buy equipment and a vehicle to use as an ambulance. The unit's most dramatic intervention was during the February 1937 retreat from Málaga, when Bethune led repeated sorties in the unit's ambulance to aid a column of civilian refugees who were being shelled by a warship and strafed by aircraft. Bethune described the horrors in the pamphlet *The Crime on the Road: Malaga to Almeria*. Bethune's courage (he insisted on aiding the refugees despite the misgivings of Hazen Sise, who accompanied him) contrasted with his political naivety. Sise would soon denounce him, in part because of his affair with the 'anarchist' Kajsa Rothman. However, there is abundant evidence that he was no anarchist sympathiser; for instance, after completing the rescue mission, Bethune was heard railing against the anarchists, blaming them for the fall of Málaga. A convert to the Communist movement late in life – he was forty-five when he joined the party – he never questioned the official line of the Comintern.

---

15   Letters reproduced in Hannant, *Politics of Passion*.

After Bethune returned from Spain, the Canadian Communist Party sent him on an extended speaking tour but told him to conceal his party membership in order to maximise public support. Bethune had no time for such political subterfuge; on the contrary, he was eager to announce his Communist affiliation and, after chafing for some time, did so. When the idea of a medical mission to China was suggested to him, he stipulated that if he was killed in action, it should be announced that he had died a Communist. Blocked from returning to Spain, Bethune welcomed the opportunity to return to active service in the fight against fascism and disdained the risks that deterred many others. A Canadian nurse, Jean Ewen, who had spent four years working for a Catholic mission in China, accompanied him as assistant and translator. The CPUSA financed the mission and appointed another surgeon, Charles Edward Parsons, to lead it. Parsons, however, turned out to be a worse alcohol abuser than Bethune and was sent home, leaving Bethune in charge.[16]

Bethune's two years in China – approximately four times as long as he spent in Spain – gave him far more scope to make an impact. But the difficulties he faced were correspondingly greater. The Eighth Route Army had virtually no trained medical personnel, and conditions in its hospitals were dreadful. Poor hygiene and lack of basic nursing care meant that wounds became infected. Even if operated on successfully, patients were likely to die because aftercare was virtually non-existent. Bethune was appalled by the number of gangrenous limbs he was forced to amputate as the only way of saving lives. The addition of one or two additional doctors would have only a marginal effect. When Bethune arrived in Yan'an, he met Mao Zedong several times, and after being reassigned to forward units, he sent Mao a series of letters and reports calling for radical reform of the army's medical service. A systematic training programme was the main need, but he also envisaged a democratic health service run by an elected central committee of medical staff, patients, and ordinary citizens.

Bethune faced endless problems with funding and medical supplies. His mission was officially under the auspices of the Canadian China Aid Council. The CAC did not send funds directly to Bethune, however, but initially to the Chinese Red Cross and later to Song Qingling's China

---

16 Parsons was the elder brother of the sociologist Talcott Parsons who despite being anti-Communist was targeted by J. Edgar Hoover.

Defence League in Hong Kong. Because it was logistically easier for the China Defence League to send aid to the New Fourth Army stationed in the Yangzi region, only a fraction made it through to Bethune.[17] A League of Nations medical mission offered to donate its supplies, but the KMT overruled it. Michael Lindsay, who was making occasional visits to guerrilla-controlled areas while at Yanjing University, advised Bethune to set up a smuggling route via Beiping. A Christian missionary, Kathleen Hall, offered to help and smuggled some supplies, but the Japanese uncovered the operation and destroyed Hall's clinic as a reprisal.

Soon after arriving in Yan'an, Bethune had insisted on serving with active military units and was sent to the Jin-Cha-Ji Border Region as chief medical advisor to its commander, Nie Rongzhen. He set about reforming the health service hospital by hospital. While he made significant progress, his bulldozing style of work sometimes crossed the line into outright bullying of staff he deemed lazy or incompetent.[18] Bethune's experience of wars of position in Europe left him unprepared for a guerrilla war with neither front lines nor fixed bases. He browbeat Nie Rongzhen into setting up a model training hospital, which was built by a huge communal effort but functioned for just over a fortnight before the Japanese razed it. He learned from the experience, which led him to write a 150-page book, *Organization and Technique for Division Field Hospitals in Guerrilla Warfare*. Thereafter, he set up a smaller, mobile centre where he carried out open-air training sessions, but he never abandoned the idea of establishing a permanent medical school. He was working on a syllabus and textbooks when he died.

Bethune had lost none of his propensity to antagonise others. He arrived in China via Hankou where he met Agnes Smedley, whose book *China's Red Army Marches* had sparked his interested in China. Smedley raised funds for his onward journey to Yan'an and arranged for a missionary doctor, Richard Brown, to replace the disgraced Parsons. But before long, Bethune had fallen out with Smedley – admittedly, not a difficult accomplishment. He called her spiteful and vindictive, and pulled rank on her by pointing out that he was, unlike her, a party

---

17   Stewart, *Phoenix*.
18   Ibid.

member. Smedley wrote to the CAC demanding that it recall Bethune from China. Bethune and Brown, who were often called upon to carry out marathon operating sessions, worked well together, but Brown told Ewen, 'The Angel Gabriel couldn't get along with Norman Bethune. He's a horrible man.' Bethune, for his part, wrote to a friend, 'I am unable to speak of the work of Dr Brown with sufficient praise.'[19] Ewen was also critical of Bethune but noted the tenderness he showed towards his patients, writing that 'no man ever removed so much lead from peoples' bone, flesh, and guts as he did, or set more broken bones or amputated so many extremities'.[20]

By late 1939, overwork and poor diet had left Bethune exhausted and emaciated. Frustrated by the continuing difficulties in obtaining money and supplies, he was planning a fundraising trip to Canada and the United States when, not for the first time, he cut his finger while operating on a wounded soldier. He died twelve days later of sepsis.

Bethune's last letters and reports reveal him as dedicated, committed, and optimistic but overworked and preoccupied with practical problems. On 4 March 1939, his forty-ninth birthday, he wrote a long letter to Tim Buck praising the Eighth Route Army's strategy of protracted warfare and the CCP as the 'best' national party he had seen. A report written in July gave details of four battles, during which his mobile medical unit carried out 315 operations in the field, including on two wounded Japanese who were returned to the enemy after recovering. Obtaining medical equipment and drugs supplies remained an immediate and pressing problem – in August, he wrote that, for three months, his unit had depended on supplies smuggled by Kathleen Hall. He held the army responsible for putting Hall's life in danger because it had failed to establish a reliable underground supply route.[21] A July letter to the head of the regional Sanitary Service was extremely critical and detailed: drug purchasing was 'careless and slipshod', as expensive, useless drugs were favoured over cheaper essentials, while careless packing meant that medicines were lost in transit. Bethune's greatest concern, however, was the need to train an entire new cadre of medical staff,

---

19   Ibid.
20   Ibid.
21   Bethune tried to recruit Hall to his unit, but she left after being threatened by the Japanese.

especially nurses. Nursing care had previously been left to teenage boys who were, he said, temperamentally unsuited to the work. Older men, university students, and women had to be trained to replace them. Indeed, training, he argued, was the most effective contribution foreigners could make – since sending foreign doctors was mere firefighting. To implement his vision, he would need funds; he wrote to a friend of his plan to travel via Yan'an, Indochina, Hong Kong, and Honolulu to San Francisco. He said the war would last another ten years, and that 'we must help these splendid people more'.[22]

Bethune was impulsive, erratic, and sometimes impossible to get on with, but he was also courageous, committed, and always on the side of the underdog. He was only a Communist for the last four years of his life and was no theoretician, but he ended up sacrificing his life for the cause. Much has been made of the excesses of his personal life, especially with regard to his expulsion from Spain, but the most serious charges against him were entirely fabricated – the product of the Stalinist hunt for oppositionists that, ironically, he supported. It is sobering to reflect that had things gone slightly differently, he might well have been shot by his own side before he ever got to China. These days, distrust of CCP propaganda is so great that some Chinese suspect Bethune's story is a legend spun by Mao Zedong. This is emphatically not the case. Bethune was a flawed hero, but a hero nonetheless.

---

22   Ibid.

13

Popular Fronters

The two great international causes of the British left in the 1930s were solidarity with Republican Spain against Franco and with Republican China against Japan. Many people were active in both campaigns, but while Spain often figured in histories, biographies, and memoirs of the period – understandably, as tens of thousands of international volunteers fought there – references to China were sparse. One of the leading activists in the China campaign in Britain, Arthur Clegg, blamed Eurocentrism, the Cold War, and the Sino-Soviet Split for the imbalance. Five decades later, he set out to fill the gap in his book *Aid China: A Memoir of a Forgotten Campaign.*

Clegg was a student at the London School of Economics and a member of the Communist Party when, in September 1937, he was appointed national organiser of the China Campaign Committee. For three years, he was a tireless and effective worker, travelling constantly to speak at public meetings and establish local support groups. But Clegg was young and inexperienced. The man who gave shape to and inspired the campaign, who built it with his society connections, and financed it with his own money, was its chairman, the publisher Victor Gollancz, founder of the Left Book Club (LBC).[1] The club's October 1937 book of the month, timed to coincide with the launch of the

---

1 An anonymous donor, believed to be Gollancz, made monthly donations of one hundred pounds sterling – worth more than 6,000 pounds in 2020.

CCC,[2] was its all-time bestseller, Edgar Snow's *Red Star over China*. Sales of *Red Star*, the LBC, and the China campaign grew in step with each other. If Gollancz was a great champion of Republican Spain, his enthusiasm for China was 'untrammelled'.[3]

The LBC, little more than a year old when the campaign was launched, was already a publishing phenomenon with 50,000 subscribers. In return for a monthly subscription of half a crown, members received a book chosen by Gollancz, Harold Laski, and John Strachey and a copy of the club journal, *Left News*.[4] The club spawned hundreds of discussion groups that attracted both middle-class radicals and trade unionists and developed into the most active political forums in Britain, eclipsing Labour Party branches and alarming Transport House.[5] They provided the foot soldiers of the China campaign and organised so many public meetings that Clegg found it difficult to meet the demand for speakers. A cadre of organisers, mainly from the Communist Party, was required to coordinate the groups. Strachey, who was a party sympathiser, wrote the editorials for *Left News*. Gollancz was a member of the Labour Party but later recalled that, at the time, he was 'as close to the communists as one hair to another'.[6]

It was the era of the Popular Front. The Comintern had officially buried the disastrous 'Third Period' line at its Seventh Congress in 1935. Georgi Dimitrov, a defendant in the 1933 Reichstag fire trial, now Comintern general secretary, instructed Communist parties to cooperate not only with the previously vilified Social Democrats but to seek broader alliances encompassing bourgeois parties. Gollancz, gregarious

---

2   According to Clegg the CCC was established in either August or September 1937. *Red Star over China* was the Left Book Club book choice in October 1937.

3   In 1938, Gollancz followed up *Red Star* with Agnes Smedley's *China Fights Back*. Gollancz's enthusiasm for the Spanish cause was tempered by guilt over deaths of British volunteers there. See Ruth Dudley Edwards, *Victor Gollancz: A Biography*, London: Gollancz, 1987, 177.

4   Laski was a member of Labour's National Executive Committee and became Labour Party chairman in 1945. Strachey was, at the time, a Communist in every respect except carrying a party card. According to some accounts, Strachey applied to join the CPGB but was turned down. Others say the party thought he would be more effective if he remained nominally independent.

5   See Kevin Morgan, *Against Fascism and War: Ruptures and Continuities in British Communist Politics, 1935–41*, Manchester: Manchester University Press, 1989, 256.

6   Ibid., 260.

and supremely well connected, was well placed to build such a movement in Britain. His popularity was attested by the barometer of political satire. After 9,000 people packed the Albert Hall for a Left Book Club
rally,[7] *Time and Tide* described Gollancz as presiding over 'an embryo
Catholic Church with [himself] as Pope'.[8] Clegg called him 'the embodiment of the Popular Front'.[9]

But Britain, unlike France and Spain, was not fertile ground for
Popular Front politics. The Labour Party dominated the workers movement, and its right-wing leaders, above all Herbert Morrison and Ernest
Bevin, were ferociously opposed to any form of cooperation with the
Communist Party. However, they faced some opposition, including
from Stafford Cripps and Harold Laski, who formed the Socialist League
to argue the case for an alliance from within Labour. At a mass meeting
in Manchester, Cripps, Harry Pollitt, the CPGB general secretary, and
ILP leader James Maxton launched a Unity Manifesto. Cripps circulated
an appeal to Labour Party members to work with those of 'all parties or
none' to throw out the National Government.[10] But the response of the
Labour Party was to disaffiliate the Socialist League and kick Cripps out
of the party.

The CPGB was haunted by its wild swings in policy, imposed by the
Comintern. Even the left-wing ILP was a reluctant partner. The
Communists had previously denounced the ILP as 'social fascist' for
calling for a United Front of working-class and socialist parties.[11] Now,
they had outflanked the ILP on the right by calling for a broader alliance
than the ILP would countenance. At its 1937 conference, the party
chairman,   veteran   anti-colonial   campaigner   Fenner   Brockway,

---

7   Ben Pimlott says it was 7,000 people. See Ben Pimlott, *Labour and the Left in the
1930s*, Cambridge, UK: Cambridge University Press, 1977, 99. Either way it was an
impressive turnout.

8   See George Orwell and Peter Davison, ed., *The Collected Non-fiction*, London:
Penguin Classics, 2017. The article, signed Sirocco, implied that only those prepared to
recite the Creed were invited to take communion. 'Why are there no [Left Book Club
books] by anarchists? Who publishes . . . nice young Trotskyists?'

9   Arthur Clegg, *Aid China 1937–1949: A Memoir of a Forgotten Campaign*,
Beijing: New World Press, 1997, 25.

10   Jean Jones, *The League against Imperialism*, London: Socialist History Society,
1966, 193.

11   Clegg recalled that several supporters of the CCC, including Harold Laski, had
been previously labelled 'social fascist' for supporting what became CCC policies. Clegg,
Aid China, 18.

reaffirmed the ILP's support for a Workers Front as opposed to a Popular Front.[12] And after Stalin exported his war of terror against the Opposition to Spain and ILP members were targeted, relations between the parties became toxic. Clegg stumbled into the crossfire when he tried to set up a branch of the CCC in Glasgow. After he 'naively' attempted to reconcile the two sides, Peter Kerrigan, the local CPGB secretary, denounced him to the Central Committee.[13]

Clegg's path to the Communist Party and the CCC was through Willi Münzenberg's League against Imperialism (LAI),[14] an organisation whose inspiration and roots, to a great extent, lay in the Chinese Revolution of 1925-27. Münzenberg's Workers International Relief organised a world-wide campaign of solidarity, culminating in a Hands Off China congress in Berlin, where Münzenberg urged the 1,500 delegates to 'form a holy alliance [of] white, yellow, black and different coloured underdogs'.[15] At the 1927 founding congress of the LAI in Brussels, the Chinese outnumbered all the other delegations apart from the Germans. According to Nehru, representing the Indian National Congress, the Chinese were 'young and full of energy and enthusiasm' and, to his annoyance, dominated the proceedings with their 'orations'.[16] The British delegation included James Maxton and Fenner Brockway from the ILP and future Labour Party leader George Lansbury, who was acclaimed as the league's elder statesman, made the keynote speech, and was elected its first chairman.[17]

---

12   James Jupp, *The Radical Left in Britain, 1931–1941*, London: Taylor & Francis, 2005, 95.

13   The party leadership recognised that Clegg was a political novice and forgave him. See Clegg, *Aid China*, 47.

14   Clegg joined an LAI offshoot – Friends of the Chinese People – chaired by an eccentric former Royal Navy officer, Edgar Young, whose pet orangutan roamed free in his St John's Wood villa, disconcerting Clegg when he paid a visit. After the war, Young chaired the friendship societies of several East European states. His activities earned him a fat Secret Service file and dismissal from the Navy Reserve. Oddly, the files reveal that he was unpopular with East European officials. See UK National Archives, ref. KV 2/3353.

15   Quoted in Kasper Brasken, *The International Workers' Relief, Communism, and Transnational Solidarity: Willi Münzenberg in Weimar Germany*, New York: Palgrave Macmillan, 2015, 58–60.

16   Michele Louro, *Comrades against Imperialism: Nehru, India, and Interwar Internationalism*, Cambridge, UK: Cambridge University Press, 2019, 53. Nehru complained that the Chinese were 'not remarkable for their lucidity' and bored the other delegates.

17   Lansbury stepped down soon afterwards because of Labour Party commitments and was succeeded as chairman first by Brockway and then Maxton.

This high point of cooperation between Labour, the ILP, and the CPGB would not last. The alliance between the Comintern and the KMT was crumbling and, after Chiang Kai-shek's anti-Communist coup, Stalin imposed an ultra-left turn on the Comintern. The new 'class against class' line declared that Communists were 'in fundamental opposition to all other parties'.[18] The absurd consequences became clear at the league's second congress in Frankfurt in 1929, when its own chairman, Maxton, was attacked by a succession of delegates (led by Stalin's lapdog Dmitri Manuilsky) and expelled soon afterwards.

The Comintern's swing to the left was a near-fatal blow to the LAI – an organisation created precisely to build alliances. However, the right turn to Popular Frontism in the mid-1930s did not revive it but rather finished it off. Since Stalin's goal was an alliance with the French and British Empires, the very name League against Imperialism, sounded a discordant note. The International Peace Campaign (IPC), set up in 1936 by the Conservative former Foreign Office minister Lord Robert Cecil and the French Radical Pierre Cot, had a more harmonious ring.[19] The league effectively disappeared into it, dissolving itself in 1937.

It was an organisation with roots in Liberalism and Quakerism that provided money, office space, and key personnel to get the CCC off the ground. The Union of Democratic Control was established at the beginning of the First World War by dissident Liberals to oppose secret treaties and annexations.[20] Charles Trevelyan, who resigned from Asquith's government in protest at the declaration of war, took the initiative to set up the UDC, with financing from the Quaker businessmen George Cadbury and Arnold Rowntree. The organisation's first chairman was E. D. Morel, whose 1906 book, *Red Rubber*, exposed the atrocities perpetrated in the Congo, then King Leopold II's personal fiefdom, and forced

---

18   See *Class against Class: General Election Programme of the Communist Party of Great Britain*, London: Communist Party of Great Britain, 1929, available at marxists. org.

19   Horrified by the carnage of the First World War, Lord Robert Cecil, a minister in the wartime government, devoted the rest of his life to international action to outlaw war. He was an early advocate of the League of Nations and helped draw up its covenant. He was awarded the Nobel Peace Prize in 1937. Pierre Cot, a member of the Radical Party, was minister for air in Léon Blum's Popular Front government.

20   See *The Union of Democratic Control: Its Motives, Object, and Policy*, London: Union of Democratic Control, 1916, available at Warwick Digital Collections: wdc. contentdm.oclc.org.

the Belgian state to buy the colony from the king. Other founder members included Ramsay MacDonald,[21] Bertrand Russell, the *Guardian* editor C. P. Scott, and Scott's close friend and *Guardian* colleague, the theorist of imperialism J. A. Hobson.[22] When Morel died in 1924, his health broken by six months in jail for anti-war activities, Hobson took over as secretary.

By 1937, when the UDC helped set up the CCC, its leading lights were two journalists broadly sympathetic to the CPGB and the Popular Front project. Dorothy Woodman, the organisation's chair, had posed as Georgi Dimitrov's girlfriend so that she could visit him in prison when he was accused of conspiring to burn down the Reichstag. Her real boyfriend and UDC colleague was Kingsley Martin, the editor of the *New Statesman*.[23] At the founding meeting of the CCC chaired by Victor Gollancz, Woodman took Arthur Clegg on as national organiser and gave him a desk in the UDC office.[24] Clegg was soon joined on the CCC's full-time staff by another young party member, twenty-three-year-old Mary Sheridan Jones. George Hardy joined as national trade union organiser in 1938. As Clegg noted, all the full-time workers for the campaign were members of the Communist Party.[25]

---

21   MacDonald, to his credit, resigned as Labour Party leader in protest at its support for the war.

22   C. P. Scott was Hobson's friend and relative by marriage – his son married Hobson's daughter – and employed Hobson for many years as a *Guardian* journalist. In 2019, the *Guardian*, noting the little-known fact that Hobson held anti-Semitic views, attacked Jeremy Corbyn for writing a preface to Hobson's classic work *Imperialism, a Study* (although it would require an extraordinarily close reading of *Imperialism* to detect any hint of anti-Semitism). Scott believed it was necessary to 'make the Jew a whole Jew [and] clear him up in his own eyes and the eyes of the world'. See 'Charles Prestwich Scott', Jewish Virtual Library, jewishvirtuallibrary.org.

23   The Nazis accused Dimitrov of masterminding the Reichstag fire. He defended himself with an outstanding speech from the dock and was acquitted.

24   Woodman's security services file gives an amusing insight into both her and the police mindset: 'Precise assessment . . . difficult. Left-wing political busy-body. Very able and persuasive. Alleged past contacts with Soviet espionage but not confirmed . . . Constant admirer of liberation movements in S.E. Asia'. UK National Archives, KV-2-1607_1, 281A.

25   Clegg, *Aid China*, 60. According to the historian Tom Buchanan, the appointment of Hardy on a recommendation from the CPGB's Ben Bradley shows that the CPGB was pulling the strings behind the scenes, and that Clegg was disingenuous in playing down Communist Party influence in his memoir. However, though the party pulled strings, it was hardly behind the scenes. Clegg and his comrades were open about their political affiliation. Furthermore, since the activities of the CCC were legal and its

Clegg worked tirelessly, even obsessively, as national organiser for three years. He 'thought only of China, morning noon and night', to the extent that colleagues thought he was 'barely human'.[26] But Gollancz praised him as the epitome of 'the quiet, unpretentious, devoted middle-class section of the left-wing England I know'.[27] His hard work and commitment were the more remarkable since he was disabled and in constant pain. While in his teens, he had climbed a tree, fallen, and broken his back in two places. He had been in a wheelchair for four years, and although he had forced himself to walk again, first with crutches, then two sticks, and finally one stick, he would limp for the rest of his life.

Clegg's fascination with China had begun when he was a child and, as with many others, it was kindled by the church. His mother had been a missionary in Ceylon and his father was a Methodist minister who preached the gospel to working-class communities in the Gorbals and Tiger Bay. A cousin who was a missionary in China sent regular letters. When Japan invaded Manchuria in 1931, seventeen-year-old Clegg volunteered to join a 'peace army' proposed by the Christian pacifists Maude Royden and Donald Soper to stand in between the Chinese and Japanese armies. That project came to nothing, but floods and famine along the Yangzi the same year kept his interest in China alive. The huge death toll from this natural disaster also tested his faith;[28] Clegg abandoned Christianity and fell out with his family.[29]

The CCC was launched at a public meeting in a Methodist church in Tottenham Court Road. Lady Dorothea Hosie, a well-known

---

aims legitimate, indeed praiseworthy, it seems of little consequence that party members caucused before meetings or reported back to the CPGB Central Committee. See Tom Buchanan, *East Wind: China and the British Left, 1925–1976*, Oxford: Oxford University Press, 2012, 69–70.

26   Clegg, *Aid China*, 32. Thanks to Arthur Clegg's daughter Jenny Clegg for these insights.

27   'Obituary: Arthur Clegg', *Independent*, 16 February 1994, independent.co.uk.

28   Estimates of deaths from drowning, disease, and starvation range from half a million to 4 million.

29   The rift lasted a lifetime for one of Clegg's sisters, who married the future Bishop of Worcester. After Arthur became a 'godless communist', the bishop forbade his family to have anything to do him. Only after the bishop died did his children seek out Arthur's children to reconcile. Arthur was not the only rebel in the family. His younger brother, Hugh Clegg, also abandoned Methodism for Communism but, after mellowing, became an advisor to Harold Wilson and set up the Prices and Incomes Board.

missionary and sinologist, spoke alongside Harold Laski and Patricia Koo (Gu Zhuzhen), daughter of Wellington Koo (Gu Weijun), the distinguished diplomat and former premier of China. 'Red Ellen' Wilkinson, former Communist, now Labour member of Parliament for Jarrow and organiser of the famous unemployment march, joined them on the platform alongside General Yang Hucheng who, with Zhang Xueliang, had staged the 1936 Xi'an coup against Chiang Kai-shek.[30]

Victor Gollancz rallied artists, actors, authors, academics, clergymen, politicians, lords, and ladies to the cause. Among those who joined the CCC were the sinologist Arthur Waley, the historians Eileen Power and R. H. Tawney, the bishop of Bristol, and the head of the Methodists, Scott Ledgett. Twenty-one bishops supported the CCC call for a 'China Sunday' to raise money for medical aid. Actors who signed up included Hermione Baddeley, Sybil Thorndike, Bernard Miles, and Cyril Fletcher. Pearl Binder, Misha Black, and James Boswell of the Artists' International Association organised an exhibition of Chinese art featuring woodcuts by Jack Chen, Eugene Chen's son. The Indian dancer Uday Shankar, Ravi Shankar's elder brother, performed at a benefit for China organised by independence leader Krishna Menon. The biggest star to perform was Paul Robeson, who sang at a CCC fundraiser in November 1937.[31]

After London, Manchester was the largest and liveliest of the local CCC groups, in part thanks to the Irish activist John de Courcy Ireland, who had been Jim Larkin's election agent and was later a founder member of Campaign for Nuclear Disarmament. Somewhat surprisingly, the genteel seaside town of Bournemouth had the second-largest regional branch. An exhibition of Chinese art there was sponsored by the local MP Sir Henry Page Croft, a high Tory. The show's opener was poet Laurence Binyon, author of the lines recited each Remembrance Sunday: 'They shall not grow old as we that are left grow old, age shall not weary them, nor years condemn.' There were still more unexpected supporters. An elderly gentleman who presented Clegg with a cheque for five pounds turned out to be Colonel Younghusband, who had led the 1903 British invasion of Tibet. Not everyone was welcome, however. Sylvia Pankhurst offered to

---

30   Chiang Kai-shek was kidnapped by Yang and Zhang Xueliang. In 1949, Chiang, copying the barbaric *miezu* (family extermination) punishment from imperial times, had Yang murdered along with his wife and children.

31   Worth roughly 15,000 pounds in 2020.

join the committee but was rebuffed by Dorothy Woodman – probably because of her 'leftist' challenge to Communist orthodoxy. Clegg later regretted that he had not dared to stand up to Woodman on this.[32]

Clegg, Willie Gallagher, and Aneurin Bevan attended an international conference of Lord Cecil's International Peace Campaign that was packed with 'French priests, English ministers of the Church . . . Catholic intellectuals [and] Communist deputies'. Clegg, who chaired one of the sessions, recalled how Nehru helped him out as he stumbled through a translation in 'abominable' French.[33] The IPC claimed a huge following worldwide. Lord Cecil said it had 15 million supporters. Others arrived at the fantastic figure of 123 million by including the membership of affiliated organisations.

Of the 'great and the good' among CCC supporters, probably the greatest contribution came from a member of another Quaker dynasty, Margery Fry of the Fry's Chocolate family, who was Gollancz's deputy as vice-chair. Fry, the former principal of Somerville College, secretary of the Howard League for Penal Reform, and a BBC governor, was a formidably connected, energetic, and efficient campaigner, 'a public figure called to mind whenever a list of distinguished women . . . [was] needed to underwrite any humane cause'.[34] She brought a new level of professionalism to the committee's work. In 1939, she saved the lives of four Chinese activists in Britain's Tianjin concession who were about to be handed over to the Japanese for almost certain execution.[35] On her initiative, the CCC took legal action to force the foreign secretary, Lord Halifax, to prevent the handover. The CCC lost the first two rounds of the case, but Fry's spirited publicity campaign ensured the appeal was won, and the militants were freed. While Clegg acknowledged Fry's talents, he lamented her hostility to Communism.[36]

32 Younghusband was infamous for a massacre of badly armed Tibetan troops during the invasion. He later became a mystic.

33 Clegg, *Aid China*, 84–5.

34 Enid Huws Jones, *Margery Fry: The Essential Amateur*, Oxford: Oxford University Press, 1966, 154.

35 Ibid., 195–6; and Clegg, *Aid China*, 122, 126.

36 It seems not to have occurred to Clegg that the Communist Party's wild policy swings were legitimate grounds for mistrust. Fry was a member of the Labour Party until she resigned in protest at the expulsion of Stafford Cripps. Asked if she would join the Liberals, she said, 'I have never been a Liberal and I can't imagine that I ever shall be . . . I have always belonged to the Labour Party.' Jones, *Margery Fry*, 193.

When, in May 1938, Japanese bombing of civilians in Canton outraged the middle class, the CCC seized the opportunity to campaign for a consumer boycott. Mary Sheridan Jones took charge, launching an appeal for a Christmas boycott of Japanese toys. Silk was Japan's main export, and Jones followed up the Christmas campaign with an appeal to women to abandon silk stockings in favour of synthetics. The actress Hermione Baddeley appeared at the campaign launch in Conway Hall wearing rayon stockings. High-society women, including Lady Gladstone and Lady Violet Bonham Carter (Asquith's daughter and sometime president of the Liberal Party) signed a no-silk pledge and joined a march down Oxford Street.[37] Soon the campaign spread to the United States, where marchers carried placards with slogans like 'Silk in her stockings paid for that bullet'.[38]

In economic terms, the campaign against Japanese imports was not particularly successful. In 1938, a Cooperative Congress in Scarborough voted for a boycott of goods from aggressor nations, without directly naming Japan. Marks & Spencer, Woolworths, and John Lewis agreed not to sell Japanese goods, *apart* from silk. Gordon Selfridge met a CCC deputation but, after expressing sympathy, declined to implement a boycott. Clegg suggested that the boycott caused a 30 per cent drop in sales of Japanese silk but admitted this may have been due to relabelling.

Along with public meetings and 'bowl of rice' fundraising dinners, protest marches through central London were among the campaign's main activities. Following the traditional route from Hyde Park to Trafalgar Square, the parades were led by a youth band from the East End. The campaign got a free publicity boost when, as marchers passed the Japanese embassy, the Japanese military attaché, a Major Takahashi, slapped Mary Sheridan Jones in the face. The major was arrested, while Jones was 'whisked away' to Fleet Street to be interviewed for the following day's headlines.[39]

---

37   Clegg, *Aid China*, 108–9.

38   Lawrence Glickman, 'Make Lisle the Style: The Politics of Fashion in the Japanese Silk Boycott, 1937–1940', *Journal of Social History*, Vol. 38, No. 3, 2005, 573–608.

39   According to Clegg, this was the only time anyone was arrested during a CCC protest. He ridiculed a claim by Margot Kettle that Philip Toynbee had been arrested on a march, although Clegg admitted it was possible that Toynbee would 'indulge in some wild gesture'. Clegg, *Aid China*, 78, 86.

It is a paradox that, during the Popular Front period, as Communist Parties were reaching out to liberals and democrats in the capitalist world, the Moscow Trials and Stalin's great purges were taking place. Many who applauded Dimitrov's fine words calling for unity against fascism at the seventh Comintern congress overlooked his chilling warning to the opposition:

> There can be no room in our Parties for factions, or for attempts at factionalism. Whoever will try to break up the iron unity of our ranks by any kind of factionalism will get to feel what is meant by the Bolshevik discipline that Lenin and Stalin have always taught us.[40]

Some old enemies of the left greeted Stalin's liquidation of the Old Bolsheviks with barely concealed delight. Churchill, for one, praised the Prosecutor Vyshinsky's 'masterful' performance at the trial of Tukhachevsky.[41] On the left, Stalin's most egregious British apologist was one of the CCC's most frequent public speakers: D. N. Pritt, king's counsel, Labour MP, Fabian, and chairman of the Howard League for Penal Reform. Pritt defended the trials in a series of articles and pamphlets that cannot be read today without eliciting bitter laughter. According to Pritt, the trials had enhanced the reputation of the Soviet judiciary. Like Churchill, Pritt had nothing but praise for 'intelligent' and 'mild-mannered' Vyshinsky (who described Zinoviev and Kamenev as 'rabid dogs' and Bukharin as a cross between a 'fox and a pig'.)[42] Kingsley Martin also thought the trials were 'free and open'. After visiting Trotsky in Mexico, he wrote a faux naïf article for the *New Statesman*, feigning surprise that Trotsky was not a 'stage revolutionary' with 'fuzzy hair' but resembled a 'dapper French artist'. After the visit, he was 'less inclined to doubt the possibility of Trotsky's complicity' and thought 'the possibility of his embarking on a crazy plot more credible'.[43] Gollancz, who was convinced, correctly, that fascism could only be

40   Georgi Dimitrov, 'Concluding Address', in *Seventh World Congress Communist International*, London: Modern Books, 1935, 10.

41   Winston Churchill, *The Gathering Storm*, London: Cassell & Co., 1948, 225.

42   D. N. Pritt and Pat Sloan, *The Moscow Trial Was Fair* (pamphlet), London: Russia Today, 1936–1937, available at marxists.org.

43   Kingsley Martin, 'Trotsky in Mexico', 10 April 1937, in *Statesmanship: The Best of the New Statesman*, Jason Cowley, ed., London: Weidenfeld & Nicolson, 2019.

defeated with Soviet help, censored criticism of Stalin in his publications. Most notoriously, he refused to publish H. N. Brailsford's *Why Capitalism Means War* because it criticised the trials.[44]

Despite determined opposition from right-wing Labour and trade union leaders, some workers took direct action in support of the boycott. In December 1937, dockers in Southampton refused to unload a 200-ton cargo of Japanese silk and toys from the *Duchess of Richmond*, a Canadian ship. They stencilled the message 'refused by Southampton dockers' to each crate, and the ship had to return to Canada with its cargo. The action was led by Trevor Stallard, a shop steward for the Transport and General Workers Union (TGWU) and a member of the Communist Party. Stallard, a former Welsh miner and professional footballer, had a long record of activism on the docks and in the unemployed workers' movement. He also organised a demonstration to run Oswald Mosley's fascist blackshirts out of Southampton. During the mêlée, Mosley was forced to hide in a tram.[45]

Dockers in Middlesbrough followed the Southampton lead by refusing to load scrap iron onto the Japanese ship *Haruna Maru*. Clegg took a night train to the northeast and organised a public meeting with the Trades Council and the local Labour Party. The *Haruna Maru* issue was morally straightforward: unlike the fancy goods on the *Duchess of Richmond*, the scrap iron was indisputably war material and public opinion was on the side of the dockers to the extent that a minister asked Clegg to address his congregation, but that did not deter TGWU officials from working with the management to crush the unofficial action. They first tried to load the iron onto another ship, the *Bhutan*, owned by P&O. When this failed, the *Haruna Maru* sailed for London, and the scrap iron was sent on by rail to meet it. Clegg raced back to London, where the employers were scheming to demoralise the dockers by offering unemployed Chinese sailors fantastic wages to sign on the *Haruna Maru*. A Chinese restaurant boss sent Clegg to a Limehouse laundry, where an elderly Chinese man, whose word clearly carried weight, assured him that no Chinese would dare sign on. Trevor Stallard

---

44 Dudley Edwards, *Gollancz*, 174.

45 See Graham Stevenson, 'Stallard Trevor', Graham Stevenson archive, grahamstevenson.me.uk; and 'Fascist Oswald Mosley Hid in a Tram to Escape the Angry Mob in Southampton', *Daily Echo*, 13 December 2012, dailyecho.co.uk.

addressed a public meeting in Canning Town Hall alongside Maude Royden and the Reverends Reginald Sorenson and Jack Putterill.[46] Tom Mann, still campaigning for China at the age of eighty-two, spoke at a mass meeting outside Customs House. The London dockers remained solid, the employers gave up, and the *Haruna Maru* sailed without its cargo.

The rank-and-file movement in Britain was echoed around the world. In Australia, dockers at several ports refused to load scrap iron on to Japanese ships. A two-month standoff over the cargo steamer *Dalfram* earned Robert Menzies the nickname 'pig-iron Bob' after he used the so-called 'dog collar act' to force dockers to load the ship. Despite his efforts, Chinese sailors and Australian dockers cooperated on several occasions to thwart shipments to Japan.[47] In France, Leon Blum's Popular Front government banned exports of manganese and iron to Japan and restricted Japanese imports. The Irish Seamen and Port Workers' Union voted for a complete boycott of Japanese goods, and the West Coast of the United States also saw boycott campaigns. The Japanese were worried enough to send the moderate trade unionist Suzuki Bunji on an international tour to argue against the strike and boycott campaign but in San Francisco, he found the mood of American workers so hostile that he abandoned attempts at persuasion in favour of threats of economic retaliation by Japan.[48]

In Britain, the *Haruna Maru* affair marked the high point of trade union action in support of China's resistance to Japan. One reason was the determined opposition of Trade Union Congress general secretary Walter Citrine and Ernest Bevin, the right-wing leader of the TGWU. Bevin, in particular, was hostile to anything that resembled a political strike, and to rank-and-file militancy in general.[49] He denounced calls

---

46   Sorenson was a Unitarian minister and a long-serving Labour member of Parliament who excoriated the British Empire. Putterill was a well-known Christian socialist.

47   The Transport Workers' Act of 1928 required all dockers to hold a government licence, nicknamed a dog collar.

48   *CCC China Bulletin*, No. 5, cited in Gordon Daniels et.al., *The History of Anglo-Japanese Relations, 1600–2000*, Vol. 5, Basingstoke: Palgrave, 2002, 276.

49   Bevin is lionised by the right for his conduct as wartime minister for Labour and as foreign secretary in the Attlee government. A phrase monotonously trotted out and intended as a compliment in right-wing literature is that he was a foreign secretary 'in the tradition created by Castlereagh, Canning and Palmerston'. Starting in the 1920s,

for action from 'bodies not connected with the Trade Union Movement', a sentiment echoed in a *Daily Herald* article that ridiculed 'professors, clerks, shop assistants, housewives and book clubs'.[50] Shortly after the Southampton action, dockers in Glasgow refused to unload a Japanese cargo, but TGWU officials forced them to back down.[51] Bevin bullied the aged Ben Tillett into refusing an invitation to speak in Middlesbrough. When the Southampton dockers refused to unload Japanese goods from another ship, the *Berengaria*, Stallard, already a marked man, was sacked along with two others. TGWU officials had labelled the *Duchess of Richmond* strike 'an embarrassing affair' and sabotaged a walkout in support of the three. Stallard was out of work for a year but treasured a letter of thanks from the Chinese embassy.[52]

Some Chinese seamen on a Norwegian ship docked in Newcastle refused to sail it to Japan, where it was to be scrapped. Unfortunately, a replacement Indian crew was found. Tom Mann and Zhu Xuefan spoke at a public meeting, and the India League sent a telegram asking the men not to serve, but they had already signed up. There was also unofficial action in Liverpool, but it collapsed under pressure from the TGWU. The National Council of Labour,[53] dominated by Bevin and Citrine, refused to back the dockers' action. Bevin claimed to be in favour of (non-existent) government action but was against the only action on offer – from the workers. Citrine opposed union action but favoured a consumer boycott, even though he admitted it would amount to no more than a 'moral gesture'. [54]

Clegg and Hardy also supported Chinese seafarers taking industrial action for their own economic demands. Clegg travelled to Liverpool in May 1941, braving heavy bombing by the Luftwaffe, to support Chinese sailors who were demanding parity with British sailors while on convoy

---

rank-and-file dockers several times set up breakaway unions to escape the TGWU, the last time being the formation of the Blue Union in Liverpool in the mid-1950s. The Scottish TGWU broke away in 1932 and remained a separate organisation until 1972. William Hunter, 'Hands off the Blue Union! Democracy on the Docks', *Labour Review*, Vol. 3, No. 1 (January–February 1958), 540, available at billhunterweb.org.uk.

50   Buchanan, *East Wind*, 71–2.
51   Clegg, *Aid China*, 46.
52   Stevenson, 'Stallard Trevor'.
53   A joint Labour Party–TUC body that existed from 1921 to 1946. It consisted of delegates from the TUC General Council, the Labour Party NEC, and the PLP.
54   Daniels, *History of Anglo-Japanese Relations*, 275.

duty. Though the Chinese were resigned to receiving lower wages than their British colleagues, they insisted they should receive the same danger bonus for serving on convoys. The action was led by Sam Chen, a Chinese activist who had settled in Liverpool, joined the Communist Party, and organised a Liverpool branch of the Chinese Seamen's Union. The seafarers won their dispute[55] but despite their contribution to the war effort, James Chuter Ede, home secretary in the postwar Labour government, 'a liberal nonconformist of the old school', later secretly and illegally deported thousands of Chinese sailors.[56]

Clegg's trip to Liverpool took place during a near-terminal crisis in the CCC precipitated by the Molotov-Ribbentrop Pact. Gollancz, for whom the struggle against fascism was everything, saw the Soviet rapprochement with Hitler as a pact with the devil, a monstrous betrayal. He also denounced Stalin's non-aggression pact with Japan, signed after the Soviet victory at Khalkhin Gol. The Communist Party's swift adjustment to the Moscow line, abandoning anti-fascism for a campaign against the 'imperialist war', disgusted and depressed him. According to Clegg, he 'was never the same again . . . the joy and self-confidence had gone'.[57] On New Year's Day 1940, Gollancz published *Where Are You Going*, an impassioned open letter to Communists. Then, in 1941, he brought out a full-length book, *The Betrayal of the Left*, with a preface by Harold Laski and essays by George Orwell and John Strachey.[58] On the other side of the divide in the CCC, the ever-faithful D. N. Pritt fronted an anti-war People's Convention organised by the Communist Party.

Gollancz stopped distributing books by Communists through the LBC. In response, party members resigned from the club's discussion groups. Since the groups had provided many of the foot soldiers of the campaign, CCC activities slackened off, and funds dried up. The

---

55 Had the sailors' action happened a few weeks later, Clegg and Hardy may well have opposed it. After Hitler attacked the Soviet Union in June 1941, the CPGB became super-patriotic and regarded industrial action as virtually equivalent to sabotage. The abrupt change of line did the party no harm. Membership reached more than 50,000 during the war and the loss of members due to the Stalin-Hitler pact turned out to be no more than a blip.

56 There were as many as 20,000 Chinese sailors in Liverpool, many of whom had married, settled down, and had children. Some were torn from their families in night raids by police.

57 Clegg, *Aid China*, 25.

58 Morgan, *Against Fascism and War*, 268.

committee gave up its office, moving back into the UDC premises. Because there was no money to pay George Hardy, he lost his job as industrial organiser. Clegg, although still active, had resigned his full-time post because of ill health, and the only staff left were Mary Jones and a typist.

There was a significant political lobby calling for some sort of accommodation with Japan to protect British interests in the East. The attitude of the government hardened, and a CCC art exhibition planned for the Everyman Theatre in Hampstead was cancelled without explanation. Following its volte-face, the Communist Party was isolated and reviled. Clegg spent two months sewing mailbags in Wormwood Scrubs – punishment for demonstrating in favour of Indian Independence on Empire Day (24 May) 1940. In January 1941, Labour's Herbert Morrison, home secretary in Churchill's government, banned the *Daily Worker*.

The atmosphere at CCC meetings became embittered; after Margery Fry accused Mary Jones of using the committee to recruit Chinese overseas students to the Communist Party, Clegg walked out in protest. At the 1941 annual general meeting, Gollancz, Fry, and Lord Listowel – a Labour peer who had hitherto been a CCC stalwart[59] – circulated an open letter to members threatening to resign unless Communist influence in the campaign was curbed. Kingsley Martin, till then a faithful fellow traveller, also threatened to resign, although Dorothy Woodman remained neutral. The crisis stopped short of an outright break-up of the committee, but Gollancz, Listowel, and Fry increasingly withdrew from active involvement. Wartime restrictions had, in any case, made campaigning nearly impossible. The Manchester regional office disbanded. Other related campaign groups, including the Peace Council and the Women's International League, also began to wind down.

Operation Barbarossa – Hitler's attack on the Soviet Union – revived the campaign's fortunes. It coincided with the arrival of China's new ambassador to Britain, Wellington Koo, whom the CCC had invited, along with US and Soviet ambassadors, to speak at a 'bowl of rice' dinner on the anniversary of the Japanese invasion. After the news of the invasion broke, there was a clamour for tickets from people eager to hear what

---

59   William Hare, Earl of Listowel, was one of the CCC's main public speakers and organisers. Formerly a lieutenant in military intelligence, after the Second World War Listowel was successively postmaster general, minister for information, and secretary of state for India and Burma in the Attlee government. His final official appointment was as governor-general of Ghana.

the Soviet ambassador, Ivan Maisky, had to say. In the event, he said nothing, but, according to Clegg, the dinner was nevertheless 'one of the high moments of the CCC'.[60] With the Soviet Union now a wartime ally, the political environment was much more favourable to the CPGB, and it reached its peak membership of 56,000 in 1942. Gollancz, although he refused to reconcile with the British Communists, set up a new organisation, the Anglo-Soviet Public Relations Association, to foster closer relations between the two countries. As with the CCC, its list of sponsors was a roll-call of prominent intellectuals and society figures – Robert Boothby, Strachey, Professor Cyril Joad of the Brains Trust, Violet Bonham Carter, Leonard Woolf, and, from the CCC, Martin, Fry, and Listowel.

As the China campaign revived, the demand for speakers again outstripped supply. Clegg was called up to speak almost every week. Gollancz largely kept his distance, leaving the running of the CCC to Fry, but the Left Book Club stepped up its China-related output, publishing Edgar Snow's account of the Nanjing Massacre, *Scorched Earth*, Agnes Smedley's *Battle Hymn of China*, and *The Chinese Communists* – a collection that included articles by Mao and other CCP leaders. Michael Lindsay sent a series of articles to the *Times* that the CCC republished as *The North China Front*. Clegg wrote a pamphlet, *China the Unconquerable*, and a book, *The Birth of New China*.

The CCC had held together during World War II, but it could not survive the Chinese civil war. Officially, the committee maintained a neutral position, but some members were unhappy about a tendency to favour the Communists. Margery Fry threatened to resign the chair but was persuaded to stay on as vice-chair after the KMT murdered two leading members of the Democratic League, Li Gongpu and Wen Yiduo, in Kunming.[61] Michael Lindsay, who had recently returned from Yan'an after five years with the Eighth Route Army, replaced her as chairman. Hilda Selwyn-Clarke, who had been interned by the Japanese in Hong Kong, became an honorary secretary. Both she and Lindsay, whose father was a Labour peer, were close to the new Labour government. Listowel, a long-term CCC supporter, was now a minister in Attlee's cabinet.

As it became clear that the Communists were going to win the civil war, the British government looked for ways to establish links with

---

60 Clegg, *Aid China*, 139–40.
61 Wen Yiduo was assassinated after delivering a eulogy at Li Gongpu's funeral.

them, and the CCC became a convenient conduit. Two issues particularly concerned the British: the status of Hong Kong and the so-called Emergency in Malaya. The British were determined to hold on to Hong Kong and, convinced the Chinese Communists were supporting the insurgents in Malaya, wanted the PRC government to 'us[e] its influence to restore peace'.[62] In October 1949, when Michael Lindsay, once a strong, if critical, supporter of the Chinese Communists, visited Beijing – ostensibly on behalf of the CCC, but also to present the British government point of view – he was not well received. In Clegg's view, the CCC was fatally compromised. It had sided with the colonial power in Malaya and abandoned a long-standing policy that Hong Kong should be returned to China. By allowing itself 'to be used as a catspaw' by the Foreign Office, the CCC had 'committed suicide'.[63] Clegg, with others including Reginald Bridgeman and Reg Birch, set about organising an alternative. In December 1949, they launched the Britain-China Friendship Society. Its supporters included Arthur Waley, the Nobel Peace Prize winner Lord Boyd Orr, and D. N. Pritt. Perhaps surprisingly, Michael Lindsay's father, Sandie Lindsay, Lord Lindsay of Birker, was also among the founder members.

After the toll of constant travelling forced Clegg to resign from full-time work for the CCC, he took up a desk job. In 1941, he was made editor of the Communist Party weekly *World News and Views*. He visited China only once, in April–May 1951, with a delegation from the Friendship Society he had helped establish. George Hardy was also on the delegation and met some of his old comrades from the Shanghai underground. As well as Shanghai, they visited Nanjing and Beijing, where they watched a May Day parade of 800,000 people. As one would expect, Clegg and Hardy were thrilled by New China. Thereafter, Clegg remained a loyal supporter of the People's Republic through thick and thin, although he joined the great exodus from the CPGB in 1956–57 following the overthrow of Imre Nagy's reformist government by Soviet tanks. It is not clear why he left the party. His daughter Jenny believes it was a protest against the invasion of Hungary, but, according to another

---

62 Michael Lindsay, draft statement to PRC government on behalf of CCC. Quoted in ibid., 182.
63 Ibid., 184.

source, it was due to a dispute over China.[64] Whatever the reason, Clegg's resignation entailed personal and financial sacrifice. He had been on the staff of the *Daily Worker* since 1947 and, by 1956, was its foreign editor. Leaving the party meant he lost his job and most of his friends. As an ex-Communist full-timer, he was virtually unemployable and relied on casual work for the Workers' Educational Association for several years.

Eventually, City University gave him a job teaching economics and political science. He wrote academic papers on the Levellers and the Diggers in the English Civil War and the role of skilled craftsmen in the development of European science. Extending the range of his writing still further, he left several volumes of poetry, at least one of which, *The Linden Tree*, was well regarded by critics. It was 'an extraordinary collage ... of miniaturesque component[s]' with 'remarkably convincing' portrayals of working-class life in 'language that is neither sentimental nor condescending'. However, the text's abundant 'sensuality and erotic male fantasy' were 'problematic' and indeed 'trying in the post-feminist 1990s'.[65] Already quite elderly by then, Clegg was becoming a man out of his time. Another volume, *Scenes from the Sixties*, published by the Artery Collective, was illustrated with woodcuts by the Flemish artist Frans Masereel, whose work had inspired Lu Xun and the Chinese woodcut movement of the 1930s. One of the poems included this poignant lament on the Sino-Soviet split:

You have torn the banner between you
leaving mankind to its plight
drowning its cry of agony
in savage polemical fight

While Clegg was a loyal defender of China, he was not tempted to join a Maoist group, perhaps because Britain was never fertile ground for Maoism.[66] Perhaps wisely, he kept his distance from the grouplets

---

64 See Graham Stevenson, 'Clegg Arthur', Graham Stevenson archive, grahamstevenson.me.uk.

65 See Pauline Polkey, 'Arthur Clegg's "The Eildon Tree" ', *Critical Survey*, Vol. 4, No. 1 (1992), 91–4, 92–3.

66 Reg Birch set up a breakaway party, but his CPB-ML never had more than a couple of hundred members, some motivated by nostalgia for Stalin rather than enthusiasm for China. Birch was a talented union negotiator respected by workers and employers alike. Had he not gone out on a limb politically, he might have been elected general secretary of the engineering union.

and remained an independent leftist. His two principles were support for all anti-colonial movements and unquestioning loyalty to the PRC. His only contretemps with China was initiated by the Chinese side. During the Cultural Revolution, the CCC and its supporters were criticised as revisionist, perhaps because of Michael Lindsay's ill-advised diplomatic démarche. Clegg was later called to the Chinese embassy to receive an apology.

Justification of the twists and turns of Chinese foreign policy did not make for popularity. Clegg blamed eurocentrism for his failure to find a British publisher for his *Aid China* memoir, but, for most left-wingers, the shine had long since gone from the People's Republic. After years denouncing détente between the Soviets and the West, Mao welcomed Richard Nixon and Henry Kissinger to Beijing during the Vietnam War. 'Soviet Social Imperialism' would soon be declared a bigger enemy than American imperialism, and China's reaction to Augusto Pinochet's coup in Chile amounted to a welcome. Most leftists were horrified by Deng Xiaoping's 1979 invasion of Vietnam. Through all of these events, Clegg doggedly defended China. His book was eventually published by New World Press in the eventful year 1989; a second edition, published eight years later, carried a preface by the former foreign minister Huang Hua, who noted, with the tact of a veteran diplomat, that 'certain circumstances prevented [friends of China] from seeing eye-to-eye with us on all issues'.[67] Clegg, however, saw precisely eye to eye with China, even on the Tiananmen crackdown, and had a furious row with his old friend David Crook, who had repented his Stalinism and supported the students.

In retirement, Clegg moved to Yorkshire, where he was active in the peace movement. There is a touching photograph of him with another elderly man and a dog, protesting against cruise missiles beside the Ripon war memorial. He was a local character who rated an obituary in the *Ripon Gazette* that described him tactfully as 'strong in his convictions and sometimes unbending'. The Chinese did not forget him and organised a memorial service in Beijing, where his daughter Jenny read the eulogy.

---

67 Clegg, *Aid China*, 5.

14

Writers on the Front Line

On the day before he died, Lu Xun visited Kaji Wataru and Ikeda Yuki, a young Japanese couple who had recently fled to Shanghai. Kaji was translating a volume of Lu Xun's essays with the help of Lu's protégé Hu Feng, who arrived together with Lu Xun in the early afternoon. It was the first time Lu Xun had been to Kaji and Ikeda's home, and they were naturally delighted. Ikeda wrote an account of the afternoon that was later published as *Lu Xun's Last Day*. The four talked for several hours. Their conversation touched on death and ghosts, but was light hearted rather than morbid. Lu Xun had brought a present for the young couple – a volume of woodcut prints by the German artist Käthe Kollwitz. He was a great enthusiast and promoter of the woodcut movement then popular among radical Chinese artists. In the late afternoon, Lu Xun went on to visit another Japanese friend, Uchiyama Kanzo, who owned a bookshop frequented by Shanghai's left-wing intellectuals. But that night, he fell ill with violent coughing fits – he had tuberculosis and was a chain smoker – and never recovered. At his funeral a few days later, Kaji was one of the chief mourners and led the cortège in the front row of pallbearers alongside the novelist Ba Jin.

Kaji had arrived in Shanghai a few months before, in January 1936, after being detained in Japan for nearly two years under the Peace Preservation Laws. It was one of several spells in jail, and each time he had been tortured. In 1933, he was arrested because, after the police beat the general secretary of the Proletarian Writers' Guild, Kobayashi Takiji, to death, they found Kaji's calling card among his possessions. Kaji later told Edgar Snow:

> The police did not charge me with any crime, I was just shifted from one jail to another. The filthy little cells held an average of twenty people. Most of them were sick. I was beaten in every jail. The police would bind me up and lift me from the floor, beat me to unconsciousness, then revive me and beat me again.[1]

Like Kobayashi, Kaji was a leading activist in the proletarian literature movement. He had been the editor of the magazine *Fighting Flag* and, in 1930, published a short novel, *Rodo nikki to kutsu* (Work diary and shoes). He joined the Japanese Communist Party in 1932.

Kaji, whose real name was Seguchi Mitsugi, was born into a well-to-do family in 1903. He got involved in radical politics while at university, where his first protest was against the special treatment accorded a classmate who was a member of the imperial family. Prince Yamanashi's desk was set higher than those of the other students, who were expected to bow to him when they entered the classroom. Disgusted, Kaji organised a class boycott and managed to sustain it for three years. After leaving university, he joined the Workers' and Peasants' Party, set up a school, and joined the movement to organise peasant unions.[2] His activism led to several arrests. When he was released from jail in November 1935, fearing that contacting his friends and associates would lead to their arrests, he decided to leave Japan. Posing as a member of a theatre troupe, he boarded a steamer for Shanghai, which, at the time, was a free port where he could disembark without a passport.

In Shanghai, he joined the loose circle of left-wing intellectuals around Sun Yat-sen's widow, Song Qingling. He befriended members of the League of Left-Wing Writers,[3] several of whom, like Lu Xun, had studied in Japan. Lu Xun took him under his wing, and his patronage helped protect Kaji from secret agents who might otherwise have spirited him back to Japan. His other friends included Rewi Alley and the

---

1   Edgar Snow, *The Battle for Asia*, New York: World Publishing Company, 1942, 189.

2   Andrew Roth, *Dilemma in Japan*, London: Gollancz, 1946, 235.

3   The league dissolved itself in 1936 after the formation of the Second United Front.

American Communists Max and Grace Granich, who published an English-language journal.

It was in Shanghai that Kaji met and married Ikeda Yuki. Ikeda, like Kaji, was a writer and a political refugee. She wrote at least one novel, *The Servant's Story*. While at college, she joined Kagawa Toyohiko's[4] Christian socialist movement and later worked with the feminist socialist Baroness Ishimoto (Kato Shizue) to organise women workers. She served even more prison time than Kaji and was also brutally tortured – interrogators broke all of her fingers. She had fled Japan before Kaji and survived by dancing with strangers for tips in Shanghai's nightclubs.[5] She was known as a brilliant wit and conversationalist.[6]

Most of Shanghai's leftists lived in the relative safety of the French Concession and International Settlement. However, that safety was about to evaporate for Kaji and Ikeda. In July 1937, the Japanese launched a full-scale invasion of China, and by August a million troops were engaged in a pitiless street-by-street battle for Shanghai. In the chaos, Kaji and Yuki were not only in danger from stray bombs and bullets but also from Japanese agents and revenge attacks by Chinese civilians. They were forced into hiding and, in despair, were considering suicide when, in November, Rewi Alley arranged for them to sail to Hong Kong.[7]

In Hong Kong, Kaji wrote articles denouncing the Japanese invasion for Hu Feng's journal *Qiyue* and other leftist publications. While in Shanghai, the couple had asked Song Qingling to arrange for them to work for the Nationalist government, but her request was rebuffed. The situation changed after the Communist poet and historian Guo Moruo was appointed head of the government propaganda department. Guo had studied in Japan and spent much of his adult life there. While he had been a propagandist for the KMT's National Revolutionary Army during the Northern Expedition, he had fled to Japan in 1928 to evade Chiang Kai-shek's White Terror. He was looking for Japanese dissidents to work in the propaganda department. The KMT, uneasily reconciled with the

---

4   Kagawa Toyohiko (1888–1960) was a Christian pacifist, socialist, trade union organiser, and campaigner for women's suffrage. He won four Nobel Prizes.

5   Roth, *Dilemma in Japan*, 1946, 237.

6   Ariyoshi Koji, *From Kona to Yenan: The Political Memoirs of Koji Ariyoshi*, Edward Beechert and Alice Beechert, eds., Honolulu: University of Hawaii Press, 2000, 104.

7   Roth, *Dilemma in Japan*, 238.

CCP in the Second United Front, saw Guo as a useful ornament for their government in a post that conferred little power. But, with Guo's help, Kaji and Ikeda were able to reach Wuhan, the Chinese capital after the fall of Nanjing.[8]

Kaji and Ikeda were hired as advisors to dozens of Japanese-speaking Chinese whose main task was to prepare leaflets and pamphlets to be air-dropped to Japanese troops. They were soon among the mainstays of KMT propaganda work. The propaganda department employed around one thousand in all [9] and, as well as leaflet drops, also transmitted radio broadcasts in Japanese. It was dangerous work. The Japanese bombed the building where Kaji and Ikeda were working, and while Kaji and Ikeda were pulled alive from the rubble, the attack killed many of their colleagues. Their work on behalf of China became known in Japan after pamphlets dropped on Kyushu in May 1938 urged Japanese civilians to follow the example of 'Mr and Mrs Kaji', who had rejected militarism.[10] When spies in Wuhan discovered their real identities, Japanese newspapers denounced them as traitors, and their house in Wuhan was targeted in a bombing raid.[11]

In early 1939, Kaji was sent to Guilin to teach Japanese at a guerrilla-warfare training school in Guilin.[12] It was probably here that he began the work for which he and Ikeda are mainly remembered – their efforts to re-educate Japanese POWs and employ them in propaganda and counter-intelligence work. Their immediate aim was to recruit prisoners to the current war effort, but their longer-term goal was to create an enlightened cadre who would take part in the reconstruction of post-war Japan.

---

8   Guo Moruo was famous for his poetry and for his archaeological work on 'oracle bones' – sheep scapulas and turtle shells inscribed with early Chinese characters and used in ancient fortune-telling rituals. He was an energetic and effective propaganda chief, but Lu Xun regarded him as a dilettante, and his reputation has suffered because of revelations about his ruthless womanising and his later years as one of Mao Zedong's most notorious literary toadies. See Stephen MacKinnon, *Wuhan, 1938: War, Refugees, and the Making of Modern China*, University of California Press, 2008, 77–80.

9   Barak Kushner, *The Thought War: Japanese Imperial Propaganda*, Honolulu: University of Hawaii Press, 2007, 144.

10   Yoshida Takashi. *The Making of the 'Rape of Nanking': History and Memory in Japan, China, and the United States*, New York: Oxford University Press, 2009, 24.

11   Roth, *Dilemma in Japan*, 239.

12   Kushner, *The Thought War*, 141.

While in prison in Japan, Kaji had shared a cell with a former soldier who told him in a matter-of-fact way, without any outward signs of guilt, about atrocities he had committed in China, including rapes and beheadings.[13] Kaji, although disgusted and appalled, attributed the man's depravity to the indoctrination of the Japanese military, and Japanese society as a whole, with aggressive imperial ideology. He believed indoctrination could be combated by counter-propaganda and proposed a re-education programme to win over prisoners of war, who would then be sent to the front lines to undermine enemy morale, encourage desertions, and recruit agents within ranks of the Japanese army. The Nationalist government, although sceptical that fanatically loyal Japanese troops could be turned, eventually agreed to the proposal.

Kaji was an unlikely recruiter of hardened and battle-scarred prisoners, but he and the still more delicate Ikeda nevertheless won over scores of Japanese troops. The renowned China scholar John King Fairbank, who was working for the Office of Strategic Services in China, described Kaji as elfin and poetic. Ariyoshi Koji, a Japanese American intelligence officer, was expecting to meet a forceful character and was surprised by Kaji's doe-eyed gentility. According to Ariyoshi, Ikeda, rather than Kaji, was 'the pillar' of the re-education programme. She was especially effective in winning over the POWs, who regarded her as a young mother figure.[14]

Their approach was to appeal to class solidarity with the simple message that ordinary soldiers had more in common with Chinese workers and peasants than with Japanese militarists and capitalists. It was surprisingly successful. In POW camps in Guilin and Hunan, Kaji and Ikeda recruited around eighty prisoners.[15] Kaji accompanied his converts to the front lines, where they used loudhailers to urge Japanese troops to desert. They reminded them of their hardships and those of their families back in Japan in a war that would only profit the rich. They also left comfort parcels containing soap and other hard-to-come-by luxuries near Japanese outposts. In December 1939, Kaji, Ikeda, and their new recruits set up the Japanese People's Anti-war Alliance

---

13   Yoshida *The Making of the 'Rape of Nanking'*, 23.

14   John King Fairbank, *Chinabound: A Fifty-Year Memoir*, New York: Harper & Row, 1982, 293, 310; Ariyoshi, *From Kona to Yenan*, 104–5.

15   Kushner, *The Thought War*, 142; Yoshida, *The Making of the 'Rape of Nanking'*, 34.

(Nihonjin hansen domei). A notable recruit was Seisaku Shiomi, former secretary of the Japanese consulate in Hanoi and a member of the Japanese secret service. After being captured in December 1938 while spying on the Chinese frontier, he joined the propaganda war, making radio broadcasts to Japan.[16]

However, Kaji and Ikeda's campaign was relatively short lived. Right-wingers in the KMT accused them of indoctrinating the prisoners with Communist propaganda.[17] The Second United Front between the KMT and the CCP was, from the outset, a fragile arrangement. By 1941, especially after the New Fourth Army Incident, when the Nationalists attacked Communist troops who had supposedly disobeyed orders, it had broken down in all but name. Kaji and Ikeda were ordered to close down the Anti-war Alliance and their POW re-education project. Their recruits were arrested and returned to prison camps. Kaji and Ikeda spent most of the rest of the war in Chongqing, where they were closely watched and kept under virtual house arrest.

Shunned by the KMT government, the couple began working for the United States Office of War Information (OWI) – mainly translating propaganda leaflets into Japanese. By early 1945, the OSS became interested in restarting the POW re-education programme and offered Kaji a salary of 200 dollars a month to set up an operation in Kunming. Kaji was willing to cooperate but insisted that he and his new organisation – the League for the Establishment of a Democratic Japan (Minshu Nihon kensetsu domei), retain their independence and that his status would be that of a consultant, not an employee, of the OSS. Given Kaji's intention that he and the league would play a role in post-war Japanese politics, his reluctance to be seen as an instrument of the Americans was reasonable. But the OSS precisely wanted to recruit Kaji as a regular agent. Negotiations broke down after Kaji and Ikeda refused to sign oaths of loyalty. Relations between the couple and the OSS were by now acrimonious, at least on the OSS side. One American agent wrote that he and others were 'thoroughly disgusted' with Kaji and suggested he be 'talked to sternly under some duress'.[18] However, by this time, it was late

---

16   Roth, *Dilemma in Japan*, 240.

17   Kushner, *The Thought War*, 142.

18   Erik Esselstrom, 'From Wartime Friend to Cold War Fiend: The Abduction of Kaji Wataru and US Japan Relations at Occupation's End', *Journal of Cold War Studies*, Vol. 17, No. 3 (Summer 2015), 159–83, 171.

July 1945. A few weeks later, the United States dropped atom bombs on Hiroshima and Nagasaki, and the issue became moot.

When Kaji and Ikeda tried to return to Japan in 1946, their departure was held up by the Americans. Kaji asked John King Fairbank for help. Fairbank wrote a letter to the army, but later recalled: 'This intervention got Kaji back home but gave me a black mark. We were already afraid of the Communists . . . Security was at work.'[19] Back in Japan, Kaji resumed his political activism. He stood as a candidate for the Diet but was not elected. He wrote extensively, including about his wartime experiences in China. In short, he was an active but not overly prominent member of the Japanese left. However, that changed near the end of the American occupation when he became the centre of a political scandal.

On the evening of 25 November 1951, while strolling in the seaside town of Kanagawa, Kaji was abducted by United States secret agents belonging to the Z Unit – a clandestine organisation headed by Colonel Jack Canon. Canon reported to Major General Charles A. Willoughby, the head of US Army Intelligence in the Far East. Willoughby's political views might be described as far right or, more straightforwardly, as fascist. He had been decorated by Mussolini, was an enthusiastic supporter of Franco, and later became a lobbyist for the Spanish dictator. An 'alarming' Texan gun enthusiast, Canon eventually shot himself in 1981. Willoughby set up the Z Unit in 1947, giving it a wide brief to carry out operations across Asia, including in Korea, China, and the Soviet Union, as well as Japan. The Z Unit staff was drawn from all countries in the region. Canon's second in command was a Korean, Yeon Jeong, who was personally assigned to the unit by the South Korean president, Syngman Rhee.[20]

Kaji was not seen again until the evening of 7 December 1952, when, at a press conference in his lawyer's house, he recounted how he had been released earlier that day after being interrogated and tortured in various secret locations for more than a year. His interrogators, both Z Unit and CIA, had accused him of spying for the Soviet Union, but their overriding aim appeared to be to recruit him to US intelligence – precisely by applying the kind of 'duress' earlier suggested in China by

---

19   Fairbank, *Chinabound*, 310
20   Tessa Morris-Suzuki, *The Korean War in Asia: A Hidden History*, Lanham, MD: Rowman & Littlefield, 2018, 173–6.

the OSS. He had been taken first to the Z Unit's Tokyo headquarters – an ornate mansion, former home of the Iwasaki family, owners of Mitsubishi. After a few days of brutal interrogation, he was moved to another safe house, the Tosen Club in Kawasaki. There, Kaji wrote a letter addressed to a friend – the former Shanghai bookshop owner Uchiyama Kanzo, now head of the Japan-China Friendship Association in Tokyo – and attempted suicide by drinking a bottle of bleach. However, he survived, and the young safe-house cook, Yamada Zenjiro, was assigned to nurse him back to health. Yamada, a former air force cadet, had been the Canon family cook before the colonel reassigned him to the Z Unit operation.

As he had in China when faced with OSS demands, Kaji refused to cooperate with his captors. His intractability presented them with a problem: given that the US occupation of Japan was scheduled to end by April 1952, holding Kaji beyond the end of the occupation would infringe Japan's sovereignty and embarrass both the United States and Japan. But it was equally difficult to see how his detention could be explained if he was released earlier. At some point, it seems, Canon hired Japanese hitmen to kill Kaji and dispose of his body, but he called them off after they demanded too high a price.[21] As this episode shows, cynical, reckless, and chaotic improvisation was the hallmark of Canon's activities. Hiring the family cook to work for a clandestine unit was amateurish enough, but assigning Yamada to look after Kaji after his failed suicide attempt turned out to be a catastrophic security lapse. The two men became friends, and Yamada sought out Uchiyama to tell him that Kaji was alive and being held by US intelligence agents. In June 1952, Yamada quit his job at the Z Unit and began working with Uchiyama and the Kaji family to expose the scandal. Towards the end of 1952, stories about Kaji's abduction began appearing in the Japanese press and, on 6 December, Yamada, Uchiyama, Ikeda Yuki, Kaji's father and sister, and the Socialist Diet member Inomata Kōzō held a press conference to demand his release. The following day, the US flew Kaji from Okinawa – where they had recently been holding him – to Tokyo and released him into the street.

The revelation that Kaji had been abducted created an uproar in Japan. If an American secret unit was operating on Japanese soil and

---

21   Esselstrom, 'From Wartime Friend to Cold War Fiend', 179.

abducting Japanese citizens, especially relatively prominent figures like Kaji, then oppositionists could claim the occupation had ended in name only. The pro-Western government of Yoshida Shigeru, contested by both left and right, was in a weak position. CIA files released in 2007 revealed a militarist plot to assassinate Yoshida.[22] More CIA documents obtained by Professor Erik Esselstrom in 2013 show that the Americans feared the Kaji scandal would bring the government down.

The US embassy's explanation for Kaji's year-long detention was that he had asked the United States for protective custody after confessing to being a Soviet agent. According to this line, he had fabricated the account of being abducted and tortured to avoid reprisals by his former comrades and was probably still working for the Soviets.[23] But the documents obtained by Esselstrom show the United States had prepared several alternative scripts for handling the scandal, ranging from 'Vigorous Defence and No Concession' to 'Partial Concession of Wrongdoing' to 'Full Admission'. Kaji's character was to be 'blackened', and his wartime resistance work in China to be recast as treason against Japan. The United States even drafted a letter of protest for the Japanese government to sign – to which the United States would issue a pre-prepared response.[24] Kaji's abduction was to be attributed to 'misguided' personnel acting 'without instructions' from 'generous humanitarian motives'.

As the US embassy tried to sell the story that Kaji was a spy, the Japanese conveniently produced a witness to corroborate the American line. They arrested a double agent called Mitsuhashi Masao. Mitsuhashi had been recruited by the Soviets while a prisoner of war in the Soviet Union, but when he returned to Japan, he was 'turned' by United States intelligence and told to continue working for the Soviets. Mitsuhashi named Kaji as an accomplice in his spy ring. Kaji vehemently rebutted the accusation and counter-charged, entirely plausibly, that Mitsuhashi was a police informer. Kaji's case dragged on for nearly two decades, eventually leading to his conviction in 1961, but he was acquitted on appeal in 1969.

*   *   *

---

22   'CIA Files Reveal Militarist Plot to Kill Yoshida in '52', *Japan Times*, 28 February 2007.

23   Esselstrom, 'From Wartime Friend to Cold War Fiend', 164–5.

24   Ibid., 176–7.

Kaji Wataru died in 1982, a year after Jack Canon shot himself. Yamada Zenjiro, Canon's cook and nemesis, continued to campaign and write about the Kaji case for the rest of his life. In 2011, he drew attention to the similarity between Kaji's detention and the CIA's black jails and extraordinary rendition programme during the so-called War on Terror to demonstrate that the methods used by United States intelligence services had not changed.

15

Changing Minds

On the Allied side, Kaji and Ikeda's POW re-education programme was the exception, not the rule. Chinese government forces were known to mistreat and kill prisoners. On one occasion, having broadcast that they had captured scores of Japanese, they had to borrow prisoners from the Communists to display to the press because the original captives had been massacred.[1] On a forced march from the Burmese border, only eighty out of two hundred prisoners survived.[2] In the Pacific theatre, US troops, wary of an enemy indoctrinated to fight to the death, initially took few prisoners. It was not just a matter of self-preservation; they were also influenced by racist propaganda that routinely depicted Japanese as rats, bats, insects, and reptiles. One veteran wrote about the battle of Tarawa: 'Marines did not consider that they were killing men. They were wiping out dirty animals.'[3] Some soldiers collected ears and other body parts as battlefield trophies. In 1944, *Life* magazine pictured a young woman gazing dreamily at the skull of a Japanese soldier sent to her by her boyfriend. These attitudes reached the top. Congressman

---

1   Barak Kushner, *The Thought War: Japanese Imperial Propaganda*, Honolulu: University of Hawaii Press, 2007, 134.

2   Ariyoshi Koji, *From Kona to Yenan: The Political Memoirs of Koji Ariyoshi*, Edward Beechert and Alice Beechert, eds., Honolulu: University of Hawaii Press, 2000, 159.

3   Andrew Rooney, *The Fortunes of War: Four Great Battles of World War II*, Boston: Little, 1962, 37.

Francis E. Walton, a notorious racist, presented President Roosevelt with a letter opener made of bone taken from a Japanese corpse. It was only after Japanese propagandists made hay with the incident that Roosevelt returned the gift.

The anthropologist Ruth Benedict, whose book *The Chrysanthemum and the Sword* was commissioned by the Office of War Information and became an unofficial manual for the occupation of Japan, suggested that barbaric ideas were being floated in leading circles in the United States:

> The Japanese were the most alien enemy the United States had ever fought in an all-out struggle ... There were violent disagreements among those who knew the Japanese best. ... were the Japanese a people who would require perpetual martial law to keep them in order? Would our army have to prepare to fight desperate bitter-enders in every mountain fastness of Japan? ... Was the alternative the eradication of the Japanese?[4]

In Yan'an, the Chinese Communists were taking a different approach. The Eighth Route Army and its affiliates had taken around three thousand prisoners. Most were returned to their units after a short period of indoctrination, but around three hundred of the ideologically most promising were kept in Yan'an to be re-educated at a so-called Workers' and Peasants' School. The head of the school was the Japanese Communist leader Nosaka Sanzo, who had arrived in Yan'an from the Soviet Union in the spring of 1940. Nosaka had originally planned to continue on to Japan but stayed in Yan'an until the end of the war. In 1944, he organised his POW converts into the Japanese People's Emancipation League.

In some ways, Nosaka was an unlikely leftist. He came from a well-to-do background and, in his youth, was known as a dandy. However, he was radicalised by the 1911 execution of the anarchist Kotoku Shusui,[5] who was hanged with eleven others for plotting to kill the emperor. The supposed conspirators were convicted on flimsy evidence in a closed

---

4 Ruth Benedict, *The Chrysanthemum and the Sword*, London: Secker & Warburg, 1947, 1–3.

5 Rodger Swearingen, *Leaders of the Communist World*, New York: Free Press, 1971, 77.

trial, and it is now widely accepted that the so-called High Treason Incident was a pretext to eliminate a generation of radical leaders. Kotoku was a significant figure in the development of the East Asian labour movement. His books *Essence of Socialism* and *Imperialism* were translated into Chinese, and the first Chinese edition of the *Communist Manifesto*, published in 1922, was based on his Japanese translation. Nosaka saw him as 'one of the greatest thinkers Japan has ever produced'.[6]

The other great influence on Nosaka was quite unlike Kotoku. Suzuki Bunji was a Christian social reformer who founded the trade union federation Yuaikai.[7] Nosaka joined the Yuaikai while at university and, after graduating, he edited the Yuaikai journal *Labour and Industry*. Suzuki was no militant. Seeing the right-wing AFL leader Samuel Gompers as a model trade union leader, he invited him to Japan to preach a 'constructive' approach to labour relations. But despite their political differences, Nosaka was one of Suzuki's favourites and, in 1919, Suzuki sent him to study the British labour movement as a 'special correspondent' for Yuaikai.

Nosaka arrived in Britain in the middle of a strike wave and widespread sympathy for the Russian Revolution. Troops mutinied against being sent to fight the Bolsheviks. Government ministers, fearing an uprising, deployed tanks in Glasgow after tens of thousands of strikers defeated the police in a street battle. Nosaka threw himself into the movement, joined its left wing, and was one of the founder members of the British Communist Party. He wrote for the party journal *Labour Monthly* and became a frequent speaker at rallies. Inevitably, he came to the attention of the Special Branch, and in 1921 he was deported. He travelled back to Japan via Soviet Russia.

During the interwar years, the Comintern's repeated attempts to launch a party in Japan were frustrated by waves of arrests that broke up each embryo party. In 1931, after several spells in jail, Nosaka and his wife fled to the Soviet Union. He was soon integrated into the apparatus of the Comintern – by now, quite a different organisation than when he was in Britain. The Opposition had been crushed, and Communists

---

6 T. Nosaka (Sanzo), *A Brief Review of the Labour movement in Japan*, Moscow: International Council of Trade and Industrial Relations, 1921, 10.

7 'Yuaikai' means 'friendly society'.

struggled to keep up with Stalin's twists and turns in policy. In 1921, Nosaka had seen the future Japanese revolution as proletarian and socialist;[8] in 1932, he was tasked with correcting a draft programme that repeated this 'Trotskyist' heresy. Japan, he wrote, was not capitalist but semi-feudal, and the main task of the revolution was to overthrow 'the Emperor system'. By the time it was published, it was irrelevant because the Communists in Japan had once again been rounded up.[9]

Nosaka spent the next nine years in the Comintern apparatus. Elevated to the Comintern Presidium in 1935, he was a key speaker at the seventh congress, where Georgi Dimitrov, on the eve of the Moscow trials, issued his scarcely veiled threat that anyone who tried to 'break up the iron unity' of the Communist ranks would be liquidated.[10] Nosaka spent four years in the United States but was mainly based in Siberia trying to keep the underground party alive in Japan. One of the aims of his Workers' and Peasants' School in Yan'an was to create a cadre to reconstruct the party after the war.

The Japanese prisoners of war were not held in camps. There were no sentries, barbed wire fences, or watchtowers. Admittedly, this was partly because the chances of a successful escape attempt were small; prisoners who tried it would soon be apprehended either by the Eighth Route Army or by local peasants, who might exact revenge for the raids carried out by the occupiers. But the psychological effect of this relative freedom was very real. The prisoners grew their own food and made their own clothes. According to several observers, they lived better than the Eighth Army troops.

The teachers at the Workers' and Peasants' School were recruited from among the prisoners. A corporal who had taught ju-jitsu to the Osaka police gave lectures on Marxism. The superintendent of the school was Takayama Susumu, a former factory worker. The basic message emphasised the shared class solidarity between Chinese and Japanese workers and peasants, but there was also a strong, quasi-religious element of moral reform. Prisoners attended regular self-criticism sessions and were encouraged to think they had been reborn through

8   Nosaka, *Brief Review*, 31.

9   Robert A. Scalapino, *The Japanese Communist Movement, 1920–1966*, Berkeley: University of California Press, 1967, 42

10   Georgi Dimitrov, 'Concluding Address', in *Seventh World Congress Communist International*, London: Modern Books, 1935, 10.

re-education. 'All of us have died once. We are now building the foundations of our new lives,' Takayama told them.

Re-education began from the moment of capture. Savage punitive raids on villages suspected of aiding the guerrillas meant that peasants often took revenge on captured Japanese. While the army treated prisoners well from the outset, it did not hide from them what local people might do to them if they were not protected. However, propaganda campaigns eventually convinced peasants that prisoners were potential allies, and by the later stages of the war, villagers were delivering prisoners unharmed.

Japanese troops based in blockhouses throughout the countryside were isolated, bored, afraid, and often bullied by sadistic officers. As such, they were ideal targets for psychological warfare. Nosaka's most 'advanced' prisoners were sent to the front line to undermine morale and encourage desertions or turn individual soldiers into agents. They tapped into telephone wires to talk directly to whoever picked up. In this way, they were able to build up pictures of the situation in blockhouses, down to the names of individual officers and soldiers, and were able to target particularly cruel officers. There were some notable successes, as when a Nosaka recruit, Corporal Shiratori, persuaded an entire unit to defect. Nosaka also ran a network of agents behind enemy lines. The intelligence he gathered was so detailed and accurate that it was said that the Japanese would sacrifice a division to eliminate him. The US Army's Dixie Mission microfilmed his collection.

Nosaka returned to Japan in 1946 to a hero's welcome from comrades who had kept the faith during the long underground struggle. Over the following decades, he led a spectacular resurgence of Japanese Communism, transforming a sect with barely a thousand members into a mass party.[11] He did so by turning the Communist Party, in his own words, into a 'lovable' organisation. The party was no longer planning a violent revolution. It remained committed to abolishing the 'emperor system', but there would still be a place for the imperial family. The party was patriotic, but not opposed to the American-led occupation, which was a benign guarantor of democratic reforms. A two-stage revolution, or rather reform, was the future mapped out for Japan. The first task was

11   Membership grew from 1,180 in 1945 to 108,693 in 1950 and to 300,000 in 1966. See Scalapino, *Japanese Communist Movement*, 67.

to abolish the imperial bureaucracy and break the power of the large landowners and monopoly capitalists. Among these, the main enemy was the bureaucracy.[12] The socialist transformation – when it eventually came, in some faraway, indefinite future – would be carried out peacefully, in coalition with the Socialist Party, or at least its left wing.[13] Nosaka's early mentor, Suzuki Bunji, might have found little to disagree with in the party programme.

International developments blew Nosaka off his moderate course. As the Cold War turned hot in Korea, Russian and Chinese rhetoric zigzagged to the left. Nosaka began to hedge, saying peaceful revolution was merely a tactic that could change.[14] But he failed to keep up. In January 1950, he was lambasted in the Cominform's magazine *For a Lasting Peace for a People's Democracy!* as an anti-Marxist. The attacks multiplied: he was a Titoist and, absurdly, a Trotskyist.[15] Nosaka responded by making a self-criticism, moving to the left, and denouncing the American occupation. The party replaced the slogan of bourgeois-democratic revolution with a call for national liberation.[16] Nosaka went underground, and some leaders went into exile in China. Some members took to sabotage, and there were even a few absurd attempts to set up rural guerrilla units. Then Stalin died, and the Korean War ended. At the sixth congress of the party in 1955, Nosaka reappeared in public. He steered the party back onto a moderate course and membership continued to grow, reaching 300,000 by 1966.

The Sino-Soviet split created more problems for the party. At first, Nosaka tried to remain neutral, then he leaned towards China before switching back to an even-handed position. He attacked General Secretary Leonid Brezhnev, but also denounced the Cultural Revolution. For this, the former friend of China was attacked in 1967 by the *Peking Review* as a 'revisionist chieftain' who 'spreads poison everywhere'. Comically, he was excoriated for travelling like a 'feudal prince' because he stayed in hotel rooms with an 'attached bath and toilet'.

There was one final twist to the Nosaka story. When he died in 1993, at the age of one hundred and one, he had long been a fixture on the

---

12   Ibid., 59.
13   Ibid., 55–7.
14   Ibid., 60.
15   Ibid., 63.
16   Ibid., 82.

Japanese political scene, regarded even by enemies as a dignified and refined old gentleman. But his fall from grace was dramatic. The Japanese Communist Party had long acknowledged that some of its members had been killed in the Stalinist terror in the Soviet Union, among them one of the party leaders, Yamamoto Kenzo. When the Comintern archives were opened, a February 1939 letter from Nosaka to Georgi Dimitrov denouncing Yamamoto was discovered. Yamamoto was shot a month after Nosaka sent the letter. There is some doubt as to whether Nosaka's letter played any role in precipitating Yamamoto's execution, since Dimitrov did not receive it until May 1939 (although, in all likelihood, it had already been read by the NKVD). Rather, it may have been a denunciation by the arch-Stalinist Pavel Mif that sealed Yamamoto's fate.[17] Regardless, the broader story was murky and sordid. It turned out that Yamamoto was himself a prolific denouncer. Notably, in a feud with the grand old man of the Japanese labour movement, Katayama Sen, he denounced Katayama's protégés Katsuno Kinmasa and Kunizaki Teido. Katsuno escaped to Japan and lived to write his memoirs, but Kunizaki was arrested in August 1937 and shot in December that year.[18] However, none of these details could save Nosaka's reputation among his erstwhile comrades. Apart from acknowledging that he had written the letter, he said nothing further. Branded a traitor and expelled from the party, he died in disgrace.[19]

---

17   Elena Dundovich, *Reflections on the Gulag*, Milano: Feltrinelli, 2003, 113–15. Mif was shot a few months later, in September 1939.

18   Kato Tetsuro, 'The Japanese Victims of Stalinist Terror in the USSR', *Hitotsubashi Journal of Social Studies*, Vol. 32, No. 1, 2000, 1–13, 6.

19   Ibid., 1–2.

16

Changing Sides

Mizuno Yasuo's parents owned a farm and a hotel but, as the youngest of three boys, he had no prospect of inheriting either, so he enlisted in the army when he was seventeen. But it was not only his lack of prospects that attracted him to the military. Growing up near a naval base, he noted that the smartly turned-out sailors were never short of female admirers. His uncle, a retired cavalryman, still wore his splendid uniform on special occasions. That, plus the emperor worship and militarist propaganda at his all-boys school convinced Mizuno to purloin his father's seal to stamp his application letter. Mizuno's mother was heartbroken, but his father allowed his deception to stand. Mizuno wanted to follow his uncle into the cavalry but was rejected because his legs were too short. He was assigned to the infantry and sent to Qingdao.

Mizuno's dreams of glory soon evaporated. Military life for enlisted men consisted of being ordered around and bullied by officers who treated their subordinates as virtual slaves. Beatings for petty offences were the norm. Recruits were made to hold their rifles above their heads for hours. Dropping a rifle earned a thrashing. Since he was a volunteer, Mizuno was given a slightly easier time by the officers than conscripts, but older enlisted men expected him to be promoted and come back to lord it over them, and treated him accordingly. After basic training, his unit was sent to Wenshang, one of many walled towns that dotted the otherwise featureless North China Plain. A small crowd was dragooned to welcome the troops with Japanese flags as they marched through the gates.

Wenshang was the headquarters of the local garrison and the centre of a network of blockhouses extending into the surrounding country-side. The blockhouses, each manned by around a dozen troops, were the front line in a low-intensity but vicious war waged by Communist guer-rillas against the occupiers. During the day, patrols that dropped their guard risked being attacked with knives, pickaxes, or whatever came to hand. At night, the troops would raise drawbridges over defensive trenches to prevent surprise attacks. Isolated and surrounded by a hostile population, every sound made them nervous.

The Eighth Route Army rarely confronted the occupiers but stationed themselves around ten to twelve kilometres away, waging war by infil-tration. The villages in between were the arenas where the armies came into contact with each other. Both sides used spies and informers to gather intelligence. The guerrillas recruited innumerable peasants and even encouraged some to become double agents, confident they could rely on their basic loyalty. The Japanese understood that 'their' agents were also reporting to the guerrillas, but they had no choice but to continue to recruit. They used money and women as incentives; there were always a few women on hand to use as bait.

When an underground Eighth Route Army man or a spy was unmasked, they would be tortured and interrogated and, when no more information could be extracted from them, killed. Sometimes the Japanese would kill their own agents when they decided they were no longer useful. Despite the high attrition rate, there was no shortage of spies. Their reports were used to plan surprise attacks on guerrilla groups. These usually turned into wild goose chases since even if the original report was accurate by the time a patrol reached the destination the guerrillas would have escaped. The usual result was that the raid would degenerate into a looting spree accompanied by the brutalisation of villagers.

On one of the raids, Mizuno witnessed an atrocity. Finding no guer-rillas, his unit set about looting. Mizuno was rounding up some chick-ens when he saw four Chinese men kneeling on the ground pleading for their lives while nearby soldiers were digging their graves. An officer stepped forward and aimed his revolver at one of the peasants, his hand trembling. After a long pause, the officer fired, and the man fell forward. After shooting the prisoner, the officer relaxed. He had proved he could shoot and kill from ten meters. Losing face was all he had worried about.

Another officer used a sword to cut off the remaining peasants' heads. He botched the first two executions, failing to sever their heads, and the men bled to death. The final execution was a clean cut, and a soldier ran forward and held up the head by its hair with a mocking grin. According to Mizuno, this sort of insane cruelty was carried out by young officers straight out of military school who were trying to prove themselves while among the enlisted men, old soldiers brutalised by five or six years of war were capable of anything – cutting open women's stomachs, thrusting knives into their vaginas, disembowelling men, or cutting their heads off. The perpetrators of these horrors lived in fear of revenge, and their fear fuelled further atrocities as a victim's family had to be wiped out.

Mizuno was captured in July 1939 after a one-sided battle at Liangshan – a mountain rising out of marshland that was the setting for the classic novel *The Water Margin*.[1] Having spotted a force of around a thousand Eighth Route Army troops dug in on the mountain, the commander of Mizuno's two-hundred-strong force, instead of retreating, ordered a suicidal uphill attack in broad daylight. The Japanese were soon pinned down by machine-gun fire and after nightfall, the Chinese counterattacked and wiped them out. According to his account of the battle, Mizuno, like most of his comrades, had saved a bullet to kill himself rather than be captured. Several soldiers killed themselves, but Mizuno tried to escape, telling himself it was his duty to report the position of the Chinese to headquarters. But, as he made a run for it through a field of sorghum, he was captured by a group of Korean soldiers.

Mizuno expected to be shot out of hand or handed over to the peasants to be torn to pieces. But a long-haired Korean, older than the others, told him, 'We're not going to kill you. Get on the horse.' After riding through the night, they arrived in a village where Mizuno saw several other Japanese prisoners squatting at the roadside under guard. He was put with the others, and they talked about the prospect of being rescued by the Japanese army that would, they felt sure, retaliate. By mid-morning, the village market was in full swing, and a crowd gathered around the prisoners. There were shouts of 'Guizi!'[2] and someone threw a

---

1   Liangshan was the setting for the famous novel, which is also known as *The Outlaws of the Marsh*.

2   'Ghosts', or 'devils'.

stone. The officer in charge looked unconcerned, but when the situation seemed about to turn ugly, he stood up to calm the crowd and decided to get the cart moving and leave the village. If the incident was staged to deter escape attempts, it did not work. Mizuno tried to work out ways of killing the officer and getting away.

They were billeted in a peasant house and interrogated by a young officer. It seemed to Mizuno that the Eighth Route Army's intelligence was excellent. All the more reason, he thought, for him to escape and report back. He dreamed he might be promoted or even decorated. But, since he did not know where they were or anything about their surroundings, escape seemed impossible. Meanwhile, the prisoners were given soap, towels, and notebooks. In the books was written, 'Dear Japanese brothers, the militarists and wealthy started this war but victory over them is coming'. It was signed by their young interrogator – Lieutenant General Yang Yong.[3]

After the interrogation, they were treated well but still hoped to be rescued or escape. When they heard Japanese bombers attacking the area around Liangshan, their hopes were raised. The Japanese had launched a counter-offensive and were attacking villages in the area, committing the usual atrocities. The Chinese told them that they were killing civilians, including children and old people who were left in the villages. Young women were being raped and sent to brothels or, if they were discovered to be students, and therefore probably Eighth Route Army spies, were being tortured to death. They also said the Japanese were digging up the bodies of their troops to take away for reburial. The prisoners were comforted by this last piece of news.

With the counter-offensive threatening their positions, the Chinese moved the prisoners to an island on a lake. The regime on the island was even more relaxed; they were allowed to walk around a village, pursued by local children shouting 'Guizi' and touching them to see if they were real. Their guards told the villagers that the prisoners were Japanese peasants who had been exploited and misled by militarists and capitalists. Again and again, they drummed this simple lesson in. It was

3   Yang Yong was appointed governor of Guizhou Province after 1949. He fought in the Korean War. During the Cultural Revolution he was persecuted but was rehabilitated, and in 1977 he was appointed deputy chief of staff of the PLA. He died in 1983.

repeated all over the front line as it was a basic tenet of Communist internationalism but Mizuno and the other prisoners dismissed it as verbiage and enemy propaganda.

One night, during a rainstorm, six prisoners made a break for it. But three of them drowned while trying to cross a river, and the remaining three, including Mizuno, gave themselves up. They were tied up and taken back to the island where an officer told them that if they ever wanted to see Japan again, they would have to trust the Eighth Route Army. If they persisted in trying to escape, they would probably be killed by the peasants or by their own side. Chastened by the death of their three comrades, they began to change their attitude.

Two weeks after their escape attempt, the remaining three prisoners were transferred to Yang Yong's headquarters in a small village set in beautiful countryside. A man who had studied in Japan and spoke the language fluently befriended them, and they were given copies of Mao's *On Guerrilla Warfare*. By this time, they had given up the idea of escape and began to reflect on the nature of the war. It was at this point that the Chinese recruited them to teach Japanese to the Eighth Route Army.

Mizuno taught hundreds of young men and women basic Japanese, compiling phrasebooks for the soldiers to shout, such as 'Throw down your weapons and come out and you won't be harmed!' He also taught courses on Japanese culture and customs. In the end, his loyalties completely switched, and he joined the Japanese People's Awakened League.[4] On 15 August 1941, he formally established the Hebei, Shandong, and Henan branches of the league. As well as teaching and compiling propaganda, the league carried out frontline activities. They threw bamboo poles painted with slogans around the Japanese block-houses. They compiled a booklet of soldiers' demands, including an end to face-slapping as punishment and embezzlement of soldiers' pay by officers. They threw gifts and cards around the blockhouses while shouting anti-militarist slogans. As he was among the most active, Mizuno became well known among the Japanese soldiers and consequently a target of the reprisal raids.

---

4   Chinese: *Riben ren juexing lianmeng*. One of several organisations set up by defecting POWs and other Japanese dissidents under CCP sponsorship that were later amalgamated into Nosaka Sanzo's Japanese People's Emancipation League.

After a period in Yan'an studying at Nosaka Sanzo's Japanese Workers' and Peasants' School, Mizuno returned to Shandong and was assigned work in the Eighth Route Army headquarters. When Japan surrendered in September 1945, he led a team of fellow prisoners to the front line to spread the news to the Japanese troops, many of whom had not heard the news. Mizuno and his comrades went from blockhouse to blockhouse calling on soldiers to lay down their weapons and persuading them not to commit suicide. It was Mizuno's last operation on behalf of the Chinese. He returned to Japan in July 1946.

Maeda Mitsushige was one of the first Japanese to join the Eighth Route Army, and a founder member of the Japanese People's Awakened League.[5] He was born in 1916 in Kyoto to a family of poor handicraft workers, who apprenticed him to a merchant after he completed primary school. He briefly joined the navy in his teens but was discharged because of poor health. In 1937, he moved to Manzhouguo to work for the Southern Manchurian Railroad Company – a huge conglomerate with interests in mining, power, docks, and grain processing, which dominated the economy of Northeast China. Sent to manage a quarry in Hebei Province, Maeda had only been in the post a few days when, on 25 July 1938, he was captured by the Eighth Route Army.

An officer who spoke Japanese, was given the task of winning him over. Maeda resisted at first, as he believed Japanese propaganda about liberating China from rule by white imperialists. However, after seeing burnt-out villages, he began to have doubts. His captors stressed that Japanese soldiers were also victims of the war and gave Maeda a book on Marxism written by Japanese Communist Jirō Hayakawa. He joined the Eighth Route Army on 1 February 1939. Later that year, with seven other prisoners, Maeda set up the Japanese People's Awakened League which later grew into an organisation of thirteen branches with 223 members, thirty-six of whom died in combat. During the 1940 Hundred Regiments Campaign, Maeda distinguished himself by carrying out propaganda work under heavy fire.

5   See Ye Lishu, *Laizi yiguo de pengyou: Zai zhongguo you guo teshu jingli de waiguoren* [Friends from abroad: Extraordinary stories of foreigners in China], Beijing: Jiefang jun chubanshe [People's Liberation Army publishing house], 1990, 293–8.

In August 1942, after attending the founding conference of the Japanese People's Emancipation League in Yan'an, Maeda was appointed Nosaka Sanzo's deputy at the Japan Workers' and Peasant's School. He stayed in China after the war, only returning to Japan in 1958. He was active in the Japan-China Friendship Association, wrote a memoir of his experiences with another old comrade, and in an interview with Chinese television in 2017, aged one hundred, he reiterated that he had not changed his views.[6]

Kobayashi Hirosumi was born in 1919. His father was the Buddhist abbot of a family-owned temple that Kobayashi would normally have inherited. However, he was conscripted in 1940, trained as a machine gunner, and sent to Shandong Province. The following year, while on a 'bandit clearing' operation in the mountains, his unit was ambushed. He and a fellow soldier, Toshikazu Shirato, agreed to help each other commit suicide. Kobayashi shot Toshikazu, but, when he tried to kill himself, he only grazed his head. He then tried to drown himself but was rescued by Chinese soldiers. Both Kobayashi and Toshikazu survived and were nursed backed to health.

After some months, out of boredom, Kobayashi began to read the propaganda pamphlets given to the POWs. An Eighth Route army officer, Jiang Kun, who had studied in Japan and spoke Japanese, convinced him to defect. Kobayashi persuaded a small group of his fellow prisoners to join him and they established an anti-Japanese alliance in Shandong, joined the Eighth Route Army, and took part in frontline propaganda operations. The Japanese put a price on his head.

After the end of the anti-Japanese war, Kobayashi transferred to the People's Liberation Army and fought in the civil war. He joined the Communist Party in 1946 and was transferred to Dalian, where he met and married a Japanese nurse. He worked as a government official and eventually became director of a hospital in Inner Mongolia. In December 1955, Kobayashi and his family moved back to Japan, where he worked for a shipping company until he retired at the age of seventy-five. Kobayashi subsequently served as the chairman of an association of Japanese veterans of the Eighth Route Army and New Fourth Army. In

---

6 'Japanese Veteran of China's Eighth Route Army Calls for Reflection upon History', New China TV, YouTube video, 15 August 2017, youtube.com.

September 2015, at the age of ninety-six, he returned to China for the seventieth anniversary of the end of the War of Resistance and was decorated by Xi Jinping.

In June 1938, a unit of the Northeast Anti-Japanese United Army led by Yang Jingyu[7] attacked a tunnel under construction on the railway line between Tonghua and Ji'an in the puppet state of Manzhouguo. They captured several Japanese, including a forced labourer called Fukken Kazuo. In line with established practice, they were planning to release their prisoners, but Fukken asked to join the army. He was accepted and trained as a machine gunner. He took part in several operations. During an attack on a lumberyard guarded by a police unit, he shot and killed the police commander while his comrades were cutting through the wire-mesh fence. The remaining police surrendered, apart from a few diehard Japanese who hid in a trench. Risking his life, Fukken ran forward and persuaded them to surrender.

Meagre rations and bitter cold were the worst enemies of the Northeast Army. Even in winter, they wore only light clothing and plimsolls, and boiled meagre rations of rice in melted snow. Fukken, who was short and slightly built, was particularly vulnerable. In the winter of 1939, Fukken's unit was facing starvation after Japanese troops discovered their headquarters and carried off their supplies. By this time, he could barely walk, and when they were ambushed shortly afterwards, he refused his comrades' efforts to carry him to safety. Instead, he told them to run while he covered them. The Japanese troops captured him, tortured him, then hacked him to death.[8]

Kagawa Takashi was born into a peasant family in 1915, the youngest of four boys. His father worked in mines and power plants while his mother and their sons farmed their land. Excelling at school, Kagawa earned a place in college, where he studied Japanese and Chinese literature. In

---

7   Yang Jingyu (real name Ma Shangde) joined the Communist Party in 1925 and formed a guerrilla band after Chiang Kai-shek's 1927 coup. He was appointed commander of the Northeast Anti-Japanese United Army in 1936. In 1940, surrounded and starving to death, Yang was killed in combat.

8   Ye Lishu, *Friends from Abroad*, 271–3. With typical candour, the Chinese account tells how he suffered an anal prolapse after struggling with constipation, which makes the manner of his death still more horrific.

1938 he was conscripted and sent to China. By the time he arrived, the Japanese had taken China's main eastern cities, but the Chinese victory at the Battle of Taierzhuang slowed their advance, creating the conditions for a long war. Kagawa was sent to guard the strategically important railway from Shijiazhuang to Taiyuan. While at school, he had uncritically accepted militarist propaganda about liberating Asia from Western imperialism, but after witnessing the horrors of 'bandit clearing' operations, he became disillusioned.

In 1940, Kagawa was captured while defending a railway bridge during the Eighth Route Army's Hundred Regiments Campaign. He briefly contemplated escaping but was impressed by the good treatment of prisoners and the discipline of the Eighth Route Army troops. Instead, he joined the Japanese People's Awakened League and was sent to Yan'an for training at Nosaka Sanzo's Workers' and Peasants' School.

Because of his higher education and knowledge of Chinese, Kagawa was not sent to the front line but stayed on to teach at the school. By now a convinced Communist, he was one of the few foreigners who took part in Mao Zedong's notorious rectification campaigns. In 1945, Kagawa joined the Eighth Route Army headquarters as an intelligence advisor. After Japan surrendered, Kagawa left Yan'an on the same plane as Nosaka bound for Changchun. He worked for a time with the Soviet army organising the repatriation of Japanese refugees before returning to Japan in January 1946. He joined the Communist Party of Japan but resigned when its relations with China soured.

Yamamoto Hideo arrived in China at the age of ten with his parents. The family settled in Heilongjiang – then part of the puppet state of Manzhouguo. After his father died, and his elder brother was conscripted into the Kwantung (Guandong) army, Hideo became the head of the family aged fourteen.

After Japan surrendered, Japanese immigrants in Heilongjiang were assembled near Harbin to await deportation to Japan. While doing odd jobs at a police station, he was recruited by an army officer who noticed he was a hard worker and was made an orderly at a battalion headquarters. In 1946, Yamamoto took part in the campaign to wipe out the notorious bandit Xie Wendong. During the campaign, he fell ill and was sent to a military hospital. After recovering, he took a job at the hospital. In November 1947 he was transferred to the Northeast Field Army headquarters and worked as a medical orderly throughout the civil war. Despite suffering from a weak heart, he served with distinction, rescuing many wounded from the battlefield, and was decorated several times.

Yamamoto stayed in China after the civil war since he had little to go home for. Both his parents were buried in China and the people closest to him were his Red Army comrades. Some relatives in Japan contacted him in 1949, but he decided not to return. He applied to join the Communist Party but was not accepted. He worked at a convalescent home in Hubei for the next twenty years as an administrator, trade union official, radio announcer, and head of the entertainment department. He applied many times, unsuccessfully, for Chinese citizenship.

Unlike some other foreigners, Yamamoto was given no special privileges. During the Great Leap Forward famine, he suffered badly. He was reduced to eating leaves and foraging for roots in freezing lakes; his limbs swelled from malnutrition. In the Cultural Revolution, he was persecuted by Red Guards who accused him of being a spy. But ironically, it was also in this period that he was finally granted Chinese citizenship. Bizarrely, since there were two Maoist factions in the convalescent home, he received two letters of congratulations. The two sides made peace for long enough to hold a joint meeting to mark the occasion. He married the same year, and in 1968 his wife gave birth. Tragically, however, the child contracted polio.

In November 1979, Yamamoto left for a six-month visit to Japan, ostensibly to visit relatives. But it seems to have been principally a propaganda trip organised as part of China's opening-up process. He addressed a series of meetings, always wearing a Zhongshan suit to display his Chinese identity. On New Year's Day 1980, his old primary school classmates held a party for him in his home village. In April 1980, he returned to China and was given a job teaching Japanese at Wuhan University. In 1983, he was finally allowed to join the Communist Party, and, in 1987, was appointed to the Wuhan branch of the Chinese People's Political Consultative Committee.

Japanese prisoners of war did not only surrender to the Chinese. Some of those taken by the Americans also cooperated to a degree that surprised their captors. Ruth Benedict, author of *The Chrysanthemum and the Sword*, puzzled over their switch of loyalties from Imperial Japan to the United States.

> They were better than model prisoners. Old Army hands and long-time extreme nationalists located ammunition dumps, carefully explained the disposition of Japanese forces, wrote our propaganda and flew with our bombing pilots to guide them to military targets. It was as if they had turned over a new page; what was written on the new page was the opposite of what was written on the old, but they spoke the lines with the same faithfulness.[9]

Benedict, for whom the Japanese were a priori alien, attributed the change of heart, tautologically, to 'peculiarities of Japanese behavior'.[10] Alternative explanations may be their political or personal background circumstances in Japan, or simply that their American captors, some of whom, as we saw above, had studied Chinese practice, had convinced them that their side in the war was in the wrong.

With the end of the World War and the onset of the Cold War, the Chinese way of treating prisoners of war, exemplified by Nosaka's Workers' and Peasants' School, was no longer seen in the West as a model to be emulated, but as a sinister exercise in the dark art of brainwashing.[11] At the end of the Korean War, twenty-one captured American soldiers declined to be repatriated to the United States. Among them was Clarence Adams, a black GI who had grown up in segregated Tennessee. After being arrested while in his teens, Adams had been given the choice of prison or the army and enlisted. He was sent to Korea twice, in 1948 and in 1950 and experienced the same sort of racism in

---

9   Benedict, *The Chrysanthemum and the Sword*, 41.

10   Ibid., 42.

11   The English term 'brainwashing' seems to have been first used in 1950 by Edward Hunter, a former OSS agent whose 1951 book *Brain-Washing in Red China: The Calculated Destruction of Men's Minds* popularised the term. According to Hunter, the term was a direct translation from the Chinese *xi nao* and referred to specific mind-control techniques practised by the CCP. See Beverly Hooper, *Foreigners under Mao: Western Lives in China, 1949–1976*, Hong Kong: Hong Kong University Press, 2016, 56. But ideas of thought reform, awakening, cleansing of the soul, and so on date back to the reform movement of the late nineteenth century and even to Confucianism and Buddhism. See Ryan Mitchell, 'China and the Political Myth of "Brainwashing"', *Made in China Journal*, 2019.

the army that he had faced in civilian life. It was not only a matter of casual racism among the rank and file; according to his account, while retreating from the Chinese-led counter-offensive that drove the UN forces from the Yalu River, his mainly black unit was sacrificed to allow white soldiers to escape. Even during his three years in a POW camp, the racism from fellow prisoners never slackened. He began to read the propaganda material distributed by his guards and seeing no reason to return to a still-segregated United States, he decided to take a chance on China, where he gained a university degree, married a teacher and raised two daughters. During the Vietnam War, like Martin Luther King, Malcolm X, Muhammed Ali, and others, Adams saw no reason why black Americans should fight poor peasants overseas while they remained second-class citizens at home. He made radio broadcasts calling on black soldiers to quit the war, go home, and fight racism.

Ironically, it was the experience of racism in China, especially the xenophobia displayed by some 'leftists' during the Cultural Revolution, that led to Adams's decision to return to the United States with his family. Although disappointed and disillusioned by events in China, Adams did not switch his loyalties back to the United States. When other defectors returned to the United States, they claimed, after aggressive debriefing, that they had only switched sides because they had been brainwashed by the Chinese. They may have made these claims because they feared imprisonment; two American prisoners of war who had planned to go to China but changed their minds at the last minute were nevertheless handed savage sentences of twenty and ten years for 'collaboration'.[12] But Adams defiantly maintained that he had made a rational choice not to return to the racism he had experienced in the United States. The authorities backed off and he was not prosecuted. His story has a relatively happy ending; he and his wife opened a Chinese restaurant and eventually built their business into a small chain.

---

12   Hooper, *Foreigners under Mao*, 54. They eventually served shorter sentences of between three and four years.

17

A Hawaiian in Yan'an

US Intelligence officers were not blind to the value of information gleaned from prisoners of war, and some even studied Kaji Wataru and Ikeda Yuki's work. Among them was a young Japanese American, Ariyoshi Koji. In the summer of 1944, Ariyoshi flew to Kunming[1] from Burma, where he had been serving in a psychological warfare unit in the Office of War Information.[2] Ariyoshi had interrogated Japanese prisoners in Burma, including some who had attempted suicide after being captured, but also others who had deserted after reading Allied propaganda leaflets. He was convinced Japanese soldiers could be won over and after arriving in China he sought out Kaji and Ikeda.

Ariyoshi met with Kaji and Ikeda several times in Chongqing. He was surprised by Kaji's slight figure and gentle, scholarly demeanour and was impressed by Ikeda's intelligence. But by the time he arrived, the KMT had closed their prisoner re-education programme down. When Ariyoshi visited a prison camp in Kunming where former Anti-War Alliance members were being held, he was encouraged to find that their morale was still high and their anti-war convictions still firm. However, conditions in the camp were bad. Bizarrely, prisoners, including Korean

---

1   Kunming is the capital of Yunnan Province in Southwest China. Around 10,000 US troops were stationed there during World War II.

2   The Office of War Information was set up by presidential decree in June 1942 to direct the United States' wartime propaganda effort. One of its remaining legacies is the state-owned international radio broadcaster Voice of America.

comfort women, were paraded around and humiliated to entertain gawping civilians. At the time, it was widely believed the war would last for several more years. Indeed, seen from China, it was far from certain that it would be won. In 1944, Nationalist forces were collapsing in the face of Operation Ichi-go. Believing all available resources should be mobilised against the invaders, Ariyoshi asked the camp commandant to release Kaji and Ikeda's recruits so that they could work for the Office of War Information but he was rebuffed.

Ariyoshi's path to army intelligence officer had been anything but straightforward. He was recruited from an internment camp in the California desert – one of those opened by President Roosevelt after Pearl Harbor, in which he ordered Japanese living in the United States to be confined for the duration of the war. In an atmosphere of anti-Japanese hysteria whipped up by the press, more than 110,000 out of a total of around 127,000 ethnic Japanese were detained. Ariyoshi, who had been a longshoreman in San Francisco, was marched off the docks at bayonet point and sent to the Manzanar detention camp. Ironically, the previous year, he had tried to join the Marines.

As a second-generation immigrant who identified as American and had an anti-fascist and leftish outlook, Ariyoshi supported the war effort and became a model prisoner. He organised a Manzanar Citizens' Federation, wrote for the camp newspaper, and even served in the camp police force. He met his wife while in the camp, and she gave birth to a baby girl behind barbed wire. But the inmates were split on generational and political lines. Many first-generation immigrants, especially veterans of World War I, supported Japan, and some were right-wing fanatics. Ariyoshi became a target. On the anniversary of Pearl Harbor, they rioted and went looking for 'collaborators'. Fortunately for Ariyoshi, he had recently left, having been recruited by military intelligence officers who had come looking for Japanese speakers. By 1943, he had been promoted to sergeant and commanded a ten-strong psychological-warfare team.

Ariyoshi was born in Hawaii in 1914 to poor Japanese immigrants who scraped a living on a small coffee farm in Kona. They leased the land from a processing firm and were obliged to sell their crop to the same firm at a fixed price. Hawaii was dominated by a white plantocracy that had engineered the annexation of the islands in 1898. A multi-ethnic workforce of native Hawaiians, Chinese, Japanese, Filipinos, and

Portuguese was the basis of the cash-crop economy of plantations and docks. Strikes, when they occurred, did so on ethnic lines and were, therefore, easily defeated by the 'Big Five' corporations.[3] One of Ariyoshi's early memories was of the eviction of Filipino workers after their strike collapsed.

Ariyoshi worked in canneries, on the docks, and even for the coffee company that exploited his parents but he aspired to be a journalist and wrote occasional articles for a local newspaper. After hearing an old-time activist, Frederick Kamahoahoa, speak at the YMCA, he joined the semi-underground International Longshoremen's and Warehousemen's Union. Encouraged by his professor at the University of Hawaii, he read the New Deal literature of Steinbeck and others and when Japan invaded China, he supported the Chinese and helped raise funds for refugees. He moved to the mainland to study journalism in Georgia, where he encountered racial segregation for the first time. After graduating, he found a job on the San Francisco docks and became a union activist.

From Chongqing and Kunming, Ariyoshi was sent to Yan'an with the US Army Observer Group – the so-called Dixie Mission. The US commander in China, Joseph Stilwell, had faced down opposition from Chiang Kai-shek to authorise the mission.[4] Chiang had half a million troops, whom Stilwell wanted to deploy against the Japanese, tied up blockading the Communist areas.[5] Stilwell planned to equip five Communist divisions with modern weapons, but he was relieved of his command before this could be implemented.[6] Chiang and Stilwell detested each other, and Chiang finally succeeded in claiming Stilwell's scalp as Ariyoshi arrived in Yan'an. General Albert Wedemeyer took over in his place.

At the outset, relations between the Dixie Mission and the Communists were excellent. The commander, Colonel David D. Barrett, was an old China hand who spoke Chinese fluently. Two of the mission's

---

3   The Big Five were Alexander & Baldwin, C. Brewer, Castle & Cooke, American Factors, and Theo Davies.

4   The mission was initially proposed by Stilwell's advisor John Paton Davies.

5   Carolle J. Carter, *Mission to Yenan: American Liaison with the Chinese Communists, 1944-1947*. Lexington, KY: University Press of Kentucky, 1997, 19.

6   Charles F. Romanus and Riley Sunderland, *Stilwell's Command Problems*, Washington: Office of the Chief of Military History, 1956, 432, 451–8. The proposal was relatively modest. By comparison, Stilwell's plan provided for equipping sixty Nationalist divisions.

four Foreign Service officers – John Paton Davies, who had first proposed the mission to Stilwell, and John Stewart Service – had been born in China to missionary families.[7] John Emmerson, a former diplomat and fluent Japanese speaker, was assigned to work with Ariyoshi. The mission personnel lived in Yan'an's hillside caves alongside the Communist leaders, mixing freely with them. They were photographed wearing Chinese-style uniforms. One of Ariyoshi's prized possessions was a photograph of him standing next to Mao Zedong. In the McCarthyite period, all this would be used as evidence that the mission had been hoodwinked by the Communists.

Ariyoshi was impressed by Nosaka's Workers' and Peasants' School. He reckoned that by the end of the war, around forty per cent of new prisoners were deserters, many won over by Nosaka's recruits. He wrote to a colleague in Burma that Nosaka had built 'an excellent war school . . . Compared to what they have our propaganda school is like an elementary school.'[8] Emmerson returned to the United States to create a school on the lines of Nosaka's at Camp Huntsville in Texas, but the war ended before it could be opened.[9]

Relations between the Dixie Mission and the Chinese worsened after President Roosevelt's envoy, Major General Patrick J. Hurley, visited Yan'an. Roosevelt had sent Hurley to China to reconcile Stilwell and Chiang Kai-shek but having failed to do so, he engineered Stilwell's removal in a manner the latter described as 'cutting my throat with a dull knife'. Nevertheless, with his confidence in his deal-making ability undiminished, he set out to reconcile the Nationalists and the Communists. A self-made millionaire and former secretary of war, Hurley was brimming with self-belief, impulsive, and given to heavy drinking. He knew little about diplomacy and less about China, and when his plans went wrong, he was quick to blame subordinates.

Ariyoshi witnessed Hurley's unannounced arrival in Yan'an on 7 November 1944. During the diplomatic niceties, Hurley, who was

---

7   Both would later be persecuted during the McCarthyite witch hunts for 'losing China.'

8   Barak Kushner, *The Thought War: Japanese Imperial Propaganda*, Honolulu: University of Hawaii Press, 2007, 152.

9   Ibid., 150–1. Although the war ended less than a year later, at this time it was assumed it would last several years; the bulk of Japan's troops were stationed in China and were on the offensive.

dressed in an extravagant uniform, waved his cap 'like a seasoned ham actor' and yelled a war cry he had learned from Choctaw Indians in his youth.[10] The Chinese, unfamiliar with displays of American exuberance, were taken aback. At the welcome dinner later, Hurley was ebullient, drank too much, and punctuated the evening with more war whoops, but by the end of the evening everyone was getting on famously.

Over the next few days, things began to go wrong as Hurley began his improvised diplomacy. Ariyoshi recalled how he overheard Hurley sitting outside his mud shack talking to Zhou Enlai and how, on Zhou's next visit following Hurley's discussions with Mao, Hurley handed over a piece of paper on which he had written five points that he said should form the basis of a settlement between the Nationalists and the Communists.[11] Shortly afterwards, in a friendly atmosphere, Mao and Hurley signed the paper. The problem was that Hurley had not discussed his five points with anyone in the Chinese government, least of all Chiang Kai-shek, and, when he presented them in Chongqing a few days later, Chiang rejected them out of hand.

Unsurprisingly, the Communist leadership felt they had been misled and made to look foolish. Around this time, Hurley also reassigned Colonel Barrett replacing him with less sympathetic officers, one of whom spent most of his time pheasant shooting. Relations worsened after the only US casualty of the mission, Captain Henry C. Whittlesey, and a Chinese photographer were killed by the Japanese. Whittlesey was reconnoitring routes to rescue downed American aircraftmen when they were ambushed. The Chinese proposed a joint funeral service but the American commander refused and the services were held separately. In turn, the Communists began bypassing the mission's commander and talking directly to the lower ranks. Zhou Enlai asked Ariyoshi to

---

10   Ariyoshi Koji, *From Kona to Yenan: The Political Memoirs of Koji Ariyoshi*, Edward Beechert and Alice Beechert, eds., Honolulu: University of Hawaii Press, 2000, 140.

11   The five points were: (1) The Chinese government, Kuomintang, and the Communist Party should cooperate and unify all their military resources to defeat Japan. (2) The parties agree to transform the Kuomintang government into a coalition government and adopt a revised version of Sun Yat-sen's Three Principles of the People. (3) The coalition government should support Sun Yat-sen's theories and construct a government of the people, by the people, and for the people. (4) The coalition government should recognise all military groups who are fighting the Japanese army. (5) The legal status of all political parties should be recognised.

pass messages to US authorities, as his relationship with the Communist leaders remained friendly despite the deep freeze at the top. General Ye Jianying told Ariyoshi that while Yan'an would continue to cooperate with the United States against Japan, it no longer officially recognised the Dixie Mission.

Even before the end of the war against Japan, civil war was already breaking out. In July 1945, Nationalist forces led by Hu Zongnan attacked Eighth Route Army positions in the Yetai mountains between Xi'an and Yan'an. The Nationalist force, which outnumbered the defenders three to one, won the initial battle, but the Communists regrouped and forced the Nationalists into a retreat that turned into a rout. While the fighting was still going on, Ariyoshi arrived with a US investigation team. After interviewing prisoners, he concluded that morale was low among Nationalist troops, many of whom had deserted to the Communists even during the initial phase of the campaign. He told General Wedemeyer that in a civil war, the political weakness of the KMT would outweigh its military superiority. Sending heavily armed troops into contested areas was simply a way of supplying arms to the Communists.

Wedemeyer told Ariyoshi to relay his concerns to Hurley. When he did so, he witnessed an extraordinary outburst. The erratic Hurley, who received Ariyoshi in a dressing gown, dismissed his report and launched into a rant against his colleagues. People were trying to knife him in the back, he said, but his knife would cut deeper. He reeled off a list of the people he had removed, including Stilwell and the previous ambassador, Clarence Gauss. Everyone was sniping at him, he said, but like a cool-headed sheriff facing a wild gunman, he would 'shoot last'.[12] Hurley believed that the 1945 Sino-Soviet Treaty had undercut Mao and left him a marginalised figure who would have to accept whatever terms Chongqing offered. In fact, the country was on the brink of civil war, and United States troops were being drawn into clashes with Communist guerrillas. But American soldiers wanted to go home and were demonstrating in their thousands, in both Asia and Europe, demanding immediate demobilisation. There were rumblings in Washington. On 25 November, six congressmen proposed resolutions calling for the withdrawal of troops. The following day, Hurley sent a bitter letter of

12   Ariyoshi, *From Kona to Yenan*, 176.

resignation to President Truman complaining that 'professional foreign service men sided with the Chinese Communist armed party and the imperialist bloc of nations whose policy was to keep China divided against itself'.[13] Hurley had struck the first blow in the 'Who lost China?' controversy.

The Dixie Mission was wound down and Ariyoshi returned to the United States. On the ship home from Shanghai, Ariyoshi was made to sign the passenger manifest as an alien, reminding him that, despite his military service, he was not fully accepted as an American citizen. But back in Hawaii, the balance of power had shifted in favour of the labour movement. In 1948, Ariyoshi achieved his journalistic ambitions by setting up the *Honolulu Record*, a muckraking, pro-labour, pro–civil rights weekly that was partly financed by local trade union branches. Before long, however, he was engulfed by the McCarthyite wave. In 1951, a former trade union militant, Jack Kawano, also a Japanese American, denounced Ariyoshi to the House Un-American Activities Committee as a Communist.[14] Although Kawano's testimony was full of errors, Ariyoshi was arrested with six others and charged with conspiring to overthrow the government. After a long trial, in June 1953, all seven were sentenced to five years. Fifty thousand workers walked out in protest, and Ariyoshi and the others were released on bail but the legal process dragged on for years. Song Qingling auctioned her wedding dress to help pay the defence costs. In June 1958, Ariyoshi and the others were finally acquitted but the trial and appeals had taken their toll; the *Honolulu Record* folded weeks later.

As with many of those persecuted during the McCarthyite period, it is not clear whether Ariyoshi ever joined any Communist organisation. Regardless, it is evident that he had neither plan nor prospects of overthrowing the government. He was no revolutionary but a New Deal radical, a political outlook that was admittedly in line with Communist Party policy for much of its history. After his newspaper was forced to close, Ariyoshi opened a flower shop that earned him the nickname the

13   Hurley's resignation letter, 26 November, 1945, is available from the US State Department Office of the Historian: history.state.gov. By the imperialist bloc, Hurley meant the old empires of Britain, France, and the Netherlands. Hurley was an Irish American and viscerally opposed to the British Empire.

14   Dan Boylan and T. Michael Holmes, *John A. Burns: The Man and His Times*, Honolulu: University of Hawaii Press, 2000, 67.

Red Florist of Hawaii. He established a Sino-US friendship society and, in 1972, in the run-up to President Nixon's visit, he returned to China to interview Zhou Enlai for a Honolulu newspaper. In his later years, he lectured part time at the University of Hawaii. He died young – still in his sixties – in 1976. In 2005, he achieved posthumous recognition when the Hawaiian Public Broadcasting Service made a documentary about his life.

18

Spitting Fire

For ten months in 1938, alongside besieged Madrid, the Yangtze port of Wuhan became an international symbol of the resistance to fascism. Big-name supporters of Republican Spain arrived to show solidarity. Christopher Isherwood and W. H. Auden visited the front, and Robert Capa and Joris Ivens recorded the fighting. The city was the base of operations for 2 million Chinese troops battling the Japanese in the most heroic but costliest period of the War of Resistance; more than a million were killed or wounded.[1] A rare victory at Taierzhuang was followed by the fall of the strategic city of Xuzhou. Chiang Kai-shek resorted to opening the dykes on the Yellow River to slow the Japanese advance – a desperate tactic that cost the lives of half a million civilians. But, at the eye of the hurricane, Wuhan experienced a degree of political freedom that was unique in Chinese history. Dozens of newspapers and journals represented all shades of political opinion.[2] The political and artistic scene was leavened by the voices of intellectuals among the tens of thousands of refugees who flooded the city.

Among the refugees was a young Japanese woman, Hasegawa Teru, better known by her Esperanto pseudonym Verda Majo. Guo Moruo had brought Verda from Hong Kong, where she had fled from the

---

1 The Chinese had air support from 2,000 Soviet pilots.
2 See Stephen MacKinnon, 'The Tragedy of Wuhan, 1938', *Modern Asian Studies*, Vol. 30, No. 4, 1996, 931–43.

fighting in Shanghai, and employed her in the government propaganda department. In Japanese-language radio broadcasts for three months, until Wuhan fell in October, she excoriated the invaders, telling the rank-and-file troops that their enemy was at home in Japan, not in China, and calling on them to revolt against the ruling clique of militarists and imperialists. She also wrote articles for the CCP paper *Xinhua Ribao* under the pen name Lu Chuan Yingzi.[3] Verda was an instinctive and uncompromising internationalist, as can be seen from her writings:

> If I had my wish, it would be perfectly fine to call me a 'traitor' to my country. I do not fear that at all. Rather, I am far more ashamed to be of the same race as a nation that simply invades the lands of others and calmly brings down hell on a completely innocent and powerless people.

She had contempt for former radicals in Japan who had succumbed to patriotism and were taking the side of their own country. 'When I see those intellectuals, who once called themselves conscientious, progressive, and even Marxist, jumping on the bandwagon of reactionary militarists and politicians, shamelessly promoting the "justice" of the "imperial army", I cannot control my angry desire to vomit.'[4]

Verda's broadcasts made her a hero in China – 'her soft voice spat thunder and lightning through the microphone' – but a traitor in her own country. Although she used a pseudonym, Japanese agents soon discovered her real identity. A newspaper printed her photograph and denounced her as a 'demon spreading poison to her fatherland' and a 'coquettish traitorous slave'. Ultranationalists tracked down her family and, in poison-pen letters, urged her father to reclaim his honour by committing suicide to atone for producing such a vile creature.

Verda was undeterred. When Wuhan fell to the Japanese in October 1938, she retreated with her Chinese husband to Chongqing, where they joined Kaji Wataru's Japanese People's Anti-war Alliance. Verda

---

3   Gotelind Müller, 'Hasegawa Teru alias Verda Majo (1912–1947)', Heidelberg: University of Heidelberg, 2013, 13.

4   Erik Esselstrom, 'The Life and Memory of Hasegawa Teru', *Radical History Review*, No. 101 (2008), 145–59, 151.

continued to work for the Esperantist section of the propaganda department but Chongqing, unlike Wuhan, was under tight political control and Chiang Kai-shek's secret police chief Dai Li made it a hostile environment for leftists. As the Second United Front disintegrated in all but name, Guo Moruo was sacked from his job as head of propaganda. Exhausted and malnourished, Verda contracted tuberculosis, and her husband fell ill with kidney disease. They were both depressed because of illness and the political repression, but, around this time, Verda gave birth to a son, Liu Xing. In 1942, she wrote a short autobiography in Esperanto, *En Ĉinio Batalanta*.

Verda Majo was born in 1912 into a conventional middle-class Tokyo household. Her father was a civil engineer, her mother a housewife. Her sister introduced her to Esperanto, kindling a lifelong devotion to the language and its associated ideals. It was through Esperanto that Verda Majo absorbed and developed her political ideas, and that she met her Chinese husband.

Esperanto is now largely seen as a failed project, but in Verda's time, it was taken seriously, especially in East Asia, where intellectuals saw language reform as a path to modernisation. The Chinese written language, which was used throughout the region, was only suitable, they believed, for a leisure class of literati and scholar-officials. To spread literacy throughout the population, they argued, characters must be replaced with an alphabet. A well-known aphorism, attributed to Lu Xun, went *hanzi bu mie, zhongguo bi wang* – 'Abolish characters or China is lost'. Some Chinese intellectuals even had the fantastic idea of replacing the Chinese language altogether, spoken and written, with Esperanto or English. In Japan, the first Meiji education minister, Mori Arinori, called for Japanese to be replaced by English. The liberal politician Ozaki Yukio favoured Esperanto. More realistically, Esperanto as a second language would allow speakers of different languages and dialects to communicate. Japan's Esperanto movement comprised both liberals and socialists and among both wings, internationalism was strong.

When she graduated from high school at the age of seventeen, Verda was offered a university place in Tokyo but chose instead to go to the Nara Women's Teacher-Training College, nearly 500 kilometres away, to escape her conservative father. In Nara, Verda joined student societies and wrote poetry and short stories, as well as for the college magazine.

She joined an Esperanto study group, championed proletarian literature, and became involved in the labour movement. However, any left-
wing activity invited repression. In 1932, she was arrested in a nationwide sweep of several hundred cultural activists.[5] Though she was
released soon afterwards, she was cruelly expelled from the university,
just three months short of graduating and returned to her parents' home
in Tokyo.

Verda might have been expected to drop out of political activity after
her arrest. Instead, she joined another Esperantist group, the Klara
circle, named after two of the group's idols – Klara Zamenhof, wife of the
creator of Esperanto, and the German Communist Clara Zetkin. She
began writing for Esperanto publications, including the Shanghai journal *La Mondo*. For the 1935 Women's Day issue, she wrote a piece on the
Japanese women's movement describing how the government tolerated
a bourgeois liberal element alongside right-wing patriotic women's
associations but suppressed organisations of working women. However,
without a proletarian revolution, she wrote, there would be no women's
liberation.[6]

Verda ridiculed ultra-rightists who demanded women stay in the
kitchen while fomenting the wars that drove them into factories. Having
been drafted into the workforce, women would inevitably launch a
struggle against the militarists and capitalists. Recalling that during the
revolutions of 1905 and 1917 in Russia, it was the women workers who
first took to the streets, she predicted they would do so again:

> They will organise themselves, create a united front with male work-
> ers, and join up with their sisters in the fields, factories and homes . . .
> they will launch a united struggle against the militarists and capital-
> ists . . . Just look at 1905 and 1917. Who was it that stood up for their
> lives and called for 'peace and bread'? . . . Lenin himself said that 'if
> not for the women, our revolution would not have succeeded'.

In 1936, Verda Majo went to Osaka to act in an Esperanto-language
play. While there, she met a Chinese exchange student, Liu Ren. Liu was

---

5   Alan Tansman, *The Culture of Japanese Fascism*, Durham: Duke University
Press, 2009, 63.
6   Müller, 'Hasegawa Teru alias Verda Majo', 5.

from the puppet state of Manzhouguo, where Japan had installed the titled nonentity Puyi as a fig leaf for the colonisation of Manchuria. Liu was also an Esperantist and moved in the same left-wing circles as Verda Majo. They fell in love and married. The wedding was held in secret because Verda's father, who shared the conventional Japanese view that the Chinese were uncouth and backward, would not have allowed it to go ahead. At the beginning of 1937, Liu returned to China to settle in Shanghai. Verda followed him there a few months later.

She would arrive in Shanghai just weeks before the simmering Sino-Japanese conflict turned into full-scale war, but she had no way of knowing this. As her ship left Yokohama, she experienced quite a conventional range of emotions. She was in tears because she was leaving her family and friends. She was apprehensive about moving to a country where she knew only her husband and spoke only a few words of the language. But she also felt the excitement and optimism of a young person on the threshold of an adventure. Surrounded by Chinese in her third-class cabin, she thought, 'Yesterday they were strangers, today they are fellow-passengers, tomorrow they will be fellow countrymen.'[7]

Verda arrived on the eve of the Marco Polo Bridge Incident, which the Japanese used as an excuse to launch their invasion. She and Liu barely had time to find accommodation before war broke out. Because Verda could not speak Chinese, they invented a rather naive cover story that she was an overseas Chinese from Malaya and that the language she spoke – Esperanto – was a local dialect. They socialised with the Chinese, Japanese, and Korean leftists for whom Shanghai was a refuge because of its foreign concession areas and free-port status. In mid-July, Verda had a brief respite from language-imposed isolation when the Chinese Esperanto society celebrated the language's fiftieth anniversary with a conference attended by 300 Esperantists from around the country. Chinese Esperantists, she wrote, saw no contradiction between patriotism and internationalism. They wanted their country to be free from oppression but had no desire to oppress others. The conference took place a week after the outbreak of war, and a large banner in the meeting hall proclaimed: 'Through Esperanto for the liberation of China'.

7 Hasegawa Teru (Verda Majo), *En Ĉinio Batalanta*, Osaka: Japana esperanta librokooperativo, 1954.

From the start, Verda took a clear-cut position on the war. After fighting broke out in Shanghai, she wrote 'Love and Hatred', in which she declared her willingness to join the battle against the invaders:

> Victory for China is the Key to Tomorrow for all of Asia . . . if one possesses a human heart and clear-headed reason, surely one will feel sympathy for China . . . I am one and the same with the Chinese people . . .
> If it was possible, I would join the Chinese army. Because the Chinese army is fighting for national liberation, not against the Japanese people, but against the Japanese imperialists. Together with my comrades I cry out to our Japanese brothers. Do not spill your blood here. Your enemy is not on this side of the sea.[8]

She took part in other movements, including the campaign to free Shen Junru (later first president of the PRC Supreme Court), one of the so-called Seven Gentlemen arrested by Chiang Kai-shek in 1936 and released only after Japan invaded.

When Shanghai fell to the Japanese, Verda and Liu Ren fled to Guangzhou, where she worked for a short time in the Esperanto section of the government propaganda department. But, after ultranationalist KMT officials discovered her nationality and sacked her, she and Liu Ren fled to Hong Kong where she wrote a despairing tract 'Japan: A Country Ruled by Savages.' It began with the words 'Is this title the exaggeration of an ill-intentioned enemy? No, I myself am Japanese.' The couple remained in Hong Kong for several months before Guo Moruo, now head of government propaganda, brought them to Wuhan.

After war, in the winter of 1946, the couple moved to Harbin, which had been taken by the Soviets in 1945 and was under Communist Party control. They were appointed professors at Northeastern University. By this time, Verda had given birth to a second child, a daughter but when she became pregnant for a third time she decided to have an abortion. Tragically, she contracted an infection during the operation and died at the age of thirty-five. She was given a state funeral. Four months later, Liu Ren also fell ill and died. Both are buried in the Harbin martyrs'

---

8   From Verda Majo, *Love and Hate*, quoted in Ye Lishu, *Friends from Abroad*, 231–2.

cemetery. Their son, Liu Xing, and daughter, Liu Xiaolan, were taken care of by the Communist Party. In 1979, a joint Chinese-Japanese TV production serialised the couple's lives, and in 1981, an edition of Verda's Esperanto works was published in China. Verda's elder sister visited China to meet her niece and nephew and took them to Japan to meet their mother's friends.

Decades after her death, Verda Majo became a symbol and an inspiration for anti-war and anti-militarist movements in Japan. Her example was invoked during the 1970s, when Japan was a base for American bombers during the Vietnam War, once again when Japan helped finance America's wars in the Middle East, and more recently as rightist politicians stepped up their efforts to revise Japan's pacifist constitution.[9] Her romantic but tragic story, with its poignant, unfulfilled possibilities, but above all her courage and internationalism, ensured her enduring popularity.

---

9   Esselstrom, 'The Life and Memory of Hasegawa Teru'.

19

Forgotten Flyers

The ninety-nine pilots of the American Volunteer Group (AVG), better known as the Flying Tigers, are celebrated and commemorated both outside and inside China, especially in the southwestern city of Kunming where they were headquartered. Less well remembered are the Soviet volunteer pilots who took part in the first phase of China's War of Resistance. Some standard English-language histories of the war play down the contribution of the Soviet volunteer force. Others fail to mention it at all. One author states that the Soviet Union made a secret agreement with Japan not to send aid to China. Yet around 2,000 Soviet airmen fought in China between 1937 and 1941, and 236 of them were killed.[1]

The Soviet Union began delivering weapons, military advisors, and financial aid to China in the autumn of 1937, soon after Japan launched

---

[1] For example, in his history of China's role in World War II, Rana Mitter, refers six times to the Flying Tigers. while suggesting that they were little more than a morale booster, but only twice to the Soviet pilots. See Rana Mitter, *Forgotten Ally: China's World War II, 1937–1945*, Boston: Houghton Mifflin Harcourt, 2013. Bruce Elleman makes a brief mention of Soviet air support in the battle of Wuhan but asserts that the Soviets made a secret agreement with the Japanese not to arm China. 'Throughout 1937 to 1945, the Nationalist and Communist anti-Japanese resistance continued, but was undermined by Soviet–Japanese negotiations . . . Moscow agreed not to arm and supply Jiang Jieshi and to muzzle the Chinese Communists' anti-Japanese activities.' Bruce Elleman, *Modern Chinese Warfare, 1795–1989*, London: Routledge, 2001, 205, 211. Other authors say Marshall Zhukov served as chief of mission in China. In fact it was Marshall Vasily Chuikov.

its full-scale assault on China following the Marco Polo Bridge Incident. Between 1937 and 1941, the Soviets supplied 1,250 aircraft including 322 bombers and 575 fighters, 82 tanks, 1,600 artillery pieces and anti-aircraft guns, 14,000 machine guns, 50,000 rifles, 180 million rounds, 30,000 bombs, 2 million shells, plus trucks and fuel. Thousands of Soviet and Chinese workers constructed a highway along the route of the ancient Silk Road from Almaty through Xinjiang to Lanzhou. The Soviets also built aircraft assembly plants and a training school for Chinese pilots and provided China with 250 million dollars in low-interest loans. From 1937 until the end of 1941, almost every Chinese military action was conducted using Soviet equipment with the assistance of Soviet advisors and volunteers.[2]

No other country delivered significant aid to China during the first four and a half years of the War of Resistance. Britain was unwilling to risk its Far Eastern colonies by confronting Japan and would have welcomed a Japanese attack on the Soviet Union. The United States remained isolationist. At the beginning of 1941, Roosevelt allowed military pilots to resign to join the AVG, but the Flying Tigers did not see action until after Pearl Harbor. Germany had been China's main military partner, supplying both equipment and advisors, but the 1936 Anti-Comintern Pact meant that China could no longer rely on German support against Japan. Chiang Kai-shek's German advisors pulled out in July 1938, as the Japanese advanced on Wuhan, China's wartime capital after the fall of Nanjing.[3]

The Chinese domestic context for the Soviet aid programme was the formation of the Second United Front between the KMT and the CCP

---

2   Yu. V. Chudodeyev, *Na Zemle i v Nebe Kitaya: Sovetskiye voyennyye sovetniki i lotchiki-dobrovol'tsy v Kitaye v period yapono-kitayskoy voyny* [On the soil and in the skies of China: Soviet military advisors and volunteer pilots in China during the Sino-Japanese War], Moscow: Institut vostokovedeniya RAN, 2017, 22. Yu Maochun of the US Naval War College, one of a few Western authors to acknowledge the scale of Soviet assistance, gives similar figures of 900 aircraft, including 318 heavy bombers, and 10,000 machine guns. Yu states that while the United States, France, and Britain did little to help China, the Soviet Union 'took immediate action on a massive scale'. Yu Maochun, *The Dragon's War: Allied Operations and the Fate of China, 1937–1947*, New York: Naval Institute, 2013.

3   Stephen MacKinnon, *Wuhan, 1938: War, Refugees, and the Making of Modern China*, Berkeley: University of California Press, 2008, 101.

in December 1936, following the Xi'an Incident.[4] The CCP's armies were incorporated into China's National Revolutionary Army as the Eighth Route Army and the New Fourth Army. Nevertheless, little Soviet military aid reached the Communist forces. On the other hand, to the CCP leadership's annoyance, they received shipments of Marxist literature and a Soviet plane carried Wang Ming, Mao's rival and faithful follower of the Moscow line, back to Yan'an.[5]

Chiang Kai-shek's quest for a Soviet alliance predated the December 1936 crisis. Indeed, he had already instructed Jiang Tingfu, China's recently appointed ambassador to the Soviet Union, to seek a mutual security treaty with the Russians.[6] In so doing, Chiang aimed to ensure that, in the event of war with Japan, the Soviet Union would be drawn into the conflict.[7] Open warfare between Japan and Russia, he reasoned, would take the pressure off China and, hopefully, mean the Japanese would be defeated.

While Chiang aimed to draw the Soviet Union into war with Japan, Stalin's aim was the opposite – to avoid war with Japan while keeping China in the war to deflect the Japanese from Siberia.[8] Stalin explicitly set out the main task of the Soviet mission to its last chief, Vasily Chuikov:

> Your task, comrade Chuikov, is not just to teach Chiang Kai-shek and his generals how to use the weapons we are sending them but to inspire Chiang Kai-shek with the confidence that the Japanese invaders can be defeated. If he has confidence in victory, Chiang Kai-shek will not come to terms with the aggressors . . . The task of all our people in China is to tie the hands of the Japanese aggressor. Only then . . . can we avoid a war on two fronts if the Germans attack.[9]

---

4   In December 1936, the warlord Zhang Xueliang took Chiang Kai-shek captive in Xi'an to force him to end the anti-CCP campaign and fight the Japanese.

5   Otto Braun, *A Comintern Agent in China, 1932–1939*, Jeanne Moore, trans., London: C. Hurst, 1982, 209.

6   John W. Garver, 'Chiang Kai-shek's Quest for Soviet Entry into the Sino-Japanese War', *Political Science Quarterly*, Vol. 102, No. 2 (1987), 295–316, 300.

7   Ibid., 297.

8   Soviet fears were justified. During the Allied Intervention in the Russian Civil War, Japan sent by far the largest contingent – 70,000 troops – to Siberia, masking territorial ambitions as an anti-Communist crusade.

9   Chudodeyev, *Na Zemle i v Nebe Kitaya*, 30.

In Nanjing on 21 August 1937, China and the Soviet Union signed, not a mutual assistance treaty, as Chiang had hoped, but a non-aggression pact. Since war had already broken out, Chiang had no choice but to take whatever the Soviets offered. Nevertheless, the pact opened the way for Soviet aid, which began arriving almost immediately.

Soviet assistance to China, then, was not disinterested. But, while not openly fighting Japan, the USSR became a de facto ally of China. For both countries, it was an alliance of convenience in which they put their own interests first. Chiang wanted more than the Soviet Union was prepared, or perhaps even able, to offer. But he was no less duplicitous than Stalin and did not declare war on Japan until after Pearl Harbor.

In December 1938, Chiang, who had relied heavily on his chief German advisor, Alexander von Falkenhausen, asked Stalin to send Vasily Blyukher, who had carried him to victory in the Northern Expedition, as his replacement. Sending Blyukher, Chiang said, would be the equivalent of sending 100,000 men.[10] Blyukher's return was, however, impossible. Stalin had already had him killed and never replied to Chiang's request. Four chiefs of the Soviet mission succeeded each other between 1937 and 1942; M. I. Dratvin, A. I. Cherepanov, K M. Kachanov, and V. I. Chuikov. All except Kachanov had served in China between 1924 and 1927 during the first United Front.

The new mission to China was not confined to air support; Soviet advisors were active in all branches of the military and took part in land battles. Nevertheless, China's greatest need was for air power. The Chinese air force had started the war with obsolete aircraft piloted by rich amateurs. According to Soviet Squadron Leader F. P. Polynin, the Chinese planes were museum pieces. Aircraft purchase was managed not by defence chiefs but by the financier H. H. Kung and the head of the air force, Zhou Zhizhou, was universally regarded as corrupt. Utterly outclassed by the Japanese, by the end of 1937 the Chinese air force had been almost entirely wiped out, and cities were defenceless against air raids.[11]

The Soviet's first chief aviation advisor in China was Pavel Vasilyevich Rychagov. Rychagov had been awarded the Order of Lenin and named a

---

10   S. L. Tikhvinsky, ed., *Russko-kitaiskie otnosheniya v XX veke* [Russian-Chinese Relations in the 20th Century], 5 Vols., Moscow: Pamyatniki istorichyeskoi misli, 2000–2010, Vol. 4, 365, available at historyrussia.org/ru.

11   Chudodeyev, *Na Zemle i v Nebe Kitaya*, 57–8.

Hero of the Soviet Union for his exploits as a squadron leader in Spain. Fighting under the pseudonym Pablo Palancar, he shot down six fascist aircraft during the defence of Madrid. In a famous incident, he was shot down but managed to bail out and landed in the Paseo de la Castellana, one of Madrid's main avenues. After returning to Russia, Rychagov was promoted rapidly. Just twenty-six years old when he arrived in China with the first wave of volunteer pilots in December 1937, he was already a brigadier general.

On average, pilots served six months in China. Since open conflict with Japan had to be avoided, they were officially volunteers, travelled to China clandestinely in civilian clothes and were instructed that, if captured, they were to say they were White Russian mercenaries. When pilots died in combat, their families were not informed.[12] How many of the pilots were genuine volunteers and how many were simply ordered to go is hard to tell. In theory, they had the right to decline the mission, but it is hard to imagine many doing so, given the possible consequences, as well as pride and peer pressure. It is also credible that young pilots (most were in their twenties or early thirties) were still motivated by the ideals of revolutionary internationalism and anti-imperialism inherited from the October Revolution or the newer Soviet patriotism associated with the doctrine of Socialism in One Country. They may have been inspired by what was a golden age for Soviet aviation. Indeed, the exploits of Soviet aviators were being celebrated at home and abroad. The famous aerobatics pilot Valery Chkalov made several record-breaking long-distance flights, including a 1937 transpolar flight from Russia to the United States, after which he was paraded through New York and met President Roosevelt.[13]

From Irkutsk and Almaty, the aircrews flew in civilian passenger aircraft and converted bombers to Xinjiang or Lanzhou. It was a hazardous journey. Flights from Almaty went over the Tian Shan mountains, while those from Irkutsk crossed the Gobi Desert. Radios were unreliable, and instruments were primitive and at high altitudes, breathing apparatus froze. Over the desert, dust storms and high winds, often lasting several days, were a huge problem. Airfields en route were primitive – in Xinjiang, they were often simply marked out on the sand. There were many accidents, and some crews never made it to China.

---

12   Ibid., 63–4.
13   Ibid., 60–2.

Meanwhile, their warplanes were dismantled, transported in kit form, and reassembled in Xinjiang or Lanzhou. In addition to the 2,000 airmen, more than 1,600 technicians and other ground staff took part in the mission. As well as maintenance work, they were often sent on hazardous missions to retrieve damaged aircraft and some doubled up as gunners on combat missions.[14]

The Soviet flyers were thrown into battle against formidable opponents. After landing in Nanjing in November 1937, the fighter pilot D. A. Kudymov had to take off immediately to repel a Japanese air raid and became involved in a desperate dogfight. He shot the enemy fighter down and was awarded the Order of the Red Banner. Kudymov became a famous ace in the Second World War but, at the time, like many of the other Soviet volunteers, he was young and inexperienced. The Japanese pilots, by contrast, had seen real combat and included many famous aces. Some of the Japanese pilots were fanatically committed. If forced to crash-land, they would commit suicide rather than surrender – perhaps because they expected a worse death at the hands of Chinese civilians. To avoid being mistaken for the enemy if shot down, Soviet pilots were given silk cloths embroidered with the message, 'This foreigner came to assist us in our armed struggle. Military and civilians should afford him all necessary help and assistance.'

Ordinary Chinese were, naturally, grateful for Soviet assistance. Squadron leader M. G. Machin recalled that after missions, peasants and street vendors would bring piles of tangerines, apples, bananas, boiled eggs, and other snacks to the airport to give to the volunteers. The Soviets also worked closely with Chinese maintenance staff and frequently flew missions with Chinese pilots and gunners.[15] But they were wary of other foreigners, above all White Russians, who were often in desperate straits and approached the volunteers looking for ways to return to Russia. Some had been recruited by the Kuomintang spymaster Dai Li. An NKVD agent, S. P. Konstantinov, claimed that, soon after he was contacted by a young Russian woman, Dai Li's agents tried to kill him in a staged car accident.

The Soviet secret police and political commissars kept a close eye on the aircrews. Party and Komsomol (Young Communist League)

---

14   Ibid., 93.
15   Ibid., 107. Machin retired as a lieutenant general in 1971. He died in 1995.

members were expected to attend meetings, which were billed as military meetings in deference to the sensitivities of the Chinese. But it was not all work and politics. The pilots, who were almost all young men, were also able to go to bars and nightclubs, drink and, of course, meet women. It seems that, on the whole, morale was relatively high. One of the pilots, Ivan Gurov, played the mandolin and organised a band. He was killed in action and was buried in Wuhan.

One of the most notable operations carried out by the Soviet volunteers was a raid on the Matsuyama airfield near Taipei, where the Japanese had been assembling a force of German and Italian warplanes to attack mainland China.[16] On 22 February 1938, Rychagov ordered thirty-one-year-old F. P. Polynin, commander of a squadron bombers based in Wuhan to prepare an immediate attack on the airfield. Polynin had already led a raid on an airfield near Nanjing that had destroyed many Japanese planes on the ground.[17] But attacking Taiwan was a much more formidable task. The distance to the target was over 1,000 kilometres, at the limit of the Tupolevs' range. On the return journey, they would have to land in the coastal city of Fuzhou to refuel. To even reach the target they would have to conserve fuel by flying at high altitude with substandard oxygen masks.

Despite these difficulties and thick cloud cover over the target on the day of the attack, the mission was an outstanding success. The Soviet and Chinese bomber crews destroyed forty enemy planes on the ground as well as hangars and fuel stores. The defenders, caught by surprise, had no time to retaliate and all the bombers returned to base safely. Humiliated, the Japanese government removed the governor of Taiwan and court-martialled the island's military commander. The commander of the airfield, which was never used to attack China, committed suicide. Chiang Kai-shek's wife, Song Meiling, hosted a banquet to honour the leaders of the raid and their commanders but, to preserve the official secrecy of the Soviet mission, journalists were told it had been carried out by Chinese aircrew. Some newspapers even claimed the raid had been led by an American volunteer.[18]

---

16   In an air raid on Hangzhou launched from Matsuyama in 1937, four Japanese bombers were shot down.

17   Peter Harmsen, *Storm Clouds over the Pacific*, Philadelphia: Casemate, 2018, 67.

18   Vincent Schmidt, who was bewildered and embarrassed when congratulated for a mission he had no part in.

Also in February 1938, Soviet bombers attacked a Japanese airbase in Hangzhou, destroying thirty aircraft on the ground, before severely damaging Hangzhou railway station. The commander of the mission was Sidor Vasilyevich Slyusarev, who served in China from May 1938 to March 1939 as head of a bomber group. Slyusarev later took part in the defence of Kiev, the Battle of Stalingrad, and the capture of Berlin. He was awarded three Orders of Lenin and the title Hero of the Soviet Union. After the war, he was a senior air force commander in Siberia. During the Korean war, he commanded Soviet pilots who flew clandestine missions to provide air cover for North Korean and Chinese troops.

When Nanjing fell in December 1937, the Soviet volunteers withdrew to airfields in Nanchang and Wuhan. Wuhan became the de facto capital of China until the Japanese took the city at the end of October 1938. The ground and naval battle for the city from June to October was one of the bloodiest of the war.[19] Soviet pilots were in constant action defending the city and it was the setting for the fiercest fighting of their mission. More than a hundred Soviet volunteer pilots were killed defending the city.

On 29 April 1938, the Japanese mounted a massive attack on Wuhan to mark Emperor Hirohito's birthday. The attack was expected, and crews were on standby in their aircraft from dawn. When Japanese bombers and their fighter escorts were spotted around ten in the morning, sixty fighters piloted by both Russians and Chinese took off to intercept them. There were some notable acts of bravery. Twenty-four-year-old Lieutenant Lev Zakharovich Shuster ran out of ammunition while attacking a Japanese fighter and rammed his target head-on. Both Shuster and the Japanese pilot were killed.[20] Another fighter pilot, Konstantin Kitaev, attacked a formation of more than twenty Japanese bombers and shot down two of them before he was shot down and killed. The Soviet ace Grigory Panteleyevich Kravchenko shot down two Japanese bombers. When he, in turn, came under attack, Anton Gubenko flew to provide cover and divert the Japanese fighters. Kravchenko bailed out and landed in a lake where he was rescued by fishermen who carried him in a sedan chair to their village; a rescue party found him drinking the local firewater with his hosts. In a later

---

19   Wuhan is an inland port on the Yangzi River.
20   Chudodeyev, *Na Zemle i v Nebe Kitaya*, 85.

battle, Kravchenko provided cover for Gubenko when Japanese fighters tried to strafe him as he descended by parachute. Kravchenko was made a Hero of the Soviet Union and promoted to squadron leader. He later commanded an air force division in World War II and fought in the battle of Khalkhin Gol, for which he was named Hero of the Soviet Union for a second time. He was shot down and killed during the siege of Leningrad. His ashes were placed in the Kremlin wall.

After the humiliation of 29 April, it was a month before the Japanese mounted another major air raid on Wuhan. On 31 May, eighteen bombers and thirty-six support fighters attacked Wuhan, but the raid ended just as badly, and they lost fourteen aircraft. During the battle, Anton Gubenko shot down one Japanese fighter and rammed another, using his biplane's propeller to wreck one of its wings. He managed to land his plane safely. The press, adhering to the fiction that Soviets were only advisors and not involved in the fighting, attributed the feat to a daredevil Chinese pilot, but Gubenko was awarded the Golden Order of the Republic of China and made a Hero of the Soviet Union. During five months in China, he shot down twelve enemy aircraft. The year after returning to Russia, he was killed in a flying accident while practising aerobatics.[21]

As well as flying missions, the Soviet pilots also trained around 1,800 Chinese pilots at flying schools established in Xinjiang and Nanchang. Most of the Chinese cadets were trained as fighter pilots, but some also trained in bombers. F. P. Polynin recalled that the Chinese were especially diligent students. 'They sat for hours on the ground without moving, listening to lectures without taking lunch or rest breaks. As for the planes, they treated them as living creatures, literally idolizing them.'[22]

It was not only Rychagov who had seen action in Spain. Bomber squadron commander Grigory Illarionovich Thor, who led missions against Japanese warships on the Yangzi River, had flown more than one hundred missions against Franco's forces. After returning from China he was promoted deputy commander of an air force division but

21   'Soviet Pilot Who Risked His Own Life to Help China', *China Daily*, 25 August 2015.

22   Chudodeyev, *Na Zemle i v Nebe Kitaya*, 87.

continued to fly. In 1941 he was taken prisoner and shot by the Gestapo.[23] Another bomber pilot and veteran of the Spanish Civil War, Timofey Timofeyevich Khryukin, was awarded the Order of the Cloud Banner by the Chinese government. Khryukin was a model Soviet success story having grown up illiterate in extreme poverty and worked as a labourer before joining the air force. Another Spanish veteran, fighter pilot, Georgy Zakharov, forced a Japanese fighter down during a dogfight and landed nearby. The Japanese pilot shot himself rather than be captured and Zakharov was ordered to fly the Japanese plane back to Russia. During the flight the engine failed, and Zakharov crashed into a mountain. He survived with minor injuries and went on to command an air regiment during the Great Patriotic War.

From December 1937 to December 1939, the Soviet pilots shot down or destroyed on the ground around 900 Japanese aircraft and destroyed around 150 Japanese ships. However, their own losses were daunting. In June 1938 alone, 162 aircraft were shot down by the Japanese. And enemy action was not the only threat. Faulty and inadequate equipment, inexperience, and difficult terrain led to a high death toll from accidents, many of which took place on flights home after volunteers completed their tours of duty. In one incident alone, a plane flying from Hankou to Xi'an caught fire and crashed, killing twenty-two volunteer pilots. Another crash killed eighteen pilots. In one two-month period in 1938, eleven plane crashes killed seventy Soviet air crew.[24] Some units were nearly wiped out by a combination of combat losses and accidents. Of the sixty volunteers sent to China in October 1938 under the command of S. V. Slyusarev, only sixteen returned to the Soviet Union alive. These are, by any standards, horrendous figures.

The high accident rate had a squalid coda. After returning from China, Rychagov continued his rise through the ranks. He was promoted to major general in 1939 and, in 1940, was appointed to the Chief Military Council of the Red Army; later that year, he replaced Yakov Smushkevich as head of the Soviet Air Force. Accidents were not confined to the China theatre and, by 1941, following Stalin's purges of senior officers, the number of pilots being lost was alarming. On 9 April

---

23   Ibid., 68–9.
24   Chudodeyev, *Na Zemle i v Nebe Kitaya*, 133.

1941, at a meeting in the Kremlin to discuss the issue with Stalin, Rychagov blurted out that the accident rate was high because 'you make us fly in coffins'. While his colleagues held their breath. Stalin, who had been pacing the room smoking his pipe, paused, and replied, 'You would have done better to keep quiet, general.'[25] Rychagov was dismissed and, shortly afterwards, the NKVD came for him. In 1953, an NKVD general testified how Rychagov was interrogated and beaten with rubber truncheons but refused to talk. He was shot without even the pretence of a trial on 28 October 1941, in the village of Barbysh near Samara. The NKVD also shot Rychagov's wife, Major Maria Nesterenko, herself a pilot and deputy commander of an air force regiment. When Rychagov was eventually posthumously rehabilitated, a street was named after him.

By the time the Soviet mission's final commander, Vasily Chuikov, arrived on New Year's Day 1941, the war in China had entered a period of stalemate. The United Front between the Communist Party and the Kuomintang was breaking down and within days of Chuikov's arrival, the New Fourth Army Incident took place. He warned the Nationalist government that supplies would be reduced or cut altogether if it stepped up action against the Communists. Although cooperation between the CCP and KMT, never strong, effectively ended, Chiang Kai-shek nevertheless appointed Chuikov his chief military advisor and de facto deputy chairman of the Military Council. As noted earlier, the Soviet Union's chief concern was to avoid a Japanese attack on the Soviet Far East. Despite Chinese insistence that Japan was planning just such an attack, Chuikov correctly assessed it would concentrate its forces on the Americans and the Pacific.

On 13 April 1941, the Soviet Union and Japan signed a non-aggression pact. Among its provisions was a Soviet agreement to respect the integrity of the puppet state of Manzhouguo in return for a similar commitment from Japan regarding Mongolia. Although the last military advisors did not leave until 1944, the agreement effectively signalled the end of large-scale Soviet aid to China. In the summer of 1941, the United States sent Air Force general Henry Clagett to China to discuss

---

25 Alec Nove, *Glasnost in Action: Cultural Renaissance in Russia*, London: Routledge, 2012, 50. See also Moshe Lewin, *The Soviet Century*, London: Verso, 2016, 93.

the provision of air support. The Soviet aid effort was winding down, and that of the United States ramping up. In February 1942, General Stilwell was assigned to command the China-Burma theatre and, shortly afterwards, Chuikov was recalled and was not replaced.

20
Farmers

Where do correct ideas come from? Do they drop from the skies? No. Are they innate in the mind? No. They come from social practice, and from it alone.

Mao Zedong, 1963

Nature and nurture conspired to make Joan Hinton a prodigy. Through her father, Sebastian 'Ted' Hinton, she was descended from outstanding mathematicians. Ted's father, Charles Hinton, explored the mathematics of multi-dimensional space and coined the word 'tesseract'. Charles's wife, Joan's grandmother, was Mary Ellen Boole, one of the five daughters of George Boole, the self-taught genius who invented Boolean algebra – one of the pillars of computer science. Boole's wife, Mary Everest, Joan's great-grandmother, devised string geometry as a way of teaching mathematics to children and wrote books on evolution and psychology. She passed on radical politics to her daughters, one of whom, Joan's great aunt Ethel, joined the Narodniks while working as a governess in St Petersburg and based on her experiences in the movement wrote the famous revolutionary novel *The Gadfly*.[1]

---

1 Ethel married a Polish revolutionary called Michael Voynich, who later became a book dealer. He is remembered for discovering the Voynich manuscript, an illustrated fourteenth-century text written in an unknown language that has, so far, not been deciphered.

Ted Hinton was a lawyer and part-time inventor. He built an elaborate climbing frame for his children and filed a patent under the name 'jungle gym' which thereafter provided a steady income for the family. But Joan and her elder siblings, Bill and Jean, barely knew their father as he died when they were young children. Joan's mother, Carmelita, told them he had succumbed to an infectious disease, but after Carmelita died in 1983, the children found out that he had committed suicide in an insane asylum.[2] Carmelita had brought the children up to think Ted's side of the family, rather than her own, was special, but Joan was not convinced. According to her, George Boole was just a teacher who dabbled in mathematics in his spare time; his algebra was left dusting on library shelves until computers came along. 'If you want to know me, know my mother,' she often told people.

Carmelita Hinton, née Chase, came from an upper-crust family in Vermont. Her father was the owner and editor of a newspaper, her mother a renowned society hostess who threw parties for the local elite. Carmelita was expected to follow her mother's path in life but rebelled and went to Chicago to work for Jane Addams at Hull House. After Ted died, leaving her with three children to raise, she took a series of teaching jobs, including one at Shady Hill in Cambridge, Massachusetts – a progressive school run on the Deweyan principle of learning by doing. Perhaps oddly for such a school, the children went on discovery holidays to Nazi Germany. In 1933 and 1934, in the manner of Miss Jean Brodie, Carmelita took groups of schoolchildren, including her own three children, on Nazi-hosted tours. The children were taken to mass rallies, including one where Joan stood not much more than a yard from Hitler. She came back with swastika badges and flags as souvenirs, and an enthusiastic twelve-year-old Nazi, to the horror of her friends and their parents. Joan's biographer excuses Carmelita because, at the time, it was 'not common knowledge that Hitler was organising the German people to believe in the superiority of the Aryan race'.[3] To be sure, that might excuse one trip; but perhaps not both.

---

2   For more on the Hintons' family background, see Gerry Kennedy, *The Booles and the Hintons: Two Dynasties That Helped Shape the Modern World*, Cork: Cork University Press, 2016.

3   Dao-yuan Chou, *Silage Choppers and Snake Spirits*, Quezon City: IBON Books, 2009, 11.

In 1935, Carmelita set up a school in the small town of Putney, Vermont. Joan spent her secondary school years there. Lessons were mainly outdoors and concentrated on practical skills of farming, livestock rearing, carpentry, metalwork, construction, sports, music, and so on. There was 'no sitting in classrooms with arms folded listening to a teacher drone on'. By the time she finished school, Joan was a talented amateur violinist and an Olympic-class skier. Only the outbreak of war prevented her representing the United States at the 1940 games planned for Japan. From Putney, she went to Bennington, a liberal arts college for women. But Joan was more interested in science than the arts. In her spare time, she made a Wilson cloud chamber and spent holidays at Cornell University working on their cyclotron.[4] From Bennington, she moved to Wisconsin University to study physics, but in 1944 she was drafted into the Manhattan Project before completing the course. Wisconsin hastily awarded her a master's degree on the strength of her cloud chamber.[5] She was one of only a handful of female scientists on the atom bomb project.

Joan's position at Los Alamos was junior, but a colleague recalled her as a 'very, very brilliant young lady'.[6] Enrico Fermi, the Italian genius who created the world's first nuclear reactor, took her on as a lab assistant. Fermi, Joan, and Bob Carter, another of Fermi's lab assistants, were all keen hikers, horse riders, and skiers. They became close friends and went on camping trips together. Carter recalled Fermi making waffles for them in his kitchen. 'There was no outward indicator that he was a Nobel Prize physicist, one of the world's wisest and best physicists. He was just an ordinary guy with a waffle.'[7] Fermi and Joan even co-authored a paper – although she later said Fermi more or less dictated it to her:

I didn't understand a thing. Then he signed it with my name and his. There's this paper in the archives with my name on it . . . A lot of these top scientists . . . were very human human beings. Fermi liked

---

4 The first Cornell cyclotron was built in 1935.

5 Joan thought this absurd, as a cloud chamber is relatively simple to make.

6 Julius Tabin, interview, Voices of the Manhattan Project, 2012, manhattanprojectvoices.org.

7 Bob Carter, interview, Voices of the Manhattan Project, 2018, manhattanprojectvoices.org.

to get a few young students around him. No airs at all. Very much part of the group.[8]

The scientists also had a chamber orchestra, in which Joan played the violin and Edward Teller, the 'father of the hydrogen bomb', played the piano. She got on well with Teller despite political differences. 'Teller was a real character. His voice, his roar, you could hear it all down the site. He went into anything with tremendous vigour, including playing the piano.'[9] She also became good friends with the project's chief scientist Robert Oppenheimer and his wife Kitty to the extent that they lent their nearby ranch to her so that she could invite Carmelita for a summer break. Joan later maintained that Oppenheimer wanted to stop the bombing of Hiroshima but was pressured into acquiescing.[10]

Neither Joan nor Bob Carter were authorised to attend the first atom bomb test on 16 July 1945. But the test location was an open secret at Los Alamos, so they rode Carter's motorbike 250 miles from Los Alamos to a mound a safe distance from the detonation point. They had to hide the bike and walk the last leg of the journey to avoid army patrols. Joan said that when the bomb was detonated around dawn, 'it suddenly felt like you were at the bottom of the ocean and the ocean was not water but light . . . [then it] concentrated into this purple mass. A terrible color of poisonous purple.'[11] Many years later, Carter said, only half-jokingly, that they might have preceded the Rosenbergs to the electric chair if they had been caught.[12]

Three weeks later, the United States bombed Hiroshima. The destructive power of the bomb famously reminded Oppenheimer of the *Bhagavad Gita* verse 'I am become death, the destroyer of worlds'. Joan, who had somehow convinced herself that the United States would invite Japanese leaders to witness a demonstration at an unpopulated location, was disabused and distressed.

---

8   Joan Hinton, interviewed by Neil Burton, taped interviews with Joan Hinton and Erwin 'Sid' Engst, 1987. Kindly provided by their son Fred Engst.
9   Fermi described Teller as the only monomaniac he ever knew with more than one mania.
10   Chou, *Silage Choppers*, 66.
11   Ibid., 59
12   Bob Carter, interview, Voices of the Manhattan Project, 2015, manhattanprojectvoices.org.

What have we done? It was such fun on the site, we had so much fun together. The atmosphere ... everyone working for a common cause ... nobody cared whether somebody's more smart ... going out and skiing and everything ... we never had the idea they were going to kill anybody ... then they brought back these samples of cement with the shadow of a human arm on it.[13]

A small minority of Los Alamos scientists, including Joan, horrified by the weapon they had helped create, set up the Association of Los Alamos Scientists to campaign for civilian control of atomic energy.

Joan and Bob Carter had been working on a uranium reactor. Two other young colleagues, Harry Daghlian and Ed Hammel, were working on a plutonium reactor nearby. Both installations, for safety reasons, were sited in a deep canyon. When Joan arrived for work on the morning of 21 August, a fortnight after the destruction of Hiroshima and Nagasaki, a GI guard ran to her car shouting, 'Harry's had an accident'.[14] When Daghlian emerged, he told Joan, 'I've just killed myself. Take me to the hospital.' He had been 'tickling the dragon's tail' – bringing a plutonium core to the brink of criticality – when he accidentally dropped a brick into the assembly, triggering an instantaneous surge in radiation. As Joan drove to the clinic, he kept rubbing his injured hand. When she later tested some coins from his pocket, the Geiger counter went off the scale. Daghlian was beyond help. Joan said 'it was like he had been burned right through his body ... he just disintegrated. His hair fell out, they put ice packs on him ... he just gradually died, it took a month.'[15] The plutonium core that killed Daghlian had been earmarked for a third bomb that was to be dropped on Tokyo, had Japan not surrendered.[16]

Joan threw herself into the campaign against nuclear weapons. She sent samples of sand fused into glass by the test explosion to the mayors of every major city in the US, with the message, 'Do you want your city

---

13   Joan Hinton, interview.

14   The soldier, Private Robert Hemmerly, who was yards away from Daghlian when the accident happened, died of leukaemia in 1978 at the age of sixty-two.

15   Joan Hinton, interview.

16   The following year, the same so-called 'demon core' killed another scientist, Louis Slotin, during a similar experiment. It was never used to make a bomb. Both accidents were attributed to the victims' bravado and lax safety standards. See Alex Wellerstein, 'The Demon Core and the strange death of Louis Slotin', New Yorker, May 21, 2016.

to look like this?' However, she was the only member of her team to join the association. She tried many times to win Fermi over. He eventually, in a friendly note, asked her to stop, saying that there were 'several points' on which he disagreed with her.[17] She could not even convince Bob Carter.

Perhaps failure to win Carter over was a factor in cutting short what might have developed into a romance. According to Carter, he held off because, in 1944, Joan was already talking about going to China, 'I felt "I don't have a right to change her life, and I don't want to go to China, so we don't have a future as a couple."' Decades later, after his wife died, he and his daughter visited Joan and her family in Beijing. While they were having dinner, Joan announced: 'You know, for two years, Bob and I did *everything* together.' Embarrassed, the strait-laced Carter replied: 'Everything we did, we did together, but there were some things we didn't do.'[18]

Joan's elder brother, Bill Hinton, was her link with both China and her future husband, Erwin 'Sid' Engst. Bill and Sid had roomed together while studying agriculture at Cornell University, and Joan had met Sid when she worked on the cyclotron there. Bill had been a pacifist, and when he was drafted after Pearl Harbor, he declared himself a conscientious objector but his other sister, Jean, who was in the Communist Party, eventually persuaded him to enlist to fight fascism. After he was found unfit for combat duty, he was assigned to the Office of War Information and sent to China, where he interviewed Mao Zedong when he was in Chongqing for peace talks with the KMT. His book *Fanshen* is an account of land reform in the Shanxi province.

Sid's parents were dairy farmers with a history of activism – having organised milk strikes to protest against low prices. His father, who had been a miner before taking up farming, dabbled in socialist ideas. Having grown up in the Great Depression, Sid was sympathetic to the left, and discussions with Bill and Jean further radicalised him. At the end of the war, he decided to follow Bill to China and, with Jean's help, in March 1946, he found a job with the United Nations Relief and Rehabilitation Administration in Shanghai. He had been carrying on a long-distance courtship with Joan and went to Los Alamos to ask her

---

17   Chou, *Silage Choppers*, 66.
18   Bob Carter, interview, 2018.

to go with him but she was still attached to her work and turned him down.

After the war, Fermi gave Joan a job at the University of Chicago's Institute of Nuclear Physics,[19] where she also studied quantum mechanics under Teller. One of her classmates was Chinese – the future Nobel Prize winner Li Zhengdao. She recalls being bold enough to correct Teller after he mistakenly conceded a point to Li. The camaraderie of the Manhattan Project transcended political differences. When Joan, disillusioned with the military's domination of nuclear research, finally decided to join Sid in China, Fermi and Teller knew exactly where she was going. CIA agents visited the head of the institute, Samuel King Allison, and demanded to know Joan's destination, but he told them to mind their own business. Even Teller, the real-life Dr Strangelove, kept silent when a single word would have thwarted her plans.[20]

Why did Joan go? A letter to Sid makes it fairly clear it was not to help the Chinese get a nuclear weapon. She relates how Allison and Fermi thought she was mad, was writing off her PhD, and told her that she would forget physics if she dropped out for even a short time – two years was her plan at the time. It is clear they regarded her as junior and not a security risk:

> I am not at all sure I want to put my whole life into being a physicist . . . I think if I want to get a degree when I get back, I will do so, (though probably at a school which is less tough than Chicago). If I do not want one then that will be OK, too . . . My point in coming here was, after all, to learn physics, only secondarily to get a degree.[21]

Sid Engst had arrived in Shanghai not knowing quite what to expect and found it 'a den of iniquity' – a phrase he used often in his recollections of Nationalist China. There was widespread hunger in across China, and one of the worst-hit areas was Hunan Province, where refugees from the countryside arriving in the provincial capital of Changsha were dying at the rate of 200 a day. UNRRA was shipping hundreds of tons of food to the region each month, but bad roads, chaotic

19   Now the Enrico Fermi Institute.
20   Chou, *Silage Choppers*, 102.
21   Letter from Joan Hinton to Sid Engst, 7 January 1948.

organisation, and corruption had hampered the operation. Sid was sent to investigate and found the incompetence of the KMT 'impossible almost to imagine'. People were dying in relief camps because they were already too weak to cook the small amounts of flour they were given. There was 'squeeze' at every level that seemed impossible to eradicate. When he got back to Shanghai, he wrote 'a very nice report' and was praised but nothing changed. He had been hired to raise a dairy herd, but the cows never arrived. Disillusioned, he resigned from the UNRRA, joined the China Liberated Areas Relief Association, and made plans to get to Yan'an. In October 1946, when the United States sent a plane to pick up its remaining three military men from Yan'an, Sid hitched a ride.

Yan'an was poor, but there were no beggars, nobody starved, and there was little gap between rich and poor. Sid was renamed Yang Zao, after a martyred revolutionary, and put in charge of a small herd of cows on a ten-acre farm. Anna Louise Strong, Sid Rittenberg, and George Hatem were among the handful of foreigners still in Yan'an. He found Anna Louise a 'terrific person' but overpowering. She would ask you what you were doing, but 'you hadn't talked very long before she was telling you'. As a newcomer, Sid had yet to prove his loyalty and was closely watched. Some things surprised him, as when he met a peasant activist who supported the Communists but bound his small daughter's feet.[22] While the CCP discouraged foot-binding, it did not enforce a ban. Indeed, the liberated areas were no utopias. The Communists took a softly-softly approach to reforming traditional customs, preferring propaganda to confrontation. Sometime after Joan arrived, a fourteen-year-old Mongolian girl was sold as a child bride against her will, despite asking for refuge on their farm.[23]

In March 1947, the KMT general Hu Zongnan took Yan'an, and Sid was forced to flee with the farmhands, thirty-odd cattle, and a couple of donkeys. They spent the next year on the run from village to village, evading KMT bombing raids. The night before they left, Zhou Enlai, Zhu De, and Mao Zedong visited the small group of foreigners still in Yan'an – Sid, Anna Louise Strong, George Hatem, Sid Rittenberg, and Bob Burton. Sid described the scene revealingly: Zhou Enlai came bouncing in and shook hands with everyone; 'He was always so fast and sharp.' Then Zhu De arrived – also very jolly and friendly; 'He always

22   Chou, *Silage Choppers*, 83–4.
23   Ibid., 153–4.

looked like the cook at the PLA.' Then the chairman came in; 'His actions and everything were so different from the premier, always. He's always slow and always sort of calculated. I shouldn't say calculated.'[24] When Mao left the room, Zhou Enlai instructed Anna Louise Strong to return to the White areas to publicise the Red resistance. She burst into tears and protested, but she had no choice.

At a village near the Great Wall, Sid met up with Bill Hinton, George Hatem, and David and Isabel Crook. Sid and the Crooks worked for a while in an iron foundry that made simple goods like ploughshares and cauldrons from whatever scrap metal could be scavenged, including unexploded KMT incendiary bombs. 'I don't know how we ever got through that without blowing our heads off,' Sid recalled. Now that the tide had turned in the civil war, the KMT had fled from Yan'an, and the government moved back there.

Joan arrived there in March 1949 and, despite misgivings, married Sid in a big ceremony with an American truck as a wedding car. The misgivings were because, although she was a nuclear scientist, it became clear that in Yan'an she was seen as a farmer's wife. Sid was consistently seen as the senior partner in the relationship and appointed to higher positions than Joan.[25] The official line was equality, but male chauvinism ruled in the party leadership. To say the PRC record on women's liberation was 'unimpressive [was] an understatement', according to Sid. There 'really is no women's movement as we think of it in the West'. The Women's Federation, like the official trade unions, performed tasks like 'distributing movie tickets free sometimes and seeing that the workers get a shower once in a while.'[26] Through their decades in China, this never changed. In 1973, when Zhou Enlai praised both Joan and Sid at an International Women's Day rally, the meeting minutes mentioned Sid but not Joan, who recalled, 'It was the only time in my life I ever got praised by the Premier, and it was all Sid and not me. I felt so crushed!'[27]

---

24   Sid Engst, interviewed by Neil Burton, taped interviews with Joan Hinton and Erwin 'Sid' Engst, 1987.

25   Joan was classed as an intellectual and Sid as a poor peasant, which in Maoist China would have worked in his favour.

26   Sid Engst, interview.

27   Chou, *Silage Choppers*, 425. Sid was also made vice-chairman of the Revolutionary Committee of the Red Star Commune, where they were working at the time.

Joan was offered a career in physics, which would have meant higher status and benefits, but turned it down. Instead, she and Sid spent their working lives designing agricultural machinery, especially dairy production facilities. Although Sid was the dairy farmer, Joan's scientific background and talent for improvisation, honed at Putney School, meant that she soon outstripped him. Sid freely admitted she was 'much more expert in this field' than he was. Nevertheless, in China, even after a century of revolutions, women remained, in practice, second-class citizens.

Sid and Joan spent the rest of their lives in China and thus lived through the entire history of the PRC from its foundation into the first decade of the twenty-first century. They witnessed the great 'red high tides' – the Anti-Rightist Movement, the Great Leap Forward, the Socialist Education Movement, and the Cultural Revolution. They were almost unique among foreigners in China during this period in that they did so, not from the comparative luxury of the Friendship Hotel in Beijing, but as farmers in the countryside, working side by side with the peasants. They never lost their commitment to the Chinese Revolution, and for the first forty years, they remained true believers and loyal supporters of the leadership.

Their first assignment was to a dairy farm on the borders of Inner Mongolia, Ningxia, and Shaanxi. Conditions were difficult. Water was scarce, as was fuel, and winters were bitterly cold. In 1949, the area around Three Border Farm was unstable. Some defeated KMT troops had turned to banditry after surrendering. While CCP cadres were mainly Han Chinese, the local people were ethnic Mongols who distrusted the Han, partly because of a long history of dealings with unscrupulous merchants. They also found CCP talk of land reform bewildering since, as traditional pastoralists, they had no concept of landownership. Almost all the men smoked opium, to the extent that it had replaced the devalued KMT banknotes as the local currency.[28] Drunken fights sometimes broke out between Mongolians and Han and between CCP and KMT supporters. Another factor was that the ethnic Mongolians in the area were Catholics, converted by missionaries who had built a church in the area using Boxer Indemnity

---

28   Some cadres wanted to let opium remain as the local currency. Sid recalled that there was 'quite a fight over that'.

funds. The priest, a Belgian Jesuit, was outwardly correct but, according to Sid, hostile and used his influence to undermine efforts to improve the livestock by vaccinations and introduction of new breeds.

A confrontation was brewing, and when it came in the form of the Three and Five Antis campaigns, the focus was the local Catholic church. In 1952, a Chinese priest was 'unmasked' as a former warlord officer and arrested. Soon afterwards, informers from among the parishioners claimed the Belgian Jesuit had plotted to poison the local party secretary and had buried a cache of arms.[29] He was arrested, sent to a jail in a nearby county town, and eventually deported to Hong Kong. A fellow Jesuit jailed with him died in detention. Sid and Joan had no sympathy with the priests. They had, after all, used reparations imposed on the Chinese by the imperialist powers to establish their influence in China. Deportation to Hong Kong was, in their view, not only what the local priest deserved but what he wanted. Their memories of Three Border Farm were of lively and relatively democratic political discussions; 'You could bring up anything . . . you could discuss anything – not the kind of study you have now.' They also recalled winning over sceptical Mongolian herders at drunken feasts, from which it was almost impossible to escape. One family threatened to set their dogs on them when they tried to leave: Sid recalled 'Mongolian dogs – boy, they're not vegetarians at all.'[30]

They were aware that the revolution claimed innocent victims. The 1957 Anti-Rightist Campaign rapidly degenerated into a witch hunt, and they were confronted with a horrific incident in their workplace. The director decided he had to find a Rightist in their midst and picked on the dairy's veterinarian – an easy target since he had previously served in a KMT cavalry regiment. After some of the dairy's cows died, he accused the vet of sabotage. The vet replied: 'If cows don't die in the dairy, where do they die?' He was hauled before a kangaroo court of the staff. Nobody dared to defend him except Joan, who, 'feeling flutters' because she was going against the current, said the vet may have

29   It is impossible to say whether there was any truth in the allegations, but the poisoning charge was flimsy. The priest had given poison to a parishioner and told him to use it to kill 'the big fox'. Poison was used to kill foxes in the area but 'the big fox' was taken to mean the local party secretary.

30   Sid Engst, interview.

counter-revolutionary ideas but was not guilty of sabotage. Her inter-vention did not affect the outcome. The vet was put under guard. Soon afterwards, he committed suicide in a horrific manner – by disembowel-ling himself. Looking back on the incident three decades later, Sid and Joan blamed Deng Xiaoping, who had directed the Anti-Rightist Campaign, but they absolved Mao Zedong.

By this time, they were working at a state dairy farm just outside Xi'an. Joan had given birth to three children: Fred in 1952, Billy in 1955, and Karen in 1956. When they arrived, conditions were primitive. There were hardly any refrigeration facilities, and there was no tarmacked road into Xi'an. Transportation of milk into the city on mule-carts along mud tracks before it spoiled was a logistical feat repeated daily. One year, during the rainy season, a bridge was washed away. Joan stood waist deep in the river with the other workers, passing empty milk churns hand over hand. The next day, they built a raft out of oil drums to deliver the milk. Joan saw it as an affirmation of the improvisation and team spirit she had learned at Putney School.

As China industrialised, women went to work in factories, and the demand for milk as baby food grew. Sid and Joan were told to draw up a five-year plan to expand production. Before long, the country was hurled into the Great Leap Forward, with a target to overtake Britain in fifteen years. They worked at the farm for thirteen years beginning in 1953. Sid recalled that 'we were under tremendous pressure . . . right up until '66 . . . we increased cow numbers . . . at the rate of 21 per cent per year and we increased milk production at the rate of 25 per cent a year'. Eventually, a road into Xi'an was built, and the farm got electricity. Joan remembered the momentum generated by the launch of the campaign in 1958: 'The enthusiasm of this year – you had to live through it to believe it.' People's communes were estab-lished to the sound of drums and gongs. Factories were being built everywhere. To begin with, the farm's production plans were 'on the whole very good, but a little bit on the optimistic side'. By 1959, however, Sid recalled, things 'got completely out of hand' and 'there were a lot of crazy things done'. Food ran short, and before long people around Xi'an were visibly malnourished. Sid and Joan were doubly protected, however. Sid was now technical director of the dairy (although it was Joan who designed and built most of the machinery.) And, as foreigners, they were entitled to extra rations. They even had a nanny to look after the children, although she returned to her village when food became scarce.[31]

We now know that, at a minimum, several million people starved to death during the Great Leap Forward, but Sid and Joan always believed that the achievements of the period were underestimated, and the losses exaggerated. They were in no doubt about who was to blame for the losses. It was 'bullshit artists' – people who initially opposed the Great Leap Forward but, after seeing which way the wind was blowing, became '200 per centers'. According to Joan, 'the only places [that] had actual starvation were places that had those eager-beaver cadres who had given false reports of how much grain they produced . . . there wasn't mass starvation'. Sid believed the right wing in the party had adopted a deliberate tactic of hijacking mass movements and taking them to extremes to discredit them. The chief culprit at the top was not Mao, but the enthusiast for the disastrous communal kitchens, Liu Shaoqi, later labelled 'chief capitalist roader' during the Cultural Revolution.[32]

When the leadership introduced bonus schemes and private plots to speed the recovery from the Great Leap Forward, Joan and Sid opposed them on both ideological and pragmatic grounds. The reforms, they argued, were not just a step in the wrong direction, away from socialism; they also did not work. Joan kept meticulous statistics of her production activities. During the Great Leap Forward, she was ordered to raise ducks and given ridiculous targets. When the workers, mainly village girls, were motivated by moral incentives only, 98 per cent of the ducks survived. When the bonus system was reintroduced in 1962, the survival rate fell to 80 per cent. It seemed obvious to Sid that introducing some equivalent of private plots into large-scale herding and dairy farming simply made no sense.

Given these views, one might expect they would welcome the Socialist Education Movement and the Four Clean-Ups Campaign launched in

31 Not all foreigners were so fortunate. Joan's friend Jane Su, who had married a Chinese surgeon and also lived near Xi'an, suffered from severe malnutrition while feeding her husband, three children, and mother-in-law. Dr Su was one of China's pioneering heart surgeons. Although non-political, he returned from the United States in 1949 to serve his country. The leadership finally persuaded him to join the party on his hundredth birthday.

32 Chou, Silage Choppers, 275, 283. Communal kitchens allowed local bureaucrats to ship grain out of areas where there were food shortages in order to meet their own inflated targets.

1963 – an initiative commonly seen as a mini red high tide and a precursor to the Cultural Revolution. However, Joan and Sid characterised it as a White Terror. Work teams sent into the farm to root out corruption 'put the fear of God into everybody'. Immediately after the Great Leap Forward, three people had been disciplined for corruption, and one of them was sent to jail. But when the work teams arrived, everyone came under suspicion. The staff were forbidden to talk to Sid and Joan, and they were excluded from meetings. Peasants were accused of selling a pig on the black market, and even of offences as trivial as pilfering watermelons. Everyone was guilty until proven innocent. Ten people supposedly committed suicide during the campaign, but Sid believed at least one of them was murdered by the work team to stop him revealing the abuses they were committing. Again, he blamed Liu Shaoqi for setting quotas for unmasking corrupt officials; Liu Shaoqi, he said, was very fond of quotas.

In 1966, Sid and Joan volunteered to go to Vietnam to fight US imperialism. But the leadership had other plans. In preparation for the Cultural Revolution, all foreigners in China were being concentrated in Beijing, given largely meaningless jobs, and housed in the Friendship Hotel. After a decade and a half at the grass roots, working side by side with ordinary Chinese workers and peasants, the Hinton family was to be cocooned in the gilded prison inhabited by the 'foreign experts' in quiescent and conformist Beijing. They protested, but only their request that they not be put in the Friendship Hotel was granted. Instead, they were housed in another fancy hotel where every morning, a chauffeur-driven limousine picked them up and ferried them to their offices.

Joan and Sid were given jobs as 'language polishers'. In a system that still operates today, editors chose suitable newspaper and magazine articles to be translated by young foreign-language graduates. The translations were often barely comprehensible and required 'polishing' by native speakers into something a foreign reader might understand. The text was then meticulously checked by the editors for political deviations or anything that might cast China in a bad light. Some of the articles were political in content. Others were lyrical descriptions of China's glorious past or its wonderful 'scenic spots'. The latter might be recycled many times over decades. Joan and Sid, unsurprisingly, found the work infuriating. Sid recalled with exasperation 'the crap about the scenic, seductive, beautiful little pagodas and serene waters and so on and so forth [of the

West Lake in Hangzhou]'.[33] The political propaganda was no better, according to Sid. It was written by 'pen-pushers', and some of it was simply ridiculous, such as an article about Mongolians – plains pastoralists – learning from the hill-farmers of Dazhai how to build terraces, and the story of Lei Feng sacrificing his life to save a piece of wood.[34]

As the Cultural Revolution got under way, Joan and Sid were still more isolated from Chinese society. They were told to stay away from the office and work from their hotel room. By late summer 1966, they had had enough and, having seen hundreds of big-character posters (*dazibao*) pasted up around Beijing, they decided to write their own. Together with Ann Tompkins, a recent arrival in Beijing, and Bill Hinton's ex-wife Bertha, they penned a list of demands, chief among which was that they be allowed to live alongside and be treated equally with the Chinese people. In the extravagant language of the period, they added that only 'snake spirits' of the Khrushchev-revisionist type could object to these simple requests. They sent one copy to the Cultural Revolution Committee and one to the Foreign Experts Bureau. Before long, they were summoned by the foreign minister, Marshall Chen Yi, who told them Mao had approved their poster and said they should take part in the Cultural Revolution.

The *dazibao* was the catalyst that drew all the foreigners in Beijing into the vortex of the Cultural Revolution. They set up their own 'fighting group', the Bethune-Yan'an Rebel Regiment. Sid was elected to its steering committee. At the end of the year, somebody discovered that Mao had written a comment on Joan and Sid's poster asking the Foreign Ministry to come up with a plan to treat foreigners the same as Chinese if they requested it.[35] Chen Yi had not told Joan and Sid about Mao's note and had done nothing about it. Israel and Elsie Epstein and a handful of other foreign experts formed a subgroup within Bethune Ya'nan called the September Eighth Fighting Group[36] to criticise Chen Yi. The

---

33   Ibid., 352.

34   Dazhai was a model commune. The model soldier Lei Feng was said to have died trying to save a telegraph pole.

35   The foreigners were warned off criticising Chen Yi in a message passed via Sid Rittenberg. Chen Yi was hauled before some criticism sessions but escaped serious persecution.

36   The eighth of September 1966 was either the date they wrote the poster or the date Mao added his comment.

upshot was an absurd meeting in the Friendship Hotel at which the 'poet general', former commander of the New Fourth Army, smoked and mumbled in front of a semi-hostile group of language polishers.[37]

Zhou Enlai was encouraging the 'fighting groups' to 'take power' in their workplaces, and foreigners, now armed with Mao's approval, were allowed to join their workplace groups. Sid described how he and a group of colleagues 'overthrew' the party secretary of his work unit. They drove an army truck to the secretary's home late at night, hammered on the door, and told him, 'Get your clothes on. You're coming with us.' After rounding up a few more senior staff, they told them that 'power had been taken away from them and that they were to report to work the next day to do whatever work they were assigned to by the revolutionary masses'. For Sid, it was an exhilarating experience. 'Those were the real days! They did exactly that; they were as meek as mice.'[38] Meanwhile, in Xi'an, fourteen-year-old Fred, who had stayed behind to complete his school year, joined a Red Guard group, and went with them to a coal-field where they 'started raising hell'.[39]

As the Cultural Revolution degenerated into faction fighting, 'chaos in the super-structure', as Sid put it, took over, and foreigners became a target. David and Isabel Crook, Sid Rittenberg, Israel Epstein, and others disappeared into jail or informal detention for years. Sid, who had been linked with Rittenberg, dropped out of political activity immediately. Joan did soon afterwards. They were spared jail and were even allowed to move out of the hotel into an apartment. The language-polishing work had dried up, but their wages were paid punctiliously right through the Cultural Revolution.[40] In 1972, they were allowed to return to agricultural work at the Red Star Commune on the outskirts of Beijing.

At the time of the Sino-Soviet split, Joan and Sid had wholeheartedly supported Mao's denunciation of the 'revisionist' Khrushchev for seeking détente and peaceful coexistence with the West. They saw no contradiction between that stance and Mao's rapprochement with Nixon in 1970–71. The visit of Henry Kissinger – carpet bomber of Vietnam, Laos, and Cambodia – did not seem to disturb them. The Chinese were

37 Ibid., 360.
38 Ibid., 361.
39 Sid Engst, interview.
40 An odd feature of the period was that foreigners continued to be paid even while in jail.

taking no chances, however. When Richard Nixon arrived in Beijing, the American 'experts' were taken into precautionary custody to prevent any hostile demonstrations or, heaven forbid, an assassination attempt. Sid and Joan were taken on a pointless tour of a model factory, even though the 'poor cusses at the commune, they knew we were not of that caliber.'[41] Warming relations between the two countries became an opportunity for family reunions. Bill Hinton was allowed to visit China for the first time since the 1950s. Carmelita brought a youth group on a tour. Jean's children, Marnie, Sarah, and Peter also visited.[42]

Not everyone was as sanguine as Joan and Sid about the new policy. Zhou Enlai gathered all the Americans in China into the Great Hall of the People to reassure them. Everyone was there, Sid recalled, from 'the Left and you might even say the ultra-Left'. Huey P. Newton of the Black Panthers, on an official visit, was in the audience. The premier said that he understood many people would be disappointed China had invited the likes of Nixon and Kissinger to China but assured them that 'the Chinese Communist Party led by Chairman Mao will never compromise the interests of the people of the world.'[43] By the mid-1970s, it had become possible for Joan and Sid to visit the United States. Sid went in 1975 and Joan followed in 1977. They were taken on speaking tours organised by the US-China People's Friendship Association to extol the warming relations between the United States and the PRC and were generally received favourably, despite being pursued from venue to venue by hecklers from the Taiwan lobby, at the time dominated by the KMT.

Back in China, Joan and Sid were appointed advisors on animal husbandry to the Ministry of Agriculture and established experimental plants in Beijing and Xi'an. They would remain on their model dairy in the Beijing suburbs for the rest of their lives. Despite being on prime real estate, the property developers have so far been kept at bay. Although still a working farm, it has since become a 'Red tourism' destination and a memorial to Joan and Sid.[44]

---

41   Chou, *Silage Choppers*, 414.

42   Marnie married Carl Crook, David and Isabel's eldest son. The foreign community in Beijing in the Mao era was a tight-knit group.

43   Ibid., 400.

44   In the 1970s both Joan and Sid began to suffer from ill health. Sid went to the United States for a heart operation in 1978. He died of heart failure in 2003. Joan died in 2010, also from heart disease.

As with many of the 'old foreign experts', the breaking point for Joan and Sid, their disillusionment with the Chinese leadership, was 4 June 1989. The crushing of students and workers was too much to bear. 'The order to shoot the people in Tiananmen was fascist', and it was no accident that it was given by one of Mao's chief enemies, Deng Xiaoping. Until 1989, Joan and Sid, with some reservations, had given Deng the benefit of the doubt. The economic reforms and the thaw with the United States had brought some benefits. After 4 June, looking back on Deng's record, they excoriated not only his economic reforms but his foreign policy. Deng's 1979 invasion of Vietnam, when the PLA was badly mauled, showed that a mighty regular army could be defeated by an armed people organised in militias to defend their country.[45] But even though the trajectory that ended in the invasion was arguably set in motion by Mao when he welcomed Nixon to China, they never criticised the chairman.

In the Cultural Revolution, according to Sid, the Gang of Four, contrary to general opinion, 'weren't ultra-left at all; they were fascists, they were ultra-right'. Jiang Qing turned against foreigners because she was a 'bourgeois nationalist'. Mao, by contrast, Joan said, was a

real proletarian leader [who was] able to understand the oppression of all people [and] could see from the struggle that it was a question of principle how you treated foreign revolutionaries . . . it was a fight between the Liu/Deng line and Mao's line: bourgeois nationalism and proletarian internationalism.[46]

Zhou Enlai also was 'completely honest . . . a great proletarian revolutionary'.[47]

Joan and Sid never lost this blind spot, their inability to find fault with the Mao-Zhou leadership. The 'red high tides' of the Great Leap Forward and the Cultural Revolution were, on the whole, positive – 70

---

45   Sid and Joan's view of the conduct of the war. Ibid., 461. In fact, Vietnamese regular troops were also involved in the fighting.

46   Ibid., 349–50. Joan speaking.

47   Ibid., 411. Joan speaking. According to Sid, on the other hand, Zhou was a canny person: 'Some people go out looking for a bear skin, but they come back without their own skin. Many people tried to skin the Premier, but in the end lost their own skin.' Sid Engst, Interview.

per cent good, 30 per cent bad, in CCP jargon. Furthermore, the negative aspects were the result of machinations by Mao's disloyal and
scheming colleagues, – Liu Shaoqi, Deng Xiaoping, and other 'capitalist
roaders'. When Mao died, Joan and Sid supported his appointed successor, Hua Guofeng. Although he had 'limited experience' of running the
country, during his short time in power he acted decisively by arresting
the Gang of Four. However, he lacked prestige with the 'old bureaucrats
who had been there since Pluto was a pup', and they deposed him.[48]

Joan preached the unity of theory and practice all her life. Indeed, her
own experience taught her that classroom study and book learning
could only take you so far. At the Putney School, she had learned how to
build a barn by building one. At Los Alamos, there was no manual
describing how to build a bomb. Books on science are written after its
frontiers have been breached. In China, she designed farm equipment
by trial and error in consultation with workers who would use it. She
was instinctively sympathetic to Mao's determination to break down the
barriers between mental and physical labour and emphasise practical
experience over book learning. Despite their vastly different back-
grounds and experience, Mao's ideas on education closely resembled
John Dewey's – the ideas that inspired and informed Carmelita's experimental school.[49] The campaign to take kids out of urban classrooms and
send them to the countryside to learn from the peasants was, to Joan, a
gigantic Deweyan experiment – a Putney School on a subcontinental
scale.

Successive dynasties of Imperial China ruled through a scholar-
gentry caste schooled in the Confucian classics. The consequence was a
profound gulf between intellectuals and productive workers. The
contrast with the pragmatic and dynamic United States was especially
sharp. Trying to introduce new ideas and designs, Sid had to battle the
inflexible planners and high-handed bureaucrats in the Agriculture
Ministry. In turn, he became nostalgic for doing things the American
way. He cited the example of Bill Hinton, who became an expert in
mechanisation, not because of his time at Harvard and Cornell but
because

---

48   Sid Engst, Interview.
49   Niu Xiaodong. 'Mao Zedong and John Dewey: A Comparison of Educational
Thought', *Journal of Educational Thought*, Vol. 29, No. 2 (1995), 129–47, 129.

he drives a tractor, and he drives a harvester. Whereas all [Chinese engineers] do is sit up in their offices over their drawing boards . . . and this is after thirty years of Socialism when Mao has been trying movement after movement.

Sid and Joan had hoped the Cultural Revolution would modernise China's old-style school system; the opposite happened. School closures and years of chaos created a reaction that killed off any hope of educational reform, and China now has among the most regressive education systems in the world. The *gaokao system*[50] teaches students there is only one correct answer to any question, encourages mindless cramming, deprives students of sleep and physical exercise, and, in many cases, robs them of their childhood. It has spawned an entire parasitic industry of night and weekend schools, many run by outright charlatans. Just as in imperial times, only those with the money to pay private tutors get their children into the top colleges. Since the ambition of many graduates is a job in government, a mandarin caste is being recreated. A dose of Putney pragmatism is long overdue but is likely to remain so.

Reading their recollections, it is hard to avoid the conclusion that Joan and Sid were optimistic to the point of naivety. When you are working to create the most powerful weapon in history, it takes a degree of self-delusion to entertain the thought that 'we never had the idea they were going to kill anybody'. Did they expect the Great Leap Forward and the Cultural Revolution could proceed without victims? Or did they think the numbers could be kept within acceptable limits?

Sid may have found the experience exhilarating, but the arrest of the Film Distribution party secretary during the Cultural Revolution was an almost comic-opera affair. Revolutions that happen with the permission of the rulers do not deserve the name. The fighters of the Bethune-Yan'an Regiment did not work in the underground to create a revolutionary organisation; they did not organise strikes or rouse the masses; they did not subvert the army. They were invited by China's supreme ruler to take part in a political movement. For many of them, although not Joan and Sid, there were consequences after the fact. Still, at the outset, they were far removed from the revolutionaries of China's past, who consciously

---

50 The annual, government-set senior high school graduation examination – effectively a university entrance examination – was reintroduced in 1977.

risked their lives daily for years on end.

To be sure, Joan and Sid risked their lives and much else in the late 1940s. The McCarthyites branded Joan a nuclear traitor, and even after the thaw of the early 1970s, it was with some apprehension that she visited the United States. Although Joan's Los Alamos colleagues had nothing but good things to say about her, there are those in official America who still think she was anything but naive. Her biography on the Manhattan Project website reads:

> An ardent Maoist, she worked as an educator and translator and spent many years working on dairy farms. Although she was implicated by Senator Joseph McCarthy as a potential Communist spy during the 1950s, she *ostensibly* retired from professional physics after her emigration.[51]

It seems that full and unconditional absolution has not been granted.

Joan and Sid's real heroism was their tireless effort to improve Chinese agriculture and raise the living standards of the masses. Indeed, the difficulties they faced are difficult to exaggerate. In 1949, outside a few cities, China had few decent roads and only a skeletal rail network. Exhausted by the war against Japan and the civil war, the people were on the brink of starvation. At least three-quarters of them were illiterate. Peasants farmed the land with the most primitive tools. Joan and Sid worked selflessly and without thought of material gain to improve the lives of rural Chinese. They deserve to be saluted for this, even if in the end many of their hopes and expectations were dashed. It was inevitable that the world market would return to knock on China's door. When China opened up, many homegrown products were swept away. Joan lamented that her design for a combine harvester was rejected in favour of imported West German machines that were four times as expensive. The authorities, she said, had an a priori belief that foreign things were always better: 'They don't believe in the Chinese people. They believe in these foreign capitalists. They think that money makes the world.'

---

51 'Joan Hinton', Atomic Heritage Foundation profile, atomicheritage.org, my italics.

21
Experts at Revolution

Sid Rittenberg, according to his own estimate, and that of some others, reached heights attained by no other foreigner in China since Marco Polo served Kublai Khan. In Yan'an at the end of the Second World War and during the upheavals of the 1960s, he was close to the top leadership – Mao Zedong, Zhu De, Zhou Enlai, and others. At the height of the Cultural Revolution, he became a public figure and briefly wielded authority when Jiang Qing appointed him head of a government radio station. He believed he was becoming 'part of history'. However, his ambition was, he later acknowledged, his undoing. Of his thirty-five years in China, he spent sixteen in solitary confinement, accused of spying for the United States, although he was never brought to trial. He was jailed for the first time in 1949, on the eve of the Communist victory, and held until 1955, when he was set free with an apology and a job offer. While in prison, he maintained his innocence, kept the Communist faith, and resolved that when released, he would stay in China and prove himself an exemplary party member. His second downfall came in February 1968. Rittenberg was not the only foreigner jailed during the Cultural Revolution, but this 'most notorious foreign expert' was held for ten years – twice as long as the others.

In the 1960s, Rittenberg was an influential presence in the lives of the 'foreign experts' who, for the most part, lived in the Friendship Hotel in Beijing. Well looked after but isolated from Chinese society and starved of information, they depended on rumour and gossip, and Rittenberg was one of their main sources. He was 'the bright star of the circle', the man on the inside track who distributed the real dope over lunch – a 'maverick of remarkable charm . . . with an undefined mystique of power'.[1] The experts, many of them young and engaged in the tedious task of 'polishing' bad English translations of wooden propaganda, valued his words like gold nuggets. But after he finally left China, hardly any of those who stayed had a good word for him. His contemporaries among the older experts were especially scathing. Some would routinely refer to him as Sidney Rottenberg. He had been friends with George Hatem since he met him in Yan'an in 1946, but Hatem, who wisely kept out the Cultural Revolution, never spoke to Rittenberg again after he got involved. According to Rittenberg, former friends called him a deserter when, in 1980, he quit China after his second jail term (though one might think being jailed for sixteen years by your own side is reasonable-enough grounds for leaving). The translator Sidney Shapiro, who loathed Rittenberg, dismissed him as an 'obvious hustler, a typical high pressure salesman . . . a slippery liar'.[2]

Shapiro quoted the Canadian journalist John Fraser as saying: 'No two people get exactly the same story from Rittenberg'. But it was a selective quotation, and Fraser's assessment of Rittenberg was more nuanced. The full sentence continues: 'which is not to say he is knowingly deceptive, but his reigning enthusiasms sometimes mean history gets rewritten a little'. Fraser said Rittenberg was 'one of the most remarkable men I have ever stumbled across . . . I never doubted the basics of any of Sidney's tales – but you do have to keep your wits about you nevertheless . . . Talking with Sidney is a bit like playing chess against a master'.[3] Like Marco Polo, Rittenberg was a compelling storyteller, not above embellishing for dramatic effect.

Rittenberg arrived in China a month after Japan surrendered. He had been drafted into the army and sent on a crash course in Chinese at Stanford University. He turned out to be a gifted linguist. A fellow student recalled that 'he became fluent . . . while most of the rest of us

1 David Milton and Nancy Dall Milton, *The Wind Will Not Subside: Years in Revolutionary China, 1964–1969*, New York: Pantheon, 1976, 101–2.

2 Sidney Shapiro, *I Chose China: The Metamorphosis of a Country and a Man*, New York: Hippocrene, 2000, 299.

3 John Fraser, *The Chinese: Portrait of a People*, Toronto: Totem, 1981, 183–6.

were trying to form a sentence.'[4] He had been earmarked for a Japanese course but, fearing a long sojourn in occupied Japan, switched to Chinese hoping for an early return to the United States. He was flown over the Hump in a Dakota troop transport from India to Kunming, in China's far southwest. The normally sleepy provincial capital of Yunnan Province had been flooded by thousands of US troops and far-greater numbers of refugees from North and East China. Entire universities had migrated to Kunming en masse, and their staff and students formed a reservoir of political radicalism with links to the Communist underground.[5]

Rittenberg was already a Communist, having been a member of the CPUSA for more than five years. His work in Kunming, settling compensation claims made against the US Army, was undemanding so, with time on his hands, he contacted the underground and helped with tasks such as ferrying activists in and out of the city in his jeep. It seems he became engrossed, as he abandoned his plan to return to the United States at the end of his posting. According to his account, the poverty, corruption, and brutality of Nationalist China changed his mind. The case of a young girl who was run over and killed by a reckless army truck driver particularly affected him. After witnessing her parents' grief and their pathetic gratitude for the pittance the army offered in compensation, he asked to be demobilised in China and moved to Shanghai, where Song Qingling found him famine relief work with the UNRRA. His growing mastery of Chinese opened doors. He was asked to interpret at truce negotiations between the New Fourth Army and the KMT and met Zhou Enlai, who told him he should go to Yan'an.[6] He set off on a roundabout journey. En route, he worked for a Communist radio station in Kalgan (Zhangjiakou). After Kalgan was threatened by

4   Ibid., 184. Rittenberg chose Chinese over Japanese because he thought he would get back to the United States sooner, since the occupation of Japan would last several years.

5   Not all the activists were Chinese; when Rittenberg arrived, Ho Chi Minh was in Kunming asking the Americans to send aid to the Vietminh. He had to settle for a signed photograph of General Claire Chennault.

6   The New Fourth Army commander Li Xiannian and his deputy Wang Zhen were unhappy that the CCP leadership agreed to their withdrawal from strategic positions around Shanghai. At one point, Wang Zhen was so enraged that he stormed out of the talks.

Nationalist forces, General Nie Rongzhen sent him on to Yan'an.[7] The 500-mile journey, on foot and by mule, took one and a half months. When he arrived, on an October evening in 1946, the leaders were at one of Yan'an's famous dance events. He was greeted by Mao, who interrupted a foxtrot to welcome him, and Zhu De but he was not in the slightest overawed. Before too many minutes had passed, he was dancing with Jiang Qing. He was just twenty-five years old.

Rittenberg inherited his courtesy, confidence, and patrician manners from his family. The Rittenbergs were part of the political establishment in the old slave port of Charleston, a citadel of the former Confederacy. One of Charleston's main boulevards is named after Sidney's grandfather, Sam Rittenberg, who made a fortune dealing in real estate and was elected to the South Carolina legislature five times. Sidney's father was a successful lawyer and sometime president of the city council. However, the family was not part of the old slavocracy. Both of Sidney's grandfathers were Jewish immigrants from the tsarist empire and his maternal grandfather supported Lenin, so there was at least one red hand on his cradle. Aged eighteen, Sidney was offered a scholarship to Princeton but turned it down to study philosophy at the University of North Carolina, which, under its liberal president Frank Porter Graham, had acquired a reputation for radicalism. Rittenberg's politics never erased the effects of his upbringing; even after decades in China, he still played the Southern gentleman, with 'the combined graciousness of Charleston and Peking'.

Rittenberg was drawn to the left by 'the blinding poverty and backwardness of the American South'. At Chapel Hill, he was vocal in student politics and volunteered to teach basic literacy to textile workers. In January 1940, a couple of months short of his nineteenth birthday, he joined the CPUSA on an impulse, after hearing that the Dies Committee had accused Frank Porter Graham of being a crypto-Communist. 'They want Communists – let's give them Communists,' he told his roommate, and enrolled both of them in the party. It was, in some ways, an odd time to join. The Soviet Union was in the midst of the Winter War on Finland and had been expelled from the League of Nations. President

---

7   Anna Louise Strong wrote to Zhu De from Kalgan to ask if Rittenberg could accompany her to Yan'an as her assistant since 'he speaks and reads Chinese like Confucius'. Zhu agreed but stipulated that a seat could not be spared for Rittenberg on her flight and he would have to travel overland. Tracy B. Strong and Helene Keyssar, *Right in Her Soul: The Life of Anna Louise Strong*, New York: Random House, 1983, 223.

Roosevelt denounced the 'dreadful rape of Finland'. Furthermore, the war was going badly for the Soviets. But the CPUSA's opposition to retaliation against the Soviets coincided with a widespread isolationist sentiment in the United States. Rittenberg said it was precisely the party's 'pacifist' stance that attracted him.[8]

He shared the puritan, ascetic ideals that were then, and remain, widespread among leftists. He was impressed by the hard work and dedication of his party comrades who were bound by a strict moral code that outlawed drugs and extra-marital sex – restrictions partly justified by fear of blackmail. The rules were rigorously enforced by the district organiser, Bart Logan, an electrician who had served jail time for trade union activities. Members who showed individualism or ambition invited suspicion and sanction. The Southern Communists of the time were, Rittenberg later said, much like the Chinese Communists of the 1940s and '50s. By contrast, he was repelled by the bohemian lifestyle of party members in New York who were, he said, 'not at all like my idea of a good Communist'.

The dedication of the membership was exploited by apparatchiks who imposed iron discipline in the name of 'Bolshevisation'. Soon after joining, Rittenberg was sent on a training school for cadres where he was 'taught to repeat word for word . . . the doctrine according to Stalin, with no ifs, ands, or buts'. The course was supposed to give him some grounding in theory and prepare him for trade union work, but although he swallowed it at the time, he later said,

> Nothing that I learned there was any use . . . The fatal flaw of American Communists was that we were taught blind faith in Stalin and the Soviet Union. When the chips were down, our Number One obligation was not so much to organise the workers to win a better life and to learn about Socialism – Number One was to get the workers organisations to pass resolutions supporting Soviet foreign policy.[9]

At this time, Rittenberg's knowledge of Marxism was rudimentary; insofar as his politics had an intellectual foundation, it was a socialist

---

8   Sid Rittenberg, interview with the author, 2018.

9   Ibid.

interpretation of Kant's ethics.[10] But he was a talented public speaker and became an effective trade union organiser, his travel and accommodation paid for by workers' subscriptions.

In Yan'an, Rittenberg was assigned to the English language service of Xinhua – the New China news agency. His job was to tidy up and polish translations of news stories and to improve the translators' English. While it was routine work, he carried it out with great dedication. He was convinced he was playing a unique role spreading the message of revolution, although he later reflected that most of the output was 'hard, metallic propaganda', expressed in a strange mixture of Chinese and English. The few foreigners in Yan'an enjoyed the same privileges as the top leadership and Rittenberg was given his own cave home and ate in the 'small canteen', where meat was served every day.[11] Eating alongside Mao and the other leaders, he overheard the latest political and military news.

Rittenberg relates how, after he interpreted for Anna Louise Strong at an interview, Zhou Enlai asked him to translate a top-secret Politburo document that Strong was to deliver personally to the first secretaries of the Communist Parties of Eastern Europe, warning them not to take orders from foreigners – in other words from Moscow.[12] Rittenberg believed this was a quasi-Titoist moment with the Chinese attempting to triangulate between the Soviet Union and the United States – a gambit that failed, he maintained, only because of American intransigence. It seems scarcely credible that Zhou would entrust such a sensitive task to two foreigners although, on the other hand, doing so might preserve deniability. Whatever the truth, Rittenberg felt he was being accepted into the inner circle and he applied to join the Chinese Communist Party – a privilege rarely granted to foreigners.[13] His application was ratified by the five members of the Central Committee Secretariat: Mao Zedong, Liu Shaoqi, Zhou Enlai, Ren Bishi, and Zhu De.

---

10   Rittenberg was a lifelong student of Kant. When he was released from his second term of imprisonment, among the books his jailers returned to him were the *Critique of Pure Reason* and the *Critique of Practical Reason*. See Sidney Rittenberg and Amanda Bennett, *The Man Who Stayed Behind*, London: Duke University Press, 2001, 416.

11   There were three levels of canteen. The basic level provided almost exclusively vegetarian food; meals in the second-level canteens, which served middle-level cadres, included some meat every week.

12   Rittenberg and Bennett, *The Man Who Stayed Behind*, 90–1.

13   George Hatem (Ma Haide) had joined before Rittenberg.

In early 1949, as Beiping[14] was about to fall to the Communists, Xinhua's editor-in-chief, Liao Chengzhi, took Rittenberg aside and told him he was being sent on a special mission.[15] Believing he was being taken to cover the PLA marching into the city, Rittenberg set off elated. However, his destination was not the new capital but a village, where he was arrested. He had been fingered by Stalin himself. Anastas Mikoyan was in China for talks with the CCP leadership when on 4 February, he received this telegram:

> To be communicated to Mao Zedong.
>   We have no doubt that the American Rittenberg, who works in the editorial office of the Central Organ of the CPC Central Committee, is a malicious American spy. We advise you to immediately arrest him and uncover the rest of the network of American agents.
>   We know for certain that the American writer Anna Louise Strong is an American spy ... she has long been in the service of the Americans ...
>
> Stalin[16]

According to Mikoyan's reply to Stalin, the news about Rittenberg startled Mao and the other leaders. Ren Bishi pointed out that Anna Louise Strong had vouched for Rittenberg. Mao mentioned George Hatem who had been with them since 1936 and Ren Bishi added that Hatem had been recommended by Edgar Snow. Mikoyan immediately extended the accusation of spying to Hatem. It is obvious, he said, that Hatem was the American station chief (*rezident*) in the Communist headquarters, and that he should also be arrested.[17] But Hatem was not

---

14   Beiping, meaning 'northern peace', was Beijing's name, while Nanjing was the capital of China.

15   Liao Chengzhi's father was the left-wing KMT leader Liao Zhongkai, who was assassinated by KMT rightists in 1925; his mother was the poet and revolutionary He Xiangning. He spent time in exile in Japan and Germany before joining the Fourth Red Army, whose leader, Zhang Guotao, jailed him for three years. Mao and Zhou Enlai freed him and appointed him head of Xinhua.

16   Letter from Joseph Stalin to Anastas Mikoyan, 4 February 1949, available at nsarchive.gwu.edu/rus, my translation.

17   Anastas Mikoyan, record of discussion with Mao Zedong, 5 February 1949, in Tikhvinsky, *Russko-kitaiskie otnosheniya*, Vol. 5, Book 2, 80. Kang Sheng also repeatedly

arrested, perhaps because the Chinese would only accept the word of the organ grinder in the Kremlin.[18]

Rittenberg had been in trouble before in Yan'an. Admiration for the Red Army's puritan ideals was not the same as living up to them. A brief fling with a woman comrade led to her demanding he marry her. He escaped with nothing worse than a stern lecture about revolutionary morality and eventually married a radio announcer called Wei Lin, whom he had met in Kalgan.

A more serious incident happened in the early stages of the civil war, when the CCP evacuated Yan'an in the face of a Nationalist advance. On the day his team was supposed to leave under cover of darkness, Rittenberg was arrested by a village militia fifteen miles from Yan'an. His explanation was that he was terrified by KMT air raids and had wandered off to find some peace. Asked what was in the notebook he was carrying, he said he had written out Keats's Ode to a Nightingale to calm his nerves. Perhaps the explanation was so odd that it was convincing. Liao Chengzhi was angry but did no more than keep him under surveillance during the evacuation. Decades later, when Rittenberg's reputation among the foreign experts was already ruined, Joan Hinton suggested he had been running to the Nationalist lines, but since she did not arrive in Yan'an until 1949, this was a second-hand account. In his autobiography, Rittenberg pleaded guilty to cowardice, but no more. 'I was helping the Chinese with their cause, not fighting for my own people's rights. I was willing to endure a lot, but I wasn't ready to be blown away by a five-hundred-pound bomb.'[19]

---

tried to incriminate Ma. One of his accusations was that Ma was negligent in treating or had actually poisoned Wang Ming, but Ma was consistently supported by Mao, Zhu De, and other top leaders. See Edgar Porter, *The People's Doctor: George Hatem and China's Revolution*, Honolulu: University of Hawaii Press, 1997, 153–5.

18   A small problem of chronology remains. In his memoirs, Rittenberg wrote that he was arrested on 21 January 1949, two weeks before Stalin's telegram was sent. None of the accounts of Anna Louise Strong's arrest date it before 21 January, although Rittenberg says he heard the news before he was arrested. Harrison Salisbury, the *New York Times* bureau chief in Moscow at the time, said Strong, Mikhail Borodin, and the entire staff of *Moscow News* were seized sometime between 28 January and 4 February. Other accounts put her arrest as late as 14 February. The simplest explanation for the discrepancy is that, after many decades, Rittenberg simply misremembered the date. Another possibility is that his arrest was recorded using the Chinese traditional calendar. That would make the date of his arrest 18 February according to the official calendar, in which case the problem disappears.

19   Rittenberg and Bennett, *The Man Who Stayed Behind*, 116.

Rittenberg gave differing accounts of his first imprisonment. He told John Fraser that he had been treated well and when Mao, in 1964, at a banquet for foreign experts, apologised for his bad treatment, he replied, sycophantically, that prison had been a 'good experience'. Incredulous, Mao said derisively, 'You had the experience of sitting in the slammer.'[20] In his autobiography, Rittenberg gave a much-fuller account of his prison time describing repeated aggressive interrogations, during which he was threatened with torture and execution. He was deprived of sleep and given hallucinogenic drugs that provoked bizarre visions of Mao Zedong as a gorilla, as Satan, and as a 'threatening homosexual'.[21] He was beaten up and handcuffed with manacles that gradually tightened and cut into his wrists and in one of the jails, a guard sexually assaulted him. After a year, his conditions briefly improved. He was allowed to socialise with the guards and given newspapers to read. But in 1951, he was put back into solitary confinement. He was allowed books, however, and for the first time seriously studied Marx. In April 1955, he was abruptly released with an apology. He was told, in a matter-of-fact manner, that his wife had divorced him and remarried.

Rittenberg was given a job in the Broadcast Administration that managed all China's radio stations, including the international service, Radio Peking. Its boss was Mei Yi, who had been a member of Lu Xun's League of Left-Wing Writers.[22] Before a year passed, Rittenberg remarried to Mei Yi's young secretary, Wang Yulin. For the next decade, the couple lived comfortable middle-class lives, and Wang gave birth to three daughters and a son. Formerly rich families were disposing of their assets at knock-down prices, and Rittenberg, who had an eye for antiques, acquired an outstanding collection of Ming-dynasty furniture.

Rittenberg admits that, while living in comparative luxury, he took part in the periodic campaigns against dissidents. In the campaign against the Hu Feng literary opposition, he played a 'tangential' role in sending a young broadcast worker, his wife and baby, plus two of their friends to a labour camp in Manchuria. The only evidence against them

---

20 The occasion was Anna Louise Strong's eightieth birthday celebration in Shanghai. Mao was about to launch the Cultural Revolution. Rittenberg and Bennett, *The Man Who Stayed Behind*, 274.

21 Ibid., 152.

22 Mei Yi's real name was Chen Shaoqing.

was that they had read Arthur Koestler and Somerset Maugham. At the
time, he justified it to himself by imagining farm work would do them
good.[23] During the Anti-Rightist Campaign, he was told he must find a
Rightist, with or without evidence. His heart 'felt like cold ashes', but he
picked out a young man with a bourgeois background who was then
sent to a farm in Hebei province. He even denounced his friend Wen
Jize, a veteran cadre who had lost an ear to frostbite in a KMT prison.
Wen had acted as matchmaker when Rittenberg was courting Yulin, and
he and Yulin quarrelled bitterly over the case.[24]

He whole-heartedly supported the Great Leap Forward. The pace of
work at the radio station was leisurely, and he had quietly fumed as his
colleagues wasted half the working day on lunch-breaks, siestas, and
idle gossip. There were 'a few overworked volunteers surrounded by a
sea of plodders'.[25] The Great Leap Forward changed all that. Everyone
competed to display diligence and commitment. Rittenberg was the
most zealous worker when, absurdly, the Broadcast Administration
built a blast furnace. He went on propaganda tours and extolled rolling
fields of wheat until, as signs of hunger began to appear in Beijing, Mei
Yi told him to tone down his enthusiasm.

While the country went hungry, Rittenberg, along with two former
State Department employees, Sol Adler and Frank Coe, the journalist
Israel Epstein, and the British Communist Michael Shapiro, was co-opted
onto the team translating the fourth volume of Mao's collected works. In
addition to the five foreigners, there were nine Chinese – all very distinguished scholars. The whole team was given special rations. Meanwhile,
back at the radio station, most of the staff were visibly malnourished, as
was Yulin, who was studying English. Out of solidarity with her classmates and teachers, she refused to share Sid's increased rations. With
little incentive to finish, and therefore lose their rations, and no doubt
taking great care to avoid mistakes, the translation team worked at a
snail's pace. They took two years to translate 500 pages. Half a page a day
was considered great progress; some days, they managed only one line.

Rittenberg's memoirs are, in part, a remarkably frank confessional.
He pleads guilty to Icarus-like ambition, cowardice, disloyalty,

---

23   Ibid., 193.
24   Ibid., 216–21.
25   Ibid., 224–5.

fickleness, callousness, and fanaticism. However, he also asserts that he was given important, even indispensable tasks by the leadership. During the Sino-Soviet split, he found himself 'more and more at the center of things'. He had a ringside seat as the rift in the Communist camp unfolded. In the Great Hall of the People, he saw Mao and Khrushchev together – both men's faces distorted by rage. By now, he was not only 'considered a crack translator' but also 'an effective conduit for strategic leaks'.[26] He became a celebrity among foreigners in Beijing on the hunt for inside information and as the country recovered from the great hunger, Rittenberg could once again play the bon viveur. He took foreign guests to the best restaurants, the opera, and so on.[27] Mei Yi briefed him that the leadership now considered Soviet revisionism more dangerous than US imperialism. Liao Chengzhi told him that he had been given

> authorization from the very top . . . to play a bold, independent role in expanding . . . the Chinese Communist Party's influence among the foreign community in Beijing, and through them to influence the worldwide contest between the Chinese and the Russians . . . The Party really needed me.

Rittenberg was delighted with his 'new mandate'. At the radio station, he had become little more than a 'pencil-pushing bureaucrat' at what resembled a 'court gazette [publishing] bulletins about the happenings of the royals'.[28] He took more and more time off work, despite the demands of his bosses, as his 'political work was just too important to be interrupted'.[29] He did not doubt what was at stake. At a thank you banquet for the translation team, he listened raptly as Mao related a conversation with Khrushchev. If the Russian leader persisted in his demand for military bases in China, Mao told him he would take to the hills again as a guerrilla.

The arena for Rittenberg's political work was the foreign experts' dining room in the Friendship Hotel – a haunt of 'cliques, klatches, and table-hoppers'. Having no doubt about which side he was on, he

---

26   Ibid., 276.
27   Ibid., 278.
28   Ibid., 259–60.
29   Ibid., 279.

faithfully relayed the latest anti-Soviet polemics, such as how the Russians were economically exploiting Cuba, and threw in political jokes for good measure. In August 1963, he was 'boosted into even greater prominence' when he was summoned to Zhongnanhai at a moment's notice by Mao himself to work on an important text that Mao was planning to read to a meeting of African revolutionaries. Rittenberg said 'Roman candles went off in [his] head', when he received the summons.[30] At the meeting, Mao pointed out Rittenberg as an example of a white man who could be trusted – an 'internationalist fighter for Communism'. The next day Rittenberg's name appeared in the *People's Daily*.

It is hard to avoid the conclusion that Rittenberg is magnifying his role in events. The PRC depended then, as it does today, on foreign experts to help translate and edit foreign-language texts. The 1960s cohort was made up exclusively of Communists, sympathetic nationalists from the Third World, and oppressed national minorities such as Afro-Americans. Rittenberg's Chinese-language skills may have made him primus inter pares – though even that is not certain – but he was probably not indispensable. He helped translate Mao's works, but as part of a team. Even when summoned to Zhongnanhai, he was not alone. Frank Coe was also called in to help and arrived there before him. Their task was simply to edit an English speech for Mao to read to the African leaders and, as things turned out, Mao read out only a few lines before getting bored. Tellingly, it was the first time Rittenberg had seen Mao since 1949. And while convincing the Beijing experts was important, it is unlikely that the leadership saw it as crucial to winning the argument in the world Communist movement. Despite Rittenberg's efforts, quite a few of the experts sided with the Soviets and left China anyway.

In November 1965, Rittenberg met Mao again, on the occasion of Anna Louise Strong's eightieth birthday. A group of the most eminent experts, including Rittenberg, Israel Epstein, Frank Coe, Sol Adler, Rewi Alley, and George Hatem, accompanied Strong to Shanghai, where Mao met them, along with other foreign Communists, for an informal pre-banquet chat. Although they did not know it, Mao was in Shanghai because he was preparing to launch the Cultural Revolution.

---

30 Ibid., 268–9.

Nevertheless, when Mao joked about being outvoted, Rittenberg picked up on the tension between him and the officials who accompanied him. Mao's message to the meeting was that the world had entered a new phase of revolution.[31] He told an Indonesian comrade that Suharto's massacre of Communists – ongoing at the time – was no more than a temporary setback, comparable to Chiang Kai-shek's 1927 coup;[32] the East Wind would inevitably prevail over the West Wind. Rittenberg was once more at the centre of things, but not alone, and as a witness to, not a maker of history.

Sensitive to the political wind, Rittenberg donated his antique furniture to the Palace Museum, began wearing workmen's clothes, and volunteered to dig ditches. He did not warn Yulin that he was planning to give their furniture away and, unsurprisingly, they had a huge argument.[33]

During the Cultural Revolution, Rittenberg became a celebrity – the most famous foreigner in China. He spoke at mass rallies to audiences of up to 100,000 people. As he travelled from engagement to engagement, he was lauded in newspapers and recognised in the street, on trains and aeroplanes.[34] He used his access to the leadership to influence developments in the Broadcast Administration – and became, as he put it, 'a kingmaker', before, at the height of his powers, being appointed to the top job himself.

His voice became one of the most radical as he rode the wave of the Cultural Revolution, but at the outset, he urged restraint. Around seventy foreigners joined the Bethune-Yan'an Regiment formed by Joan Hinton and others to demand the right to participate in the movement. But when they put foreign minister Chen Yi in their sights, Rittenberg told them they had overstepped the mark. According to Hinton's account, he 'pulled up in his chauffeured car one day and read [them] the riot act ... He was furious.'[35] Not long afterwards, however, Rittenberg and a group of radical foreigners ran into George Hatem in the street. Hatem, who had known Rittenberg since their time together

---

31 Ibid., 289.
32 It is not clear whether this assessment was simply delusional or reflected the fact that Mao intended to concentrate his efforts on China's internal affairs.
33 Ibid., 296.
34 Ibid., 338.
35 Chou, *Silage Choppers*, 360.

in Yan'an in the 1940s, wanted nothing to do with the Cultural Revolution, telling him, 'Sid, you gotta tell these boys to cut this out. They are interfering in China's internal affairs.' But by this time, Rittenberg, although he never formally joined the Bethune-Yan'an regiment, had switched his allegiance to the radicals. 'We all gathered round George and argued back with him.'[36]

Rittenberg said he was propelled to fame on 1 October 1966, when, along with half a dozen other foreign experts, he was invited to join Mao on the Tiananmen Gate Tower for China's National Day celebrations. At the end of the ceremony, he pushed through the crowd to ask Mao to autograph his Little Red Book. A television film crew caught the moment, and he appeared on the evening news. Afterwards, everyone wanted to shake hands with the man who had shaken hands with Mao. It was the moment, Rittenberg said, that 'Mao turned me into a personage'. He later recounted that Deng Xiaoping, Liu Shaoqi, Wang Guangmei, and Chen Yi were all present but looked shrivelled and dejected. Zhou Enlai was running around doing Mao's bidding. Rittenberg claimed that he sat down to talk to Deng because he felt sorry for him.[37]

Like almost all the other foreign experts, Rittenberg claimed unbroken loyalty to, and friendship with, Zhou Enlai. But his detractors, who later included the majority of foreign experts, accused him precisely of plotting against the premier. The substance behind the charge was that Rittenberg had seized power in the Broadcast Administration against Zhou's express instructions that organisations directly controlled by the central government were untouchable. As Sid Engst put it:

> The premier said definitely that the Red Guards should not take power in these several places . . . one of which was radio . . . But Jiang Qing specifically supported Rittenberg to do this . . . Rittenberg of course always painted himself as an ardent supporter of the premier. It just

---

36   Porter, *The People's Doctor*, 258.

37   Rittenberg and Bennett, *The Man Who Stayed Behind*, 329–33. Parts of Rittenberg's account, such as the conversation with Deng, stretch credulity. He was not the only foreigner who got his book signed, as is evident from films of the event. See, for example, '1966 China National Day – Part 1', uploaded 19 May 2013, YouTube video, youtube.com.

doesn't fit with the facts, that's all. As I say, Rittenberg is a person with a very creative memory.[38]

According to Rittenberg, however, the change of regime in the Broadcast Administration was approved by Zhou Enlai. His old friend and boss, Mei Yi, had been ousted and replaced by Ding Laifu, a high-ranking PLA political commissar.[39] When student rebels from the Broadcast Institute turned on Ding as their next target, Ding called in a platoon of troops to rough them up. Rittenberg supported the students, and, at a mass meeting called to show solidarity with Vietnam, he seized the opportunity to ask Zhou Enlai for help. According to Rittenberg's account, Zhou immediately instructed the PLA's chief political commissar, Xiao Hua, to stand the troops down, saying, 'The rebels have a complete right to make a Cultural Revolution at the Broadcast Administration.' At the same mass meeting, finding himself sitting behind Jiang Qing, Rittenberg wrote a note asking her to help defeat representatives of the 'bourgeois reactionary line'.[40] She told him to bring two leading representatives of the rebels to meet her.

Once the rebels received the backing of Jiang Qing, Ding Laifu's days were numbered. He was ousted as a 'capitalist roader' and, following a brief interregnum, Wang Ziqiang and Cao Renyi, the rebel pair Rittenberg had taken to meet Jiang Qing, 'took power', after being given permission to do so by the Cultural Revolution Group. Before long, however, Wang and Cao were denounced as bureaucratic and reactionary by a new wave of rebels. Rittenberg threw in his lot with the new wave. According to his memoirs, he made an impassioned speech denouncing head-shaving, beatings, dunce caps, the 'airplane' stress position, and other mistreatments meted out to opponents.[41] The next day, the Cultural Revolution Group appointed him head of the Broadcast

38   Sid Engst, interviewed by Neil Burton, taped interviews with Joan Hinton and Erwin 'Sid' Engst, 1987. Kindly provided by their son Fred Engst.

39   Rittenberg watched as Mei Yi was beaten and had his head shaved. He admitted that, partly out of fear and partly out of sympathy with the young rebels, he kept silent as his friend was tortured. Rittenberg and Bennett, *The Man Who Stayed Behind*, 323.

40   Rittenberg and Bennett, *The Man Who Stayed Behind*, 345.

41   This is Rittenberg's account of what he said. But he admits that he 'shouted along with the others' in mass meetings when deposed officials were mistreated.

Administration. He was nominally in charge but as head of a triumvi-
rate that included a young male journalist, Kang Shuji, and a female
announcer, Li Juan. It soon became clear that Kang Shuji held the real
power; Rittenberg was little more than a figurehead.

It is reasonable to ask why the Chinese leadership appointed
Rittenberg, a foreigner, to such a prominent and sensitive position in
their propaganda apparatus. Although the Cultural Revolution represented, in many respects, a turn inward and a disengagement with the
outside world, in the 1960s the CCP retained an internationalist perspective. It welcomed revolutionaries from around the world as visitors,
long-term guests, and refugees. Furthermore, Beijing was competing
with Moscow for leadership of the world Communist movement. It was
important to demonstrate that foreign comrades in China fully
supported Chairman Mao and his 'anti-revisionist' line. In the early
stages of the Cultural Revolution, the Chinese press praised foreign residents for joining the movement in articles with headlines like 'Foreign
Friends Acclaim China's Great Cultural Revolution', and 'They Fight
Side-by-Side with Us'.[42]

Rittenberg later wrote that around this time, January 1967, Zhou
Enlai told him with almost childlike enthusiasm that China's democracy, where high officials could be dislodged by ordinary people, was far
superior to the version on offer in Lyndon Johnson's America. The
implication is that Rittenberg had Zhou's full support. Against that, in
1973, when all the other foreign experts who had been detained during
the Cultural Revolution were released, Zhou Enlai publicly apologised
to them but denounced Rittenberg as 'a bad man who has made serious
political mistakes' and would never be set free.[43] Rittenberg, who, it
seems, had an answer for everything, interpreted this as his 'old friend'
Zhou defending him from the much more serious charge of spying.[44]
He told John Fraser that Zhou, who had to be circumspect while Jiang
Qing still held power, had saved his life. Had the spy charge been made
to stick, he said, 'I would have been a goner.'[45] By the time Rittenberg
was released, Zhou Enlai had died, but he later said that Zhou's wife,

42   Anne-Marie Brady, *Making the Foreign Serve China: Managing Foreigners in the
People's Republic*, Lanham, MD: Rowan & Littlefield, 2003, 157.
43   See Milton, *The Wind Will Not Subside*, 304, 372.
44   Rittenberg and Bennett, *The Man Who Stayed Behind*, 443.
45   Fraser, *The Chinese*, 193.

Deng Yingchao, assured him that the premier had always thought highly of him.[46]

One of the specific charges (or rather, reasons for his arrest, since he was never charged) against Rittenberg was his attendance at a literary conference in Tianjin and promotion of a play, *Madman of the Modern Age*, about Chen Lining, a Cultural Revolution activist who was briefly famous for his extreme speeches. The leadership later denounced the conference as a 'counter-revolutionary black meeting'.[47] But Rittenberg was not alone. Michael Shapiro, Israel Epstein, and Epstein's wife, Elsie Fairfax-Cholmeley, had taken over the Bethune-Yan'an group in a radical coup and were also involved. Although Rittenberg never formally joined the group, it was believed that he was directing the leftist faction from behind the scenes.

Michael Shapiro (no relation to Sid Shapiro) was a British Communist who joined the Young Communist League in 1931, during the Third Period of 'leftist' Stalinism, and the main party in 1934. After the Second World War, he became a housing activist and was elected as a Communist councillor in the London Borough of Stepney. An intellectual from a secular Jewish background, he studied at the London School of Economics but was unimpressed with the 'thoroughly bourgeois' education he received there. It seems he was unhappy with the CPGB's abandonment of its original revolutionary programme Soviet Britain in favour of the reformist line later enshrined as the British Road to Socialism. He regarded Stepney's Communist member of Parliament, Phil Piratin, a defender of party orthodoxy, as an unprincipled bully. His heretical views led to him being reported to Harry Pollitt as a malcontent. He was particularly opposed to Pollitt's extension of the wartime 'class-collaborationist' policy of opposing industrial action into the post-war period. Disillusioned, he moved to China in 1949 to work for Foreign Languages Press. In letters sent home from China, he denounced the British party as revisionist.[48]

Israel Epstein was born in Warsaw during the First World War as German troops advanced on the city. Then part of the Russian Empire,

---

46   Rittenberg and Bennett, *The Man Who Stayed Behind*, 443.

47   Milton, *The Wind Will Not Subside*, 281.

48   See Neil Redfern, 'Michael Shapiro: A Communist Life in Britain and China', n.d., available at academia.edu.

around a third of Warsaw's population was Jewish. Epstein's parents were comrades in the Bund. His mother was exiled to Siberia during the reaction following the 1905 Revolution but escaped and travelled to Paris. In 1907, Epstein's father represented the Bund at the RSDLP Unity Congress in London. They were reunited in Paris and married in Vilnius. When the Germans took Warsaw, Epstein's father was in Japan working for a trading firm. To avoid a long separation, his mother took their infant son on the Trans-Siberian Railway to join him. After the February Revolution, Epstein's father returned to Petrograd, planning to resettle the family in the revolutionary capital. However, because of the prolonged civil war in Siberia and political differences with the Bolsheviks, the family settled first in Harbin and later in Tianjin, then a patchwork of foreign concessions, where Epstein received his education in Russian and English. (As a refugee, he remained stateless until he took Chinese citizenship in 1957.) His socialist parents were focused on Europe; even the great May Fourth Movement of 1919 scarcely made an impression on the family. In his mid-teens, he began working for an English-language newspaper in Tianjin. He would remain a journalist for the rest of his life. The Japanese invasion of 1937 forced him to focus on the fate of his country of residence. While working as a war reporter for United Press, he covered the battles of Nanjing, Wuhan, and Guangzhou and joined Song Qingling's China Defence League. From then on, his loyalties never wavered. After 1949, his writings rarely, if ever, deviated from the official line of New China. He wrote extensively on Tibet, defending the PRC position that it had carried out a necessary, belated social revolution to eliminate a reactionary theocracy. The national dimension of the issue he dismissed as separatism stirred up by forces, including the CIA.

Elsie Fairfax-Cholmeley came from a family of minor Catholic gentry in Yorkshire. Her father had liberal views; he married his gardener's daughter, improved his estate by installing running water and telephones, and set up a dairy cooperative. An admirer of William Morris and Bernard Shaw, he instilled in Elsie a love of poetry, particularly of William Blake. Tall, blonde, good looking, and educated at a public school on England's south coast, Elsie effortlessly glided into a job with the Institute of Pacific Relations, a Wilsonian think tank that was later thoroughly colonised by leftists. The post took her first to New York and then to Hong Kong, where, while working for the international arm of

the Chinese Industrial Cooperative Association (Indusco), she met
Epstein. They became lovers after escaping together from a Japanese
internment camp and married in Chongqing in 1943. They made a
rather memorable couple as Elsie towered over Epstein, who had inherited his father's tiny stature.

By the end of 1967, the radicals' position was becoming precarious,
and Rittenberg became a target. A big-character poster in the radio
headquarters' courtyard asked: 'How Is It That an American Adventurer
Seized Red Power at Peking Radio?'[49] He was arrested on 21 February
1968 along with Epstein, Fairfax-Cholmeley, and Shapiro. All of them
were accused of plotting against the premier. But, while Rittenberg was
held for ten years, the others were released after five. They had, according to Zhou Enlai, been 'misled'. Their jobs and status were restored, and
thereafter they were welcomed back into the community of foreign
experts. Epstein, in particular, although he had allegedly plotted against
Zhou Enlai alongside Rittenberg, was highly esteemed by the other
foreigners in Beijing, who universally referred to him affectionately as
'Eppy'.

For the first few years, Rittenberg was held in solitary, threatened
with torture and execution, deprived of sleep, and kept continually
hungry and cold. He heard prisoners being beaten in nearby cells. Some
were defiant; others pleaded for mercy. The cell peephole meant he had
no privacy. Throughout his ordeal, Rittenberg showed extraordinary
toughness and resilience, surviving through mental discipline and
Taijiquan exercises.[50] After Kissinger's visit in 1971, his conditions
improved. He was moved to a new cell, given better rations, and allowed
to read newspapers. Six months after Nixon's visit, his books, including
Kant's *Critiques*, were returned to him. After Lin Biao's flight, he heard
one of Lin's imprisoned supporters screaming for Zhou Enlai to be
executed; when the Gang of Four were arrested, he heard Jiang Qing
protesting her loyalty to Mao.

In November 1977, Rittenberg was released and reunited with Yulin
and their children, who were by then teenagers. The family was housed
in a suite in the Friendship Hotel. While Rittenberg was shunned by the

49   Milton, *The Wind Will Not Subside*, 303.
50   Characteristically, he wrote a self-help book, *How to Manage Your Mind*, based
on his experience.

other experts as a suspect and dangerous figure, he was sought out by foreign journalists, and it was at this time that Fraser met him. While Rittenberg's colleagues among the foreign experts regarded him as aloof and self-serving, Fraser concluded that what distinguished him was that he had become 'more of a Chinese than he is a foreigner'.[51] Tuned in to Chinese reality to a far greater extent than the other experts, he adapted to the changing political currents as a Chinese person would. Perhaps surprisingly, Fraser sensed that Rittenberg, even after his second jail term, retained an ambition to stay at the centre of things. But Yulin, who had been beaten and imprisoned with the children for eight months and then sent to work in rural labour camps, was determined to leave. In 1980, the family relocated to the United States. According to Rittenberg, their decision to leave China was triggered by the suppression of the Beijing Spring when, in 1978-79 for roughly a year, citizens were allowed to post demands for reform on 'Democracy Wall.'

As China opened up to foreign investors, Rittenberg set up a consultancy business advising multinationals on how to gain a foothold in the Chinese market. Once again, he appeared as a man with privileged access to Chinese power holders. This stung those experts who had remained in China despite being mistreated during the Cultural Revolution. The fact that this time he was using his top-level connections to profit financially added to their resentment and confirmed their view that he was an unprincipled opportunist. Many of the old experts, while initially welcoming Deng Xiaoping's reforms, detested the drift towards outright capitalism, and Rittenberg's smooth adaptation to it became another reason to despise him. In Rittenberg's defence, he too was shocked by the generalised corruption of the new order but later decided that Deng's reforms had given the Chinese a high standard of living and more freedom than ever before. And those who stayed behind might privately grumble but eventually had to adjust to the system.

The suppression of the student demonstrations at Tiananmen on 4 June 1989 was a severe test for those among the old experts who remained in China as well as those who left. Two of Rittenberg's daughters narrowly escaped death when their Beijing apartment was strafed with bullets. But his condemnation of the brutal crackdown was equivocal. Writing for an American audience, he said he was sure

---

51   Fraser, *The Chinese*, 189.

that the Chinese government would eventually repudiate the massacre. On the other hand, the students, although idealistic, were 'quixotic'. They were not 'the last best hope for democracy' in China but were 'manipulated by people in both power factions'.[52] China would eventually evolve 'a form of political democracy' without 'another great upheaval'.[53] This sounds very much like an echo of Deng Xiaoping's line that the student demonstrations were heading for a rerun of the Cultural Revolution. Epstein went further. The students were indeed manipulated, although not by Chinese factions but by the CIA and other Western agencies. He praised the government's initial restraint and condemned the students for 'baiting' Premier Li Peng. Not only had they disrespected Li; they had done so while wearing pyjamas. The implication was that they had called disaster down on themselves. His only veiled criticism of the government was that if Zhou Enlai had been in post, he would have used his authority to resolve the situation without violence.[54]

A memoir of any sort cannot but focus to an extent on its author. But while most foreigners who wrote political memoirs regarding this period of Chinese history did so from the point of view of an observer, Rittenberg wrote from the point of view of a protagonist. His text is an odd mix of mea culpa and outright bragging, peppered with phrases that emphasise and exaggerate his role in shaping events. His 'fame was growing', and his 'political work was just too important' for him to spend his time in the office doing his day job. He was 'a conduit to the top' who could make or break careers.[55] The other foreigners, when he takes note of them, appear as also-rans, extras in his biopic. However, although Rittenberg invests the tasks he undertook with great significance, many of them were rather routine and mundane, and were carried out by teams, not individuals. On whom should the Chinese rely to help them produce foreign-language propaganda, translate Mao's works, and so on, but foreign sympathisers? Was the Friendship Hotel really the arena in which the Sino-Soviet political struggle played out? Like the other foreigners in China after 1949, Rittenberg's impact was tiny compared

---

52   Rittenberg and Bennett, *The Man Who Stayed Behind*, 452.

53   Ibid., 452.

54   Israel Epstein, *My China Eye: Memoirs of a Jew and a Journalist*, Beijing: New Star Press, 2015, 427.

55   Rittenberg and Bennett, *The Man Who Stayed Behind*, 344–55.

to, for example, Mikhail Borodin, who brought with him funds, advisors and weapons to equip an army; or Vasily Blyukher, who led that army to victory over the warlords and, inadvertently, handed power to Chiang Kai-shek.[56] To those two we might add the names of Grigory Voitinsky, Henk Sneevliet, Vladimir Vilensky, and others. It must be admitted that some scholars, who see the Chinese Revolution solely through the Maoist prism, also magnify the role of the Yan'an generation of foreigners, including Rittenberg. However, in one of his franker moments, Rittenberg assessed himself as 'a flash that panned'.

Having established Rittenberg's realistic proportions as a historical figure, we should also do him political justice. It is not clear why he, rather than others mentioned in this chapter, should have been so ostracised by the old experts. Perhaps he paid too-careful attention to what his audience wanted to hear. He exaggerated, boasted, and bent the truth to make a good story. But these are, arguably, the venial sins of a raconteur. Rittenberg also admitted turning against former friends during the Cultural Revolution – a serious matter, no doubt, but who among his detractors was qualified to cast the first stone? Perhaps his unforgivable offence in the eyes of the loyalists was to have repudiated Mao as a 'great criminal', a 'scheming tyrant' responsible for 'the deaths of millions, or perhaps tens of millions'.[57]

Rittenberg's denunciation of Mao was, however, qualified. He had perhaps brought 'misery and death' on a grand scale, but he had united China and rescued 'hundreds of millions from pauperdom'.[58] Although he left China, Rittenberg never stopped defending, in broad terms, not only the country but also its revolution. He actively engaged with academics, journalists, diplomats, and others, arguing patiently for a policy of peaceful cooperation with China, although he withdrew from the debate in the last year of his life, when the raised voices of new cold warriors, encouraged by Donald Trump's 2016 election victory, drowned out moderate opinion. Despite the heated rhetoric, he did not believe there would be a war between China and the United States; according to him, 'the two behemoths will continue, each to develop along its own

---

56   Without Stalin's mistaken strategy, Chiang Kai-shek would not have taken power and arguably, had Chiang not chased him into the mountains of Jiangxi Province, Mao would have remained a second-rank CCP leader.

57   Ibid., 450.

58   Ibid.

track according to its own logic, collaborating and contending as they go.' He blamed both sides for the worsening relations. Xi Jinping's political programme amounted to Make China Great Again – a mirror image of Trump's posturing. Old-style internationalism that was never quite extinguished under Mao had been replaced by idiotic nationalist ravings amounting to ' "Down with Japanese workers because they're Japanese" and "No Japanese film star can kiss our Chinese actress in a film." '[59]

Rittenberg said that he remained on the left and continued to believe that society would develop towards 'some sort of Socialism', although 'not any time soon'. Viewing the political scene in the United States, he gave qualified support to the Occupy movement but said it had allowed itself to be 'sidetracked by anarchists'. Bernie Sanders, he said, had succeeded in 'waking up sections of the youth'. The rise of Sanders on the left and Trump on the right showed that the duopoly of the Republicans and Democrats – 'two political groupings who do not represent the will of the public' – was beginning to break down. In 2018, two years before supporters of President Trump stormed the US Capitol, he predicted a 'showdown between a semi-fascist right-wing mob and democratic-minded American people'.

He said that he remained a Marxist but rejected Leninism and the concept of the dictatorship of the proletariat. Marx, he said, 'never would have associated his name with a "socialism" that was less democratic than capitalism'. But, oddly for someone who rejected Leninism, he regarded Earl Browder's partial dissolution of the CPUSA in 1944 as the 'Great Betrayal of the American progressive movement'. Having built a 6-million-strong trade union movement, the party relinquished leadership of it and 'deliberately dissolved' its huge mass organisations 'to reduce the Roosevelt administration's concern about the American left so that it would form a closer alliance with the Soviet Union . . . it was a terrible betrayal from which the American progressive movement has still not recovered'.[60] If not an entirely coherent perspective, it indicates a nostalgia for the selfless activists of the CPUSA and the CCP rank and file he met in Yan'an.

---

59   Sid Rittenberg, interview.
60   Ibid.

Afterword

Between 1919 and 1927, a small number of foreign revolutionaries substantially affected the direction of Chinese history. They were mainly, though by no means exclusively, Russians, and all were inspired by internationalist ideals. It was a period when the interests of the Soviet state coincided with the Bolshevik Party's mission to spread world revolution. In 1919, Soviet Russia, facing British, French, American, Japanese, and other interventionist forces, welcomed and encouraged movements that might weaken or divert the attention of the imperialist powers. Colonised India and semi-colonised China were fertile territories for revolutionary action. In China, left divided and bullied by imperialists after the abortive revolution of 1911, radicalism was revived by the cynical award of Qingdao to Japan at Versailles.

Vladimir Vilensky, Grigory Voitinsky, and Henk Sneevliet were indispensable in transforming the Chinese Communist Party from a tiny discussion group in Shanghai into a national party that recruited tens of thousands of members, created trade unions and peasant organisations, and sparked mass movements like the great Hong Kong–Canton strike. Soviet diplomat Adolph Joffe negotiated the historic agreement between the Soviet government and Sun Yat-sen; Lev Karakhan won over Chinese intellectuals during his stint as ambassador in Beijing. The much-maligned Sneevliet, criticised for his tactical errors, was a veteran anti-colonial fighter who insisted on an anti-imperialist strategy that served the party well throughout its history.

The foreign internationalists helped build not one, but two parties. Mikhail Borodin's reforms transformed the KMT from a clique around Sun Yat-sen into a modern political party. Vasily Blyukher and other military advisors created a new model army, the National Revolutionary Army, and led the Northern Expedition that defeated the warlords and unified China. The outcome was not, as the Comintern hoped and expected, a friendly bourgeois government, or a coalition government of the KMT with the Communist Party. Many in the CCP had hoped for a more or less immediate transition to some form of socialist or workers' government; some saw the KMT as a Trojan horse under which a concealed takeover by the Communists could take place. Disagreements among Chinese and Soviet leaders meant that they had no consistent strategy; indeed, when confronted by events that did not fit the schema the Comintern had set out for the Chinese revolution, they improvised.

The revolution reached its peak when a working-class uprising, led by the Communist Party, seized power in Shanghai. What followed was a disaster for the party and for Soviet influence in China. But, although the left was almost completely wiped out, a 'bourgeois-nationalist' government was installed, as foreseen by Moscow – albeit in the misshapen form of a KMT dictatorship. Soviet arms and military advisors had propelled Chiang Kai-shek, a small-time gangster turned minor warlord, to power.

Stalin and Comintern leader Bukharin were in denial after Chiang's coup. Accordingly, they tried to breathe life into the revolution's embers by ordering adventurist insurrections. Blyukher helped plan the takeover of Nanchang, and Vissarion Lominadze and Heinz Neumann were sent from Moscow to organise the suicidal Canton Commune. After the inevitable defeats, foreign activists like veteran labour militants George Hardy and Arthur Ewert were restricted to clandestine activities, keeping the depleted, underground CCP alive by passing on Comintern funds and instructions. It was hazardous work, as demonstrated by the Noulens' case, and demanded great courage.

The Nanchang and Canton debacles were the first steps in an ultra-leftist turn of the Comintern – the so-called Third Period – that was not seriously challenged until its absurdity was demonstrated by Hitler's appointment as chancellor. In China, the Third Period was exemplified by Li Lisan's 1930 takeover of Changsha, an adventure that lasted just over a week. The Chinese Soviet Republic was proclaimed the following year, with Mao Zedong as head of state, even though it controlled only tiny and remote patches of territory. The leftist line was reflected in the actions taken by the Comintern's military advisors – such as Manfred Stern's construction of an airstrip to receive Soviet arms that never arrived, and the tactics of his subordinate Otto Braun.

The 'iron discipline' of enforced unanimity, backed up by terror, had not yet been imposed either in the Soviet Union on the Comintern. Although Trotsky was expelled from the Soviet Union in 1929 and 'Trotskyism' was officially anathemised, it was impossible to stifle debate on the reasons for the crushing defeat of 1927. In Moscow, hundreds of Chinese students at Sun Yat-sen University were won over to the opposition by Karl Radek and others, and in Shanghai opposition supporters like Frank Glass and Harold Isaacs worked together with and debated with the official Comintern.

By the mid-1930s, reality had caught up with the Comintern's Third Period folly. Nazi Germany and Fascist Italy armed Franco and sent 'volunteers' to Spain while the democracies stood by. The Comintern U-turned from refusing to cooperate with social democrats to seeking alliances with the liberal bourgeoisie, but even Leon Blum's Popular Front government refused to support Republican Spain.

In China, as Japanese encroachment turned to open aggression, exasperation with Chiang Kai-shek's war against the CCP provoked a military coup that ended in compromise and a renewed KMT-CCP alliance. When Japan invaded in 1937, the Soviets once again poured arms and advisors into China; as in the 1920s, the bulk of the aid went to the KMT, not the CCP. Between 1937 and 1941, around two thousand Soviet pilots served in the armed forces of the KMT government. They were officially volunteers, and although in reality they may have had little choice, there can be no doubt that many saw their mission as an internationalist duty. Until Pearl Harbor, the Soviet Union, alone among the great powers, gave military support to China. Civilians including Edgar Snow, Agnes Smedley, Anna Louise Strong, Arthur Clegg, Victor Gollancz, and others publicised, raised funds for, and took part in China's war effort. Japanese Communists and anti-imperialists Nosaka Sanzo, Verda Majo, Kaji Wataru, Ikeda Yuki, and scores of disaffected Japanese troops risked their lives to undermine morale in and desertions from the Japanese army.

Paradoxically, the Popular Front turn coincided with the Great Purges. To appear as reliable allies to liberals and bourgeois democrats, the Comintern progressed from the suspension of class struggle to its outright suppression – up to and including the liquidation of revolutionaries and working-class militants. Rank-and-file Communists were recruited to the secret police to spy on their comrades. David Crook volunteered to fight fascism in Spain – and, to his credit, returned to the fighting after being wounded – but was recalled from the front to spy on the anarchists and the POUM in Barcelona. When he was sent to China, it was not to foment revolution but to infiltrate a tiny group of foreign Trotskyists. Debate inside the Comintern was shut down, and members were expected to believe the wildly implausible conclusion of show trials that the leaders of the October Revolution had been traitors from the start. Fellow travellers, with varying degrees of reluctance, adapted to the official line. For example, Kingsley Martin, editor of the *New Statesman*, wrote a vicious caricature of Trotsky after meeting him in Mexico. For others, siding with Moscow was a matter of choosing the lesser evil; as Edgar Snow put it, faced with a plague of rats – the Nazis – it was impossible to remain neutral.[1]

The Great Depression and the seemingly intractable capitalist crisis that followed led some Fabians and other moderate socialists to re-evaluate the Soviet experiment. The success of the Five-Year Plans, they surmised, might lead other countries to adopt socialism by emulation without the need for the unpleasantness of revolution. Compared with the prospect of a new, more advanced stage of human history, the elimination of an earlier generation of Bolsheviks, along with their out-of-date ideas, might be regarded as a detail.

On the question of war and peace, the Popular Front line was a profound change to Communist policy. The founders of the Third International seceded from the Second International because of its failure to oppose the First World War. However, faced with the threat of fascism, Communists called on the democracies to rearm and take preemptive action. They were no longer opposed to, but advocating a new world war and decried pacifists who, they claimed, opposed the idea of

---

1   Quoted in John Maxwell Hamilton, *Edgar Snow, a Biography*, Bloomington: Indiana University Press, 1988, 229.

collective security.[2] Although the Bolsheviks had organised soldiers' soviets in World War I, when David Crook joined up, the CPGB told him to just be a good officer. Clearly, the Second World War was not a rerun of the First, but whatever the reasoning and justification for it, the new policy, together with other aspects of the Popular Front line, changed what it meant to be a Communist. CPGB membership peaked during the war years, but the beliefs of the membership were very different from those of the first generation of Communists. Over time, the tenets of Popular Frontism became embedded in party programmes like the British Road to Socialism and expressed in Japan's 'lovable' Communist Party, the Historic Compromise in Italy and so on.[3]

In China, as recounted by Otto Braun and others, Mao Zedong was pressured by the Comintern to cooperate closely with the KMT and was even accused of 'Trotskyism' by his factional enemies in the CCP. But Chiang Kai-shek's 1927 coup had taught Mao that political power comes out of the barrel of a gun. No matter what the Comintern prescribed, the CCP leadership would never again place itself at the mercy of its enemies by dissolving or relinquishing control over its own armed forces. 'The party must control the gun' had become an article of faith.

If the 1920s was the period when foreigners had the most impact on Chinese politics, after 1949, their influence dwindled to virtually zero, especially after Khrushchev withdrew Soviet technical experts in 1960. A few sympathisers outside China, such as Edgar Snow, could still affect international public opinion, but those foreigners who remained in the country were restricted to routine tasks such as translating, editing, foreign-language teaching, and so on. For all their talent and energy, Joan Hinton and Sid Engst had only a model farm to show for their efforts. 'Foreign experts' were, for decades, segregated from the Chinese population, and insofar as they had a political function, it was as decoration for the regime. Of course, they did not seek influence – the most basic goal of the Chinese revolution was that China should run its own affairs. Still, they shared the socialist ideals of their predecessors, chafed under the restrictions, and threw themselves into political campaigning

---

2   Apart from the twenty-two months of the Molotov-Ribbentrop Pact, when the war was tagged as imperialist before reverting to an anti-fascist crusade when Hitler invaded the Soviet Union.

3   In Britain this logic led to former GB intellectuals becoming cheerleaders for New Labour and Tony Blair.

when given the opportunity during the Cultural Revolution. Believing they were taking part in a world-historic movement, it does not seem to have occurred to them that a revolution carried out with official permission is not a genuine revolution. Despite the insignificant effects of their actions, they were manipulated, betrayed, and suffered badly at the hands of their own side – none more so than Sid Rittenberg, who, more than any of the others, overestimated the importance of his personal role.

Almost all the old experts were disillusioned by the repression of the Tiananmen protests in 1989. Some called it a counter-revolution and the restoration of capitalism, but, by now elderly, they had nowhere else to go. China's subsequent economic success brought praise from the World Bank, and a new generation of supporters attracted by the prospect of making money.

Perhaps out of inertia, the state persists with the odd, self-defeating Friend of China awards, which destroy the credibility of recipients as soon as they are conferred. However, only a tiny minority of the new 'friends' are political activists or pundits, for whom this might be a drawback; business executives who receive the honour value the doors it opens. It must be said that China has some contemporary supporters on the left – those who see the Belt and Road Initiative as rallying the Global South against the 'rules-based order' dominated by the United States. For some of the old experts, this is a continuation of the anti-colonial revolution by other means and a consolation that partially compensates for the failure of China's attempts to construct socialism.

Appendix A: *China and Soviet Russia*, by Vladimir Vilensky

China and Soviet Russia:
On the Question of Our Far Eastern Policies
By V. I. Vilensky (Sibiriakov)

Contents

Preface from the Editorial Board

The revolutionary movement of the peoples of the Far East presently taking shape under national banners, has as its basic task the creation of unified nation states capable of fighting for economic and political liberation. But the movement has been complicated from the outset by inevitable internal class struggles of the oppressed and exploited against their oppressors.

Soviet Russia, straddling West and East and directly bordering the Far East, faces an urgent question – how to relate to this revolutionary movement.

The Eighth Congress of our Party placed the alliance of proletarians and semi-proletarians of different nations at the centre of the revolutionary struggle to overthrow capitalism. The Congress also urged extreme sensitivity to the remnants of national feelings among the toiling masses of the oppressed nations.

The Russian proletariat cannot content itself with setting an example to the awakening Asiatic peoples but must actively assist their burgeoning revolutionary movement.

But, in order to do so, we must first study the concrete conditions in the Far East. Only then will we be able to respond to the tasks set before us by the revolutionary movement. This series of booklets published by the Agitation and Propaganda Library of Siberia and the Far East, aims to present an accurate picture of events in Asia and along the Pacific coast.

On the Ruins of the Great Qing Empire

The Great Qing Empire, the last dynasty of Imperial China, was swept away in a revolutionary wave that gave birth to the new Chinese Republic. The history of the Great Qing is that of the collapse and plunder of what had once been the mightiest and oldest state in the world; a state that created order and civilisation two thousand six hundred years before Christ, at a time when Europe was mired in darkness and barbarism.

The revolution that overthrew the Empire was fuelled by racial resentment that had smouldered throughout the history of the dynasty since the Manchus usurped state power under the Great Qing banner. The most vivid expression of this racial revolution was the Taiping rebellion that began in 1849 in Guangxi Province under the leadership of Hong Xiuquan. Hong ruled his Heavenly Kingdom of Great Peace until 1868, having overrun several provinces and led his forces to the gates of Beijing. The Taipings were eventually suppressed with the help of foreign troops.

China, at the time, was already a target for the imperialist powers. A general plunder followed, as capitalist predators from England, France, America, Japan, Russia and others stretched out their greedy paws to snatch the tastiest titbits from the failing dynasty.

In the Sino-Japanese war of 1894–95 Japan stole the island of Formosa and, on the pretext of maintaining the balance of power in the Far East, an alliance of imperialist predators, Russia, England, and Germany shared out other spoils. In 1898, tsarist Russia 'leased' – in other words seized – Port Arthur and pronounced its right to build a railroad across Manchuria. At the same time and in the same manner, England took Weihaiwei and Germany grabbed Jiaozhou Bay and the port of Qingdao.

Tsarist Russia's great-power foreign policy was to race to the Pacific Ocean to capture ports as part of a grandiose scheme to create colonies throughout the fading Qing Empire in Chinese Turkestan, the Uryankai region, Tibet, Kokonor, Mongolia, Manchuria, and elsewhere. Russia would have achieved its goals had the Mikado's army not snatched some of Nikolai Romanov's prized Chinese possessions from his hands in the Russo-Japanese War. Taking advantage of Russia's defeat, Britain, secured Tibet for itself in the Anglo-Russian Treaty of 1907, cutting off one of tsarist Russia's planned routes into Asia.

China was a helpless spectator to this brazen theft of its territory. But Japan's victory over Russia inspired and energised the entire East, including China. The revitalised Chinese revolutionaries quietly abandoned the slogan 'China for the Chinese' and, by degrees, transformed the racial struggle against the Qing dynasty into a political struggle to abolish the monarchical system altogether. When the dynasty finally fell, they proclaimed the Republic of China on its ruins.

Revolutions in China

China's Revolution did not end with the formation of the Republic. A simple change of political forms could not solve the country's problems. Agrarian China had, imperceptibly, been drawn into the world market. Foreign capital in the form of loans and concessions poured into the country creating capitalist enterprises that employed tens of thousands of workers. Railway lines spread rapidly, growing from 11 kilometres in 1880 to 5,953 kilometres in 1906 – i.e., by a factor of 540.

Capitalist development changed the character of the revolution. Social forces elbowed their way into the revolutionary movement and forced both leaders and masses to reflect on their aims. Sun Yat-sen, one of the main leaders of the Chinese Revolution, described its nature as follows:

> Our goal is not just to establish democracy, but also to change the conditions of social life. This is difficult for Europe and America but incomparably easier for China. If Europe and America cannot solve their social problems, it is because they are unable to solve the problem of agriculture.
>
> We want a revolution of national liberation because we refuse to put up with a situation in which a clique of Manchus controls our country's resources.
>
> We want a social revolution because we do not want a bunch of capitalists to monopolise the country's wealth.
>
> The social forces involved in the revolution were stumbling blocks that separated the revolutionary south from the more conservative north which was influenced by Imperial Japan.

South China is the citadel of the Chinese Guomindang revolutionaries. Since the time of the Taipings, there has existed a network of secret societies, united in two large unions. The first is the Triads (Sanhehui), widespread in Guangdong, Guangxi, Fujian and Zhejiang; the second is Elder Brothers Society (Gelaohui) concentrated in Hunan and the Yangzi provinces. Years of struggle between southern and northern China were a great fighting school for Chinese revolutionaries. The Red Forces of the south strengthened and armed themselves and, despite the colossal material aid to the north from Japan, were a constant threat to Beijing's reactionaries.

Just as in the days of the Great Qing Empire, northern China tries to channel popular discontent into hatred and hostility to 'foreigners' – while applying the same label to the southern revolutionaries. Of course, hostility to foreigners is not entirely wrong – when directed by Chinese revolutionaries against the imperialist agents and industrial condottiere who, in the eyes of the toiling masses, embody the economic and political enslavement of China.

Indeed, the capitalist world of Europe and America did its best to present its worst side to the Chinese people. During their entire time in China, the capitalist exploiters regarded the Chinese as barely human. Under the protection of European cannons, the behaviour of the 'civilisers' was so unbridled that the Chinese came to regard these white 'barbarians' with utter contempt. It is not surprising therefore that, in the eyes of many Europeans, the Chinese revolutionary movement against capitalism and world imperialism, took on a chauvinistic character.

We noted above that the leaders of the Chinese revolution, represented by Sun Yat-sen, believe that the main domestic issue of the Chinese revolution is the resolution of the land question. The revolution's theorists believe that, to achieve social justice, surplus land in China's agricultural heartlands should be transferred to the state.

Trying to combine the interests of the toiling masses of rural China with those of the nascent Chinese proletariat, China's revolutionaries are working out their own concrete programme. China's remoteness and the 'Chinese wall' of its language sometimes prevents us from seeing clearly and understanding what is going on there. But one thing is certain – China has been woken from its deep sleep by world imperialism and is presently looking around, trying to determine who are her enemies and who are her friends.

Japan and China

Japan found herself with one of the few surviving armies after the world war and was honoured to be included among the Five Great Powers who were to establish peace on earth while dividing it among themselves. Japan had concrete aims and prepared a list of demands to present to the peace conference. These were outlined 'off the record' by an adviser to

Japan's Versailles delegation, who said Japan was seeking British and American approval for its expansion in the east. Specifically, Japan wanted recognition of its commercial rights in Siberia, China and elsewhere, and the abolition of America's discriminatory laws against the Japanese.

Japan had even more definite plans for China. The defeat of Russia and the seizure of the Kwantung Peninsula opened up dizzying prospects for imperialist Japan in China. She no longer had any serious rivals in the Far East apart from Britain, with whom she was allied. Japan's exports to China have increased almost fivefold since 1912, mainly at the expense of Britain and America. And, given the enormous importance of finance capital in the modern economy, Japan set itself the task of securing control over the largest Chinese banks. The Bank of China whose influence in China can be compared with the role of the National City Bank in America, is now dependent on Japan. In recent years, Japanese banks have loaned it ten million dollars to remove expired credit notes from circulation. The Transport Bank/Bank of Communications is also under Japanese influence as, in instalments over the past few years, it has borrowed twenty million yen. The bank employs a consultant specifically to look after Japanese interests. One of the largest Chinese banks, the Territorial Development Bank, is on the point of collapse and will inevitably fall under Japanese control. When that happens there will be only one independent bank left in China. The financial conquest of China by Japan is proceeding full steam ahead. In its drive for profit, Japanese imperialism has relentlessly sought loans and concessions using all sorts of tricks and stratagems [learned from the European bourgeoisie]. In recent years, almost all Japanese governments have based their policies on supporting one or another of China's warring parties with finance and weaponry – intending to reap handsome compensation of course. And, in order to manipulate public opinion, Japan has concentrated the main telegraph companies in its hands to deliver news to all the Beijing and Shanghai newspapers, not to mention provincial titles. Other telegraph companies cannot compete with the extraordinarily low prices charged by the Japanese. Japan controls all the main newspapers in Beijing, Shanghai, Tianjin, Fuzhou and elsewhere. All these papers benefit from extraterritorial rights that permit them to talk about subjects forbidden to the Chinese press and are heavily subsidised, directly and by advertisements, so as to destroy the competition.

Using such methods, Japanese imperialism is rapidly expanding its economic clout. A consortium of Japanese banks has acquired important concessions to build several railroads in China in return for an advance of forty million dollars to the Chinese government. Newspapers have recently reported the formation of a major Sino-Japanese mining joint venture. In return for this concession the Japanese forgave a million-dollar loan it had made to Yuan Shikai. Without even waiting for government approval, the Japanese have already begun working the mines and acquiring the land for the railroads.

But the main factors in the success of Japanese imperialism in China were the so-called 'slave treaties' made public by the Chinese delegation to Versailles. It turns out that the Japanese tried to impose such draconian terms that even the normally compliant Chinese government cried foul. Even the Japanese were embarrassed by the disclosures, as can be seen by the lengths they went to – stealing copies of the treaties from the Chinese delegation's luggage when it passed through Japan, and even going so far as to threaten an armed confrontation – to prevent their publication at the peace conference. From August 1914, when Japan issued its ultimatum to Germany, to the moment when the Japanese ambassador to China, politely demanded the withdrawal of the Chinese delegation from Versailles, the record of the Japanese in China looked like this: They took Qingdao and the southern half of Shandong Province, imposed the infamous 21 demands, conspired to overthrow Yuan Shikai, encroached in southern Manchuria, made a secret treaty with Russia, demanded control of the Chinese armed forces as a precondition of China joining the war against Germany, supported the northern militarists, made loans in return for control of China's natural resources, organised a Japanese controlled administration in Shandong, signed a military alliance in 1918 that included a whole string of secret provisions, and concluded the Lansing-Ishii agreement. All these were part of a consistent policy to eliminate China's independence and 'reform' it in accordance with the aims and objectives of Japanese imperialism – in the name of the so-called doctrine of 'Asia for the Asians'. Japan has also tried other approaches – for example, in the Beijing and Tianjin Daily News, a prominent Japanese professor has called for the formation of a Sino-Japanese defensive and offensive alliance. He writes that only with Japan's help can China be spared from dismemberment and that neither country can survive without mutual economic cooperation. In view of the current situation in Russia, the author writes, Japan was forced to take vigorous measures to preserve the peace and protect its interests in Korea, Manchuria, and Mongolia! As Russia is fragmented and weak, protection of the common Sino-Japanese border with Russia is all that is required. But to achieve this, Japan must control the railways – which will also permit the peaceful development of southern and northern Manchuria.

In the current international situation, with the rapid growth of the fleets and land armies of the United States, England, and France, as sister powers in East Asia, China and Japan should cooperate to pursue their common interests. If China could trust Japan it would be able to redirect its heavy military expenditure into exploiting its rich natural resources, expanding education, developing industry and so on.

Given the global situation, it would seem, on the face of it, that the Chinese ought to cooperate with their fellow Asians – the Japanese – to advance Asian civilisation. But the 'fraternal' assistance offered to China by Japan has little in common with the aim of developing 'Asian civilisation'. For example, the *Peking Leader* newspaper, in its article 'Is Japan Dealing with China Honestly?' describes how morphine and opium is being flagrantly smuggled into China. In 1913, nine million taels of morphine were imported into Dairen; by now of course the volume is much greater. There is virtually no morphine left in Europe. Japan has a monopoly of supply. In recent years, the Japanese have become the main, almost the only, buyers of opium in Persia and India. The opium is shipped to Kobe and from there to Qingdao. There is evidence that, from 1 January to 1 October 1918 alone, around 2,000 crates were delivered via this route. But is the Japanese government interested? In fact, Chinese customs do not have the right to check parcels sent to Japanese postal facilities in China – parcels that sometime contain illegal drugs. The Japanese state even makes a profit by imposing duties on imported opium.

The Chinese government cannot enforce the law in its own country. In the Japanese-controlled railway zones, Japanese gendarmes prevent Chinese police from enforcing the law against opium smoking. In southern China, things are even easier. Many opium dealers there hold Japanese passports stating that they are natives of Formosa and carry on their trade in complete security.

What is China supposed to do in this situation? Shouldn't it demand the destruction of foreign trade offices established solely for political reasons? Cooperating with smugglers is a violation of international law. Shouldn't extraterritoriality be abolished? Who can seriously oppose the immediate termination of a situation that threatens the health of China's population and disrespects the dignity of its institutions and authorities?

According to one American journalist, China is the Balkans of the Far East, a land of opportunity, ripe for division among Japan, America, Russia, and other European imperialist predators. The current flood of opium confirms this analysis.

America is arming itself and Japan is not far behind. In 1919, the Japanese government proposed a military budget sufficient to put 41 divisions in the field, a massive increase from the 25 divisions proposed to the Diet the previous year. Storm clouds are gathering over the Far East. They threaten to engulf Japan, America, China, Russia and perhaps the European imperialists in a war as bloody as the one we have recently emerged from. It is the logical outcome of the conference at Versailles. Who can prevent it?

China and the Lessons of Versailles

China, both south and north, has every reason to be unhappy with the outcome of the Versailles Conference. Before this 'peace' conference convened, China was promised a great deal. So much so, that revolutionary southern China made a temporary agreement with reactionary northern China to send a joint delegation, led by Lu Zhengxiang, to Versailles.

The main points of China's programme at the peace conference were:

1) Qingdao must be returned to China.
2) The former German possessions in the Guandong (Kwantung) region to be given to China, not Japan.
3) Russia must hand over the China Eastern Railway. The involvement of Japan or any other power in this matter is unacceptable.
4) Extraterritoriality must be abolished.
5) All foreign garrisons must leave Chinese soil.
6) China has the right to manage its own debt obligations and to impose and levy taxes without the intervention of foreign powers.

7) All secret treaties and agreements concluded between the former Chinese Empire and the Japanese capitalists to be annulled, whether or not they were concluded with the knowledge of the Tokyo government.
8) Foreigners will be allowed to live in China's interior outside of concessions or spheres of influence.
9) The same goes for trading rights throughout the Republic of China.
10) Renegotiation of all previous treaties and agreements with foreign powers, since they were signed by China under duress or the threat of foreign invasion, by Chinese governments that did not understand the norms and practices of modern diplomacy.

In the runup to the Versailles Conference, Chinese newspapers declared that, if the peace conference failed to deliver on these demands, then all the talk of freedom, justice, and law from the victorious powers would amount to empty chatter in the eyes of the Chinese people. But even this modest programme, inadequate in the eyes of the revolutionaries of southern China, was unacceptable to Wilson, Lloyd George, and the rest. China for them remained a 'place to be carved up'. The only question was who among the 'big five' would be the winners and losers. The overall international balance of forces dictated that Japan would get the lion's share, and it got Shandong along with all the other German concessions. The rest of the imperialist predators guaranteed their interests by organising a banking consortium through which America, Great Britain and France could take part in the looting of China.

The Chinese delegation refused to sign the 'peace treaty' and left Versailles with feelings of irreconcilable anger towards the European barbarians. Inside China, these hatreds are brewing up a new revolutionary storm. The South is again under arms as the northern reactionaries prepare to hurl their regiments against it. But the Versailles lesson has not been lost on the masses of the north. The Beijing reactionaries have been given a taste of the unrest fermenting among the lower classes on whom they previously relied. The Japanese, as evidenced by the words of their war minister, are also worried about maintaining stability in the north. Everything points to the revolutionary fire spreading from the south to the north. If so, revolutionary Russia will find in China a reliable ally against the imperialist predators who are soaping the rope for the peoples of the Far East in Versailles, because the Chinese are beginning to see clearly who their friends are and who are their enemies.

Soviet Russia and China

Having just crossed the Urals to crush Kolchak and the other Siberian reactionaries, we hear on the radio that a bloody clash among the imperialists is about to take place in the Far East. An American radio station reports that, in the United States, there is growing outrage at the granting of Shandong to Japan that may lead to the decision being revisited or reversed. Our military experts believe that Japan is no match for the United States army which has proven its combat capability on battlefields of Europe. China, the Balkans of the Far East, has turned out, as expected, to be the bone of contention between hardened predators. America, contender for the role of hegemon of the Pacific and its coastlines, has lost patience with its yellow rival and, despite its usual reticence, is now threatening to expose every dirty deal that was cooked up at Versailles. On 14 July, American radio reported that two of Wilson's Peace Commissioners, Henry White and General Tasker H. Bliss, had protested against the transfer of Shandong to Japan. They handed a memorandum to President Wilson immediately after the decision, stating that they could not agree to the way the issue was resolved. The president told them that he had to make concessions to ensure Japan's participation in the League of Nations, since as Italy had already threatened to withdraw, the conference could not allow the loss of another great power that might even ally with Germany. The Versailles kitchen served up a 'concession' to Japan under pressure and now the 'Big Five' are having to reckon with the consequences. The situation is extremely serious; a radio report of July 21 stated that 'the mood of the Japanese delegation is alarming'. A member of the Japanese delegation complained that a speech by a US senator was highly offensive to Japan's national dignity, but he hoped that the good sense of the American people would prevail and a conflict between Japan and the United States would be avoided.

But it is not only the United States and Japan who are itching for a fight. Other members of the Big Five have interests in the Far East. The

London newspaper *Export* recently reported that Britain is sending a fleet comprising a heavy cruiser, four light cruisers, 18 destroyers and 11 submarines into Chinese waters. The news has enraged public opinion in Japan. Two hours after the publication of the report, the Japanese Admiralty announced that the Japanese fleet in Chinese waters was being put on full alert.

This then is the situation in the Far East, where, by the way, the Siberian reactionaries are heading in full flight and are destined to perish. We have always based our Far Eastern policy on the assumption that the imperialists will fight among themselves. Clashes between these hardened robbers are inevitable and can only benefit the Russian revolution and the revolutionary movements in the Far East. Following this rule of thumb allowed us to maintain Soviet power in the Far East until September 1918, when the 'Far Eastern contradictions' were blunted by a temporary truce between Tokyo and Washington. Now events are bringing this truce to an end.

What should our policy be? The answers are clear. The first is to lance the boil of imperialism in the East as we did in the West during the world war. The second is to reach out to those peoples likely to become genuine allies. They include the Koreans who are fighting for independence from Japan, autonomous Mongolia, and, above all, revolutionary China. The Versailles robbers have done everything in their power to alienate the Chinese. The so-called peace agreement – a worthless scrap of paper the Chinese delegates disdained to sign – has imposed on China the necessity of waging a defensive war. China, now doomed to partition, can and should ally with Soviet Russia. There are no serious differences between the sides. China's demands at Versailles were the return of the China Eastern Railway and the revision of old unequal treaties. Soviet Russia can, with a light heart, settle both issues in favour of China. In doing so we will acquire an important ally. Creating an alliance with revolutionary China is a task we must immediately undertake with all the means at our disposal. Such an alliance would be the foundation for a fraternal union of the proletarians of the Far East to transform modern capitalist society on socialist lines.

Appeal to the Chinese People and to the Governments of Northern and Southern China [The Karakhan Manifesto]

On the day when Soviet troops smashed the counter-revolutionary Kolchak's army along with his foreign-backed despotism, and triumphantly entered Siberia to unite with its revolutionary people, the Council of People's Commissars sends these fraternal greetings to all the peoples of China:

Soviet Russia and the Soviet Red Army have, after a two-year struggle of incredible proportions, crossed the Urals into the East not for the purposes of conquest or enslavement – as every Siberian peasant and worker knows – but to liberate the people from the yoke of foreign bayonets and foreign gold under which all the peoples of the East, especially the Chinese, are suffering. We offer help not only to our working classes but also to the Chinese people and take this opportunity to remind them of what we said at the time of the Great October Revolution of 1917, but was perhaps hidden from them by the corrupt American, European, and Japanese press.

As soon as the workers' and peasants' government took power in October 1917, on behalf of the Russian people it issued an appeal to the peoples of the world to establish a lasting permanent peace. The fundamental principle of this peace was the relinquishing of all foreign conquests and annexations. Every nation, big or small, whether formerly independent or not, has the right to live freely and govern its own affairs; no power has the right to forcibly hold another nation within its borders. The workers' and peasants' government followed up this announcement by abrogating all secret treaties signed with Japan, China and its former allies – treaties that the tsarist government imposed by violence and bribery to enslave the peoples of the East for the benefit of Russia's capitalists, landowners and generals. Simultaneously, the Soviet government invited the Chinese government to enter into negotiations on the annulment of the Treaty of 1896, the Peking Protocol of 1901, and all agreements with Japan from 1907 to 1916, that is to say on the return to the Chinese people of everything that was stolen from them by the tsarist government either on its own, or in concert with Japan and others. Negotiations on the issue continued until March 1918 when the Allies grabbed the Beijing government by the throat, showered the Beijing mandarins and the Chinese press with gold, and forced the Chinese government to cut all links with the Russian workers' and peasants' government. Without waiting for the return of the China Eastern Railway, Japan and the Allies seized it for themselves, invaded Siberia, and even forced Chinese troops to assist them in this criminal and unheard-of robbery. The Chinese people, workers and peasants were never told the truth about this attack on Manchuria and Siberia by the European, American, and Japanese predators.

Now we turn to the Chinese people once more in order to open their eyes.

The Soviet government renounces all the conquests made by the tsarist government whether in Manchuria or other areas of China. Let the people living in these areas decide for themselves which state they want to belong to and what form of government they want.

The Soviet government returns the East China Railway to the Chinese people without recompense, along with all the associated mountain, forest, gold mining and other concessions seized by the tsarist government, the [colonial] Korean government, or the robbers Horvath, Semenov, Kolchak and other Russian generals, merchants, and capitalists.

The Soviet government reaffirms for the third time that it will not accept indemnity payments from China due under agreements signed after the Boxer Uprising of 1900.

The Soviet government renounces all special privileges and treaty ports granted to Russian merchants on Chinese soil. No Russians, whether officials, priests or missionaries should dare to interfere in China's internal affairs, and if they commit crimes, they must be tried in a Chinese court.

In addition to these main points, the Soviet Government is ready to negotiate with the Chinese people, represented by the plenipotentiaries, on all other issues, so as to eliminate, once and for all, the injustices and acts of violence committed against China by former Russian governments in league with Japan and other allies.

The Soviet government is well aware that the Allies and Japan will do everything in their power to prevent the voice of Russian workers and peasants reaching the Chinese people, and that in order to return to the Chinese people all that has been stolen from them it will first be necessary to settle accounts with the predators presently sitting in Manchuria and Siberia. Therefore, it now sends this message to the Chinese people along with the Red Army, which is crossing the Urals to free the Siberian peasants and workers from the bandit Kolchak and his Japanese allies.

If the Chinese people want to become free like the Russian people and avoid becoming another Korea or India – the fate prepared for them by the Allies at Versailles – they must understand that their only reliable allies and brothers in the struggle for freedom are the Russian workers and peasants and their Red Army.

The Soviet government invites the Chinese people, represented by their government, to open a formal dialogue with us and send representatives to meet our army.

[Signed,]
Karakhan, Deputy People's Commissar for Foreign Affairs

Appendix B: The Far Eastern Republic Mission to China

The Bolsheviks sent their first diplomatic mission to Beijing, not in the name of Soviet Russia, but in that of the Far Eastern Republic, a short-lived, nominally independent, Siberian state spawned by civil war and foreign intervention. The FER was conceived by the Bolsheviks as a buffer state that would allow them to avoid open war with Japan and give their young revolutionary regime time and space to recover. By early 1920, the Red Army had defeated Admiral Kolchak, and the American intervention force in Siberia left soon afterwards. However, Japan still had 70,000 troops in Siberia and was transparently pursuing territorial ambitions under the pretext of an anti-Communist crusade. For Moscow, the new state would serve several purposes – not only to avoid war with Japan, but also to rally patriotic forces against the invaders, and to persuade the United States to pressure Japan into quitting Siberia.

The Americans had their own interests in the region and opposed Japan's expansionism. Furthermore, their leaders of their intervention force had been disgusted by the conduct of the Japanese military. The American commander in Siberia, General William S. Graves, had stuck to a narrow interpretation of his mission and detested Japan's brutal proxies Ataman Grigory Semyonov and Baron Ungern von Sternberg.[1]

---

1 Graves later told a congressional committee that Semyonov was responsible for the 'wiping out of whole villages [in a] deliberate campaign of murder, rape and pillage' that claimed the lives of 100,000 men, women, and children. Graves's senior officer, Colonel Charles H. Morrow, told the committee: 'Had it not been for the influence of

The Bolsheviks calculated that Japan would find it difficult to justify prolonging its Siberian campaign if its opponent was a democratic state. Therefore, the FER had neither soviets nor commissars but a parliament and a council of ministers. Its government was a coalition of Bolsheviks and moderate socialists. The Red Army in Siberia was rebadged as the People's Revolutionary Army. Trotsky put it succinctly: 'You want democracy, we'll give you democracy.'

The FER's delegation was kitted out with all the trappings of a bourgeois diplomatic mission. A large crowd saw them off as they left Kyakhta in a black Cadillac that had been confiscated from a French general. A troop of Cossack cavalry accompanied them to the Mongolian border, where they were met by Chinese cavalry. After diplomatic niceties in Urga,[2] the delegates drove their Cadillac across the Gobi Desert to Kalgan[3] and from there completed the journey to Beijing by rail. Once in the Chinese capital, they took rooms in the grand Peking Hotel until they were able to buy a suitable residence, since the Russian embassy was occupied by tsarist-era diplomats who claimed to represent the defunct provisional government.

Ignaty Yurin, a former Polish army officer, headed the mission.[4] His deputy was an old Bolshevik called Gromov, a factory worker who had spent years in exile in America. The mission's translator was twenty-one-year-old Marc Kazanin, who had grown up in Harbin and studied Chinese in Vladivostok. A cipher clerk and a treasurer who was a former Siberian partisan, brought the total to five.

None of them had any experience of diplomacy; they were revolutionaries improvising in fancy dress. They hired an English tailor to make them frock coats, top hats, and evening suits. Yurin stood firmly on ceremony, insisting on being treated as the representative of a state and refusing to present his credentials to anyone of lower rank than the Chinese foreign minister. He and his comrades kept up the appearance

---

another power [meaning Japan], we would have disarmed all of Semenoff's forces.' See Jamie Bisher, *White Terror: Cossack Warlords of the Trans-Siberian*, London: Frank Cass, 2005, 214; and 'New Bail Bond or Jail for Semenoff', *New York Times*, 13 April 1922.

2   Ulan Bator. Mongolia was at this time part of Chinese territory after a 1919 invasion ended eight years of independence under a Buddhist theocratic regime backed by tsarist Russia.

3   Now Zhangjiakou.

4   Yurin's real name was Dzevaltovsky.

of being independent of Moscow, even though all sides knew it to be a convenient fiction. Since Yurin was keeping himself in diplomatic purdah, the task of exploratory negotiations fell to Kazanin. Much of the mission's success was due to this remarkable young man. Wily Chinese officials tried to catch him out, but he proved more than equal to the task. Before long, the Chinese withdrew recognition from the old tsarist diplomats. It was an important first step.

The cultivation of relations with other foreign missions in Beijing's legation district was at least as important as efforts to gain diplomatic recognition from China. The fiercely anti-Bolshevik French were downright hostile, and the British were not much better. Surprisingly, the Japanese were cordial and punctilious. Most importantly, however, the Americans, the mission's main target, were the friendliest. They were characteristically very keen to discuss practical matters regarding trade and oil concessions, and President Wilson's envoy in China, Charles Crane, was a millionaire Slavophil who had business interests in Russia. He was soon on excellent terms with the delegation.

Another task was to win over public opinion. Kazanin found it easy to cultivate the Beijing press corps, as journalists eager for a story were only too keen to meet and interview the new arrivals. They happily relayed the FER, that is to say, by extension, the Soviet point of view to the public. They were also excellent sources of intelligence. Kazanin recalled that the 'thoroughbred' journalists of the *Times* and Reuters particularly enjoyed showing off their insider knowledge and were free with useful gossip.[5]

With China in chaos, some of the world's leading intellectuals arrived in Beijing to offer advice on how the country could be saved. Kazanin played tennis with John Dewey. He thought Dewey's protégé Hu Shi seemed mainly interested in obtaining a top government post, which he later did, as ambassador to the United States. But the FER envoys became great friends with Bertrand Russell and his mistress Dora Black. The unmarried couple created a minor scandal in Beijing – Russell had not yet obtained a divorce from his first wife. The revolutionary diplomats teased Dora about her liberal views, but she wept at the train station

---

5   Marc Kasanin (Kazanin), *China in the Twenties*, Moscow: Nauka Publishing House, 1973, 102–3.

when it was time to part.[6] Russell wrote later about his affection for Yurin, Kazanin, and their colleagues:

> I ought perhaps to confess that I have a bias in favour of the Far Eastern Republic, owing to my friendship for their diplomatic mission which was in Peking while I was there. I never met a more high-minded set of men in any country. And although they were communists, and knew the views that I had expressed on Russia, they showed me great kindness.[7]

The envoys also met the great scholar and social reformer, Liang Qichao, a hero of the 1898 reform movement. It turned out that Liang was knowledgeable about Russia, especially the reforms of Peter the Great, and was curious to know how the Soviets had managed to defeat the great power interventionists.[8]

When Crane left in 1921, Yurin arranged for him to travel home via Russia. Crane's affectionate farewell to the delegates of the FER at the railway station discomfited the British minister, whose face turned puce, 'resembling a rotten pear'. Crane's replacement, President Harding's man Schurman, was rather charmless, but by that time relations with the Americans were good enough for the mission to negotiate a concession with Sinclair Oil, pointedly located in an area on which the Japanese had designs.

Military success at home strengthened the standing of the mission. The Japanese tried to shore up their position by engineering a right-wing coup in Vladivostok in May 1921, but elsewhere their proxies lost ground. By the autumn, Semyonov had fled Russia and Ungern Sternberg was captured and executed after recklessly invading Mongolia. Relations with the Chinese improved markedly. Yurin was invited to meet Li Yuanhong, the once and future president of China, who had been the reluctant figurehead of the Xinhai Revolution in Wuhan. Official banquets and receptions followed where Yurin was addressed as 'your excellency'. Soon afterwards, they were invited to meet the prime

---

6   Ibid., 110–14.
7   Bertrand Russell, *The Problem of China*, London: George Allen & Unwin, 1966, 157.
8   Kasanin, *China in the Twenties*, 1922, 104–8.

minister, General Jin Yunpeng (according to Kazanin, 'a semi-literate upstart'). By the summer of 1921, the FER representatives were negotiating a trade deal with China. While it fell short of diplomatic relations, it was another significant milestone.

International affairs were dominated by preparations for the Washington Conference called by President Harding. Although it was ostensibly an arms control conference, the Americans used it to clip Japan's wings in the Far East and force Britain to abandon its alliance with Tokyo. The Japanese knew they could not sustain their position in Siberia in the face of American opposition, not least because Japan was heavily dependent on Wall Street loans. To appear reasonable, in August 1921, the Japanese opened negotiations with the FER in Dairen.[9]

At the talks, Yurin leaked suggestions that the FER might make concessions to Japan and might even go so far as to cede Northern Sakhalin. It was, according to Kazanin, a deliberate ploy to manipulate the Americans.[10] Schurman was alarmed and wrote to Secretary of State Charles Hughes suggesting that the FER be invited to send at least a commercial mission to Washington.[11] So it was that the FER's delegation to China achieved its greatest diplomatic coup: an invitation to the fringes of the Washington Conference.

The Far Eastern Republic was nearing the end of its usefulness. Its mission in Beijing was soon replaced in Beijing by a new delegation led by Alexander Paikes, who represented Soviet Russia in its own right. As Kazanin put it: 'The small tug had towed the large vessel into harbour.' But first, in Washington, its delegation created a sensation when it alleged, based on intercepted cables, that France was collaborating with Japan to transport Wrangel's defeated army from the Crimea to Vladivostok. It made a bad situation worse for the Japanese, who were already on the defensive. In the summer of 1922, they agreed to leave Siberia, completing their withdrawal that October. Moscow's diplomatic stratagem had worked. The FER was absorbed into Soviet Russia a few weeks later on 15 November, a month and a half before the foundation of the Soviet Union.

---

9   i.e., Dalian.

10   The threat of concessions to Japan seemed real enough to the Mensheviks and SRs. They resigned from the FER government in protest.

11   Paul Dukes, *The USA in the Making of the USSR: The Washington Conference, 1921–1922, and 'uninvited Russia*, London: Routledge, 2012, 95.

Although the FER was effectively a client state, it had some aspects
that differentiated it from Moscow. Its government was a coalition that
included Mensheviks and the Socialist Revolutionary Party (the SRs)
who had been pushed into the arms of the Bolsheviks by the Japanese
invasion and the brutality of the Whites. Chicherin warned the Politburo
that the state had some centrifugal tendencies.[12] Quite a few of the Far
Eastern Republic's officials regretted its passing. One of them was Yurin,
who argued for its continued existence in his report on the mission.
However, when Kazanin took Yurin's report to the Foreign Ministry, he
was told bluntly that the republic's fate was sealed.[13]

---

12 Ibid., 93.
13 Yurin later defected to Poland and died shortly afterwards. His family claimed
he was poisoned by Soviet agents.

Appendix C: The Decimation of the China Hands

This story would not be complete without relating what happened to the Soviet diplomats, advisors, and Comintern agents after their service in China in the 1920s.

Karakhan left China in 1926 and resumed his career in the foreign service. In 1937, while serving as the Soviet representative in Turkey, he was recalled to Moscow and executed the same year on unspecified charges. He was rehabilitated during the Khrushchev years.

Vilensky was head of the Society of Former Political Convicts and Exiles (OPK), which was formed in 1921 by former prisoners of the tsar from all revolutionary parties, including Anarchists, Social Revolutionaries, and Mensheviks, as well as Bolsheviks. Its main purpose was to record the history of the common struggle against tsarism in its journal, *Katorga i Ssylka* (*Hard Labour and Exile*), but it was also a welfare organisation that provided pensions and housing for revolutionary veterans. Although Bolshevik rule developed into a one-party state, the OPK remained a relatively free space where old revolutionaries could air contentious opinions. Vilensky seems to have managed the organisation well, but, when he declared for the Opposition in 1926, he was ousted and replaced by the shamelessly opportunist hack Yemelyan Yaroslavsky.[1]

---

1   Yaroslavsky, who years earlier had extravagantly praised Trotsky, threw a book at Trotsky's head while he was making a speech to the Central Committee in October 1927. See Victor Serge, *Memoirs of a Revolutionary*, New York: New York Review of Books, 2012, 262.

Vilensky was expelled from the party in 1927. Like many Oppositionists, he recanted but was arrested in 1936. He was sentenced to eight years and died in a labour camp on 2 July 1942.

Voitinsky was one of the few Soviet China hands from the 1920s to survive Stalin's terror. But he outlived the dictator by only a few months, dying on the operating table in June 1953. Although death by surgery was one of Stalin's methods of disposing of his victims, Voitinsky's death is not thought to have been suspicious. According to friends, he nevertheless spent his last years in constant fear of being arrested.[2]

Roy was recalled to Moscow in disgrace and made a scapegoat for the collapse of the United Front. While in Moscow for the ninth plenum of the Executive Committee of the Comintern in 1928, he feared he was about to be arrested. Mikhail Borodin helped him leave the country.[3] In 1929, he was expelled from the Comintern for opposing Stalin's 'Third Period' policy. He returned to India in the early 1930s and, after a failed attempt to form a left current inside the Congress Party, founded the Radical Democratic Party in 1940. In 1948, he retired from politics. In a book about China, he continued to criticise his friend Borodin as 'the preceptor of the policy which killed the Chinese Revolution':[4]

> Borodin distrusted Chiang Kai-shek. He also failed to see that the boldness of leading the revolutionary democratic masses in a frontal attack upon incipient military dictatorship was the only guarantee against the impending disaster. Instead of basing the fight for the overthrow of the would-be dictator upon the revolutionary mass movement, he sought to carry it on through the instrumentality of an opportunist combination of elements who were no less hostile to the revolution than Chiang Kai-shek.[5]

Henk Sneevliet opposed Borodin's military-bureaucratic version of his 'bloc within' tactic. It was one thing to work alongside KMT members involved in the labour and popular movements, but quite another to

2   Conversation with A. V. Pantsov, whose grandfather was a close friend of Voitinsky.

3   Dan Jacobs, *Borodin: Stalin's Man in China*, Cambridge, MA: Harvard University Press, 1981, 307.

4   M. N. Roy, *M. N. Roy's Memoirs*, Bombay: Allied Publishers, 1946, 565.

5   Ibid., 429.

lavish money, arms, and advisors on its militarist and conspiratorial leadership. After returning to the Netherlands, Sneevliet sided with the opposition to Stalin in 1926. In 1933, he signed a manifesto supporting Trotsky's call for a new International although, characteristically, he later quarrelled with Trotsky, and they parted ways in 1938. During the Second World War, Sneevliet was a leader of the Dutch resistance. Along with a group of young comrades, he was executed by the Nazis in 1942. They walked to their deaths hand in hand, singing the Internationale. He is honoured as a war hero in the Netherlands. In Amsterdam, a street and a metro station are named after him.

Adolph Joffe, who had been a revolutionary since his schooldays, had spent five years in exile under the tsar. He was the chairman of the Military Revolutionary Committee that organised the overthrow of the Provisional Government in October 1917. Ten years later, as a member of the Opposition, although gravely ill, he was refused permission to go abroad for treatment. He shot himself on 16 November 1927, four days after Trotsky was expelled from the party. Trotsky's eulogy at his funeral was the last time he was allowed to speak in public in the Soviet Union. Joffe's daughter Nadezhda continued to work for the Opposition for the rest of her life. She spent twenty years in a camp in Siberia, from 1937 to 1957.

For Stalin and Bukharin, the architects and defenders of the strategy of alliance with the KMT, the China debacle was an embarrassment to be forgotten as quickly as possible. When Borodin arrived back in Moscow, he was ordered to stay out of sight. He confided in Eugene Chen, 'I am on parole, for the most part due to you and Madame Sun. It is not convenient to sentence me to death now.'[6] Eventually, the Politburo decided that, although he must be kept away from political work because of 'major political mistakes of an opportunist character during his period in China', he could safely be allowed to work for TASS.[7]

Anna Louise Strong continued to haunt Borodin. In 1930, Borodin asked her to help set up the *Moscow News*, an English-language newspaper aimed at the many foreigners who fled the Great Depression to work

---

6   Chen Yuan-tsung, *Return to the Middle Kingdom*, New York: Union Square Press, 2008, 267.

7   Resolution of the Politburo, 23 May 1929, RGASPI, 17.3.741.5.

in the Soviet Union. Jack Chen and Millie Bennett from the *People's Tribune* also joined the staff. Borodin had promised an 'American type' newspaper, but censorship made that impossible, crippling the paper. Strong, who effectively ran the paper, threw tantrums and clashed repeatedly with its nominal editors. Borodin tried to calm her moods, but she was only mollified after her complaints earned her a meeting with Stalin. Strong left Moscow in 1937 but returned in late 1948, having written a book praising Mao's guerrilla warfare strategy and attacking dogmatists (that is to say, the Moscow loyalist Wang Ming). It was very bad timing; Stalin was battling Titoism, and anything that smacked of independence in the world Communist movement was anathema. Both Strong and Borodin were arrested, and while Strong was deported to Poland after a few days, Borodin was not so lucky. It had become 'convenient' to dispose of him, and he disappeared into the gulag, where he died on 29 May 1951. He was rehabilitated in a 1964 article that described him as a revolutionary Leninist.

After returning from China, Vasily Blyukher was appointed commander of the Red Army in the Soviet Far East. In 1929, he crushed the forces of the 'Young Marshall' Zhang Xueliang in a brief war after the latter seized control of the China Eastern Railway. In 1935, he was promoted to marshall of the Soviet Union. He was listed as a member of the military tribunal that condemned Marshall Tukhachevsky to death in 1937, but there is some doubt that he actually took part. He realised that his turn could not be far away and began drinking heavily. On 1 August 1938, while battling a Japanese incursion from Manzhouguo, he received a chilling phone call that exemplified the crudity and racism of the Soviet dictator.

STALIN: Tell me, Blyukher, why is the order of the defense commissar for aerial bombardment of all our territory occupied by the Japanese including the Zaozernaya Heights not being implemented?

BLYUKHER: Reporting. The air force is ready to take off. The takeoff was delayed by adverse meteorological circumstances. This very minute [air force commander Pavel] Rychagov has ordered planes into the air to attack, not taking weather into account . . . but I fear that we will hit our own units and Korean settlements with this bombing.

STALIN: Tell me honestly, comrade Blyukher, do you wish to fight with the Japanese for real? . . . What do the Koreans matter to you, if the Japanese are hitting batches of our people? What does a little cloudiness mean for Bolshevik aviation if it is really going to defend the honor of its Motherland? I await an answer.

BLYUKHER: The air force has been ordered into the air . . . Your directives are being implemented and will be implemented with Bolshevik precision.[8]

Less than three months later, on 22 October, while Blyukher and his wife were staying at Voroshilov's dacha, they were seized by NKVD agents. Blyukher was, absurdly, accused of spying for Japan since 1922. Specifically, he was accused of facilitating the defection of the NKVD general Lyushkov to the Japanese.[9] He was either shot or, according to some accounts, beaten to death while being interrogated.

Andrei Bubnov, who negotiated the settlement with Chiang Kai-shek after the March 1926 coup, joined the RSDLP in 1903 and was arrested thirteen times by the tsarist regime. In October 1917, he was one of seven members elected to the first-ever Bolshevik Politburo. He was arrested in October 1937 and shot in August 1938. The fact that he had signed the founding document of the Left Opposition in 1923 likely helped seal his fate.

Solomon Lozovsky, a member of the RSDLP since 1901, had been, along with Trotsky and Joffe, a member of the Mezhraiontsy (Inter-district organisation) that fused with the Bolsheviks at the end of July 1917. Though briefly expelled from the party after the October Revolution, he remained a leadership loyalist after being readmitted. In 1939, he was appointed deputy people's commissar for foreign affairs. During World War II, he was vice-chairman of the Soviet Information Bureau and was popular among foreign correspondents as an accomplished and affable press spokesman. He was arrested in 1949 and executed in 1952 after the trial of the Jewish Anti-Fascist Committee.

What of the less well-known, rank-and-file advisors to the KMT?

---

8 Quoted in Dmitri Volkogonov, *Stalin: Triumph and Tragedy*, London: Weidenfeld & Nicholson, 1991, 327–8.

9 Alvin D Coox, 'L'Affaire Lyushkov: Anatomy of a Defector', *Soviet Studies*, Vol. 19, No. 3 (1968), 405–20.

Forty years later, as the Khrushchev thaw came to an end, Vera Vishnyakova, who had translated for Soviet military officers, published a memoir containing illuminating and touching portraits of her colleagues. Vishnyakova was still studying Chinese when she began work as a translator for Soviet military advisors, first in Kalgan and then in Canton. It was the fulfilment of a dream for Vera, who was in love with all things Chinese. Though she was too young to have taken part in the events of 1917, she was a child of the revolution. She adopted a revolutionary style, cutting her hair short and wearing a Lenin-style cap.

To avoid accusations of political interference, rank-and-file advisors were under orders not to fraternise with the Chinese. To Vishnyakova's regret, she did not even get to know the members of the strike committee, who passed by her office almost every day on their way to consult with Borodin. She did, however, have one brush with greatness. A friendly but mysterious Vietnamese man called Li gave her language lessons. She knew only that he was on the run from the French. Years later, when she met him again in Moscow, she discovered that her teacher had been Ho Chi Minh.

Vishnyakova's boss in Canton was Mira Sakhnovskaya, a civil war heroine and one of only two women among the military advisors. Born in Vilnius, but for the revolution she would have followed her parents into teaching. Instead, she went to work for *Pravda* and enlisted in the Red Army. She worked as a nurse on a propaganda train commanded by Bubnov, took part in the defence of revolutionary Petrograd against the German army in March 1918, and subsequently fought with distinction on several civil war fronts. After the civil war, she became the first woman to graduate from the Frunze Military Academy. She was outwardly austere, a tall, thin chain smoker, but she doted on her adopted daughter and a baby son who was born in Canton. Her husband, Raphael Sakhnovsky, was also a military advisor. In 1917, while a private in the tsarist army, he was elected to the soviet in the city of Saratov and became a leader of the city's Red Guards. He joined the Red Army and fought throughout the Civil War. Like Mira, he graduated from the Frunze Academy.

The other female military advisor was Liza Goreva, who had joined the Red Army while in her teens and fought throughout the civil war. Her husband, Vladimir Gorev, was also a military advisor. The couple brought their young son to China. Vladimir Gorev was a serious student of Chinese who devised a method of classifying Chinese characters that was used in several Russian-Chinese dictionaries. Though he had been an anarchist while a student, he joined the Red Army in 1918. He was subsequently captured by the Whites but escaped. In China, Gorev was chief advisor to the KMT generals Tang Shengzhi and Zhang Fakui. He established a counter-intelligence organisation, fought with the Ironsides – the Fourth Division of the National Revolutionary Army – and was awarded the Order of the Red Banner. After returning to Russia, he taught at the Communist University of the Toilers of the East and wrote a book on the Chinese army. He was promoted to brigadier general and was awarded the Order of Lenin for organising the defence of Madrid during the Spanish Civil War.[10]

After returning from China, Mira Sakhnovskaya resumed her intelligence work, but in 1928 she was expelled from the party for being an 'ardent Trotskyist' and sentenced to three years exile in Siberia. Raphael Sakhnovsky, now chief of staff of an infantry division, was accused of being an organiser for the opposition and exiled. After Mira's sentence was rescinded the following year, her party membership was restored, and she was promoted to major general, making her the first female general of modern times. Raphael, however, remained in Siberia working on railway projects. Mira was re-arrested in March 1937 and executed on 31 July. Raphael was executed a few months later. The other female military advisor, Liza Goreva, was shot the same year, along with her husband, General Vladimir Gorev.[11]

Soviet Sinology was decimated by the purges. Vera Vishnyakova lists ten colleagues who served with her in China who were later executed: V. I. Melnikov, T. I. Vladimirova, F. Bokanenko, V. Voyloshikov, N. M. Yakovlev, B. S. Perlin, Ye. S. Yolk, E. M. Abramson, V. A. Vasilev, and Novoselov.

It is with sadness that I write most of these names remembering the terrible years of Stalinist repression. How many young and talented

---

10   C. Martin Wilbur and Julie Lien-ying How, *Missionaries of Revolution: Soviet Advisers and Nationalist China, 1920–1927*, Cambridge, MA, Harvard University Press, 1989, 432.
11   Ibid.

Chinese specialists perished, men who were loyal to the party and
their work, and who laid the foundation of Soviet Sinology.[12]

Z. S. Dubasova and P. Ye. Skachkov spent years in exile. Marc Kazanin,
translator for the FER diplomatic mission who returned to China to
work for Blyukher, was arrested in 1937 and spent eighteen years in
camps. While in China, Vera married the military advisor Vladimir
Akimov, who also spent many years in camps accused of fictitious
offences.

In their encyclopaedic study of the Soviet mission in China, C. Martin
Wilbur and Julie Lien-ying How were able to determine the fate of 117
of the advisors. Of these, at least forty-nine and perhaps eight more were
executed or died in prison, and a further seven were exiled for long periods. Among the military advisors who were executed or died in prison
were A. I. Gekker, A. I. Egorov, A. Ya. Lapin, R. V. Longva, N. V.
Kuibyshev, V. K. Primakov, and V. M. Putna.[13]

The playwright Sergei Tretyakov, who so spiritedly and light-heart-
edly entertained the staff and visitors to the Soviet embassy in Beijing,
was executed in 1937, perhaps because he had dedicated his first play,
The World Turned Upside Down, to Trotsky.

    12   Vera Vishnyakova-Akimova, *Two Years in Revolutionary China*, Cambridge,
MA: Harvard University Press, 1971, 31.
    13   Wilbur and How, *Missionaries of Revolution*, 425–430.

Appendix D: Biographical Notes

Addams, Jane 1860–1935
United States social reformer, campaigner for women's rights and anti-imperialist. A pioneer social worker, Adams founded Hull House in Chicago in 1889. She won the 1931 Nobel Peace Prize.

Aung San 1915–1947
Burmese anti-imperialist and revolutionary; father of Suu Kyi. During World War II he accepted Japanese aid but later switched sides. In negotiations with Britain's Labour government he secured Burmese independence. His party won the country's pre-independence general election, but he was assassinated along with most of his cabinet before the formal handover of power.

Barbusse, Henri 1873–1935
French novelist. Barbusse won the Croix de Guerre during World War I but wrote the anti-war novel *Le Feu* based on his experience at the front. He moved to Moscow in 1918 and joined the Bolsheviks. A Stalin loyalist, his uncritical biography of the Soviet leader was published in 1936.

Barrett, David 1892–1977
Long-serving military attaché in China. A fluent Chinese speaker, Barrett was the first commander of the United States Army Observation Group, aka the Dixie Mission, in Yan'an. Opponents of military cooperation with the Communists blocked his promotion to general.

Berkman, Alexander 1870–1936
Russian anarchist, lover of Emma Goldman. Berkman was jailed in the
United States for attempting to assassinate a factory manager during a
lockout. Deported with Goldman to Russia in 1917, he became disillusioned with the Bolsheviks. He committed suicide while suffering from
cancer.

Berzin, Yan Karlovich 1889–1938
Latvian Communist, guerrilla leader, and Cheka agent. Berzin was head
of the GRU (Soviet military intelligence) until 1935. He was a military
advisor in Spain from 1936 but was recalled in 1937, accused of
Trotskyism, and executed the following year.

Bo Gu (Qin Bangxian) 1907–1946
Bo Gu joined the CCP in 1925. The following year, aged nineteen, he was
sent to study at Sun Yat-sen University in Moscow where, with Wang
Ming and others, he formed an orthodox faction under the influence of
Pavel Mif. He returned to China in 1930 and was CCP general secretary
from 1931 until he was ousted by Mao Zedong in 1935. He died in a plane
crash, along with other senior CCP leaders including Ye Ting, Deng Fa,
and Wang Ruofei, while returning from negotiations with the KMT.

Browder, Earl 1891–1973
A syndicalist in his youth, Browder was jailed in 1917 for opposing the
world war. He represented Kansas miners at the 1920 founding conference of the RILU in Moscow, headed the PPTUS in Shanghai from 1928
to 1929 and was general secretary of the CPUSA from 1930 to 1945. In
1944, during the wartime coalition, he sought to transform the CPUSA
into a Communist Political Association – in effect a left-wing pressure
group within the Democratic Party. He was expelled from the CPUSA
in 1946 for 'liquidationism'.

Chattopadhyaya, Virendranath (Chatto) 1880–1937
Indian revolutionary, common-law husband of Agnes Smedley. During
World War I, he established the Berlin Committee to channel German
aid to Indian opponents of British rule. After Germany's defeat, he turned
to Soviet Russia for aid, joined the KPD, and was general secretary of the
League against Imperialism. He was executed on Stalin's orders.

Chen Duxiu 1879–1942
Founder and first leader of the CCP; one of China's leading intellectuals and leading light of the New Culture and May Fourth Movements. He was scapegoated for the defeat of 1927 and expelled from the party in 1929. He led the Chinese Trotskyists from 1929 until he was arrested by the KMT in 1932. Freed by an amnesty following the Japanese invasion in 1937, in his last writings he began to question Leninism.

Chen, Eugene 1878–1944
An overseas Chinese born in Trinidad. Chen trained as a lawyer in London where he met Sun Yat-sen. He moved to China after the Xinhai Revolution and set up the nationalist *Peking Gazette*, becoming a foreign minister of the KMT governments in Canton and Wuhan. After the British Concession in Wuhan was occupied by nationalist crowds in 1927, he negotiated the Chen–O'Malley agreement, a milestone in China's recovery of territories from the imperialists. Following a period in exile in the Soviet Union, he reconciled with Chiang Kai-shek but supported the 1933–34 Fujian rebellion. While in exile in Hong Kong, he was captured by the Japanese but refused to collaborate.

Chen Jiongming 1878–1933
Nicknamed the 'anarchist general', Chen was elected to the Guangdong Provincial Assembly in 1909, took part in a failed revolt in 1910, and was appointed governor of Guangdong Province after the Xinhai Revolution. Although initially allied with Sun Yat-sen, he opposed Sun's plan to unify China by force and expelled him from Canton in a 1922 coup. After Sun regained control in 1923, Soviet-backed KMT forces wiped out Chen's army and he took refuge in Hong Kong.

Deng Yanda 1895–1931
NRA officer during the Northern Expedition; opposed Chiang Kai-shek in 1927. After a period in exile, he formed a third party (now a legal entity in the PRC called the Chinese Peasants' and Workers' Democratic Party) to occupy the political space between the CCP and the KMT. He was arrested by the imperialist police in Shanghai and handed over to Chiang Kai-shek, who had him shot.

Ding Ling (Jiang Bingzhi) 1904–1986
Celebrated Chinese author. The KMT executed her first husband, the poet Hu Yepin, and held her under house arrest from 1933 to 1936. In 1942, during Mao's Rectification Campaign in Yan'an, Ding was forced to apologise for a feminist essay that criticised the party. She was denounced during the Anti-Rightist campaign and jailed during the Cultural Revolution.

Feng Yuxiang 1882–1948
Nicknamed the 'Christian general', Feng Yuxiang was a notorious turn-coat. While an officer in the Qing Army, he supported the Xinhai Revolution. After betraying Wu Peifu in the Second Zhili-Fengtian War, he accepted Soviet aid but backed Chiang Kai-shek against the Communists in 1927. He later broke with Chiang and was on a ship to the Soviet Union when he died in a fire.

Goldman, Emma 1869–1940
Russian-American anarchist thinker and activist. Goldman was jailed in the United States for opposing the draft in World War I, then deported to Russia. She supported the Bolshevik Revolution until she became disillusioned by the suppression of the Kronstadt revolt. In Barcelona during the Spanish Civil War, she edited the CNT-FAI Bulletin.

Guo Moruo 1892–1978
Writer and archaeologist who did important work on the so-called oracle bones. Guo was educated in Japan and lived there for much of his life. He joined the CCP in 1927 but returned to Japan after Chiang Kai-shek's crackdown. He was propaganda chief of the KMT govern-ment during the Second United Front. In his later years, Guo was noto-rious for his slavish devotion to Mao Zedong. He was also criticised for his treatment of the women in his life.

Hatem, George (Ma Haide) 1910–1988
Lebanese American physician. Hatem set up a practice in Shanghai and was recruited to the Communist cause by Agnes Smedley. In 1936, he accompanied Edgar Snow to the CCP's base in Northwest China and thereafter remained loyal to the CCP. He was credited with eradicating leprosy and syphilis in the PRC.

He Zizhen 1910–1984
Guerrilla fighter, Mao's Zedong's third wife and companion on the Long March; lived in the Soviet Union from 1937 to 1947 after separating from Mao.

Hinton, Bill 1919–2004
Elder brother of Joan Hinton; American agriculturalist; author of *Fanshen*, an account of land reform in a Chinese village.

Hu Feng 1902–1985
Member of the League of Left Wing Writers and a close friend and associate of Lu Xun. Hu opposed Mao Zedong's policy of dragooning literature into serving the needs of the party. In 1955, he was accused of leading a 'counter-revolutionary clique' and jailed until 1979.

Hu Hanmin 1879–1936
Close associate of Sun Yat-sen, founder member of both the Tongmenghui and the KMT. Seen as a rightist, Hu was suspected of ordering the 1925 assassination of the prominent KMT leftist Liao Zhongkai. Chiang Kai-shek arrested him and engineered his removal to the Soviet Union, where he served as KMT representative. After returning to China, Hu opposed Chiang from his power base in southern China.

Hu Shi 1891–1962
Liberal intellectual and language reformer; one of the leaders of the New Culture and May Fourth movements; Republic of China ambassador to the United States 1938–42. Hu Shi moved to New York in 1949 and to Taiwan in 1958.

Hurley, Patrick J. 1883–1963
United States brigadier general; decorated for bravery in World War I; secretary of war, 1929–33; presidential envoy to China, 1944; ambassador to China, 1944–45. Hurley was born in Ireland and detested the British Empire. He spent time with the Choctaw Nation. A heavy drinker, he was prone to diplomatic blunders for which he blamed others. After World War II, he supported Senator Joseph McCarthy's witch hunt for Communists in the State Department.

Katayama Sen 1859–1933
Pioneer of the Japanese labour movement; founder member of the Japanese Communist Party. After being arrested for leading a tram workers' strike in 1912, he spent most of the rest of his life in exile, first in the United States and later in the Soviet Union.

Koo, Wellington (Gu Weijun) 1888–1985
Diplomat; member of Chinese delegation to the Paris Peace Conference and Chinese representative at the League of Nations; ambassador to France and Britain and judge at the International Court of Justice. In 1926–27, he briefly served as president of the Republic of China.

Kopp, Georges 1902–1951
Belgian-Russian engineer; George Orwell's commander in the POUM militia. Kopp was arrested and tortured by the Stalinists in 1937. He served in the French Foreign Legion in World War II.

Landau, Katia (Julia Lipschutz) 1905–1984
Austrian Communist; POUM militant during the Spanish Civil War; wife of Kurt Landau. Jailed by Stalinists in Barcelona, she went on a hunger strike when she heard of her husband's disappearance. She campaigned until her death to find out what happened to him.

Landau, Kurt 1903–1937
Austrian Communist. Landau joined the party in 1921, becoming a district chairman in Vienna, but was expelled in 1927. Worked for the Left Opposition in Paris and, in 1936, joined the POUM in Barcelona. He was abducted and murdered by the Stalinist secret police.

Li Dazhao 1889–1927
One of the leaders of the New Culture and May Fourth movements; co-founder of the CCP along with Chen Duxiu. Li was chief librarian and later professor of politics at Peking University. He was lynched by warlord troops who stormed the Soviet embassy where he had been hiding.

Li Lisan 1899–1967
One of the CCP's most successful labour organisers in its early years. Li was elected to the Politburo in 1926, argued for the 1927 Nanchang

Uprising, and led the disastrous Changsha rising in 1930. He was made a scapegoat for the failure of Stalin's ultra-left line, and Pavel Mif engineered his removal from the leadership. During the Cultural Revolution, he was accused of being a Soviet spy and tortured by Red Guards.

Li Jishen 1885–1959
NRA general; member of the KMT CEC; supported Chiang Kai-shek's purge of Communists in 1927 but took part in the 1933–34 revolt against Chiang as chairman of the Fujian People's Government. Li reconciled with Chiang during the anti-Japanese War but set up the Revolutionary Committee of the KMT in 1948 and was later appointed vice-chairman of the PRC National People's Congress.

Liao Zhongkai 1877–1925
Chinese revolutionary; born and educated in the United States; joined the Tongmenghui while studying in Japan. A member of the KMT CEC from 1924, Liao was a strong supporter of Mikhail Borodin and the Soviet-KMT alliance. He was assassinated while on his way to a CEC meeting.

Lominadze, Vissarion 1897–1935
Georgian Bolshevik; first secretary of the Georgian Communist Party, 1922–24. Sent to China in 1927 to implement Stalin's 'left turn', he organised the Canton Commune uprising together with Heinz Neumann. In the early 1930s, he criticised the excesses of forced collectivisation in the Soviet Union and contacted the Trotskyist opposition. Facing arrest, he committed suicide.

Lu Xun (Zhou Shuren, Zhou Zhangshou) 1881–1936
China's most celebrated twentieth-century author. Lu Xun was a founder of the League of Left Wing Writers. Although claimed as a loyalist by the CCP, he never joined the party and remained on friendly terms with oppositionists.

Mann, Tom 1856–1941
British trade union leader, socialist, and internationalist; member of the Social Democratic Federation. Mann Quit the SDF because of its support for World War I. A founder member of the Communist Party of

Great Britain, he visited China in 1927 as part of a Comintern delegation with Earl Browder and Jacques Doriot. In 1933, defying the official Comintern line on Chen Duxiu, who had been expelled from the CCP, Mann supported a campaign to free Chen from a KMT prison.

Mif, Pavel (Mikhail Fortus) 1901–1939
Succeeded Karl Radek as rector of Sun Yat-sen University and carried out a purge of Trotskyists among its Chinese students. His protégés took over the leadership of the CCP in 1931. Despite his zealous pursuit of oppositionists, he was arrested and executed.

Münzenberg, Willi 1889–1940
German Communist; leader of the Young Communist International in 1919; founder of Workers' International Relief and the League against Imperialism. Münzenberg was a propaganda genius who built a media empire and led major international campaigns. After falling foul of Stalin, he left the Comintern. He was arrested in the south of France in 1940 but escaped. Months later his body was discovered in a forest. It is unclear whether he was murdered or committed suicide.

Neumann, Heinz 1902–1937
Joined the KPD in 1920; by 1922 he was editor of *Die Rote Fahne*. A long-time supporter of Stalin, during a six-month spell in China in 1927 he helped organise the disastrous Canton Commune. In Germany, he initially supported the KPD's ultra-left line of concentrating fire on the SPD but, having understood the Nazi danger, changed his mind and was purged from the leadership. Deported from Switzerland to the Soviet Union in 1934, he was shot during the Great Purge.

Nie Rongzhen 1899–1992
One of the ten marshalls of the PLA. Nie was recruited to the CCP in 1923 by Zhou Enlai while in Belgium and France on a work-study programme. A leading military commander during the anti-Japanese war and civil war, Nie later headed the PRC nuclear weapons programme.

Piatnitsky, Osip 1882–1938
Joined the RSDLP while in his teens; sided with Lenin at the 1903 London Congress. Assigned to Comintern work in 1921, Piatnitsky

became head of its International Liaison Department (OMS). He was executed for speaking out against Stalin's purges.

Pritt, Denis Nowell 1887–1972
Barrister and Labour member of Parliament. In 1932, acting for Ho Chi Minh in Hong Kong, Pritt foiled a French extradition request. He was defence lawyer for Kenyan anti-colonial leaders, including Jomo Kenyatta. Pritt was a notorious apologist for the Moscow Trials and was awarded the Stalin Peace Prize in 1954.

Semyonov, Grigory 1890–1946
Cossack warlord notorious for excesses while fighting for the Whites during the Russian Civil War. Indicted for war crimes in the United States but acquitted, he worked for Emperor Puyi in the Japanese puppet state of Manzhouguo. He was captured and hanged after the Soviets invaded Manchuria.

Slutsky, Abram 1898–1938
Volunteered for the tsarist army during World War I; joined the Bolsheviks in 1917. Slutsky joined the Cheka and later headed the international department of the NKVD. An enthusiastic pursuer of oppositionists, it is not clear whether he died of natural causes or was poisoned.

Song Qingling (Rosamund Soong Ching-ling) 1893–1981
Song defied her father, Christian businessman Charlie Soong, to marry Sun Yat-sen, who was twenty-six years older than her. As Sun's widow, she was a leading figure in the Left KMT. She spent two years in exile in the Soviet Union following Chiang Kai-shek's 1927 coup. After returning, she helped organise Comintern operations in China. She later held a series of high-ranking honorific posts in the PRC, including head of state. Her sister Song Meiling married Chiang Kai-shek; another sister, Song Ailing, married the financier H. H. Kung. Her brother T. V. Soong (Song Ziwen) served as finance minister and foreign minister under Chiang.

Sorge, Richard 1895–1944
German Communist, Comintern agent, Red Army colonel. Sorge was recruited to the GRU (Soviet military intelligence) by Berzin. From

1930 to 1933, Sorge was assigned to work in China. Later, posing as a Nazi-sympathising journalist in Japan, Sorge infiltrated the German embassy and informed the Soviet Union of Hitler's 1941 invasion plan, but Stalin dismissed his warnings. Sorge was arrested in Tokyo later that year and hanged in 1944.

Soria, Georges 1914–1991
French journalist and playwright; author of *Trotskyism in the Service of Franco: Facts and Documents on the Activities of POUM*, a compendium of NKVD forgeries published by Lawrence & Wishart in 1938.

Stilwell, Joseph 1883–1946
Commander of US forces in the China-Burma-India theatre, 1942–44. Stilwell regarded Chiang Kai-shek as incompetent and clashed repeatedly with him and his strongest supporter in the US military, Air Force general Claire Chennault. Chiang engineered Stilwell's removal in 1944. Although he held robust right-wing views, Stilwell was vilified by the so-called China lobby as one of those responsible for the 'loss of China' because he favoured cooperation with the Eighth Route Army against Japan.

Sun Chuanfang 1885–1935
Warlord based in Eastern China; leader of the so-called League of Five Provinces. Sun fought against the Northern Expedition but fled in 1927 after a Communist-led uprising in Shanghai. He was assassinated by the daughter of a man whose head he had displayed on a spike.

Sun Fo 1891–1973
Sun Yat-sen's son from his first marriage. Sun was a long-serving member of the KMT CEC and held ministerial posts in KMT governments. In 1937, in negotiations with Stalin, he secured Soviet military aid for the war against Japan. He left China after the civil war because of differences with Chiang Kai-shek but returned to Taiwan in 1965.

Sun Yat-sen (Sun Yixian, Sun Zhongshan; born Sun Deming) 1866–1925
Born in Guangdong; attended secondary school in Hawaii; qualified as a doctor and became a Christian after returning to China. Sun adopted revolutionary and pan-Asianist ideas and organised several failed uprisings. He became famous after being kidnapped by the Qing dynasty

legation in London in 1896. He established the Tongmenghui, forerunner of the KMT, in Japan in 1905. During the 1911 Revolution, he was named provisional president of the Republic but handed the presidency to Yuan Shikai. A leader of southern governments based in Canton, in 1923 he signed a cooperation agreement with the Soviet Union.

Suzuki Bunji 1885–1946
Japanese Christian reformer and trade union leader. A moderate who admired Samuel Gompers, he was a founder of the centre-left Social Democratic Party.

Tang Shengzhi 1889–1970
KMT general and supporter of Chiang Kai-shek; commander of the Eighth Army in the Northern Expedition. In 1937 he was commander of the Nanjing garrison when the city was besieged by the Japanese. He was blamed for the disorderly retreat and the subsequent massacre and retired from active service. After the civil war he remained in the PRC.

Trepper, Leopold 1904–1982
Communist and Red Army agent, head of the 'Red Orchestra' spy ring; arrested by the Gestapo in 1942 but escaped. Jailed for ten years by the Soviets after World War II, he returned to his native Poland but emigrated to Israel in 1974.

Waley, Arthur 1889–1966
British Sinologist and aesthete famous for his translations of classical Chinese novels and poetry, most notably *Monkey*, a partial rendering of the classic novel *Journey to the West*. Although Waley sympathised with Chinese progressives, he never went to China, fearing a visit would tarnish his idealised view of the country's past.

Wang Jingwei 1883–1944
Joined the Tongmenghui in 1905 while a student in Japan; jailed in 1910 for attempting to assassinate the Qing dynasty prince regent, Zaifeng. A leader of the Left KMT during the First United Front, he later reconciled with Chiang Kai-shek. He defected to Japan in 1938 and in 1940 was made head of state of a puppet regime in Nanjing. He died of illness in Japan.

Wang Ming (Chen Shaoyu) 1904–1974
Joined the CCP Youth League in 1924; studied at Sun Yat-sen University
from 1925 to 1929; protégé of Pavel Mif and an enthusiastic persecutor
of oppositionists. His group, the so-called Twenty-Eight Bolsheviks,
predominated in the CCP until he was ousted after the Long March.
From 1956 until his death, he lived in the Soviet Union, where he wrote
regular anti-CCP polemics.

Werner, Ruth (Ursula Kuczynski) 1907–2000
German Communist and Soviet spy known as Agent Sonya; in China
from 1930 to 1935, where she worked with Richard Sorge. She held the
rank of colonel in the Soviet Army.

Wu Peifu 1874–1939
Qing dynasty army officer; a leader of the Zhili clique of warlords after
Yuan Shikai's death; viewed favourably by the CCP until he massacred
railway workers during a 1923 strike. Supported by the British and
Americans thereafter, Wu was defeated by Zhang Zuolin in the Second
Zhili-Fengtian War and by the NRA during the Northern Expedition.
He died of complications following a dental operation.

Xu Kexiang 1889–1964
Joined the Tongmenghui in his youth; took part in the Xinhai Revolution.
Xu was an NRA general during the Northern Expedition. On 21 May
1927, he carried out an anti-Communist coup in Changsha. He fled to
Macau in 1949 and later to Taiwan.

Xue Yue 1896–1998
A prominent NRA commander during the Northern Expedition, Xue
offered to arrest Chiang Kai-shek on the eve of the 1927 Shanghai
Massacre but later took part in the suppression of the Canton Commune.
He commanded the Nineteenth Army during the 1937 Battle of
Shanghai. Left to defend Hainan Island at the end of the Civil War, he
fled to Taiwan.

Yang Hucheng 1893–1949
Veteran of the Xinhai Revolution. While commander of the KMT
Northwest Army, together with Zhang Xueliang, Yang organised the

1936 coup against Chiang Kai-shek in Xi'an. In September 1949, Chiang had Yang killed, along with his wife and children.

Yuan Shikai 1859–1916
During the Xinhai Revolution, Yuan commanded Qing dynasty forces, but after defeating the rebels he changed sides, forced the infant emperor to abdicate and became the first president of the Republic of China. After the KMT won national elections in 1913, he ordered the assassination of its leader Song Jiaoren. Yuan died under unclear circumstances following a failed attempt to proclaim himself emperor in 1915.

Zhang Fakui 1896–1980
Commander of the Ironsides – the elite Fourth Army corps of the NRA – during the Northern Expedition. Considered a supporter of the Left KMT, he nevertheless suppressed the Nanchang Uprising and the Canton Commune. An army commander in the war against Japan and the Civil War, he retired in Hong Kong.

Zhang Guotao 1897–1979
A student leader during the May Fourth Movement, Zhang led the party's work in the labour movement before becoming Mao Zedong's deputy in the Chinese Soviet government in 1931. During the Long March, he commanded the Fourth Red Army but lost most of his troops during operations in Sichuan. He defected to the KMT in 1938 and eventually moved to Canada, where he converted to Christianity.

Zhang Qiubai 1887–1928
Minor KMT politician who attended the Congress of the Toilers of the Far East as Sun Yat sen's representative. While serving as construction minister in the Nanjing government, he was assassinated, supposedly by the notorious Axe Gang.

Zhang Xueliang 1901–2001
Nicknamed the 'young marshall', Zhang Xueliang was the son of Zhang Zuolin and inherited his father's position as ruler of Manchuria. In 1936, while in Xi'an under orders to eliminate Communist forces in northwest China, he staged a coup against Chiang Kai-shek to force him to agree to a truce with the Communists and prioritise the fight against Japan.

After the dispute was settled, Zhang was kept under house arrest in mainland China and Taiwan until Chiang Kai-shek died in 1975. He moved to Hawaii in 1995.

Zhang Zuolin 1875–1928

Nicknamed the 'old marshall', Zhang Zuolin ruled Manchuria for two decades with Japanese support. His Fengtian clique of warlords took control of Beijing in 1924 after defeating the Zhili clique in a short war. In 1927, his troops stormed the Soviet embassy and lynched Li Dazhao, who had been sheltering there. In 1928, Zhang was assassinated by Japanese officers who blamed him for abandoning Beijing as Chiang Kai-shek's troops moved north.

Zheng Chaolin 1901–1998

Chinese revolutionary, poet, translator, and historian; studied in Moscow at the University of the Toilers of the East; leading CCP propagandist and editor of the party journal *Bolshevik*. Zheng joined the Trotskyists in 1931 but was jailed by the KMT until 1937. He was jailed again in 1952, on Mao's orders, along with all Chinese Trotskyists. He refused to recant and was not released until 1979.

Zhu De 1886–1976

PLA commander-in-chief from 1949; studied at Kunming Military School with future Yunnan military governor Cai E; supported Cai E in the Xinhai Revolution and the 1915–16 National Protection War that unseated Yuan Shikai; recruited to the CCP in Germany by Zhou Enlai. Zhu joined Mao Zedong in Jiangxi as commander of the armed forces of the Chinese Soviet Republic. Commander of the Eighth Route Army during the war against Japan, he generally supported Mao but was demoted to a regional command for six years during the Cultural Revolution.

Zhu Xuefan 1905–1996

Chinese trade unionist, member of the KMT and the CCP; PRC minister of post and telegraph; later vice-chair of the Standing Committee of the PRC.

Chinese Transliteration and Glossary

I have used Pinyin spelling throughout, except, for reasons of familiarity, in the cases of Chiang Kai-shek, Sun Yat-sen and the Kuomintang (KMT). Describing the Soviet-backed KMT government based there, I have referred to the city of Guangzhou as Canton, as was common in English-language writings of the time.

ACFTU	All-China Federation of Trade Unions
AFL	American Federation of Labor
Border-region governments	Communist local governments recognised by the ROC during the War of Resistance against Japan
Canton	historical name in English for the city of Guangzhou
CCC	China Campaign Committee
CCP	Chinese Communist Party (in quotations sometimes CPC)
CEC	Central Executive Committee (of the Kuomintang)
Cheka	Extraordinary Commission – the name of the Soviet secret police from 1917–22
Comintern	Communist International
CPGB	Communist Party of Great Britain
CPPCC	Chinese People's Political Consultative Conference

CPUSA	Communist Party of the United States of America
ECCI	Executive Committee of the Communist International
Eighth Route Army	Communist forces in North China after incorporation into the NRA in 1937, following the outbreak of the War of Resistance against Japan. Also known as the Eighteenth Route Army.
FEB	Far Eastern Bureau of the Comintern
FER	Far Eastern Republic
First United Front	Alliance between the CCP and the KMT, 1924–27
FOCP	Friends of the Chinese People – an offshoot of the League against Imperialism
GDR	German Democratic Republic (East Germany)
Ghadar Party	Indian nationalist party formed in the United States in 1913
GRU	Main Intelligence Directorate (Soviet military intelligence, often referred to as the Fourth Department)
ILP	Independent Labour Party
Indusco	China Industrial Cooperatives, a cooperative promotion organisation established by Helen Foster, Rewi Alley, Edgar Snow, and others with support and sponsorship from Song Meiling (Madame Chiang Kai-shek)
IWW	International Workers of the World, commonly known as the Wobblies
KGB	Committee for State Security, the name of the Soviet secret police, 1954–91
KMT	Kuomintang – Nationalist party. The Pinyin spelling Guomindang is closer to its pronunciation in Chinese.
KPD	Kommunistische Partei Deutschlands, German Communist Party
KUTV	Communist University of the Toilers of the East – Moscow training school for revolutionaries
LAI	League against Imperialism and Colonial Oppression – established by Willi Münzenberg in 1927

LBC	Left Book Club – established by Victor Gollancz in 1936
Lianda	National Southwest Associated University, established by refugee professors and students in Kunming in 1938
Manchuria	The three provinces of Northeast China – Heilongjiang, Jilin, and Liaoning. The name is not used in China.
Manzhouguo	Puppet regime established by the Japanese in Manchuria in 1932 with Puyi, former emperor of China, as head of state.
MIT	Massachusetts Institute of Technology
New Fourth Army	Name of Communist forces in the Yangzi River region after incorporation into the NRA in 1937
NKVD	People's Commissariat for Internal Affairs. The NKVD ran the Soviet secret police from 1934 to 1946 and was commonly used to refer to its secret police functions.
NRA	National Revolutionary Army – army of the KMT-controlled Republic of China
OGPU	Unified State Political Administration – name of the Soviet Secret Police from 1922 to 1934
OMS	International Liaison Department of the Comintern
OPK	Society of Former Political Prisoners – Soviet organisation headed by Vladimir Vilensky
OSS	Office of Strategic Services – forerunner of the CIA
OWI	Office of War Information – US propaganda organisation during World War II
PLA	People's Liberation Army – name of Chinese Communist forces after 1945. Now the armed forces of the PRC.
popular front	Comintern tactic of allying with bourgeois parties against fascism – adopted in 1935
POUM	Partido Obrero de Unificación Marxista – Workers Party of Marxist Unification
PPTUS	Pan-Pacific Trade Union Secretariat

PRC	People's Republic of China
Profintern	Trade Union International (commonly used term for the RILU)
RILU	Red International of Labour Unions
ROC	Republic of China – name of China from 1912 to 1949, still the official name of Taiwan
RSDLP	Russian Social Democratic Labour Party
SACP	South African Communist Party
Second United Front	Alliance between the CCP and the KMT, 1937–1941 (officially dissolved in 1945)
SPD	Sozialdemokratische Partei Deutschlands – Social Democratic Party of Germany
SWP	Socialist Workers Party (USA) – Trotskyist party formed by James P. Cannon in 1938
TASS	Telegrafnoye Agentstvo Sovietskogo Soyuza (formerly Soviet, now Russian, news agency)
TGWU	Transport and General Workers Union
Third Period	Leftist turn adopted by the Comintern, 1928–34
UDC	Union of Democratic Control – British pacifist organisation formed in 1914 to oppose secret treaties
United Front	Comintern tactic of allying with Social Democratic parties, and with bourgeois nationalists in colonial and semi-colonial countries. Adopted in 1921.
UNRRA	United Nations Relief and Rehabilitation Administration (active 1943–47)
WIR	Workers' International Relief – Internationale Arbeiter-Hilfe in German – a Comintern version of the Red Cross established by Willi Münzenberg
Yangzi River Patrol Force	United States naval force that patrolled China's inland and coastal waters for nearly a century from 1854 to 1949
Yuaikai	Japanese trade union federation established by the reformist Suzuki Bunji

Index